P9-DTA-944

Advice on Nutrition

A healthy diet and exercise are the starting points for supplying proper nutrition to your brain.

Be cautious when anyone recommends strange herbs or drugs.

Supplementing the diet with additional B vitamins as well as vitamins C and E might help keep the brain healthy.

Keep an eye out for other supplements that will be available in the near future.

For more information about nutrition, see Chapter 9, "Nutrition and Memory."

The Letter Equivalents

In the numeric alphabet, certain consonants represent each number from 0 to 9. They are:

0 = S or Z	5 = L
1 = T, D, or Th	6 = Sh, Ch, or J
2 = N	7 = K, (hard) G, or Q
3 = M	8 = F or V
4 = R	9 = P or B

Remember, it's the sound that counts.

Numeric Alphabet Key Words

Here are the first 20 words in our numeric alphabet. You can use this chart as an aid for memorizing lists.

1 = Hat	11 = Dad
2 = Hen	12 = Den
3 = Ham	13 = Dome
4 = Hair	14 = Door
5 = Hole	15 = Tail
6 = Hash	16 = Dish
7 = Hook	17 = Dike
8 = Hoof	18 = Dove
9 = Hoop	19 = Tape
10 = Toes	20 = Nose

alpha
books

Picture the Brain

Memory researchers fall into two broad categories: brain mappers and behaviorists. How the human brain works, however, remains a mystery.

The Human Brain

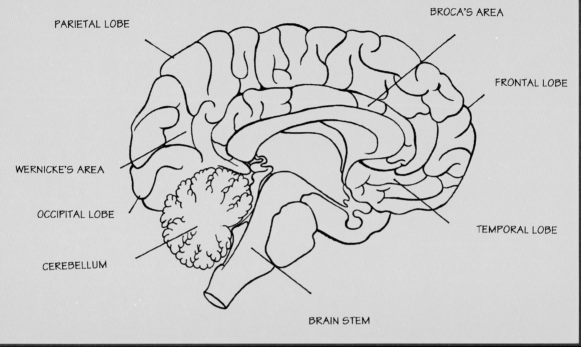

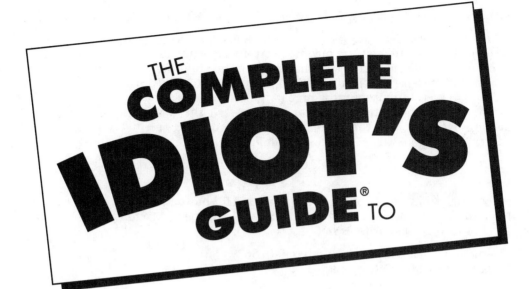

THE COMPLETE IDIOT'S GUIDE® TO

Improving Your Memory

by Michael Kurland and Richard A. Lupoff

alpha
books

A Division of Macmillan General Reference
A Pearson Education Macmillan Company
1633 Broadway, New York, NY 10019

Macmillan Publishing books may be purchased for business or sales promotional use. For information please write: Special Markets Department, Macmillan Publishing USA, 1633 Broadway, New York, NY 10019.

International Standard Book Number: 0-02862949-3
Library of Congress Catalog Card Number: 99-60667

01 00   8 7 6 5 4 3 2

Interpretation of the printing code: the rightmost number of the first series of numbers is the year of the book's printing; the rightmost number of the second series of numbers is the number of the book's printing. For example, a printing code of 99-1 shows that the first printing occurred in 1999.

Printed in the United States of America

Alpha Development Team

Publisher
Kathy Nebenhaus

Editorial Director
Gary M. Krebs

Managing Editor
Bob Shuman

Marketing Brand Manager
Felice Primeau

Acquisitions Editor
Jessica Faust

Development Editors
Phil Kitchel
Amy Zavatto

Assistant Editor
Georgette Blau

Production Team

Development Editor
Alexander Goldman

Production Editor
Christy Wagner

Copy Editor
Amy Lepore

Cover Designer
Mike Freeland

Photo Editor
Richard H. Fox

Illustrator
Brian Mac Moyer

Book Designers
Scott Cook and Amy Adams of DesignLab

Indexer
Tonya Heard

Layout/Proofreading
Jerry Cole
Natalie Evans
Linda Quigley

Contents at a Glance

Contents

Foreword

The other day, as I was preparing to write these introductory comments, I came up with a witty joke to start things off. Unfortunately, I can't remember what it was.

Okay, I apologize for the above. Take comfort in the fact that it's probably the last time in this book that you'll suffer through such an obvious gag. (I can only promise "probably" because I have read the book in galley form, and who knows what Michael and Richard may slip in between now and the final publication. But I digress.)

The point is, the gag is obvious precisely because we *do* forget things. Although there have been a few people born with virtually total recall, most of us have limitations. But, as you're about to see, it's possible to move past those, once you understand certain time-tested mnemonic techniques.

For me, mnemonics are a part of daily life; not only to bolster my work performing in theaters and on television, but for retaining names, dates, phone numbers, passwords, and other details plucked from the ever-increasing flow of data that bombards us. In this interactive Information Age, as our lives become even more complex, memory systems can provide essential help.

I've spent many years studying diverse and curious aspects of the human mind. Toward that end, I have read many texts on memory systems. Some of these are rather confusing; some are simply confused. A few books stand out as practical tools for learning. With *The Complete Idiot's Guide to Improving Your Memory*, Messrs. Kurland and Lupoff have created a new entry in that latter category. You *can* improve your memory skills, and this book will show you how.

It's also an enjoyable read. They delve into some literally heady stuff involving scientific theories and brain research, but the authors know how to make it fun. That doesn't mean you have no work ahead of you. Just reading this book is not going enhance your memory. It's not enough to know how mnemonic techniques function; you have to practice using them. My friend Harry Lorayne, arguably the greatest memory expert of this era, is famous for his demonstration of memorizing the names of every member of an audience, which can number many hundreds of people. However, even Harry can forget the name of someone he meets socially, if he doesn't make active use of mnemonics.

Fortunately, unlike most forms of exercise, memory training never gets boring. There's no limit to how strong a set of "memory muscles" you can develop—and you don't need expensive designer sneakers.

So, let's raise a glass of pingerberry juice and toast our convivial tour guides, as we prepare to meet a gallery of memorable characters, from Comrade Shereshevsky to Madame Schumann-Heink, and to explore an amazing world that resides right between your ears.

I'd sign this, if I could remember where I put my pen.

—Max Maven

Hailed by *Entertainment Tonight* as "the master mindreader," Max Maven has astonished audiences in over two dozen countries. *People* magazine called his work "a new form of participatory theater." He has appeared on hundreds of television and radio programs, including guest starring on *Fresh Prince of Bel-Air* and *General Hospital*, as well as his own series in Canada, England, and Taiwan. He's also hosted eight network specials in Japan—working entirely in Japanese.

A pioneer of interactive media, he created the critically acclaimed video *Max Maven's Mindgames* for MCA, and the award-winning *Max Magic* game disc for the Philips CD-i system. His ongoing exploration of the mysterious side of human nature led to *Max Maven's Book of Fortunetelling*, published by Prentice Hall. He has also created customized "Maximize" seminars on mental efficiency and nonverbal communication for executives and salespeople from top corporations.

Introduction

One of the greatest fears of our society as we drag our twentieth century bodies into the twenty-first century (along with "Is liposuction really painful?" and "Are bald men really more virile?") is "Am I losing my ... whatchamacallit ... you know ... oh, yeah ... my memory?"

Probably.

But probably not as badly as you think. With practice and by using the proper techniques, you can make your memory better than it ever was.

There are lots of myths and misinformation about how memory works and what you can do to make yours work better. For example, you've probably heard that you only use 10 percent of your brain and that certain techniques can raise that to 15 or 20 percent, which would make you twice as smart as anyone else.

Well, there's no scientific basis for that myth. As a matter of fact, nobody knows how much of your brain you actually use, and nobody knows how to find out. But nothing else our body carries around is useless, so there's no reason to assume we're lugging around a brain that's 10 times larger than necessary. And injuries to any part of the brain seem to do damage to the memory, the personality, the emotional centers, the senses—something—and no part has been proven to be unused.

So don't waste your money on anything that promises to help you use the unused part of your brain. Instead, concentrate on improving the parts we know you already use.

You've probably also heard that your memory gets worse as you get older—that you have all the brain cells you're ever going to have when you're one year old, and after that, they gradually die and aren't replaced. You're just doomed to get more and more forgetful, and there's nothing you can do about it.

Well, there is some slight deterioration in the short-term memory of a healthy older person. This is partly from disuse—when you retire the demands on your memory go way down—partly from insufficient physical exercise, which decreases the blood supply to the brain, and partly from the general wear and tear that goes with aging.

It's clear, however, that a 70-year-old who stays in shape and does not have the misfortune of developing a brain-robbing illness can think just as effectively as a 20-year-old. It just may take him a bit longer.

Most scientists believe that neurons—the brain cells in charge of memory and intellect—do die off gradually during the course of your life. By the time you're 100 years old, you will have lost somewhere between 5 and 10 percent of the neurons you started with. That might be, but consider that you started with something over 100 billion neurons. At age 100, you'll still have more neurons left than there are stars in the Milky Way galaxy.

Recent research on the brain has shown that some brain cells are replaced and that new ones are being added all the time. We'll talk more about this in Chapter 7, "In Sickness and in Health."

Why does it take longer to access information (that's the high-tech way of saying "remember something") when you're old than when you're young? Once more, science is not really sure (as is so often the case). "I guess I'm just slowing down in my old age" is not a real explanation.

Most likely, you're not really slowing down. Rather, your memory is like a library. The more "books" you add, the more you know. But finding a particular book—no less a particular fact—will naturally take a little longer since you have so many "books" to scan as you search for that one book—or one fact.

In this book, we're going to show you how a person of any age can develop a prodigious memory. Many techniques are available for this purpose. People have worked on this subject for thousands of years, and the amount of literature about memory is itself huge.

Some of the methods we will present involve mental exercises that actually can strengthen your brain. This may sound like an extravagant claim, but recent research (reported by psychologist Robert Dustman of the Neuropsychology Research Laboratory at the Veterans Affairs Medical Center in Salt Lake City) indicates that the neurons in your brain can be improved by mental exercise just as the muscles in your arms and legs can be strengthened by physical exercise. Curiously, the physical exercise that strengthens your body also helps strengthen your brain—if only by assuring a plentiful supply of oxygen and other nutrients.

Other methods are more down-to-earth and pragmatic, including techniques for learning lists of facts, dates, names, and numbers and for recognizing people you've met only once—and recalling their names! These have real value. They can help you in both your career and your social relationships.

Still other techniques are pure fun—you can use them as party stunts or to entertain family and friends.

By the way, here's a little piece of advice. Any time you pick up a nonfiction book—whether it's a scientific text, a biography, or a how-to guide—you should look at the book with these questions in mind:

➤ Who wrote this book?

Is the author knowledgeable on the subject? Has he written other books on this or related subjects?

➤ For whom did the author write this book?

Is the book aimed at a specialized audience—perhaps one already familiar with the subject—or is it written for the intelligent lay person?

➤ Is the book readable and useful?

Glancing through the book, does it seem to be written in a clear and informative manner?

➤ Is the information up-to-date?

If knowledge in the field is rapidly growing and changing, does this book have the latest information?

Fair enough? Okay, here are our answers to these questions:

The authors of this book, Michael Kurland and Richard Lupoff (that's us, gentle reader), have written a combined total of more than 70 books plus assorted screenplays, magazine articles, essays, and reportage. We have written a variety of nonfiction works (you probably don't really care about our novels and short stories right now), from books about computers to books about modern police forensic techniques and courtroom procedure, which included sections on memory recall and hypnotic regression techniques. One of us even developed a memory course used by the United States Army in an advanced officers' program.

We've also, between the two of us, conducted courses or appeared as guest lecturers at universities from coast to coast including Columbia University, the University of New Mexico, the University of California (Berkeley), UCLA, and Stanford University.

Our consulting expert, Max Maven, is well equipped to catch any little errors, to point out facts we have overlooked, and to lead us gently in the direction of the greater truth. Max is a professional stage mentalist who has made a very good living for many years by thinking faster, better, and more accurately than anyone else in the room.

We wrote this book for anyone interested in learning about the human brain and, in particular, about memory. Your interest may be pure curiosity. After all, the human brain is one of nature's most complex mysteries, and we are just beginning to unwrap its secrets. Or your interest may be more practical. We all use our memories daily. As with anything else useful, we want our memories to be in the best condition possible. This book will show you how to keep your memory shiny, quick, and accurate.

Like the other books in the *Complete Idiot's Guide®* series, *The Complete Idiot's Guide to Improving Your Memory* isn't *really* written for idiots. It's intended for an intelligent, curious person (somebody a lot like you!) who is seeking information in a clear and informative format. *Idiot's Guides* keep it simple without being patronizing.

Readable? Useful? Just give it a try! You're dealing with two authors who have spent a lifetime studying, writing, and teaching a variety of related subjects.

The information in *The Complete Idiot's Guide to Improving Your Memory* is as up-to-date as we could make it. Even as we were writing this book, we both scanned scientific journals and news reports for the latest developments in this remarkably fast-changing field. We interviewed psychologists and spent countless hours surfing the Internet, tracking down the latest data.

Asides

There are facts and then there are facts. Most of the facts we'll be sharing with you in this book will flow naturally in the body of the text. Some of the more interesting bits of information, however, will not fit neatly into place. These will be inserted in special boxes where appropriate, for your reading and learning pleasure.

Words to Remember

Boxes like this contain the definitions of words with which you might not be familiar or that are being used with a specialized meaning in this book.

Remember This!

Here you will find little warnings about things not to do or things to be watchful for while training your memory.

Instant Recall

This box is for all the little tips and asides that will add to your enjoyment and provide useful information. Our goal is to expand your knowledge while increasing your memory potential.

Refresh Your Memory

In these boxes, you will find quotes from psychologists and memory experts as well as from poets, philosophers, and others who have commented on the brain and memory.

Some Memorable Facts

Boxes like this contain nuggets of history, science, psychology, and anthropology as well as random bits of fascinating information that will give you better insight into the workings of the human brain and how we learn about it.

Acknowledgments

This is the space reserved for the authors to give credit to their research associates, administrative assistants, spouses, spices, fact checkers, guides, critics, elementary school teachers, editors, and agents for all the help they've provided. The problem is, once you start a list like that, it's hard to stop.

It would be simpler just to say, "Thanks to everyone who helped—you know who you are!" Come to think of it, we do want to thank everyone who helped. And you do know who you are.

And some of you are:

Michael Conant, who talked us through some of the technical stuff.

Patricia Lupoff of Cody's Bookstore, who gathered information.

Tom Ogden, Master Magician, who was there at the beginning.

Michael Pearce of the San Francisco Exploratorium, who was a helpful guide.

Trina Robbins, who drew the pictures for us and understood what we were trying to say.

Linda Robertson, who read it and wept.

Jack Scovil, who is an agent and friend.

Paula Solomon, Ph.D., who passed along some very useful information in a Mexican restaurant.

T.A. Waters, who told us about the ants.

Special Thanks to the Technical Reviewer

The Complete Idiot's Guide® to Improving Your Memory was reviewed by an expert who double-checked the accuracy of what you'll learn here to help us ensure that this book gives you everything you need to know about improving your memory. Special thanks are extended to Max Maven, Thief of Thoughts, who kept us honest.

Part 1
Memories Are Made of This

What is memory? Stop and think about it for a minute. The answer seems obvious, but in fact it's one of those tricky things like "the truth," "civilization," "intelligence," and "beauty." Everybody knows what they are—well, everybody thinks he or she knows what they are—until they try to define them. Then things get tricky. And what about memory? When you look at an orange and then look away, yet you still remember seeing that orange, is there a tiny replica of it inside your brain? A microscopic picture of it? If you peel the orange, take a big bite of it, chew it up, swallow, and then remember that experience, is there a tiny version of you sitting in your head eating an even tinier version of that orange? Probably not. But there's some kind of record of the orange you saw, the texture you felt, the flavor you experienced, and so on. What's going on here? Does your pet Weimaraner have a memory? Yes? Does a bumblebee have a memory? Maybe? Does a birch tree have a memory? No? Are you sure? Think about it!

Chapter 1

28 Chapters to a Better Memory

> ### In This Chapter
>
> ➤ Napoleon Bonaparte and Franklin Delano Roosevelt
>
> ➤ How memory works
>
> ➤ A better memory is good for you
>
> ➤ Short-term and long-term memory
>
> ➤ Making the most of your brain

Developing a good memory is one of the most useful social—and business—skills a person can master. Forgetting the name of someone you've just met at a party can be both embarrassing and particularly frustrating if the person is someone you'd like to get to know better.

Forgetting the name of someone you've been introduced to in a professional setting, such as a business lunch or an important meeting with a new client, can really hurt your career.

On the other hand, you can impress people by remembering their names and a few important facts about them. "Dorothy Gale, isn't it? And how is your little dog, Toto?"

Of Bonaparte and Roosevelt

This story is about 200 years old. Maybe it's true. It goes like this:

Whenever the French emperor Napoleon Bonaparte reviewed his troops, he walked up and down the ranks and greeted individual private soldiers by name.

Instant Recall

If you want to impress people with your intelligence and your caring nature, ask them questions about themselves and ask their advice about a professional problem. They will remember you as a brilliant conversationalist and as an exceptionally bright and knowledgeable person.

"Bonjour, Jacques!"

"How are you feeling, today, Henri?"

"Not too cold for you, is it, Albert?"

Every soldier in the ranks felt the commander knew him personally and cared about him. As a result, Napoleon's troops were fanatically loyal to their commander.

A similar story is told about former President Franklin Delano Roosevelt, who led the United States out of the Great Depression of the 1930s and through the challenges of World War II. He achieved all this while confined to a wheelchair. He was able to stand only with the aid of steel leg braces, and he could "walk" only a few painful steps at a time while clutching the arm of an aide, leaning on a cane, and swinging his paralyzed legs like two dead weights.

We know this story to be true.

In reception lines, Roosevelt greeted each person by name and asked a little question or recited a little fact that showed he really knew and cared about the person.

"How's your wife, Chester? Did she recover from that little tennis mishap?"

"Say, Walter, I heard your boy finished third in his class at Groton. Wonderful! My old school, did you know that?"

"Millicent! What a pleasure to see you. Eleanor told me that your daughter was the loveliest bride she'd ever seen. I was devastated that I had to miss the wedding."

Napoleon Remembered

Napoleon Bonaparte's method was to memorize the rosters of his units. He knew the name of the fourth man from the left in the second rank of the fifth company of the third infantry brigade. He must have checked with the battalion commander, however, to make sure the soldier wasn't out sick or missing on that day. Otherwise, Napoleon's technique wouldn't have worked; his soldiers would have seen through the trick.

Roosevelt Cribbed

Franklin Roosevelt used a different method. His chief political advisor, James Farley, kept a file of index cards listing every important person and potential campaign donor in the country. Whenever Roosevelt attended functions that required him to "meet and greet," Farley briefed him beforehand. Roosevelt memorized a key question or comment for each person he met to show his interest.

Just as Napoleon's roster studies won him the loyalty of his troops, Roosevelt's (or rather, Jim Farley's) index cards helped FDR cultivate one of the most successful political careers in the history of the world. He was elected President of the United States not once, not twice, but four times.

Did They Have Superior Brains?

These men did not have superior brains. Clearly, they both were very intelligent, but there was nothing mysterious or exotic about them. They didn't take magic memory pills or have the benefit of superior powers or the assistance of computers. They did, however, use certain methods to help them remember people, names, and facts, and these methods paid off handsomely.

Remember It Well

Some individuals seem to be born with extraordinary powers of absorbing and retaining information. These are people with *eidetic*, or "photographic," memories. Other people effortlessly can tell you what day of the week any date fell on or all the batting averages and other statistics of every baseball player who ever played for any league, from triple A ball to the major leagues.

Psychologists have tried to understand the phenomenon of eidetic memory as well as other unusual mental abilities such as those of *savants* or "human calculators." So far, psychologists' efforts have yielded only limited results, and nobody is sure just how those with unusual mental abilities manage it.

This book is not going to teach you how to look at a page in the telephone book for 10 seconds and then recite every name, address, and phone number on the page. What it can do, however, is fill you in on the latest research and theories about what memory really is, how it works, and how you can make your memory work much better than it does today.

What Is Memory, Anyhow?

How does memory work? How do we absorb information, "store" it, and then call it back when we want it? And why is it that we sometimes can't get it back?

At the Beginning

Do you remember the first year of your life? Chances are, you don't remember anything about those 12 months, at least not consciously. Yet you were taking in a wealth of information in the form of sensory impressions. You saw your surroundings. You heard people speak, dogs bark, telephones ring, and music play. You certainly tasted food. You played with your toys. You were taken for walks. Aunts and uncles, admiring friends, and strangers on the street and in the park peered into your face and said,

"What a darling baby! Why, just look at those big, bright eyes! What a wonderful smile! Oh, you're such a lucky parent to have such a marvelous baby!" Why don't you remember this taking place? Or do you? Are these sensory impressions stored away somewhere in your brain, just waiting to be tapped?

Think about this. Even though you have no conscious memories of your first year of life (maybe a little flash here or there, an especially vivid image or the comforting recollection of what it was like to be held and carried—warm, secure, loved), you most certainly did learn during that year. You probably learned as much or more than in any year since. And you do retain what you learned.

You laid the foundations of language, and you learned motor skills that prepared you for every physical skill you've ever acquired, from holding objects and standing upright to flying a jet plane or performing delicate surgery. You have not forgotten what you learned—you use it every day. You just don't remember the experience of learning it.

Who Could It Be?

Here's a scene from everyday life:

You're an automobile salesperson. You're walking down the street, and a person rushes up to you, calls you by name, says how happy she is to see you again, and asks how you are. You know that you know her, but you can't for the life of you remember her name or who she is. A high school classmate? A teammate on the soccer squad? Your dentist? Your boss? Maybe you have that "it's right on the tip of my tongue" feeling. But what does that feeling mean? What causes it? And when it happens to you, how can you get the information from the tip of your tongue to your mind where can you use it?

Then it comes back to you! You realize who the tantalizingly familiar person is.

"Ah, Ms. Henderson," you say to her, "I'm happy to see you, too. You look just wonderful today. You know, I was wondering about that convertible you were test-driving the other day down at the dealership. Really a beauty! Have you decided to buy it?"

Of course, Ms. Henderson replies that the car was indeed a beauty, that she's decided she definitely wants to buy it, that the price you quoted sounds very fair now that she's had a chance to sleep on it, and that, if you want to draw up the papers, she's ready to sign. You make your quota for the week, earn a fat commission, and receive a handshake from the boss. You also get a nice little bonus for selling the most expensive car on the lot.

What if you didn't remember Ms. Henderson's name and who she was? What if you smiled weakly, said "Uh, nice to see you too; sorry I have to run," and took off in the opposite direction? Perhaps Ms. Henderson would have bought a car from your competitor. Maybe failing to sell the car would have led to you missing your monthly sales quota. It just goes to show how important it is to remember people.

Your Senses and You

Think about this little triad: learning, remembering, forgetting. Here's another triad: receiving information, transferring it from your brain's short-term storage area to its long-term storage area, and calling it back when you need it.

Anything that comes to you through any of your senses—sight, hearing, scent, taste, or touch—is information.

The Eyes Have It

Studies have shown that humans obtain the greatest portion of their information through their eyes. We see our everyday surroundings—furniture, buildings, trees, automobiles, the sun, a peanut butter and jelly sandwich, and, of course, our fellow humans—and we learn. We also see images, photographs, paintings, drawings, motion pictures, videos—and we learn. One other thing sets us apart from every other creature on the face of the earth—we can read.

This is not to say that vision is our only important means of gathering information. Hearing comes in second, although the other senses trail far behind.

Some Memorable Facts

Different species have different senses, and the importance of these senses varies from one species to another. Bats have a form of radar. Fish have a sense of balance that helps them stay upright in an environment in which "up" and "down" are not as obvious as they are to us. (Humans have a comparable sense, by the way. Most of us aren't conscious of it, but if you've ever suffered inner-ear damage that affected your balance, you know how important this sense is.) Dogs have a sense of smell many times more sensitive than that of humans, and they use this sense far more in their everyday lives than we do. Snakes pick up vibrations through their tongues, a type of "hearing" that is very different from our own. Cats use their sensitive whiskers as balance aids and as feelers, part of their famous ability to "see" in the dark.

Is It All Just Electricity?

What actually happens when you receive a sensory impression? You have millions upon millions of nerve endings in your body. Your nerves are specialized, and

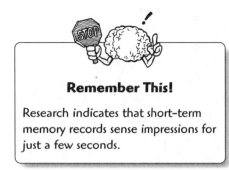

Remember This!

Research indicates that short-term memory records sense impressions for just a few seconds.

physiologists have developed a whole vocabulary for different types and parts of nerves—*ganglions*, *neurons*, *axons*, *dendrons*, and so on. Later, we'll talk about these nerves and the mysterious, almost miraculous things they do for you. For the moment, however, there's no need to get deeply involved in studying them. They are concentrated very densely in your eyes and very sparsely, for instance, in your ear lobes.

The point is that these nerve endings pick up sensory impressions: the sight of a face or a printed word, the sound of an automobile horn or a doorbell, the scent of freshly baked bread, the feeling of a loved one caressing your skin. These nerve endings transmit messages through a wonderfully complex network to your brain, where the messages are stored briefly in short-term memory.

The Fatal Moment

Your short-term memory, as you might guess from its name, doesn't hold these impressions for very long. After a time, they can be either transferred to long-term memory or simply lost. Lost. That's an important moment. If you keep the information, you can integrate it into the whole body of knowledge that you possess. You can call it back up, can manipulate it in various ways, and can put it to use. It might be the answer to a test question, a formula you need in your work, the route to a friend's house, a telephone number or e-mail address, or a line in a play.

In reading this book, you'll learn methods of ensuring that important new information is stored in your long-term memory and not lost. And we'll show you many techniques you can use to ensure that information gets stored safely in your long-term memory and that you can retrieve it when you want it.

I Know I Know It, But...

Most people have experienced this feeling. It's like walking into a great library but not understanding the shelving system. You know the book you want is there, but where is it? Or it's like opening a file drawer and discovering that the folder tabs are all blank or are in a language you can't read. You know the paper you're searching for is in one of the folders, but which one? Or it's like creating a computer file, saving it at the end of your day's work, and then not knowing where it's gone. You know this much: It's on the hard drive. But where? And how can you get it back?

Don't feel alone! In fact, these bothersome moments are virtually universal. The good news is that there are ways to improve your memory so you'll not only get better at storing information and keeping it—you'll also get better at retrieving it.

How Important Is This, Anyway?

Back in the days of vaudeville shows, "memory" acts were common. In these acts, entertainers with titles such as Professor Memory or The Walking Encyclopedia performed amazing feats of memory nightly. These acts have largely disappeared, although professional magicians and mentalists still use some of their techniques. These techniques, and other more modern methods based on what we now know of how the brain works, can be adapted to teach you practical, down-to-earth methods of remembering and retrieving information—methods that can help you.

These methods can be vitally important in situations of sheer survival. ("Now, how do I distinguish a nourishing mushroom from a toxic toadstool?") They also can be useful in social relationships. People like to be remembered. It shows that you value them and that you care about them, and they usually return the favor. These methods can be useful in school, whether you are trying to remember crucial dates for a history course, the positive or negative valences of the elements for a chemistry class, a mathematical formula for a course in geometry or trigonometry, or the rules for spelling. They also can be useful in business, whether they involve recalling the names and faces of associates or the procedure for a particular transaction.

Improving Your Memory

You say I can improve my memory, but can I really? Yes, you can! You can improve your memory through better nutrition, exercise, and concentration. You can use a variety of *mnemonic* techniques, which we'll be teaching you in later chapters.

The Complete Idiot's Guide to Improving Your Memory borrows time-tested techniques, from the knowledge of the ancient Greeks to the latest scientific research and psychological theories of memory.

Just a Matter of Concentration?

Well, maybe it is and maybe it isn't. Some skeptics contend that all the memory systems in the world serve only to force us to concentrate on the material we're trying to learn. These folks insist that all memory is purely a matter of concentration, effort, and repetition.

Words to Remember

Mnemonic means "of, or pertaining to, memory," but it also is a device that can help you remember things. The science of **mnemonics** has been around for a very long time—so long, in fact, that it's named after an ancient Greek goddess. **Mnemosyne** was the goddess of memory, the daughter of heaven and earth (Uranus and Ge), and the mother of the Muses.

We happen to think they're wrong, but let's give them the benefit of the doubt. Even if they're right—even if using the techniques you'll learn in *The Complete Idiot's Guide to Improving Your Memory* does nothing more than help you concentrate your mental powers—so what? Science does not understand the brain. We don't know why these methods work, but they do work—if you work hard, too.

Just between you and us, we think these skeptics are bending over backward to be cautious. Bending *too far* backward. Their motto might as well be "Work harder, not smarter." This doesn't make much sense to us.

Remembering Your Lines

We asked an actor friend the other day how he learns his lines, and he made a remarkably eloquent statement that actually told us more than he realized. Here's what he said:

"There's no magic formula. You just read through the whole script once to get a general sense of it, then you read your own part, then you read it again, and again, and again. You read it for meaning and that helps impress it on your mind. You read it aloud. You read it with a friend who helps you learn your cues. You read it with the rest of the cast to get the flow of it. You read it on the stage to impress the sense of place and the feel of it. After a while it starts to come. After a while longer, you realize that you have it cold."

We asked our friend if he ever forgets a role after he has learned it. Here's what he said:

"When a play closes and you go on to the next one, the first play fades away pretty fast. A few weeks into the next production, the last one is as distant as another life."

But is it really lost? Or is it just tucked away in "dead storage" to be recovered if you ever need it again? What if, for example, you were called upon to re-create a role in a new production of a play you'd been in before?

"I'd have it back in one evening," our friend told us. "One run-through with the rest of the cast and I'd know my lines again. Two or three rehearsals and I'd have my part in hand and my blocking back. I'd be ready to go in a week, whereas the first time through it takes a month or longer to get ready."

Our friend thought he was just telling us about the acting profession, but he also was telling us—maybe more than he realized—about memory.

Sense Memory Makes Sense

Our friend was using *eye memory* when he read his script. He was using *ear memory* when he heard himself speak his lines. He was using *body memory* as he mouthed his lines and as he moved through his blocking (the positioning and movements he makes on the stage). By doing these things, he was creating multiple neural paths to the same information—his lines. This is very important, and we'll come back to this point later. (If we forget, remind us.)

He also was using the principle of *repetition*. Repetition strengthens existing neural pathways instead of making new ones. This is another important point that we will come back to later. And, yes, we'll concede this much to the skeptics. Our actor friend certainly concentrated his mental energy on his lines, and that concentration surely helped him to learn them. Fair enough.

Tuned to the Neural Network

Neural paths, which will be discussed at length later in this book, are nerve paths that lead from your sense organs to your brain and that network around inside your brain. They are very, very important to memory.

For now, though, we're going to play a visualization game. You've been reading through some fairly dense material so far, and it's time to take a break for a while.

Meeting Your Date

Imagine a sports stadium of 50,000 seats, and every seat is sold out for the big game. You've been set up on a date, whom you've talked with on the telephone and have arranged to meet during the game. You've never met previously, but a mutual friend described your date.

Unfortunately, your date forgot to tell you where the seats are. How can you find someone you've never seen? Well, of course you know her name, and you could conceivably walk through every section of the stadium looking for her and calling her name. You might get lucky and come across her, but this is a pretty unreliable and inefficient way to locate her.

You know she's wearing an intensely bright red shirt to the game. That should help you spot her. Hmmm, unless red is the theme color of one of the teams and half the people in the stands are wearing red. You've also been told she is unusually tall; this might make her visible from a distance. When you spoke with her on the telephone, she told you that she is planning to bring a handmade sign featuring a picture of her school's mascot, a yellow-striped capybara, to wave between plays. She also told you that she loves ice cream and that she always buys ice cream to eat during games.

You now have no fewer than five possible clues to help you find your date: her name, her bright red shirt, her unusual height, the sign she's planning to wave, and the fact that she'll be eating an ice-cream cone. Any of these five clues might lead you to her. If you walk through the stands, you're likely to see many women wearing red shirts, many eating ice-cream cones, a fair number who are quite tall, and even several waving yellow-striped capybara signs. But if you find one tall woman who is wearing a red shirt, eating an ice-cream cone, *and* waving a capybara sign ... the chances are good that she's your blind date. Ask her. The odds are all in your favor.

Meeting Your Elusive Memory

What, you ask, was the point of that silly story?

If you were searching for elusive memory rather than for a young woman in a sports stadium, you would improve your chances of "finding" that memory by laying down multiple neural paths to it, just as you developed multiple *clue paths* to the person in the stadium.

When you establish a memory, you establish a neural path to it. You have millions of memories in your mind, however, and many millions of neural paths. You might not always be able to find the one you're looking for. If you establish multiple neural paths to a given memory, however, you increase the likelihood that you will find it when you want it.

Use It or Lose It

If you've ever begun an athletic training program—say, as a member of a school track team—you know something about developing your muscles. Or perhaps you've seen a documentary on television about how athletes prepare for the Olympics. You start out running the 100-yard dash in a certain amount of time. After working at it day after day, your time comes down steadily. You build up muscle strength in your arms and legs, you improve your lung capacity, and you strengthen your heart muscles. If you stop training, just sit around, and avoid exercise, however, your muscles get flabby.

The same is true of your brain, although it isn't a muscle in the same sense as your leg muscles. It doesn't stretch and contract as you take each step. Your brain is more of an electrochemical muscle. The more you use it, the more you build up the neural networks within it; the more nourishment it demands, the more your body feeds oxygen-bearing blood to the brain. If you don't use your brain, the neural networks deteriorate, less oxygen-bearing blood reaches it, and your brain becomes less effective, powerful, and useful.

In a laboratory experiment, two groups of rats were kept in similar conditions. They had the same general surroundings, the same type and amount of food, and the same amount of physical exercise and rest. The only difference in their living conditions was that one group of rats had toys that provided mental stimulation; the second group was kept in a calm, boring environment.

When their brains were examined, the brains of the mentally stimulated rats were actually larger and heavier than the brains of the calm, bored rats. If friends have advised you to keep active and interested, it's good advice. Any muscle becomes stronger and works better if you use it regularly. This also is true of your brain.

The Least You Need to Know

➤ Both Napoleon and FDR used memory aids to impress their constituents.

➤ You can remember what you have learned even when you have forgotten how and when you learned it.

➤ Information reaches you through all your senses, but the most important sense is vision (followed by sound).

➤ Information travels from your senses to your short-term memory and then to your long-term memory, moving along neural networks.

➤ To help retrieve information from memory, you can establish multiple pathways to a given fact.

➤ It is possible to improve your memory and, in the process, literally strengthen your brain.

Chapter 2

To Live Is to Remember

In This Chapter

➤ The strange case of "HM"

➤ Why an oak is an oak and an elm is an elm

➤ Learning and remembering

➤ The medium is the memory

Consciousness is one of those peculiar terms that seem very easy to understand until you actually try to define it. You probably haven't spent much time thinking about consciousness, but give it a moment's thought now. Just what do we mean when we say something is conscious? Is a gorilla conscious? Is a whale? What about an octopus, a dog, a black widow spider, or a rosebush?

Some philosophers (called *solipsists*) maintain that one cannot be really sure that anybody or anything in the universe is conscious (or, for that matter, even exists) except oneself. Leaving the spider and rosebush question alone for a while—we'll get back to it later—we're going to take the commonsense position that all humans do have consciousness and that all our minds work more-or-less in a similar manner. We can't prove that this is so; we can't even prove that we experience the most common phenomena in the same manner. Two people look at a red lollipop. Do they really have the same experience? Is one person's red the same as another person's red?

We can't really tell, and we probably will never know. But if they both look at the same red lollipop and agree that it's red—and that it's a lollipop—that's all they really need to do to successfully communicate. Likewise, the assumption that all humans have the same sort of intelligence—however you define it—is unprovable. For our purposes, however, this assumption works and seems to be true, so we'll go with it.

But we need to define what we're talking about. What really is consciousness? What is intelligence? What is memory? What is mind?

Richard here:

A while ago I visited the wonderful Steinhart Aquarium in San Francisco and was fascinated by something I saw there. The aquarium has a huge tank that is happily shared by a mixed population of sea lions and dolphins. One whole wall of the tank is made of glass so visitors can sit or stand and watch the creatures' activities. I saw a young father holding a baby walk to this glass wall and hold the baby close to the glass. First a sea lion swam over and looked at the baby. The sea lion's face and conduct were remarkably suggestive of a friendly, curious dog's. After a few seconds, the animal swam away.

Then a dolphin swam over to the father and the baby. The dolphin turned so one of its eyes was right up to the glass. The dolphin stared at the baby for the longest time, and the baby (who was maybe six or eight months old) was fascinated by the dolphin. I don't know what passed between the dolphin and the baby, but if I believed in telepathy, I would be convinced that they were "talking" to each other—that the dolphin was passing on some ancient wisdom to the baby.

Of this I'm convinced: the dolphin had consciousness, intelligence, surely a memory, and just as surely a mind—however we define these things.

Instant Recall

As we pointed out in the introduction—which you didn't read, did you?—in asides such as these, one of the authors will relate a humorous, insightful, illuminating tale from his own experience. These stories are told either by the brilliant but humble Richard Lupoff or the shy, multitalented Michael Kurland.

In this chapter, we'll take a look at these concepts. All of them are part of our everyday lives, and all of them are surprisingly subtle and slippery when we try to pin them down. First, however, we'll look at one of the most remarkable people who has ever lived, an individual known to the scientific world solely as "HM."

The Man Without a Memory

Memory is one of the great mysteries of life. As physicist Stephen Hawking once asked, "Why do we remember the past and not the future?" This is a disarmingly simple question with a very simple answer—or so it seems—until we think about it and try to pin down our reactions.

Psychologists and physiologists have worked for many years to identify which portion of the human brain actually contains our memory—except it isn't that simple. Once more, we run into a case in which things get more complicated the more closely we examine them.

A unique opportunity for memory research was presented in 1953 by an individual known only as "HM" (in order to protect his privacy and that of his family). HM had suffered for years from severe epileptic seizures, convulsions resulting from periodic "electrical storms" taking place within or on the surface of the brain. A variety of treatments are available for this condition, including medication. In extreme and intractable cases, however, surgery offers the best—sometimes the only—hope for alleviating the condition. In HM's case, a portion of the brain called the *temporal lobe* was removed.

Words to Remember

Amnesia: A total or partial loss of memory usually resulting from shock, psychological disturbance, brain injury, or illness.

Retrograde: Moving or tending backward. In cases of amnesia, refers to all events and experiences occurring *prior to* the onset of amnesia.

Antiretrograde: Moving or tending forward. In cases of amnesia, refers only to events and experiences occurring *after* the onset of amnesia.

This kind of treatment is reserved for "last resort" cases. It is known to present the risk of dangerous side effects including *amnesia*. Still, the risk seemed worth it as compared to a life of constant and debilitating seizures.

The surgery was undertaken. It was successful in relieving HM's seizures. Unfortunately, and completely unexpectedly, it resulted in amnesia of a peculiar (and fascinating to study) sort called *antiretrograde* amnesia.

His Event-Memory Retention Was Gone

HM retained the memories he had before his temporal lobe was removed. He remembers his childhood, his school days, his relatives and friends, and everything up to the operation itself, but he is unable to remember anything that has happened to him since. He still wakes up each morning as though it were the day after his 1953 operation, even though half a century has gone by. His ability to remember new events was destroyed in the operation.

His Motor Memory Remained

In a later test, HM learned *mirror drawing*, a skill in which he could see his own hand and the picture he was working on only in a mirror. If you think this sounds easy, just try it. All you need is a mirror, a sheet of drawing paper, a pencil, and a piece of cardboard that prevents you from directly viewing your hand and the drawing but not the mirror image.

Remember This!

Amnesia is a favorite device for writers of TV movies and soap operas. Heroes and heroines seem to get hit on the head and forget who they are at the drop of a hat. This makes for wonderful melodrama, but in real life, amnesia is a very rare condition.

Once HM learned to do this, he was able to repeat the skill. If you asked him when or how he learned it, however, he had no idea. His memories of the time spent learning this new skill were wiped away, but the skill itself remained.

Think about your own first year or two of life. How did you learn to feed yourself, to walk, and to talk? You still have these skills. You remember what you learned, but you don't remember learning it!

From this, we can learn about different types of memory. One type is the memory of specific events or experiences. Another is the retention of knowledge or skills attained through these experiences. As a very young child, you had not yet developed your *event memory*, but you had a powerful *skill memory*. When HM's temporal lobe was removed, he lost the ability to form new event memories, but he retained to some extent the ability to form new skill memories. Remembering learned physical skills is called *motor memory*. These memories must be stored in a different part of the brain than event memories.

We will return to HM in Chapter 6, "A Hole in the Head," which further explores this strange and fascinating case and others that have given us insight into how the mind and memory work.

Do Trees Really Remember?

This is another of those obvious questions with an obvious answer that keeps slipping away. If you walk up to a tree (or any other bit of plant life) and talk to it, it's really hard to believe that the plant hears you at all, or that it remembers what you said, or that it cares.

Words to Remember

Tropism: The turning or bending movement of an organism or a part toward or away from an external stimulus such as light, heat, or gravity.

Just give it the right amount of light, warmth, and water and the right kind of soil, and it will grow very nicely, thank you all the same. Oh, and keep those nasty bugs away.

But wait a minute! What about the light, warmth, and water? And what about those bugs? Plants do react to their surroundings. There are examples all around us. Some flowers open each morning, turn toward the sun, follow it throughout the day, and close again in the evening when the sun disappears. Biologists call this type of action a *tropism*.

Some plants emit chemicals that bugs or other predators find unpleasant. These plants cannot brush off the pests or flee from them, so they have cleverly found a way to make themselves unattractive to the predators. It has been observed that some trees, after they have been attacked by a particular type of pest and have "learned" to emit a substance that repels or kills the pest, "remember" this event. When the same type of pest attacks again, the tree produces more of the repellent and produces it more quickly than it did at the time of the first attack.

And of course, there are carnivorous plants, the most famous of which is the Venus flytrap. These plants, instead of chasing bugs away, emit chemicals to attract them. That's how they get their dinner.

Some Memorable Facts

The Venus flytrap (*Dionaea muscipula*) is native to the coastal plain of the Carolinas. It attracts insects with a sweet-smelling chemical. Its sensitive leaf blades have hinges that close and entrap its prey, which it then digests. This may sound like a monster out of a science-fiction movie, but it actually exists. Luckily for humans, it's far too small to eat *us* for dinner.

But Do They Remember?

Whether it's a sunflower (*Helianthus annuus*) turning toward the sun, its source of energy, or a Venus flytrap luring a bug to visit and inducing it to stay for dinner, we still have to ask, "Is this memory?" Does the sunflower remember that the sun rises in the east? Does it remember to follow the sun across the sky? Does the Venus flytrap remember to set its chemical bait and to close around its prey?

Aren't these actions tropisms? (They are.) Are tropisms the result of memory? This is debatable, but we contend that they are. The instructions to follow the sun or to emit a chemical lure and then trap a tasty insect are built into the sunflower and the flytrap. They are coded into the plants' *DNA*. They are information, and information is memory.

Words to Remember

Deoxyribonucleic acid (DNA): A complex chemical that carries the genetic information in a cell and is capable of self-replication.

Words to Remember

Hard-wired: As applied to computer technology, a program that is part of the hardware and not subject to change. By extension, in biology, the term applies to organic functions or behavior that is coded into the organism's DNA.

Soft-wired: In contrast to hard-wired, a soft-wired program is actually stored as data and is subject to change depending on circumstances. In biology, the term applies to functions or behavior that can be changed in response to new learning.

So we can observe that plants "remember," that they "know" how to act. Only a few people believe that they are conscious or have minds (although, of course, it's impossible to prove that they *don't*). And they probably can't learn. To borrow a term from the computer world, they're *hard-wired*.

Then How Did They Learn This Stuff in the First Place?

Hey, this is a terrific question! And here's the answer: The information was there in their cells, in their DNA, from the moment they came into being. Every living organism has DNA, including you. You started out as a tiny, one-celled creature living inside your mother's womb. How did *you* know how to make your body? How did you know how to make your bones, your muscles, your eyes? How did you know you were supposed to have one heart with four chambers, two lungs, and a brain with two lobes? Who told you to start growing teeth when you were a few months old, to use them for a few years, and then to get rid of them and make a second and larger set of teeth?

The answer to these questions—and to the millions of other questions biologists, anatomists, physicians, and physical anthropologists like to ask—is the same: Your DNA told you. You weren't aware of it, you never thought about it, but you did it nonetheless.

This brings us to that other question, "Why is an oak an oak and an elm an elm?" How does each tree know what shape of leaves to grow and how to distribute its seeds? For that matter, how does it know how to process chemicals from the earth into bark and sap and roots and leaves and wood? It's all in the DNA.

Don't Mess with Your DNA

If we could look inside our own cells and read the coding in our DNA, we could learn a lot about ourselves. But we wouldn't learn the multiplication tables or the alphabet, we wouldn't learn to recognize people's names and faces any better, and we wouldn't be able to name the 50 states or the presidents of the United States or the kings and queens of England. The good news about hard-wired information is that it comes with the territory—you don't have to learn it. The bad news is that, once it's there, it's extremely difficult—if not impossible—to change or add to it. If you transplanted an oak tree to a place with a lot more sunlight and much less water, it couldn't "learn" to live like a palm tree. It's hard-wired to be an oak, and it couldn't change to save its life.

By the same token, a whale couldn't learn to live on land where wolves get along very happily. And you couldn't learn to live on an ice floe in the Arctic Ocean even though polar bears think that environment is just peachy. Or could you? If you could change your DNA, you might grow a thick, waterproof fur coat, develop claws ideally suited for catching fish, and make a very nice life for yourself as a "polar human."

But people do live near the North Pole. They have learned how to do it, not by changing their hard-wired DNA but by learning and remembering. They have used their *soft-wired* brains to make a way of life for themselves. They wear warm clothes, build efficient shelters, and catch food with spears and hooks because humans are not fast and agile enough to hunt and fish the way bears and wolves do. This is where humans' "soft" memory makes the difference!

Who Has a Soft Memory?

It would be simple to generalize that plants have "hard" memories and animals have "soft" memories, but, in fact, the truth is a lot more complicated than that. More accurately, every creature that carries DNA coding—that is to say, all of us—has hard memory. We aren't aware of it, we can't call it up to our consciousness, but it's there just the same.

What about soft memory? Or intelligence? Let's try to establish a more comprehensive idea of what we mean by these terms. How do memory, *consciousness*, learning, *intelligence*, and mind fit together?

Words to Remember

Consciousness: A sense or awareness of personal identity, especially the complex of attitudes, beliefs, and sensitivities held by or considered characteristic of an individual or a group.

Intelligence: The ability to acquire, organize, and evaluate data and to make meaningful decisions based upon this data.

Consider a common spider spinning her web in a tree in your backyard. The hungry spider sits in the middle of her web waiting for some unsuspecting prey to collide with the sticky strands of the web. If a soft-bodied fly or moth gets tangled in the spider's web, the spider scurries from her position, either stings her prey into immobility or wraps her prey in strands of fresh spider's silk until it is unable to escape, and thus has herself a nice, juicy dinner. But if the creature that blunders into the spider's web is a hard-shelled beetle, the spider ignores it, leaving the beetle to escape (if it can) or to die and remain in the web. Question: Is the spider intelligent? It would certainly seem so.

Consider these facts: The spider acquires data. (Something has landed in her web, and the spider is sensitive enough to differentiate between, say, a moth and beetle by the feeling of its impact on her web.) She organizes and evaluates data. (Is it a beetle? If so, it's worthless to the spider. Is it a moth? Yummie!) She makes a meaningful decision based on the data. (She scurries over and secures her prey if it's a moth; she ignores it if it's a beetle.) But the spider cannot learn (at least as far as anyone knows). She has a memory. She remembers how to spin a very complicated web, how to trap and secure her prey, and just which insects are worth trapping, which are useless to her, and which should be avoided.

Does she have consciousness? Does the spider have a *mind*? Probably not. It seems certain that all her "memories" are hard-wired and unchangeable. The advantage of soft-wired memory is that it enables you to learn from experience. All mammals from mice to whales can learn from experience. Goldfish can learn from experience—they can be taught to actively avoid a shocking situation. The spider's reactions, however, seem to be entirely instinctive.

Androcles' Lion, Konrad Lorenz's Goose, and Your Dog

Many generations of schoolchildren have been raised on *Aesop's Fables*, including the one about Androcles and the lion. In this story, a young man comes upon a lion suffering from a thorn stuck in its paw. The young man removes the thorn, relieving the lion's pain. In later years, the lion is out hunting and comes upon the same man. Instead of killing him and eating him for dinner, the lion spares the young man's life in gratitude for the kindness he showed the lion long ago.

Konrad Lorenz, the great naturalist, having studied the behavior of animals for many years, observed that some—including many species of ducks and geese—form permanent relationships with their mates. When one mate dies, the survivor spends weeks wandering around looking for its dead partner, apparently puzzled and saddened.

As for your dog, you can probably tell us as many stories as we can tell you. Certainly, your dog gets to know you and remembers people, places, and words.

Richard here:

> My son Tom taught our dog Ramona to "buy" food by bringing him toys and exchanging them for dog biscuits or other treats. When Tom holds up a dog treat and says, "Bring me a toy, Ramona," she brings him a toy, even if she has to run upstairs and get one from the room where she sleeps. She has a number of toys including a rubber ball, a pink squeaky porcupine, and a plastic bone, and she brings whichever of these she finds first to use as "money" to buy her treat.
>
> Clearly, she understands the concepts of "buy" and "toy." She remembers that she can get a snack in exchange for a toy. Even if she doesn't remember where

each of her toys is at all times, she knows which rooms of the house they are likely to be found in. Interestingly, she has never brought another object, such as a shoe or a newspaper, when Tom asks her to bring him a toy.

Is Ramona intelligent? Is she demonstrating the ability to acquire data, to organize and evaluate it, and to make a decision based on it? I think so. And, unlike the spider who is genetically hard-wired to react to fresh prey in her web, Ramona clearly is exhibiting the ability to learn and remember what "Bring me a toy" means.

Michael here with another dog story:

Despite what they say, you can teach an old dog new tricks. When my Norwegian Elkhound Sam was about nine years old—that's over 60 in human years—I got tired of him coming into the house and leaving the door open. So I taught him to close the door. It took about a week, and he really didn't see the point, but he learned it and he did it.

Remembering with Your Body

We'd like you to try a little experiment. If you've ever learned to play a musical instrument, to hit a baseball or a tennis ball, or to operate a computer or even a typewriter, you can do this. At the very least, if you have a telephone handy, you can use it as equipment for the experiment. In fact, let's try it with a telephone.

We'll assume your phone has a keypad for punching in telephone numbers rather than the old-fashioned rotary dial. Think of a person or location you call frequently—your home, your office, or a best friend. Go ahead and pick up the handset and let your free hand move toward the keypad. Chances are, you curled three fingers and your thumb, extended a single finger, and held it poised over the first digit of the number you intended to call. It was all pretty much automatic. You didn't think, "Oh, my friend's number is 555-1234, so the first digit is 5. Ah, there it is on the keypad." If you were calling an unfamiliar number, you might have looked it up first, thought just that, and consciously looked for the 5 key, and then punched it. But to reach a familiar number, the actions were automatic.

Similarly, if you've ever taken piano lessons, your teacher probably urged you not to look at the keyboard when you played. She wanted you to learn the feel of the piano and she wanted you to learn where each white or black key was located. Ultimately (if you stuck with it!), you didn't look at a note on the sheet music, tell yourself, "Ah, that's a C-sharp," look at the keyboard, find C-sharp, and strike the note. You might have done that at first, but before long, you had trained yourself to see the note on the sheet music and respond automatically without thinking, "That's a C-sharp" or looking for the proper key.

Words to Remember

Motor: In terms of the nervous system, of, relating to, or designating nerves that carry impulses from the nerve centers to the muscles. Involving or relating to movements of the muscles.

Conditioned: In psychology, an action or response learned through physical repetition.

Reflex: In physiology, produced as an automatic response or reaction.

Conditioned reflex: An action that takes place automatically and without conscious thought in response to a given stimulus. This action is learned through frequent repetition.

You built a neural path (remember our old friends the neurons?) that connected a visual signal (the printed note) with remembered information (the layout of the keyboard), generating a motor response that caused your finger to strike the proper key. The same principle, involving motor response or motor memory, applies in other situations. If you practice hitting a baseball until you're good at it, you don't analyze a pitch and think, "Ah, that's a fastball letter high over the outside of the plate. I'll swing at it." If you did that, the ball would be in the catcher's mitt before you ever moved your bat. Instead, you developed a *motor memory* (and a set of *conditioned reflexes*) that took care of these decisions. It started your bat around in time to hit the ball coming toward you at nearly 100 miles per hour from a distance of only 60 feet, 6 inches.

You could think of examples to your heart's content. Typing on a typewriter or keying text into a computer would be a clear example of this type of conditioning and body memory. As a beginner, you might have thought, "I am going to enter the word 'elephant.' Now let's see, 'e' and here's the e key, 'l' and here's the l key..." and so forth. When you got good at it, all you had to do was think "elephant," and your fingers took care of the rest. So you see, your memory is not located only in your brain.

How many types of memory are there? Does a bee have a memory? Does a book? In the next chapter, we'll examine these questions, and you'll see how the answers apply to you as well.

Oh, remember that pesky rosebush? We were wondering whether it has consciousness, intelligence, and memory. By this time you're probably able to form an opinion regarding those matters.

But if you're wondering what we think, well ... Consciousness? Almost certainly not. Intelligence? Very, very little, if any. It does respond, to a degree, to sunlight, but this is a mechanical-like tropism, not an intelligent act. But, *memory*—unquestionably! Otherwise, how does it "know" how to grow thorns, leaves, those lovely flowers? It's in the DNA. It's "information." It's memory.

The Least You Need to Know

➤ All living things have genetic memory in the form of DNA that tells their bodies how to grow and develop.

➤ Intelligence involves acquiring, processing, and using information.

➤ "Hard" intelligence and memory are genetically determined and cannot be changed by experience or learning.

➤ "Soft" intelligence and memory are subject to development and growth and can be changed by experience and learning.

➤ Many animals have intelligence and memory. Insects and spiders have only hard intelligence and memory, while most or all mammals have both hard and soft intelligence and memory.

➤ Motor or body memory can be learned through repetition and is highly useful in many everyday activities.

Chapter 3

Birds Do It,
Bees Do It

In This Chapter

➤ Memory as the product of evolution

➤ Cephalopods, the unsuspected geniuses

➤ The dance of predator and prey

➤ Memory and communication in bees and other insects

➤ "Birdbrain" isn't such an insult!

One of the great puzzles of life is when and why intelligence evolved. Part of the problem is that we're not exactly sure just how long ago life first appeared on this planet. Most scientists believe that the earth itself is some six to seven billion years old and that life in one form or another has existed here for at least half that length of time.

Some Memorable Facts

In *Annales Veteris et Novi Testamenti* (*Annals of the Old and New Testament*) published in 1650, James Ussher, Archbishop of Armagh, worked out the chronology of the Bible and determined that the creation occurred in the year 4004 B.C. (Four years later, theologian John Lightfoot refined this determination further to 9:15 in the morning on October 26, 4004 B.C., a Wednesday.) If you choose to believe the bishop, we can only suggest that God must have planted many false clues such as fossil records, the radioactive decay of uranium, and the movement of the continents in an attempt to convince us otherwise. Perhaps it would be an act of politeness and religious faith to pretend to believe what God obviously wants us to believe.

This doesn't mean, however, that if you had a time machine and could travel back three or four billion years, you would encounter exotic civilizations peopled by glorious men and women. Neither would you find giant dinosaurs roaming about the countryside while astonishing pterodactyls soared overhead and monstrous plesiosaurs lifted their scaly crests from the primordial seas. As ancient as the dinosaurs were, they were much more recent than that. In fact, for most of the history of life on earth, the only living things were very small, very simple organisms that would make pond scum look complex—and bright—in comparison.

Evolutionary biologists like Stephen Jay Gould point out that the blossoming of much larger, infinitely varied, and hugely complex species is a relatively recent phenomenon. That is, it has occurred only in the past few hundred million years. And compared to the millions of species that have arisen on this planet, the development of complex minds, equipped with high levels of intelligence and memory, has been a still more recent and unusual event. Why did it happen?

No one really knows. Perhaps it was a chance occurrence. (Such events *do* occur.) Why do we have five fingers on each hand and five toes on each foot rather than four or six? Nobody knows the answer to that one either, but in all likelihood, it just happened that way. At least, there seems to be no evolutionary advantage to the number five nor does it happen with particular frequency.

Some Memorable Facts

Having five digits seems to be part of the pattern of being a mammal. Even such diverse species as dolphins and horses, which have no visible fingers or toes, have internal bone structures that suggest five digits on each of four limbs.

Bilateral Symmetry

You have two ears and two eyes—and with good reason. These features can provide stereoscopic vision, which is a useful skill for carnivores. If you have to leap on your prey's back to kill it, you have to be able to judge just how far away that back is. Herbivores, which exist by avoiding becoming the meal of a carnivore, have eyes placed well around on the sides of their heads. This gives them an almost 360-degree view of the world around them, making it hard for a carnivore to get within leaping range. For them also, two eyes are better than one, but as you can see, for a different reason.

Two ears are also useful. They provide directional hearing so you know from just which clump of bushes that suspicious rustling sound is coming. Perhaps these senses were more

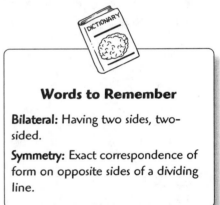

Words to Remember

Bilateral: Having two sides, two-sided.

Symmetry: Exact correspondence of form on opposite sides of a dividing line.

useful for our hunter ancestors, but they can still come in handy today. You have four limbs—two arms and two legs. You have two lungs but only one liver. You have one heart, but your heart has four chambers. You have only one brain, but it has two hemispheres. There's survival value in replication of organs, and it seems a reasonable inference—but it is not by any stretch a proven fact—that this is the reason why so many of our organs come in pairs. As creatures, we humans have *bilateral symmetry*. The same is true for most but not all members of the animal kingdom.

The Ability to Think

What was the survival value in our early ancestors being able to remember sights they had seen and events they had experienced? And what was the survival value in being able to call up these images and manipulate them, to speculate about possibilities, to make plans—in short, to think? Some scientists have suggested that our complex brains with all their electrical circuits—remember our old friends the neurons?—came about almost by accident. They suggest the development of the human hand, evolving from an animal paw, was an immense advance. And, of course, there's no disputing that. Think of going through life with paws instead of hands. Think of the impediment to human progress this would have been.

It's in the Hands

If you'll forgive the play on words, hand-in-hand with the development of the hand came the necessity to develop a hugely complex set of control circuits. Think about it. Next time you go to the kitchen and make yourself a peanut butter and jelly sandwich, try watching your hands. Notice all the complex, precise, and incredibly varied movements they make. As this wonderful "machine," the human hand, evolved, the control circuits necessary to use it efficiently and effectively did the same. But when you're not using your hands to perform complex tasks such as playing a musical instrument, typing on a keyboard, or making a peanut butter and jelly sandwich, what do you do with these circuits?

Rather than just shutting off their brains, this theory holds that our ancestors started doing other things with these circuits. They started thinking—and remembering—and remembering—and thinking. And out of all this arose human consciousness.

Or Is It?

This is just one theory, and, like many theories, it has some problems.

➤ **Problem #1: Monkeys**

Take a good look at a monkey. He's got hands pretty much like yours. In fact, he's got better toes than you do, to the point where some people might say he's got four hands. So he should be at least as smart as your are, right? If not smarter? But he isn't.

➤ **Problem #2: Dolphins**

A lot of research has been done about these wonderful creatures in recent years, and it looks as if their brains are at least as good as ours—maybe better. We're not sure how smart dolphins are, but there's a strong case to be made for them being truly intelligent—perhaps more intelligent than humans. And dolphins don't have any hands.

➤ **Problem #3: Octopuses**

Oh yes, that bright little *cephalopod*, our friend the octopus. There are several thousand species of octopus in the world, ranging from little fellows who could fit comfortably in the palm of your hand to giants who could eat you for dinner. Most octopuses (or octopi—either plural form is correct) are harmless critters and are rather shy. They are inclined to squirt a cloud of ink, forming a sort of submarine smoke screen, and skedaddle when they see humans rather than stick around and quarrel. Their nickname, "devilfish," is really undeserved. Well, except for a few fellows like the little Australian blue-ringed octopus. Touch him and you won't feel a sting, but a few hours later you'll just quietly stop breathing. You may never want to eat calamari again.

Words to Remember

Cephalopod: Any mollusk (shellfish) of the class *cephalopoda* having tentacles attached to the head, including the cuttlefish, squid, and octopus. Of all the cephalopoda, the octopuses are generally believed to be by far the most intelligent.

There is a great deal yet to learn about the octopus, but marine biologists who have studied these creatures have found them to be remarkably intelligent. They like to live in caves, and when they retire to their dens, they sometimes build barriers of rocks across the entrance to keep predators from attacking them. They communicate by changing color, and this seems to involve real expressions of emotion—maybe even ideas—not just reactions to their surroundings, as is the case with chameleons.

In laboratory aquariums, octopods have been known to learn how to unscrew the lids of jars in order to get at food. Pretty smart critters—and no hands! But wait a minute. An octopus uses its tentacles to grasp and work, just as we use our hands. The elephant uses its trunk for the same purpose, and elephants are pretty smart, too. And remember the old maxim, "An elephant never forgets."

Michael here:

A circus friend told me a story about Maybelle, an elephant who held a grudge against a particular elephant handler. Ten years after the handler retired, the circus came through Chicago, where the handler lived. When the handler came to visit, Maybelle snuck up behind him and doused him with a trunk full of water. She seemed, according to my friend, very pleased with herself. Maybelle never forgot.

The Eyes Have It

We might call the idea of developing complex neural circuits to operate hands, tentacles, or trunks, the *tool controller* theory of brain evolution as the origin of intelligence. A variation on this theory is the idea that we developed those complex circuits to *decode* stereoscopic vision. Try covering one eye and looking at a scene that has objects at different distances. Everything looks oddly flat, and it's hard to judge distances. Open both eyes and you can see in three dimensions. The octopus has a visual system remarkably similar to that of humans, and dolphins also have depth perception. So maybe there's something to that theory, too.

Strangely, the octopus, which is more unlike us than almost any animal you can think of, has eyes that are constructed a lot like our own eyes. Some Creationists have used this similarity as an example of how improbable evolutionary theory is. Could two separate paths of evolution create the same eye? Well, why not? The mammalian eye is efficient and works pretty well. If the octopus came up with it on its own, why then good for the octopus.

A Deadly Game of Tag

In the late 1970s, a brilliant scientist and student of ecology and evolution advanced a very different idea about the origins of memory, intelligence, and language. This man, Paul Shepard (1925–1996), saw the growth of these talents as tools in the endless contest between predators—hunting animals—and their prey. Shepard credited an earlier researcher, Harry J. Jerison, for stimulating many of his ideas. In this manner, Shepard was typical of scientists, each investigator advancing the work of earlier men and women. The image of the scientist as a lonely genius, working in total intellectual isolation, is more the invention of bad science-fiction writers and low-budget film-makers than it is a reflection of the way real scientists work.

It Takes Brains to Survive

Shepard suggested that, as the small furry creatures who were our remote ancestors scurried through the primeval forests, chasing or being chased, they used their memories and their intelligence to help them survive. If either predator or prey had gotten too good at its job, the result would have been disastrous. If the prey, typically herbivorous (plant-eating) creatures, had gotten too smart, they would have learned to evade the predators. The carnivorous (meat-eating) predators would have become extinct. The population of herbivores would have then grown until the food supply was completely consumed. The whole ecosystem would have collapsed.

Let's go the other way. If the predators had gotten too good at their job, they would have caught all the herbivores, consumed them, and then starved because their food supply was gone. Thus, in a remarkable balancing act, herbivores and carnivores slowly increased their mental powers over the span of millions of years. Jerison developed a way to measure brain development in various species. He called it the *encephalization quotient*. He worked out the relative "EQs" of carnivorous (predatory) and herbivorous (prey) animals over a span of several million years.

It went something like this:

Period	Carnivore	Herbivore
60+ million years ago	.44	.18
30–60 million years ago	.61	.38
13–30 million years ago	.76	.63
Recent (less than 13 million years ago)	1.10	.95

You'll notice that, in all eras, the hunters were smarter than the prey. But you also should notice that each era shows an increase in "smarts" for both groups. Don't be misled into thinking species evolve by choice. It's actually a process called *natural selection*. Whatever characteristics help organisms survive get "bred into" the species. Characteristics that cause them to die young get weeded out. It may be a cruel process, but it's the way nature works. Shepard pointed out that, in some creatures that have been around for a very long time—such as frogs—vital information processing takes place in the sense organs themselves, without much (or any!) involvement of the brain.

A frog's eye is so constructed that it will ignore flying objects that are too large or too small to make a good frog meal. When a dinner-size bug flies past the frog, however, a circuit closes, a signal goes from the frog's eye to the frog's long, sticky tongue, bypassing the frog's brain, and—wow!—dinner is served. Our eyes don't work that way. Neither do the eyes of any mammals or of most "higher" creatures.

In and Out of the Light

According to Paul Shepard's theory, our early mammal ancestors changed from daylight-dwelling creatures, to nocturnal creatures, and then reverted back to daylight-dwellers. Remember that, by *ancestors*, Shepard wasn't talking about Cro-Magnons, Neanderthals, or any other so-called "cave men." He wasn't even talking about the earliest *hominids*, which were *primates* that appeared on the plains of East Africa somewhere between 3.5 and 5 million years ago. He was talking about tiny, *quadrupedal* (four-legged), fur-covered creatures that evolved over a period of tens if not hundreds of millions of years into larger *bipeds* (two-legged)—the "cave man" ancestors we usually have in mind when we use that term.

Words to Remember

Hominids: Primates of the family *Hominidae*, of which *Homo sapiens* is the only extant (surviving) species.

Primate: A mammal of the order *Primates*, which includes the anthropoids, characterized by refined development of the hands and feet, a shortened snout, and a large brain.

Anthropoid: Resembling a human being, especially in shape or outward appearance.

It was during that period of living in the dark that we developed a lot of our abilities. It's a strange image to contemplate—our ancestors, incredible thousands upon thousands of generations ago, back when we were little beings scurrying beneath the leafy floor of the forest. Even with large, dark-adapted eyes, they lived in an environment in which they had to function in nearly complete darkness. Even though they had good eyes, their other senses grew sharper. This was particularly true of hearing, for the other senses (touch, smell, and taste) work only "up close." Vision depends on light, and light was unavailable for many hours at a time.

But they could hear as well in darkness as in light, and they could hear sounds coming from a distance—a very useful sense! They could use their eyes to find their way around, to search for food, to learn the pathways and byways of their territory, and to learn their way from their dens to their favorite watering places or food sources. If they had only been able to do this in "real time"—that is, while actually seeing the places and objects—they would have been helpless at night.

Imagine yourself living in such a world. Wouldn't it be useful to have a map of the neighborhood and a flashlight by which to read it in the dark? Our little ancestors didn't have paper maps or flashlights, but they developed something equally useful. They learned to make mental maps of their world.

If these creatures could somehow learn to store the images of paths, rocks, trees, and streams and then summon back the images to help them find their way in the darkness, they would be at a great advantage. Through the process of evolution-by-natural-selection, Paul Shepard argues, our ancestors became able to do precisely that.

Shepard came to agree with his predecessor, Jerison, in making one more point that we should consider. We've been dividing all animals into herbivores (prey) and carnivores (predators or hunters). That's a very nice, neat division, but it isn't quite accurate.

Some Animals Will Eat Anything

A third category exists—omnivores. This category includes creatures as varied as crows, raccoons, bears, and humans. Our ancestors (here we do mean cave people not prehuman quadrupeds) ate berries and nuts and fruit they picked off trees. Later, they learned to cultivate food plants and became the first farmers. But they also hunted wild animals, animals as small as birds and rabbits (and even smaller) and as large as *mammoths* and *mastodons*.

Eventually, our ancestors learned to domesticate and control food animals as well and became the first cattle ranchers, sheep herders, and chicken farmers. Even though, in this capacity, they were no longer hunters, the mental pattern had already been set. Shepard suggested that herbivores—prey animals—developed one kind of mentality. They were outwardly tranquil and passive but were always on the alert for the first sign of danger. This danger, of course, was represented by the appearance of a predator. Carnivores—predators—developed a different mentality. They were active and aggressive, always seeking out prey.

Omnivores—animals with a diet of both meat and vegetables—had a mixture of both kinds of mind. They were capable of both the herbivore's cautious, quiet, alertness and the carnivore's active, prowling outlook on life. In both situations, whether playing the part of hunter or of prey, they found it useful to remember their surroundings and the paths to food or safety. Learning itself is useful, but these creatures had to retain what they learned, and they had to be able to recall what they had retained. Every bit of learning had the potential to be useful—if they could only remember it.

But also, creatures that developed along a very different evolutionary path from our own developed the power to remember. One such example is the humble goldfish. These are attractive and colorful fellows, and many people find them amusing and rewarding pets—but hardly bright. Yet, if you happen to own goldfish, you might want to try this experiment. (If you don't own goldfish, ask a friend who does.) Every day when you feed them, sprinkle their fish food on top of their watery world at the same spot. Before long, whenever you approach their aquarium, the fish will head for the spot where they know their food will be delivered!

Some people might argue that this means the goldfish understand that you are going to feed them and know where their food is going to be placed. Others would call this *anthropomorphizing*. They would argue that the fish are simply acquiring a conditioned reflex. In either case—whether the action is the result of real under-standing or mere reflex—the fact remains that they learned and remembered where their food was delivered.

Words to Remember

Mammoths and **mastodons:** Large relatives of the modern elephant. The woolly mammoth, which was covered with long hair and lived far enough North to be surrounded by snow and ice, became extinct recently enough that woolly mammoth carcasses still are occasionally found frozen in the Siberian ice.

Words to Remember

Anthropomorphize: To attribute human motivation, characteristics, or behavior to inanimate objects, animals, or natural phenomena.

Entomologist: A person engaged in the scientific study of insects.

Bee My, Bee My Bay Bee!

A number of insect species display what seems (at least to humans) to be the strangest of all minds. Their intelligence and their memories are apparently held in common. Take the case of ants, for instance. *Entomologists* have studied the many varieties of ants at great length, both as individuals and in communities.

Millions of children have owned ant farms at one time or another and have watched in fascination through the glass walls as the little creatures went through their daily routine of obtaining food, breeding, caring for their young, and engaging in competitions of various sorts up to and including occasional ant wars. In communities, ants have a highly developed, complex, and intelligently managed social order. As individuals, however, they display almost no intelligence.

Some Memorable Facts

Some entomologists have suggested that an individual ant is like an individual neuron with feet. They suggest that, when ants get together, they form a sort of mobile ant brain, perhaps exchanging information by some sort of chemical signaling system. This hypothesis presents as many problems as it solves, such as: Can this ant brain have a collective memory? If individual ants are killed, does the colony lose part of its reasoning power? Can more ants think better? It does seem clear, however, that an ant colony is much smarter than any individual ant.

Bees present another fascinating study. Like ants, they live in large, complex communities. They have different jobs, and their anatomy is specialized for the work they perform. Bees exhibit especially fascinating behavior in their search for food. Each day, bee "scouts" leave the hive and fly throughout their surrounding territory in search of suitable nourishment. When they find it—a nice blossoming flower is always lovely—they return to the hive.

But how do these scouts report their findings to the rest of the bees? Silly as it might sound, they perform a complex dance. With their wings, legs, antennae, and bodies, they apparently are able to tell the other bees whether they have succeeded in finding food. If they were successful, they communicate where and how much food they found. Depending on the dance performed by the returning scouts, other bees fly to the food supply and bring back nourishment for the hive.

Is this amazing conduct purely the result of "hard" intelligence in the bees? Even if it is, they must be able to acquire, remember, and recall information. How do they do this? No one is really sure, but scientists are busy investigating intelligence and memory in the world of insects (ants, bees, and other six-legged bugs) and arachnids (spiders and similar eight-legged bugs).

Some Birds Aren't So Stupid After All

After many years of debate, evolutionary biologists are increasingly in agreement that the ancestors of all birds were actually feathered dinosaurs. At least one ancient bird, archaeopteryx ("ancient wing"), is frequently described as having reptilian features, including teeth. No modern bird has teeth.

Some Memorable Facts

The "hard memory" in the DNA of every modern bird was passed down from the dinosaurs of 65 million years ago. But do birds have intelligence? Do they have "soft" memories? Are they capable of learning new things, unlike, for instance, our clever friend the spider?

We know that birds do have "hard" memories. They know how to seek food, eat, mate, build nests, and care for their young. Apparently, however, they do not teach their young (as, for instance, lions teach their cubs how to hunt). If the elements of bird culture are not passed from generation to generation by social means, they must be genetically coded—that is, part of the birds' "hard memory" stored in their DNA.

But we know that birds are capable of learning, as evidenced by talking birds. Many species of birds learn to mimic human speech, the calls of other birds, or other sounds. Best known for imitating other birds is the mocking bird (*Mimus polyglottus*). Various types of parrot (members of the order *Psittaciformes*), from the familiar parakeet to the great colorful pets so often associated with pirates, have been known to develop extensive vocabularies.

Richard here:

> I once had the pleasure of owning a wonderful little parakeet named Kivi. He would sit on my shoulder while I sat at my typewriter each day, doing my work. (This was before desktop computers were common.)

One day, my wife heard me typing busily away. She thought this was odd because I'd left the house earlier and she hadn't seen me return. She entered the study and found no one there, yet she still heard the sounds of typing—clickity-clack, click-click-clack, the ding of the bell at the end of each line, the zip of a carriage return, and then clickity-clack once again. Was this a ghost?

There was no ghost. It was Kivi, sitting contentedly on his perch, imitating the sound of his friend—me—busily at work.

Most observers insist that "talking birds" merely mimic the sounds they hear and have no understanding of what they are saying. A minority cling stubbornly to the belief that birds do understand what they're saying.

Michael here:

Once in Hawaii I was standing on the lanai (porch) in front of a restaurant waiting for my date to emerge. Next to me was a big cage holding a large white macaw, which was quietly muttering to itself. An eight-year-old boy walking into the restaurant with his father paused in front of the cage. "Can these birds talk?" the boy asked his father.

"No," his father told him. "All they do is imitate sounds they've heard; they don't understand what they're saying."

"Oh," the boy said. He walked over to the cage and looked up at the bird. "Hello, bird," he said. "What's your name?"

The bird cocked an eye at the boy. "Arnold," the bird said. "What's yours?"

I'm afraid the boy will never believe his father again.

Our point is that the birds clearly are capable of acquiring, storing, and retrieving information—in this case, words. They definitely have "soft" memories. But do they have intelligence? That's another question. Plenty of anecdotal evidence suggests that crows are remarkably smart creatures (which, intriguingly, carries us back to Paul Shepard's theory that omnivores have "double intelligences"—both the active type of carnivores and the quieter, passive type of herbivores). Time and again, stories are told about crows posting a lookout while they take their dinner in a cornfield.

If three hunters approach, the stories go, the lookout crow sounds a warning call. The rest of the crows fly away and stay away even after the hunters hide. When the hunters leave, the lookout crow sounds another call and his companions return.

Suppose three hunters approach and hide, and the lookout crow sounds the alarm. Then suppose only two of the hunters leave and the third remains hidden. What happens? The lookout crow does not sound the "all clear." What conclusion can we draw from this story? How about that crows can count—at least to three!

Some Problem-Solving Birds

A British researcher conducted a fascinating experiment about the ability of wild birds to solve problems. He owned a country house and had observed many small wild birds, nuthatches, and paridae in the neighborhood. His experiment proceeded through several stages. To attract the birds, he put out some peanuts in a little wooden matchbox. The birds could come and take the nuts at will—and, of course, they did.

In the first test stage, the matchbox was mounted vertically, and the birds had to peck the tray portion of the box down to get at the nuts. They quickly learned to do this.

In the second stage, he drilled a hole in the matchbox and inserted a matchstick. This prevented the birds from pecking down the tray unless they first removed the matchstick. They quickly learned to do this.

In the third stage, after the matchstick had been removed and the tray pecked down, the nuts rolled into a second tray. The birds had to remove a second match and move the second tray to get the nuts. They quickly learned to do this.

In the fourth and final stage of the experiment, after the second tray was moved, the nuts rolled down a chute. The birds had to jump or fly down to this chute and press a lever to open a door. Then they got the nuts. The birds learned to perform all these tasks. The experimenter concluded that they not only had the intelligence to solve the problems, they had the memory capacity ("soft" memory!) necessary to remember all the steps of the process.

One bird, however, was more clever than the others (or perhaps less honest). He waited at the bottom of the chute while his companions earnestly pulled matchsticks and pecked trays until the nuts rolled down the chute. Then, before the poor hard-working fellows could jump or fly down to the bottom, this bird opened the door and took the nuts!

The Least You Need to Know

➤ Memory and intelligence are survival skills that have evolved over many millions of years.

➤ Memory without intelligence and intelligence without memory are equally useless.

➤ Both memory and intelligence can be divided into "hard" (inborn and largely unchangeable) and "soft" (learned and definitely changeable).

➤ Humans are not the only beings with memory and intelligence. Many creatures are remarkably clever, including canines (dogs and wolves), dolphins and whales, octopods, and many birds.

➤ Spiders (which are arachnids not insects) act in a manner that meets the usual requirements of intelligence. Their intelligence and memories are apparently completely "hard-wired," however, so they are incapable of new learning.

➤ Several species of insects (arthropods), including ants and bees, act in a manner that appears to be intelligent in terms of their communities but appear to have little or no intelligence as individuals.

➤ Not all birds are birdbrains.

Chapter 4

Even Educated PCs Do It

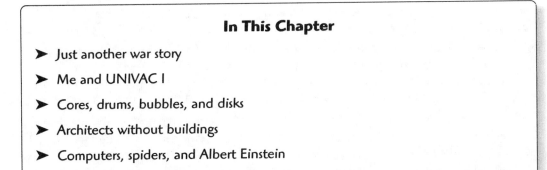

In This Chapter

➤ Just another war story

➤ Me and UNIVAC I

➤ Cores, drums, bubbles, and disks

➤ Architects without buildings

➤ Computers, spiders, and Albert Einstein

Remember the story of Rip Van Winkle, the lazy husband who took such a long nap that he didn't wake up for decades? If old Rip had fallen asleep 50 years ago and woke up this morning, he might have taken a stroll down any city street, met a 10-year-old boy or girl, and gotten into a conversation something like this:

Rip Van Winkle: This world seems very strange to me. I wonder if there's something wrong with my memory.

Ten-year-old: That could be serious. Do you think your disk crashed?

Rip: Disk? You mean, a dinner plate?

Ten: No, your memory. Did you remember to back up your work?

Rip: Back up my work? What do you mean?

Ten: Save it.

Words to Remember

Memory: In computer lingo, the machine's capacity for storing information as well as the device in which the information is stored.

Rip: Save it? I was raking leaves. Why should I save them?

Ten: No, I mean save your work on floppy disks.

Rip: Are we back to dinner plates?

Ten: (Getting annoyed.) Never mind the dinner plates. Maybe something happened to your RAM. How many megs you got? Gosh, do you think you could have fried a chip?

Rip: RAM? Megs? Fried a chip? Is that something I could put on my floppy disk and have for dinner?

Ten: It might be a problem with your hard drive. How many gigs you have, old-timer? Maybe you're running out of disk space. What software were you trying to run?

Rip: This is all too much for me. I think I'll just go take another nap.

Poor Rip Van Winkle and his young acquaintance could go on like this for quite a while, and Rip still wouldn't have the foggiest idea what they were talking about. Electronic computers have only been around since 1950 or so. For someone who lived and died before they arrived, the modern world would be a strange and puzzling place.

Of all the changes in the modern world—airplanes, submarines, spaceships, television, cell phones, medical advances, and so on—probably nothing has changed our every-day life as much as computers. And, believe it or not, we're just starting to feel their impact!

Computers have memories; there's no question about that. They probably are intelligent, too, although most people in the field believe computers have no real consciousness. (There is some disagreement about that, though.)

One of the most interesting things about computers and their memories is that they give us a fresh and fascinating way to look at ourselves and our own, human memories. In this chapter, we'll talk about computers and computer memories, and we'll use them as a mirror for studying ourselves. Keep an open mind; this is going to be fun. And you'll probably learn something useful!

Just Another War Story

The Second World War started in Asia in the early 1930s with the Japanese invasion of China. The European phase began in 1939 with the invasion of Poland by Germany. The United States entered both the Pacific and European campaigns in December 1941, following the Japanese bombing of Pearl Harbor in what was then the Territory (now the state) of Hawaii.

The war effort spurred research in many areas. One of these areas was a problem shared by both the army and the navy. It went something like this:

If a gun crew was ordered to fire a *howitzer* at a target, they could adjust their aim laterally (left or right) using a map and a compass. But the shell was fired in a high arc so it would drop onto its target from above, rather than directly at the target. How could the gun crew make sure the shell came back to earth at the right point?

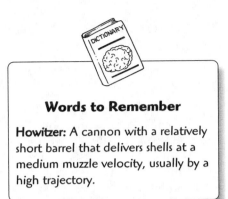

Words to Remember

Howitzer: A cannon with a relatively short barrel that delivers shells at a medium muzzle velocity, usually by a high trajectory.

Needed: Firing Tables

For every possible angle of elevation, every possible shell weight, and every possible charge of gunpowder, the *range* (distance to impact) varied. The military needed to develop a set of charts, called firing tables, that contained this information for gun crews in the field. There wasn't time to do all the computation necessary every time a howitzer was fired. So the military set whole groups of mathematicians to work, calculating firing tables.

Some Memorable Facts

The mathematicians used by the military, slaving over primitive mechanical calculators to come up with the range tables, were called "computers." Today's computers, made of silicon, metal, and plastic, rather than flesh and blood, can do in seconds—perhaps fractions of seconds—what it took a human computer months to do.

This was so time-consuming and expensive, however, that the army contracted out the development of a machine to do the work. Mechanical calculators already were in widespread use. The largest in existence at that time, called *Automatic Sequence Controlled Calculator Mark I*, was completed in 1944. This machine could perform wonders of number crunching, but the workings of gears and slides limited the speed of even the best mechanical calculators.

Needed: An Electronic Machine

What the military needed was a machine that did its work by electronic rather than mechanical means. Electricity, after all, moves at or near the speed of light—186,300 miles per second. No mechanical calculator can achieve anywhere near that speed.

The result was a machine called the *Electrical Numerical Integrator and Calculator* (*ENIAC*). It was a huge machine that filled an entire building. All data had to be entered manually by setting switches, and all results had to be copied down by hand from panels of lights. By modern standards, ENIAC was the dinosaur of computers. When it was turned on and actually functioned for the first time, however, it was a grand success.

The war ended in August 1945, and ENIAC wasn't ready to go until early 1946—but then, that's just another war story. Just as every modern organism from the tiniest microbe to the largest whale carries the DNA of ancient ancestors, every modern computer from the lightest handheld unit to the most powerful mainframe is descended from ENIAC.

How Computers Remember

Mark I stored information using a system of slides and gears. ENIAC used electron tubes, an immensely faster medium. In fact, ENIAC contained 18,000 tubes, was 100 feet long, and weighed 30 tons!

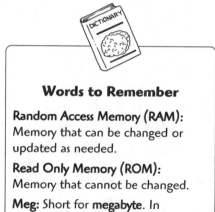

Words to Remember

Random Access Memory (RAM): Memory that can be changed or updated as needed.

Read Only Memory (ROM): Memory that cannot be changed.

Meg: Short for **megabyte**. In computer memory, one million units or characters of storage capacity.

By 1950, the first commercially available computer was on the market. The first unit delivered to a customer actually began operation in June 1951. It was called *UNIVAC I* (which stood for *Universal Automatic Computer*).

Richard here:

> In 1958, when I was a very, very young man, I got a job as a computer programmer. Desktops and laptops were far in the future at that time. The only computers that existed were mainframes, and the mainframe in the building where I worked was a UNIVAC I.
>
> We would-be programmers sat in a classroom all day, developing flowcharts and writing programs on huge sheets of "coding paper" that looked a lot like graph paper. We were told that UNIVAC I had 1,000 "words" of memory and that each word was 12 characters long. In modern language, we would say that UNIVAC I had 12,000 bytes of *RAM*. Compare this to today's common desktop machines that might have 64 or more *megabytes* each.

Back then, we students would turn in our coding sheets at the end of each day. They would then be converted either to punch cards or to magnetic tape by data-entry clerks. The cards or tape would be fed into UNIVAC I, the results would be printed out, and we would find them waiting on our desks when we arrived the next morning.

One day our instructor asked us, "How many of you have ever seen a computer?"

No one had!

"All right, I'll set up a tour of the computer for us. I'm afraid it might be at an inconvenient hour."

Was he ever right! A few days later, our sleepy-eyed class assembled at 4 A.M. for a tour of the computer, which filled an entire floor of our office building. The control console looked like a huge pipe organ, the tape drives were the size of refrigerators, the printer was as big as a washing machine and dryer combo.

In the middle of the room stood a structure that looked like a small gray barn with a glass door on one side. Our instructor led us to the "barn" and opened the glass door. We all stepped inside. He closed the door behind us; it sealed with a rubber gasket.

"You are now standing inside the computer's memory," he told us.

UNIVAC I used a device called a *mercury delay line* as its memory. Running around the inside of the barn-like structure was a tube perhaps 30 feet long that looked very much like a garden hose. Instead of water, however, this tube held liquid metallic mercury.

Data was input to the memory by electrical pulses shot through the mercury at "write gates." It was retrieved at "read gates." This may seem like a weird system, but it was the precursor of modern computer memories.

Some Memorable Facts

In the endless search for newer and better ways to build computers, engineers at one laboratory built a hydraulic computer. It operated using fluid that filled and emptied cylinders. When it was tested, this water-powered machine actually worked, but water does not flow as fast as electrons, and it was dubbed "the world's slowest computer." Unfortunately, no one could think of a use for the hydraulic computer, so the project was shelved.

Architects Design More Than Houses

Most computers have the same general pattern of units and functions that, when taken together, is called the machine's *architecture*. The people who design computers at the *system* level are called architects.

Almost any computer will have the following units:

➤ Input

➤ Processor

➤ Storage (or memory)

➤ Output

The *input unit* is used to get information into the computer. The most obvious input unit on your desktop or laptop computer is the keyboard. An Internet connection, however, also can be an input unit, as can a CD-ROM drive, a scanner, a floppy drive, or a tape unit.

The *processor* is computersmade up of the circuits that actually perform mathematical and data-processing functions. In early computers, these were made of tubes and wires. Later generations of computers moved to transistors mounted on printed circuit boards. Modern computers rely on silicon chips.

The computer's *memory*, as previously discussed, can be a silicon chip, a hard disk, or some other storage device. It's important to remember that a single computer can have several memories (or levels of memory). The main storage, or random access memory (RAM), is fast but is limited in size. The secondary storage, usually in the form of a hard disk, has a much larger capacity (often measured in *gigabytes*, or billions of units, compared to *megabytes*, or millions of units). The hard drive is not as fast as the main memory.

Of course, you also can have unlimited amounts of information stored "off-line" on floppy disks, tapes, CD-ROMs, and other devices.

Output devices include the monitor, the printer, and the Internet connection.

Why, That's a Lot Like Me!

You bet it is! If you think about it, you'll realize that you have the same types of "units" as your computer. Your own input devices are your five senses—seeing, hearing, touching, tasting, and smelling—and the organs that feed into them.

Your processing device is your brain. That's where you do your thinking. You can work on formal problems, a process comparable to your computer's number crunching. You also can dream, imagine, summon up memories, and create and manipulate images—all of which are comparable to your computer's data-processing function (and they're a lot more interesting!).

Your storage device also is your brain, for the most part. It even stores *body memory* or *motor memory*, the memory of how sets of muscles work together. How to swing a baseball bat properly, for example, is stored in the brain. Your brain also resembles your computer (and vice versa) in that your brain also has different levels of memory, which generally are divided into short-term and long-term.

Your computer can transfer data from input to RAM to the hard drive, can summon it back, can work with it, and then can return it to storage or send it to an output device. Your brain does all the same things. Your output devices are your body, your hands, and your power of speech.

What's the Latest Update on Your Software?

When using your desktop or laptop computer, you don't really have to worry about what type of circuits are inside the box. You just worry about using the computer. You're only concerned about entering, storing, and retrieving data—the computer's version of learning, remembering, and recalling information.

Let's say you're writing a novel and you have a very large computer file that contains the whole manuscript. This might be the equivalent of 400 typewritten pages. You're trying to remember the color of a character's eyes.

If you had only a hard copy of the manuscript, you would probably have to work your way through the whole 400 pages, looking for the word "eyes." But if the file is on your disk, all you have to do is open it and tell your software to search for "eyes." The computer will find every mention of "eyes," and you can then check their color.

Instant Recall

Even the most careful authors have been known to inadvertently change a character's eye or hair color in the middle of a manuscript. Sometimes they even change a character's name!

We don't know as much about the way our brains work as we do about the way computers work. This is because our brains are much more complex than even the biggest and most advanced computers in the world. Scientists are constantly studying our brains, how they're constructed, and how they work, and they've made a fair amount of progress.

Who Was the Second President?

When you learn a given fact—say, the name of the second president of the United States—that piece of information gets stored away in your brain. Let's say you're taking an exam and you need that piece of information. You "know that you know it," but somehow it doesn't pop right up. How do you find it?

Unfortunately, you can't do a word search for the second president's name because the president's name is exactly the piece of information you're trying to find. But you may have a "file" of presidents' names in your mind. If you are verbally oriented, you might just have a list of their names in your mind.

You can "open the file" and read it: Washington, Adams, Jefferson, and so forth. There he is, John Adams, second president of the United States.

If you are more visually oriented, you might have a kind of portrait gallery of famous persons in your mind. A section of the gallery might be devoted to presidents of the United States. When you open this file, instead of reading its text, you will find yourself looking at the pictures.

What's the Story?

Still another way to access the information might work best if you are good at remembering stories. History, of course, is itself one great, long story made up of an infinite number of smaller stories. You may have studied the late Colonial period, the American Revolution, and the early years of our Republic. You probably remember events such as the Boston Tea Party, the Continental Congress, the Declaration of Independence, the appointment of George Washington as commander of the American Army, the Constitutional Convention, and the formation of the Federalist and Anti-Federalist parties.

John Adams played a dramatic role in many of these events, and you'll remember the fact that he became president when George Washington retired after his second term.

There are so many ways to remember. You may make up rhymes, acronyms, or coded sentences to help you retrieve facts that might otherwise get lost in your memory. We'll tell you about many of these useful techniques in later chapters.

What's the Difference Between a Computer, a Spider, and a Genius?

The first electronic computer, ENIAC, received its program (or instructions) through a device called a *plugboard*. This actually was an old telephone switchboard that was borrowed and installed on the computer. Cables ran from terminal to terminal on the board, carrying various instructions. To change the program in any way, it was necessary to rewire the board.

Some Memorable Facts

Once computers got into serious production, there weren't enough surplus telephone switchboards to go around. Engineers designed much smaller plugboards specifically for use in computers. This major advance was used for several years before being abandoned in favor of "stored"—rather than "wired"—programs.

You can see old telephone switchboards in lots of old black-and-white movies. Think of having to remove the switchboard, replug all its cables, and remount it on your computer every time you wanted to make any change in your software program.

In this way, ENIAC had a mind like a spider's. It processed data that was given to it "intelligently," but it couldn't change its instructions. (Remember the spider in Chapter 2, "To Live Is to Remember," that does such a good job distinguishing between moths and beetles but can't learn anything new?)

Beginning with UNIVAC I, this concept changed. The program was now stored in the computer's own memory—first in the mercury delay line, then in cores, drums, and now chips. The computer could change its own program by performing logical tests and by taking different paths depending on the results.

In this manner, the computer's "mind" became more like your own (and like Albert Einstein's) and less like a spider's. It switched from a "hard-wired" program to a "soft" program, and the concept of software was born.

This is one of the great things about your own memory and the way you use it. You can keep inventing new methods and devices and can keep making new neural paths to help you remember what you need to remember!

The Least You Need to Know

➤ The first electronic computer, ENIAC, began operation in 1946. It arrived too late for use in World War II, its original purpose, but it became the ancestor of all computers built since then.

➤ ENIAC used electron tubes for its memory. The first commercial computer, UNIVAC I, used a mercury delay line.

➤ In the years since these machines were built, many different forms of computer memory have been devised. These days, silicon chips are used for most computer RAM or "main" memories.

➤ Additional computer memory is available in a variety of forms. Most modern computers use large-capacity hard disks for this purpose.

➤ Computer system design is called architecture. In most systems, the main components are input, storage, processing, and output.

➤ The earliest computer received its instructions from a "hard-wired" plugboard. This made it work like a spider or an insect—incapable of learning or changing its behavior.

➤ Since 1950, computers have stored their programs in their own internal memories, where they can be modified to meet changing conditions. In this regard, they resemble the "soft" minds of humans, and computer programs have come to be called software.

Part 2
Body and Soul

Where is your memory? You're probably ready to answer that it's in your brain, and you're probably right. Mostly. In the past, however, some people thought that the locus of human consciousness—including intelligence, emotion, and, yes, memory—was the heart. We still use expressions like "I know it by heart." Besides, any skilled pianist will probably tell you that at least part of her musical talent and skill—and memory— is in her hands. Still, the best evidence shows that most of our memory is located in the brain. It's a good idea to have at least a bit of information about the brain, how it's made up, and how it works. It's also a good idea to know how to take care of your brain. If you take good care of it, it will serve you well all the days of your life. You ought to know something about nutrition and the brain, exercise (both physical and mental) and the brain, and the way your brain processes information. As your dear old grandmother used to say, "Use it in good health!"

Chapter 5

The Brain and Why You Have One

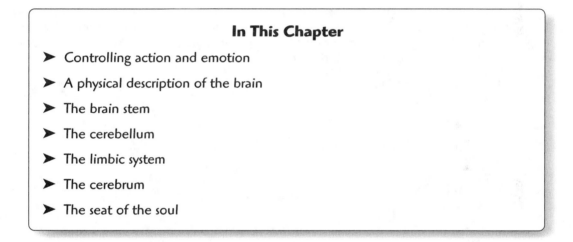

In This Chapter

➤ Controlling action and emotion

➤ A physical description of the brain

➤ The brain stem

➤ The cerebellum

➤ The limbic system

➤ The cerebrum

➤ The seat of the soul

As we've seen, just about every animal—from a sand flea to a hippopotamus, from a squid to a human being—has a brain. It seems to be one of the earliest things animals acquire on the road from being single-celled organisms to becoming hammerhead sharks, crocodiles, musk oxen, or members of Congress. A few simple sea creatures such as starfish, jellyfish, and sponges get along with only a rudimentary nervous system but no real brain. Animal evolution on the whole, however, has definitely moved in the direction of larger and better brains.

How the brain works is a deep and abiding mystery, even though we know much more about it than we did 25 years ago and immeasurably more than a century ago. We now have a pretty good idea of what the brain does. Most of *how* the brain does what it does remains unknown, however, although recent research has provided some tantalizing hints and has overturned some long-held beliefs.

Some Memorable Facts

One of the problems with brain research is that we have to use our brains to study our brains. This makes us captive to our own perceptions. For example, it is not obvious from the way we think we see things that the eye sends images to at least five different centers in the brain, dividing up the image by line, color, and different sorts of motion. Nor is it obvious from the way language seems to work that damage to a specific part of the brain can prevent us from recalling proper nouns or verbs or can destroy our ability to speak or understand speech but not to write or understand written sentences.

The brain not only is where we do our thinking, it is where we store our memories and the attitudes and habits that make up the indefinable something we call our personality. The brain also is in charge of just about everything having to do with controlling and commanding the body's functions, including (but not limited to):

➤ Internal housekeeping:

Breathing

Heartbeat

Blood pressure

Swallowing

Appetite

The cough reflex

The sneeze reflex

➤ Standing and balance

➤ Motion

➤ The senses:

Vision

Hearing

Smell

Taste

Touch

Temperature sensing

Body location

Body orientation

➤ The emotions:

    Love

    Hate

    Fear

    Anger

➤ And, of course, memory:

    Motor

    Short-term

    Long-term semantic

    Long-term episodic

A Digression on Memory

Psychologists (and biologists and other scientists) who study memory make a distinction between semantic memory and episodic memory. *Episodic memory* is your memory of events that happen regularly and routinely, such as eating breakfast or driving to work everyday. Although you are aware of having done these things, specific meals or trips get lost in the tedium of routine. In this type of memory, repetition of the event blurs the memory of any specific instance of the event.

Semantic memory is your memory of facts without regard to how the facts were acquired. You may, for example, know that the French word for umbrella is *parapluie* without having any idea when or where you learned the word. (You probably don't remember exactly when you learned the English word "umbrella" either, for that matter.) If you have been driving to work for the past few years, and if it's any distance away, you probably know all the shortcuts and side roads. You probably could draw a map of how best to travel that route in different road conditions and at different times of day, although your episodic memory of just which trips took you on which alternate paths probably is dim. Semantic memory also is the memory for poetry, specialized vocabulary, or memorizing long passages of Shakespeare. It actually improves with repetition—the more often you recite Henry IV's Crispin Day speech, the better you'll know it.

Refresh Your Memory

Specific episodes of repetitive events, if enhanced by powerful emotion, will remain clear. If during breakfast you hear the news of your favorite uncle's death or your daughter's engagement, the details of that breakfast probably will remain clear in your memory. You'll remember just which bit of oatmeal you choked on when your daughter announced she was marrying Sherman—the boy with the shaved head and the tattoos.

Let's Get Physical

Before we get into a deeper discussion of memory, let's begin with a physical description of the brain. The human brain is a two-and-a-half- to three-pound pink mass of nerve cells (mostly *neurons*, which are gray, and *glial cells*, which are white—the pink color comes from the continuous blood supply). It resembles a large, soft walnut that fits compactly inside the human skull. Although the skull seems to be one large, solid bone, it actually is made up of 22 separate bones that fit together tightly along a zigzag pattern of suture lines. In babies, the bones are not truly connected. This allows room for the head to grow. The bones fuse together as you grow up; the eight on top form the hard, protective *cranium*, or skull case, that encases and protects the brain within.

Words to Remember

Neurons: The cells that transmit information and sensory impulses (vision, hearing, pain, heat, touch, and so on) around the body. They are discussed further in Chapter 6, "A Hole in the Head."

Glial cells: Cells that provide support, protection, and nourishment to the neurons.

The brain is connected at its base to a thick rope of nerve cells called the *spinal cord* that descends through a hollow in the spine to the base of the backbone. The nerve cells all over your body that carry sensations of pain, hot, cold, and so on connect to the spinal cord, which transmits their information to the brain. The brain–spinal cord combination is known as the *central nervous system*.

The brain is cushioned within the protective bony plates of the skull by three layers: the *dura mater*, a tough, fibrous layer directly under the skull; the *arachnoid*, a web-like structure that fits over the brain like a skull cap; and the *pia mater*, a membrane that fits tightly into every crevice on the brain's surface. The space between the arachnoid and the pia mater is filled with a clear liquid called *cerebrospinal fluid*. This all serves as an efficient cushioning system against shocks.

The brain has been divided into many different parts with different names by different scientists of different sorts, depending on what functions of the brain they are analyzing. Most of these parts are not overly important for our present discussion, but it's a good idea to be familiar with the more important regions of the brain and what they do. We will now briefly look at (from bottom to top): the brain stem, the cerebellum, the basal ganglia, the limbic system, and the cerebrum.

The human brain.

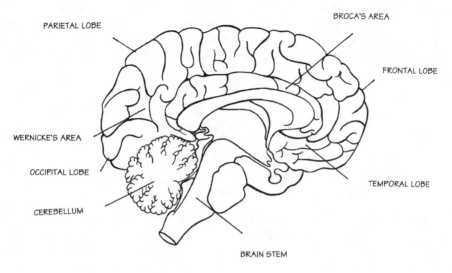

The Brain Stem

The Brain Stem

The brain begins at the top of the spinal cord just past the neck with an area called the *brain stem*, which is also called the *reptilian brain* because it is the most primitive part of the brain and is essentially the same in reptiles, birds, and mammals. It is made up of, in ascending order, the *medulla oblongata*, which actually connects to the spinal cord; the *pons*, a thick bundle of nerve fibers that feeds information from the medulla to the cerebellum above; and the *midbrain*, which controls some basic body functions.

Medulla

The medulla takes care of many of the most basic control functions of the brain. Blood pressure, heart rate, breathing, swallowing, vomiting, and even speech are regulated from the medulla, although some of these functions also can be controlled by conscious effort. Take

Words to Remember

Medulla oblongata: Latin for "elongated marrow." Although the actual object isn't all that elongated, it takes up the first inch of the three-inch brain stem. The word "oblongata" usually is dropped off when discussing this organ. (Henceforth, we will drop it as well.)

Pons: Latin for "bridge." It serves as a bridge for information and instructions between the spinal cord below and the brain above.

The **midbrain** was presumably named because it sits atop the brain stem, surrounded by the rest of the brain.

breathing, for example. When it happens without you being aware of it, the medulla is controlling it. When you think about your breathing, it comes under your conscious control. You can breath deeply or shallowly or even hold your breath. Note, however, that you can only hold your breath for a short time—two minutes or so at the very most—before the automatic control system in the medulla takes over and forces you to breathe.

Some Memorable Facts

Japanese pearl divers, Greek sponge divers, and other divers who use no underwater breathing equipment can hold their breath for more than five minutes, but this takes years of practice.

You may have heard that the left and right sides of the body are controlled by the opposite sides of the brain: The right side of the brain controls the left side of the body and vice versa. This is true, and it is in the medulla that most of the crisscrossing of nerve fibers from one side of the brain to the opposite side of the body takes place. We'll look at the two halves of the brain and how they differ later in this chapter.

Pons and Midbrain

The pons, a thick white bundle of nerve fibers about an inch long, has connections to various parts of the brain, mainly the cerebellum (which is discussed in the following section). The midbrain, also about an inch long, serves as a relay point for a variety of sensory inputs. It also controls a few basic, usually unconscious, responses such as the reflex that widens and narrows the pupil of the eye according to the amount of light available.

Cerebellum and Basal Ganglia

Tucked away behind the brain stem is a small but important brain structure called the *cerebellum*, which means "little brain." It usually is a little more than 10 percent of the total brain size, and it controls all the precise body motions you do without consciously thinking about them, such as posture and balance. When you drink from a cup, dribble a basketball, touch your nose, or walk without staggering, your cerebellum is in control. It is aided by the *basal ganglia*, four clusters of nerve cells that relay information to and from the cerebellum and that help smooth out complex motions.

Some Memorable Facts

The cerebellum is well developed in sharks, certain birds, and fish. When a pelican snatches a fish out of the water while skimming the surface or an eagle power dives on an unsuspecting pigeon and grabs it in mid-air, the cerebellum is controlling these fine movements. Human athletes, musicians, and dancers owe their best moves to their cerebellums. When a quarterback double-steps around a tackle, an ice-skater accomplishes a triple lutz, or a pianist manages a difficult passage in one of Liszt's *Hungarian Rhapsodies*, it is their cerebellums they should thank.

The Limbic System

Around the top of the brain stem are a series of structures shaped roughly like a wishbone that make up the *limbic system.* (The individual parts, for you completists, are the *amygdala*, the *corpus callosum*, the *fornix*, the *hippocampus*, the *mammillary body*, the *olfactory bulb*, the *supracallosal gyrus*, and the *thalamus*.) Pretty much the same in humans as in other mammals, the limbic system evolved early in mammalian history and sometimes is called the "old mammalian brain."

The limbic system is in charge of some of our basic emotions, mainly the so-called "fight or flight" responses. When you feel pleasure, rage, hatred, love, anxiety, or elation (to name a few), it is the result of some stimulation acting on your limbic system. Usually the stimulation is external, such as when you get angry because someone has done something you didn't like. Sometimes, however, the stimulation can be caused by an imbalance of the chemical stimuli your brain uses for internal control. It has been shown, for example, that depression can be the result of a lack of serotonin, a chemical your brain produces to control moods.

The Cerebrum

The *cerebrum*, the outer layer of the brain that covers the others like a wrinkled helmet, has a deep fissure (the *longitudinal sulcus*) down the middle that splits it in two. The two halves are known as the right and left *cerebral hemispheres.* Each hemisphere is further subdivided into "lobes" known (from front to back) as the frontal lobe, the parietal lobe, the occipital lobe, and the temporal lobe. Although the brain functions as a whole and these divisions were contrived by anatomists so they could use names for the different areas of the brain when they point to them, there is some division of labor within the brain that corresponds roughly to the different lobes.

➤ The *frontal lobe* seems to oversee learned social behavior and traits such as curiosity and planning.

➤ The *parietal lobe* interprets information from various senses (except smell, which travels from the receptors in the nose by way of a pair of *olfactory bulbs* to the thalamus in the limbic system).

➤ Although the *occipital lobe* is at the rear of the brain, it receives information from the eyes and is concerned with vision. This is one of the most complex jobs the brain is responsible for, involving as it does, decoding information involving size, shape, color, distance, texture, and movement; all of which are combined into a seamless whole within the brain.

➤ The *temporal lobe* is involved in the processing of hearing and memory.

Because of the crossover of nerve bundles coming into the brain, the two hemispheres control opposite sides of the body. That is, the left hemisphere controls the right hand, leg, and even the right side of our field of vision and vice versa. The reason for this is not known, but it is a trait we share with other mammals. The hemispheres usually work together so well that this division of responsibility is impossible to observe. They share and exchange information through a thick trunk of nerve fibers called the *corpus callosum* deep within the brain.

The two hemispheres, although they appear to be identical mirror images of each other, have different functions. This was discovered when *neurobiologists* studied patients who had their corpus callosum severed to correct severe epilepsy or another serious brain disease. With the corpus callosum cut, one half of the brain literally doesn't know what the other half is doing.

In most people, the left side of the brain seems to be dominant. This is why most people are right-handed. (Some left-handed people have right-brain dominance; others share some sort of neurological difference we don't yet understand.) The left hemisphere works at language skills including reading, writing, speaking, and working out verbal logic problems. The right hemisphere controls nonverbal skills such as understanding shapes and other visual images. The right side also is better at understanding facial expressions and both expressing and interpreting emotions.

Refresh Your Memory

Vision requires a lot of mental processing, and it is treated somewhat preferentially by the brain. Thus, it is not surprising that large areas of the brain are dedicated to sight. But why does smell, which in humans is an underutilized sense, have special pathways and its own olfactory bulbs? The answer is unknown. Perhaps it is because smell is an ancient sense or because so many other mammals make much greater use of it—it is said a dog's sense of smell is a million times more acute than a human's— that it comes as standard mammalian equipment.

As previously mentioned, however, these differences are minor in those of us who haven't had our corpus callosum severed since the two hemispheres are constantly exchanging information. Attempts to explain behavior or abilities on the basis of left-brain or right-brain activity are mostly bunkum.

The Seat of the Soul

Until comparatively recently, we didn't know any of this information about the brain. Aristotle taught that the heart controlled thought and emotion and that the brain was merely an organ for cooling the blood. For many centuries, it was believed that the seat of the mind—or the seat of the soul, as sometimes the two were seen as the same thing—was the heart or possibly the liver.

This was based, at least partly, on religious and philosophical considerations. If you believe in the survival of the personality after death, whether it ascends to heaven or waits around to be reincarnated, then that personality or "soul" must be immaterial, residing within but separate from the body. Survival of the personality also implies survival of the person's mind and memory.

If the body is merely a vessel for the soul and the mind is the part of the soul that carries the person's intelligence and memory, there is no point in looking for intelligence or memory within the body, brain, heart, liver, or kidneys.

This belief died hard, and indeed is not entirely dead even today. But it has lost much of its force. In 1746, Dr. Julien Offray de la Mettrie, who was serving as a physician in the French army, wrote a book called *The Natural History of the Soul* (*Histoire naturelle de l'âme*, as they say in French), in which he denied the existence of a soul. The brain, de la Mettrie wrote, is the mind. Possibly his experience with brain injuries in soldiers guided him to this truth. Unfortunately de la Mettrie was before his time—he was kicked out of the army and all copies of his book were ordered burned. He fled to Holland

Words to Remember

Neurobiologist: Someone who studies the brain from the neurons and other brain cells to how thoughts and memories are formed. The root *neuro* (nerve) also is used in the words *neurologist,* a doctor who treats diseases of the brain; *neurosurgeon,* a doctor who operates on the brain; *neuropsychologist,* a specialist who tests for brain impairment; *neurophysiologist,* a scientist who studies how the brain works; and even *neuroscientist,* anyone who studies the brain in any way without a more specific title.

Refresh Your Memory

The son of a physician and a student of Plato, the Greek philosopher Aristotle (384–322 B.C.) founded the Lyceum in Athens, which was one of the most important early sites of learning. He systematized the study of the sciences of biology, zoology, physics, and psychology as well as the fields of metaphysics, ethics, politics, rhetoric, history, and a few others. For 2,000 years, he was regarded as the final authority on any imaginable subject, and his philosophy and system of logic are still being taught.

and rewrote his book. But the Dutch, liberal as they were reputed to be, were not ready for such heretical ideas, and once again his book was burned.

Brain Is Mind Is Brain

Over the past two centuries, as doctors have noted that specific brain injuries cause specific mental disabilities, it has become clear that the brain and the mind occupy the same space. Whatever happens in the next life, in this one you are dependent on your brain for thinking, memory, and that elusive thing we call personality.

Cutting Away the Will

In the 1830s, a French physician named Marie-Jean-Pierre Flourens used his surgical skills to cut away parts of the brains of various animals including dogs, rabbits, and pigeons. He discovered that the animals lost their will to move or to perform any voluntary actions, although they still were capable of action if stimulated. He also found that the exact location of the area removed didn't seem to matter as much as the amount of brain matter excised. He performed these experiments over a period of many years, removing larger and more varied parts of the brain from his unlucky subjects to see the results. He developed a theory that he was removing the animal's "will," although what he actually was doing was removing the brain sites for controlling motion—and just about everything else. He doesn't sound like the sort of man we would like to have teaching our children.

Words to Remember

Aphasia: The inability to speak or to understand words due to a brain disease or trauma.

Broca's Area

In 1861, another French doctor named Paul Broca had a patient who had lost the power of speech and could only say "Tan, Tan." When the patient died, Broca did an autopsy of the man's brain and discovered a lesion (injury) about the size of a hen's egg in the left frontal lobe. Broca deduced that this part of the brain was responsible for the ability to use language, and it has been known as *Broca's Area* ever since. The inability to speak anything but a repetitive random syllable is known as *Broca's Aphasia*.

Wernicke's Area

In 1871, a German neurologist named Carl Wernicke diagnosed a different type of aphasia in several of his patients. They could respond to specific questions, but their response did not make sense and might include nonsense syllables in place of words. For example, if you asked one of Wernicke's patients where he lived, he might respond by saying, "Yes, of course. Sadly wishkepit do seldom nensitt. But if you say spedly, why that's the motive, then steck."

Autopsies of several of Wernicke's patients revealed another area, close to Broca's, that seemed to cause this particular type of aphasia. Wernicke was rewarded by having the illness and the area named for him.

Where the Action Is

In the more than a century since Broca and Wernicke located two speech centers in the brain, many more areas have been found that localize specific actions, abilities, and even memories. This convinced some researchers that the brain is hard-wired—that is, that the brain's functions originate in specific locations within the brain, that they are there from birth, and that every brain has these functions in more or less the same place. But nothing about the brain is as simple as it seems.

Some Memorable Facts

For many years the perceived wisdom was that, after the brain grew to its full size, no new brain cells were born. The old ones supposedly died off at a steady rate that increased as you got older. This was used to explain, among other things, the declining mental abilities of the elderly. Recent experiments show that at least some parts of the brain can, and do, grow new brain cells to replace those that die. Most of the mental decline of the elderly can be attributed to various diseases and to a decreased flow of blood to the brain caused by clogged arteries. This is explored in detail in Chapters 7, "In Sickness and in Health," and 9, "Nutrition and Memory."

If an adult, through an accident or a disease, loses an area of the brain that regulates some function like understanding verbs or remembering the names of musical instruments, that knowledge or ability is gone and can never be recovered. However, if a young child loses his speech center, for example, there is a strong likelihood that another portion of the brain will take over its job, and the child will grow up with perfectly normal speech.

So the brain's "wiring" is at least tentative, and rearrangement is possible at an early age. Perhaps, as we discover more about how the brain works, we will learn how to shuffle these skill centers in the adult brain to relieve some of the anguish caused by brain damage.

The Least You Need to Know

➤ The brain is in charge of body motions, emotions, thoughts, and memory.

➤ Among the major parts of the brain are the brain stem, the cerebellum, the limbic system, and the cerebrum.

➤ The brain stem, also called the reptilian brain, is made up of the medulla oblongata, the pons, and the midbrain. These control basic functions such as breathing and heart beat.

➤ The cerebellum controls precise body motions and enables you to ice skate or play basketball.

➤ The limbic system controls our emotions.

➤ The cerebrum is responsible for thinking and memory, and it oversees vision and other senses.

➤ Damage to an area of the brain can cause very specific mental defects, such as loss of the ability to speak, although understanding and writing may be unaffected.

➤ Children often can overcome damage to or the loss of a specific brain area, but adults seem to have outgrown this capability.

Chapter 6

A Hole in the Head

In This Chapter

➤ Phineas Gage's accident

➤ The brief vogue for prefrontal lobotomy

➤ Revisiting HM, who won't remember

➤ Long-term potentiation

➤ Zapping the brain for memories

➤ Retrieval problems

➤ Sense memories

➤ PTSD

Over the past few thousand years, we have learned much of what we know from the mistakes or misfortunes of others. When Og stuck his hand in a fire, his fellow cavemen learned not to do this or they'd get burned. We've lost some members of the community while discovering which mushrooms are good in an omelet and which are deadly poisons. (Someone once said that the bravest man who ever lived was the first man to eat an oyster.) We've learned over the course of centuries how to treat diseases that once were invariably fatal by testing treatments on the dying until we found one that worked. As a result, many diseases are now treatable and at least one major scourge, smallpox, has been completely eradicated.

This process has been used extensively in our studies of the human brain. We've discovered much of what we know about where the various human faculties that make up our intelligence, emotions, perceptions, and sense of identity are located within the brain by noting the effects of the damage or destruction of specific cerebral areas. Since it would be unethical, immoral, illegal, and not very nice to purposely damage the brains of our fellow humans, neuroscientists have to wait until nature does it for them. But almost any sort of accident is bound to happen if you have the patience to wait around for it.

The Misfortune of Phineas Gage

A Rutland & Burlington Railroad work team foreman named Phineas Gage entered the medical record books on September 13, 1848, when a black powder charge he had been tamping into a hole in a rock was set off by an accidental spark. The resulting explosion sent the three-and-a-half-foot-long iron tamping rod into Gage's cheek, through the frontal lobes of his brain, and out the top of his head. The rod landed about 30 feet away.

Refresh Your Memory

"The equilibrium, or balance, between [Gage's] intellectual faculties and animal propensities seems to have been destroyed. He is fitful, irreverent, indulging at times in the grossest profanity (which was not previously his custom), manifesting but little deference for his fellows, impatient of restraint or advice when it conflicts with his desires, at times pertinaciously obstinate, yet capricious and vacillating, devising many plans of future operation which are no sooner arranged than they are abandoned..."

—Dr. John Harlow

The blast threw Gage backward, and he landed hard on his back and lay unconscious where he had fallen. At first, his work crew thought he was dead, but he amazed them by coming to a couple of minutes later and was actually able to utter a few words. The crew put him on an oxcart, where he sat holding his head with both hands, and they rushed him as fast as the ox would travel back to Cavendish, Vermont, the nearest town. Two doctors, astonished that he was still alive, did what they could to keep him that way.

Dr. Edward Williams and Dr. John Harlow settled Gage into an attic room at the Adams Hotel and cleaned out his wound, removing bits of skull, hair, skin, and brain from the sizable hole. In the process, Dr. Harlow discovered that he could put his index finger straight down into the exit hole in Gage's skull without encountering any part of Gage's brain.

The doctors had a difficult time stopping the bleeding. After a short period of being (much to the doctors' further astonishment) completely lucid, Gage became delirious and began running a fever. The doctors dosed him, according to the medical wisdom of the day, with castor oil, calomel, and rhubarb.

Personality Impaired

Gage managed to fight off the initial infection (perhaps it was the rhubarb) and steadily improved over the next two months until he was able to walk around town and plan a trip to visit his mother in Lebanon, New Hampshire.

The accident, which had surprisingly little effect on the 25-year-old railroad foreman's intelligence, caused profound changes in his personality. Before the accident, he was easygoing, energetic, well liked, and capable. He was described by his friends and his employer as a shrewd and capable businessman, a good companion, and a valuable employee. After the accident, however, he became stubborn, irrational, impatient, unreliable, and capricious. He also apparently lost the ability to foresee the consequences of his actions or to care much. His friends were puzzled and declared that "Gage was no longer Gage."

The accident effectively ended Gage's life, although he lived for another dozen years. The railroad refused to give him back his job because they now found him to be undependable. Back then, the idea that the railroad perhaps should take some of the responsibility for his on-the-job accident would have struck everyone as radical to the point of insanity. Gage moved to Boston, where he was studied by doctors for a few years. He spent most of his remaining years as a sideshow performer in P. T. Barnum's circus, sitting in a chair and holding in his arms the tamping rod that had pierced his brain and destroyed his personality.

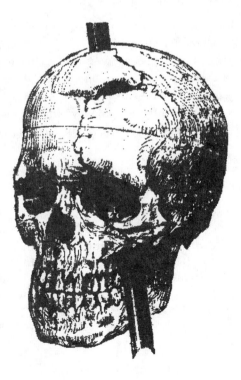

A drawing of Phineas Gage's skull done after Gage's death by Dr. John Harlow, one of the doctors who first treated Gage after his accident. The heavy black tubular line shows the path the tamping rod took through Gage's head.

Gage's Tragedy, Neuroscience's Good Fortune

In a very real sense, although Gage might not agree, his life was not wasted. The careful observations of the doctors who studied his personality changes gave neurologists their first insight into the inner workings of the brain. The frontal lobes (technically, the *orbitofrontal complex*) in both hemispheres of Gage's brain had been destroyed, and this wrought the drastic change in his personality. This was a strong indication that personality—and possibly other facets of a person's mental abilities that make up the "mind"—is stored in very specific areas of the brain.

At that time, one theory of how the brain worked was the "unitary" theory, which held that memories and emotions were somehow stored all over the brain. Gage's unfortunate experience indicated otherwise. When a couple decades later, Paul Broca and Carl Wernicke showed that language resides in yet another area (see Chapter 5, "The Brain and Why You Have One"), the case for the compartmentalization of the mind into different areas of the brain grew even stronger.

Some Memorable Facts

Gage's accident was not the only indicator early researchers had as to the function of the frontal lobes. Toward the end of the nineteenth century, neurologist Leonore Welt had a 37-year-old patient who had fallen from a fourth-floor window and smashed in his skull on the front of his head. Like Gage, he recovered physically, but his personality was drastically altered. Before the accident, he was a peaceful, hard-working furrier. Afterward, he couldn't control his temper and quarreled incessantly and violently with anyone around. Unlike Gage, he gradually improved although never regaining his full faculties, and was ashamed of his previous bad behavior.

Chimps Lead the Way

About 100 years later, when anesthetics and sterile procedures had transformed the operating room and surgeons had some hope of operating on the brain without killing the patient, neurosurgeons began trying to emulate Gage's accident, although in a less emphatic fashion. In the 1930s, C. F. Jacobsen, a physiologist at Yale, decided to see what an operation on the frontal lobes would do for a pair of intractable and nasty chimpanzees he was working with. The chimps, Becky and Lucy, reacted to the operation by losing their viciousness and becoming gentle. It wasn't that they now liked being handled, but they no longer seemed to care.

In 1935, Egas Moniz, the clinical professor of neurology at the University of Lisbon, decided to attempt the operation on some of his more intractable patients. After all, humans aren't that different from chimpanzees. The operation, which became known as a *prefrontal lobotomy*, was a success if you were interested in making patients in mental hospitals easier to handle. Patients who were given to violent fits of anger and, in some cases, physically assaulting their keepers, became docile and placid. Unfortunately, the placidity came at the cost of major changes in personality. As with Gage, the patient's friends and relatives complained that the patient no longer was the person they had known.

These operations no longer are performed today, and it would be considered unethical to do so. It is now recognized that, although different parts of the brain perform different functions, it is the brain as a whole that makes us who we are. Although thoughts, memories, emotions, and abilities may be focused in one part of the brain or another, they are thoroughly entwined in that indefinable thing called the mind.

Refresh Your Memory

"Patients [given a prefrontal lobotomy] ... were not merely calmer—much of the time they were reduced to being placid 'zombies.' Many postoperative patients lacked ambition, tact, and imagination; although the patients themselves may have felt more comfortable, their families did not. Anxiety was relieved but at the price of a loss of self-respect and of empathy with others ... A major difficulty was that the psychosurgery, which mutilated irrevocably a part of the brain, was final. Not a dispensable part, such as the appendix, is removed, but an area essential to the human being—his personality—is forever destroyed."

—Dr. Franz G. Alexander and Dr. Sheldon T. Selsnick, *The History of Psychiatry*

HM Revisited

In Chapter 2, "To Live Is to Remember," you were introduced to a man known as HM. It was on September 8, 1953, that his doctors performed the operation for epilepsy that would forever change his life and that would teach us a valuable lessen about memory. But at what an awful cost!

HM (the "H" is for Henry, the "M" is a well-guarded secret to preserve the patient's privacy) suffered badly from epileptic seizures. His doctors decided that the seizures were life-threatening. After other remedies failed, the only hope for relief was to remove a section of his brain.

Some Memorable Facts

Epilepsy has, with surprising accuracy, also been called "brain storms." It seems to be a sort of electrical storm in the brain; the natural electricity of the brain is overcome by a random, powerful burst that effectively short-circuits thought and volition and causes the sufferer to lose control. In severe **grand mal seizures**, the sufferer falls to the ground and writhes in a manner that can be frightening to watch. In ancient Greece, epileptics were believed to have been touched by the gods and were looked upon with awe as soothsayers and favored people. Alexander the Great might have been epileptic. In the middle ages, opinion shifted. Epileptics were thought to have been touched by the devil and were often burned at the stake as witches.

Drill, Spatulas, and a Silver Straw

The neurosurgeon, armed, as Rebecca Rupp tells us in *Committed to Memory*, "with a rotary drill, a pair of metal spatulas, and a silver straw," performed what he called a *bilateral extirpation* of HM's brain matter. He removed the hippocampus from both cerebral hemispheres, along with a bunch of gray matter around them including the amygdala and the inner surface of the temporal lobes.

When HM awoke the next morning, his epilepsy was gone—and so was his ability to remember anything new from that day forward. He had developed, as you will remember from Chapter 2, *antiretrograde amnesia*. For the past 46 years—as of this writing HM was still alive—he has awakened every morning with his memory intact up to the operation, but he remembers nothing since.

HM can name the presidents up to Eisenhower, but he can't identify photographs of Kennedy, Johnson, or Reagan. For that matter, he can't identify Bruce Willis, Bill Gates, or Bart Simpson either. If you spend the morning with him and then leave to have lunch, by the time you get back, he will have forgotten ever meeting you.

Hidden Memory

In Chapter 2, you learned about HM's skill in mirror-drawing. He also has learned the moves in the Tower of Hanoi puzzle, in which five donut-shaped game pieces of increasing size must be moved from the first of three pegs to the third according to rules which specify that a smaller piece may be placed on a larger but never a larger on a smaller. After playing the game for a while, HM learned to do it in close to the minimum of 31 moves. If you show him a Tower of Hanoi puzzle now, HM does not remember ever seeing it before, but he still can solve it in close to the 31-move minimum. His conscious mind does not remember, but somewhere in his unconscious mind, the rules of the game are stored along with the best playing strategy.

One of the fascinating things that psychologists and neurologists have been puzzling over after studying HM and similar cases is that the hippocampus seems to process memories for long-term storage, but the storage itself happens elsewhere in the brain. The older a memory is, the more deeply it seems to be stored. When a brain disease robs someone of their memories, it often does so in last-in-first-out order. Recent memories go first, then mid-term memories, and then finally the patient is left with only the memories of childhood. He ends his days as an eternal child, not recognizing his own wife and children or perhaps mistaking them for his parents and siblings.

Over the Long Term

A strong contender for how long-term memories are formed in the hippocampus is a process first observed in 1973 by Timothy Bliss and Terje Lømo, two scientists studying the brains of rabbits in Oslo, Norway. They found that, when they stuck fine wires in the rabbits' brains and "stimulated" neurons in the hippocampus with fairly strong electric impulses, the neurons became very sensitive to even much milder electronic stimulation. The sensitivity could last for quite a while.

This reaction is called *long-term potentiation* (*LTP*) and could be made to last for up to four months. A lot of work has been done on exactly how this process works, and the complex chemical exchanges between and within neurons are fairly well understood. It's a good bet that LTP

Remember This!

Psychologists call the two different types of long-term memory **declarative memory** (which we called **event memory** in Chapter 2) and **procedural memory**. Declarative memory is your memory of things that happen to you and of things you purposely memorize such as poetry or a list of the kings of England. Procedural memory (**skill memory**) is your memory of how to ride a bicycle or drive a car—or solve the Tower of Hanoi puzzle in about 31 moves.

Refresh Your Memory

"Bliss and Lømo discovered that, following strong stimulation of nerve pathways leading into the hippocampus, postsynaptic responses of neurons in the hippocampus were potentiated. That is, the responses of hippocampal neurons to weak stimuli were increased significantly after a strong potentiating stimulus. If the strong input stimulus was repeated several times, the potentiation of the responses could be induced to last for days or even weeks."

—John E. Dowling, *Creating Mind*

has something to do with implanting long-term memories in the brain, but knowing the chemical pathways involved in potentiation is but the first step in what will probably be a long and intricate journey leading to a full understanding of how you remember that Aunt Celia gave you a book about whales for your sixth birthday.

ZAP! It's a Summer Day, and I'm Five Years Old

Sometimes a neurologist may gain physical access to a living patient's brain. When an operation has to be performed to remove a brain tumor or surgically treat epilepsy, and the brain is going to be exposed anyway, the neurologist might politely and hopefully ask the patient if he might perform a few tests—nothing dangerous, honest! One of the first to take advantage of this unique opportunity was a Canadian neurosurgeon named Wilder Penfield. During the 1940s and 1950s, Penfield used fine wires to electrically stimulate the brains of his patients while they were fully conscious on the operating table so he could ask them about the experience.

Penfield operated on epileptics and used the electrical stimulation to locate the abnormal brain cells causing his patients' seizures. In the process, he located many areas of the brain that were responsive to sight or touch—his patients reported that they could see flashes of light or feel pressure when he probed certain areas. Stimulating other areas caused a slight involuntary motor response such as the twitch of a finger or the jerk of a leg. The same area in the brain always produced the same response. This eventually enabled Penfield to map out the brain, showing where the different parts of the body were controlled.

Even more surprising was that stimulating parts of the temporal lobes, which are off to the sides of the cerebrum, caused a memory to suddenly be replayed, sometimes so vividly that the patient felt he or she was reliving the experience. The memory was complete in sight, sound, and even emotional texture. One woman recalled a piece of music being played by an orchestra—she could hear the separate instruments. It was so real she thought a phonograph was playing in the next room. Another patient saw his mother talking to his brother on a summer day when they were children.

Some patients have only fuzzy memories when similarly stimulated; for others, the electrical zapping produces no recall at all. This has caused some neurologists to doubt that the experiences are true memories and to think they may be some sort of hallucination provoked by the probing. They note that the memories produced by some of the patients are similar (or even identical) to images that occur during the epileptic seizures of which they are being cured. Why couldn't it be a true memory and still be evoked by the seizure? We don't know. We have no opinion on this and will await further information.

That Reminds Me of the Time...

Memories lie dormant in your brain until you call for them. Even then, they may or may not come on call. "What was the name of that actor in that movie—you know the one. Humphrey Bogart played this café owner, and this other guy was a French policeman. Now what was his name?"

You ponder. Suddenly, from whence you cannot tell comes the word "Casablanca." A moment later, you remember the name Claude Rains. Now you've got the movie and the actor—you knew you knew it all along.

One of the many questions concerning memory is how do you know that a fact is in your memory when you have yet to retrieve it? Someone might ask you, What was the name of Han Solo's ship in *Star Wars*?" You might say "I

Instant Recall

Sense memories are not always pleasant. For years after World War II, the sound of an airplane overhead made some refugees—particularly children—have to fight off the overwhelming urge to dive under the nearest table for fear of falling bombs.

don't know," or you might come up with the answer immediately. You also might say, "Wait a minute. I know this, it's right on the tip of my—I'll get it, give me a minute." Then 10 minutes later, when everyone has forgotten the question, you suddenly blurt out, *The Millennium Falcon*!

The general questions, of course, are where did the memory come from and why did it take you extra time to access it? But there's also the question of how did you know your memory contained the information you were seeking if you couldn't bring it immediately to mind?

The Smell of Past Loves

It is an interesting question that, as far as we know, no one can answer yet. It has been shown, however, that memories often are keyed to sensory impressions. The taste of fresh strawberries might suddenly bring back a memory of sitting on the bank of a stream when you were a child, eating fresh-picked strawberries. The smell of baking pastry might take you back to that Paris café when you were young and so much in love—what ever happened to Babbette anyway?

Curiously, taste and smell seem to be the senses that provoke memory responses most often and most strongly. This may be because the receptors for taste and smell go directly into the brain through the olfactory bulbs of the hippocampus (which we discussed in Chapter 5, "The Brain and Why You Have One"). Vision, on the other hand, goes through a lot of processing to organize and interpret what you're seeing before the information reaches the hippocampus where it might stimulate a memory.

The Perturbing Power of Stress

Strong emotions also can evoke powerful memories. The trauma of combat or other powerful stressors can produce a syndrome called *post traumatic stress disorder (PTSD)*, in which the stress of being put in an intolerable situation, particularly one in which you feel powerless, can etch the memory of an event so deeply in your mind that it comes back unbidden time and again for the rest of your life. These "flashbacks" can be so powerful that you might seem to be reliving the event, and they can trigger highly inappropriate, even violent, behavior.

Luckily, this syndrome is not caused by more common, even if overwhelming, types of stress. Losing a job, a divorce, or the death of a loved one does not normally cause PTSD, even though these are painful episodes from which it may take years to recover. Only severe stress on the order of being in imminent danger of death or great harm, seeing a friend die under conditions of military combat, or a violent criminal attack, or experiencing a severe hurricane, earthquake, or other natural disaster can cause this syndrome. Unlike most of us who strive to improve our memories, sufferers from PTSD want nothing more than to forget. They avoid talking about the experience or doing anything that might remind them of it.

If you fear that you or someone close to you may be suffering from PTSD, you should know that it is treatable. PTSD support groups can be found through local clinics or on-line if you have access to the Internet. If possible, you should begin by consulting a psychologist or other mental health professional.

The Least You Need to Know

➤ The rod that went through Phineas Gage's head in 1848 changed his personality, and it was not an improvement.

➤ In the 1930s, prefrontal lobotomies were performed on certain intractable mental patients. It made them entirely too passive, seemingly removing their will and turning them into "zombies."

➤ An operation for epilepsy removed HM's ability to add any new memories into long-term storage, although he kept the memories he had. For HM, it is always 1953.

➤ HM has retained the ability to add new information into his procedural (or skill) memory. He can, for example, learn to play new games. Although he forgets the learning experience, he remembers the rules.

➤ A process called long-term potentiation (LTP) seems to be involved in long-term memory storage.

➤ Electrical stimulation of the brain can provoke recall of specific memories.

➤ The senses, particularly taste and smell, are powerful aides in calling up memories of past events.

➤ Post traumatic stress disorder (PTSD) is a mental illness caused by powerful trauma and a feeling of helplessness.

Chapter 7

In Sickness and in Health

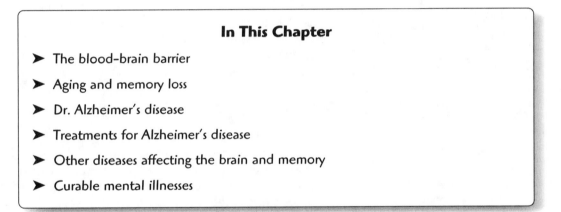

In This Chapter

➤ The blood–brain barrier

➤ Aging and memory loss

➤ Dr. Alzheimer's disease

➤ Treatments for Alzheimer's disease

➤ Other diseases affecting the brain and memory

➤ Curable mental illnesses

Considering how many different ways there are to be ill, it's amazing that most of us are well most of the time. Our immune system and other defenses against sickness do an impressive job of keeping us healthy. Sometimes the defenses break down, however, and sometimes an illness can strike the brain. This can affect our ability to control our bodies, to think, to plan, or to remember.

Of all the ills to which humans are heir, those that involve the brain are in many ways the most frightening. Other misfortunes may deprive you of the use of a limb or of one of your senses, or disable you in a bewildering number of unpleasant ways. These can be horrible handicaps, and we do not mean to make light of them. But a mental disease or brain injury, as we saw in Chapter 6, "A Hole in the Head," can deprive you of memory, personality, and cognition (the ability to think)—everything that makes you uniquely and unquestionably you.

Our Well-Protected Brains

This is why the brain is the best-armored and -protected organ in the body, sheathed in the solid bony vault of the skull and guarded from chemical or biological assault by the aptly named *blood-brain barrier*. The defenses are not perfect, however. Unfortunately, many diseases affect cognition and memory. Fortunately, many of these can be treated and the bad effects halted or reversed.

As with most illnesses, the faster you realize something is wrong and seek help, the better your chances of recovering rapidly and completely. Two common attitudes conspire to prevent or delay people from seeking needed help. The first is the fear of discovering something you don't want to know—that you have *Alzheimer's disease*, a brain tumor, or something else horrible and incurable. The second attitude, which in some ways is the opposite of the first, is the belief that memory loss is inevitable as you get older. Since there's nothing you can do about it, why make a fuss?

Serious Memory Slippage Is Not Natural

You probably don't have anything that will require more treatment than a trip to the doctor's office, a couple of pills, and maybe a regular exercise regimen. If it is something more serious, the faster you get it diagnosed the better. Most brain tumors today are operable, and the success rate is very high. There are drugs today that can slow the ravages of Alzheimer's; other, even better drugs are in the pipeline and should be available in a couple of years if not sooner. Although no current treatments can reverse it, researchers have been making some interesting breakthroughs. As you continue to read this chapter, you will see there is reason to be hopeful.

A little memory loss as you age is natural—particularly as you pass 65—but only a little. If your memory really seems to be slipping, it probably is the result of an illness or a physical condition that may be easily treatable. If you're an older person and your memory for recent events seems to be getting worse and worse, this isn't natural. You should see your doctor about it as soon as possible. Don't forget!

In our society, aging creates its own expectations that are not always based in fact. The older generation is expected to look, dress, and behave in a certain way, and as we get older, we tend to go along with this. This is okay if your age and wisdom (you couldn't have lived this long without learning something!) gets you the respect to which you're entitled. But believing the preconceptions could lead to trouble. If you discover that you can't walk as far or as fast as you used to, you might attribute it to advancing age instead of the fact that you haven't had any serious exercise in the past five years. Get out there and join a gym! If you forget a couple of words or an address and someone

Remember This!

Someone once proposed this useful, if humorous, rule of thumb regarding the severity of memory problems: "If you forget your keys occasionally, that's normal; if you forget what they're for, see a doctor."

makes a joking remark about getting old, you might worry that your brain is over the hill. What you should remember is that you've been forgetting things all your life—we all do. And this book will give you the techniques to take care of that!

All Is Forgotten

Some diseases of the brain have such total and devastating consequences that if you're capable of wondering whether you're ill with them, you're not. Certain forms of *encephalitis* can destroy memory as can a severe stroke, a serious concussion, the ingestion of certain dangerous chemicals or drugs, or Alzheimer's disease in its advanced stages.

Words to Remember

Encephalitis: An inflammation of the brain, usually caused by a virus, that can be serious or even fatal if not promptly treated. Unfortunately, its early symptoms (headache, stiff neck, and fever) can be misdiagnosed as a case of the flu.

Dr. Alzheimer's Disease

In 1906, Dr. Alois Alzheimer performed an autopsy on a 51-year-old patient he had been treating for *presenile dementia*. It was the prevailing wisdom at that time that *dementia*—loss of mental abilities including problem-solving, judgment, and memory—was a more or less natural consequence of aging that affected most of the elderly, although some managed to escape its effect by luck or good genes. Indeed, *senile dementia* (dementia of the aged) was not regarded as an illness, but as an inevitability. The very word *senility*, which merely means "old age," has acquired a second meaning, which the *Chambers Concise Dictionary* gives as "the imbecility of old age."

So presenile dementia, from which Dr. Alzheimer's 51-year-old patient died, meant that the patient was getting old and stupid before her time. Had she been 80 years old, the good doctor might not have bothered with an autopsy. Because she was younger than she should have been to exhibit those symptoms, Dr. Alzheimer took a look.

The autopsy showed an unnatural mass of plaques and tangles in certain areas of the brain. This seemed to have greatly reduced the number of neurons and possibly their ability to pass electrical and chemical signals, which is how neurons store and retrieve information. As the first to describe both the symptoms of the patient in life and the characteristic appearance of the disease in the brain at autopsy, Dr. Alzheimer had the dubious honor of having the disease named after him.

Epidemic Among the Aging

Alzheimer's disease is indeed a *disease*, not a normal condition of aging. It usually strikes people over age 65, but it has been found in people in their 40s and even younger. It is easy to see, however, why senile dementia was considered a normal part of aging—the disease is so widespread that it would be considered a major epidemic if it struck a younger population. It is estimated that more than 10 percent of the population in the United States over age 65 is afflicted with Alzheimer's, and the number rises to between 25 and 50 percent of those over 85. Other diseases (discussed later in this chapter) mimic its symptoms, and this raises the percentage of the slightly demented among the aged to well over half. Many of these other conditions are now treatable, which is why it is important to find out the specific cause of dementia in any patient.

Some Memorable Facts

Some long-term alcoholics develop a characteristic memory disease called **Korsakoff's psychosis**, which robs them of their ability to create new memory (in a way reminiscent of HM, who was discussed in the last chapter). If you go away after talking to a victim of Korsakoff's psychosis, he will not remember you five minutes later. But if you tell the patient that you met and spoke with him, he will fill in the gaps and describe the event in detail. He will do this even if you made up the story about meeting him before. Korsakoff's psychosis patients are highly suggestible and will agree with and expand upon any story you tell them. Five minutes later, they will have forgotten the whole incident.

Nobody knows what causes Alzheimer's disease. It was thought for a while that since traces of aluminum are found in the characteristic plaques but not in normal cells, aluminum in the diet, possibly from using aluminum foil and cooking in aluminum frying pans, might be the culprit. That theory has since taken a backseat to a couple of other possibilities.

There seems to be a less-than-normal supply of a *neurotransmitter* called *acetylcholine* in the brains of Alzheimer's victims. When drugs that block the action of acetylcholine are given to volunteers, the ability to form new memories is temporarily affected. Experimenters are now trying to determine whether something is killing the cells that normally make acetylcholine or whether there is some other cause for its absence in the brains of Alzheimer's victims.

Other scientists are exploring *chromosome* abnormalities linked to Alzheimer's disease. Some Alzheimer's sufferers have an abnormality on chromosome 21, some others with a version of early onset Alzheimer's have an abnormal *gene* on chromosome 14, and some people who develop the disease, mainly descendants of some Germans who lived near the Volga River, have an abnormal gene on chromosome 1.

Words to Remember

Neurotransmitter: A chemical that carries nerve impulses from one neuron to the next.

Chromosome: The part of a cell that transmits hereditary information.

Gene: A specific site on the chromosome that encodes specific hereditary information.

A couple of other possible causes being investigated include a virus infection or some sort of chemical from environmental pollution. The question is still open, however, and the answer may lie in an entirely different direction.

Symptoms

The first symptoms of Alzheimer's disease may include memory loss (particularly for recent events), occasional disorientation about names and places, and a lessening ability to make good decisions. Also listed as symptoms are loss of initiative, anxiety about the symptoms, and possibly an increased reluctance to deal with people and public situations. These last characteristics might not be symptoms of the disease itself but rather a natural reaction to the effects of the disease. These early symptoms are regarded as signs of what is considered to be the first stage of the disease, a period that usually lasts two to four years.

Remember This!

The symptoms of the early stages of Alzheimer's also are the symptoms of a host of other illnesses—many of which are easily controllable or curable if caught early. So don't make assumptions. If you or someone you love has these symptoms, see a doctor as soon as possible.

At the moment, no simple test exists for Alzheimer's, and a definite diagnosis can be made only at autopsy. A doctor diagnoses Alzheimer's in living patients by methodically and carefully eliminating all other possibilities. This can involve a battery of tests including a *computerized tomography (CT) scan*, *magnetic resonance imaging (MRI)*, and the use of other wonder machines of modern medicine. At the end of the testing, even if the doctor has eliminated all the other possibilities she can think of, she is still only 90 percent sure it's Alzheimer's.

Second Stage

The second stage, called *moderate Alzheimer's*, can last as few as two or as many as 10 years. The memory loss becomes ever more severe, and the patient on occasion may fail to recognize friends or relatives, may forget to perform routine tasks such as bathing or dressing, and may become completely untrustworthy in business and social situations. Language problems may become serious as the patient forgets words and can no longer think logically.

Third Stage

The third stage—which may include the inability to speak logical sentences or to recognize a spouse or children and finally complete physical breakdown leading to death—may last a year or as long as three or more years. These stages are not absolute, and an individual patient may have different symptoms.

Treatments for Alzheimer's

Until recently, there were no treatments for Alzheimer's disease. Studies of the disease are starting to pay off, with the discovery of several drugs that can slow its progress and the possibility of stronger treatments to suppress the symptoms. The disease is not well enough understood yet, however, to expect a complete cure in the near future.

Since 1993, doctors have been able to prescribe the drug tacrine, which increases the amount of acetylcholine available in the brain by slowing the chemical's breakdown. It has been shown to improve the mental functions of many patients with mild to moderate Alzheimer's, but it does not stop the progression of the disease. A few other drugs, such as exelon and acetylcarnitine, are coming out of the testing phase and are poised to enter the market.

Selegiline, a drug marketed under the trade name Eldepryl and used to treat Parkinson's disease, has been shown to slow the progression of Alzheimer's by about six months, as has large doses of vitamin E (2,000 IU [International Units] daily). Selegiline has not yet been approved for treatment of Alzheimer's, but it is approved for Parkinson's and a doctor can prescribe it. The drug should be used cautiously because it can have severe side effects including fainting, nausea, dizziness, and low blood pressure. It shouldn't be used if the patient is taking antidepressants or narcotics.

Remember This!

Please check with your doctor before taking large doses of vitamin E—or any other vitamin, mineral, herb, concoction, home remedy, patent medicine, or health food—even if it did wonders for your Uncle Sydney.

Vitamin E has no known side effects at the dosage used for prevention of heart disease (200 IU). The dose for Alzheimer's is 10 times that level, however, and there have been some reports of bleeding at very high doses. It is a good idea to avoid taking high doses of vitamin E if you are taking blood thinners such as warfarin (Coumadin) or heparin. Vitamin E is easily available and is comparatively cheap.

Estrogen, ibuprofen, and the hormone DHEA also are being considered as possible treatments. In the future, neurologists may be able to graft brain cells that produce acetylcholine into the brains of Alzheimer's patients. This almost certainly will delay the progression of the disease, but whether it is a cure remains to be seen.

Remember This!

Experimenters have tried enhancing a rat's brain power by grafting acetylcholine-producing brain cells from another rat. They found that the rat with the extra cells can improve its maze-running time and accuracy. People given drugs that increase the acetylcholine available to their brain have temporary improvements in their short-term memory. Such drugs, if shown to be safe, might prove to be very popular—especially at universities around exam time.

Other Diseases That Affect Memory

The discussion of Alzheimer's disease was extensive because Alzheimer's has become one of the most feared possibilities of old age and rightly so. In its later stages, it robs its victim of mind and memories. Some other diseases can be just as debilitating, but with most of them, there is at least the hope of a cure if caught early enough.

Brain Tumors

Brain tumors—the uncontrolled growth of cells in the brain—can occur in any part of the brain, and the effect depends largely on their location. In one location, a brain tumor may impair walking and balance; elsewhere, vision or speech may be affected; still elsewhere, memory could be damaged or destroyed. Most tumors occur in the glial cells—the cells that support and nourish the neurons—and are called *gliomas*. The growth of a tumor puts pressure on the parts of the brain located around it and may cut off the blood supply to a vital area. The usual treatment is to surgically remove the tumor. If the tumor is too deep in the brain to be reached by a scalpel, a hot needle can be carefully inserted to destroy as much of it as possible. In an extreme case, carefully aimed X rays may be used.

Strokes

There are three different types of *stroke*: cerebral thrombosis, when a *thrombus* (medical talk for a blood clot) blocks a blood vessel in the brain; cerebral hemorrhage, when the wall of a blood vessel breaks and spills blood into the brain, where it clots; and cerebral

Remember This!

Some evidence now suggests that some neurons in some parts of the brain are replaced by new ones, but notice how carefully we're hedging that statement. Even if this turns out to be true, the new cells are untutored and do not carry the information that was contained in the missing cells.

Instant Recall

Bovine Spongiform Encephalopathy, a degenerative disease of the brain found in cows and often called "mad cow disease," is believed to be transmittable from infected cows to people who eat meat from these cows, and to cause a disease much like **Creutzfeldt-Jakob disease** in the people infected. The disease may have been started by feeding the cows a processed feed accidentally contaminated with sheep protein containing Scrapie, a similar disease among sheep. More than a dozen cases of people so infected have been found in Great Britain, and thousands of cows have been destroyed to halt the spread of the disease. No cases are known to have occurred in the United States.

embolism, when a clot moves from somewhere else in the body and settles in an artery in the brain, clogging it and blocking the blood supply. Strokes block the blood supply to the affected part of the brain. Brain cells need a constant supply of *glucose*, the nutrient they use for energy, as well as oxygen, which is supplied by the red blood cells. If a blocked artery or a large internal blood clot deprives the cells of oxygen or glucose for even a short length of time, they will die and are not replaced.

Although there seems to be some redundancy in brain function, as a general rule when brain cells die, the body loses the ability to do whatever that area of the brain controlled. If the neurons that send instructions to the right leg die, a perfectly healthy leg will be rendered useless. Strokes can affect memory, speech, movement, balance, vision, or any of the other senses. A severe stroke can send the victim into a coma.

Drugs now exist that, if administered early enough, can limit the damage of a stroke. Some drugs (including aspirin) are even believed to help prevent strokes. Medical procedures can locate the area affected by the stroke, and the clot may be surgically removed. Any brain cells that died, however, will have taken the information or instructions they contained with them. The patient will have to relearn the skills that were lost. This takes time and a lot of hard work, but in many cases, recovery can be almost complete.

Other Possibilities

Some other diseases that can lead to memory loss and dementia include:

➤ **Parkinson's disease** affects muscular control and causes tremors that get worse as the disease progresses. Later stages can be marked by mental deterioration and memory loss.

➤ **Creutzfeldt-Jakob disease**, a rare disease for which there is currently no treatment, is caused by an infection. The victim loses muscular control, suffers personality changes and failing memory, and usually dies within a year.

➤ **Multi-infarct dementia**, sometimes called *vascular dementia*, is caused by the cumulative effect of many little strokes in the brain. Progression of the disease sometimes can be halted by lowering the blood pressure with drugs or diet.

➤ **Pick's disease** is a strong mimic of Alzheimer's disease, and is also incurable and fatal. Luckily, it is very rare.

Reversible Dementia

The possible causes of the memory loss, confusion, difficulty in problem-solving, and a wonderfully vague symptom known as "inappropriate behavior" that are the defining symptoms of dementia are varied. The National Institute on Aging says that about 100 of these symptoms, which it calls *pseudodementias*, are reversible conditions if properly diagnosed and treated. The possibilities include:

➤ **Reactions to medications** regularly prescribed for the elderly—such as pain killers of various sorts, sleeping pills, and antidepressant medications—can include varying degrees of mental confusion, short-term memory loss, and other symptoms that might be mistaken for dementia. The cure, of course, is to change medication.

➤ **Strong depression or emotional upset**, possibly organic (that is, with no known external cause) or possibly as a result of the death of a loved one, retirement, divorce, or even moving to a new house or apartment, can create withdrawal from social activities, mental confusion, and seeming memory loss (possibly due to inattention)—symptoms that look very much like dementia. There are drugs now that can help this, along with psychological help and the passage of time.

➤ **Atherosclerosis** (hardening of the arteries) can slowly cut off the blood supply to the brain, preventing the brain from working to its full ability. An operation now exists in which an artery removed from (usually) the leg can be inserted to increase the brain's blood supply. The results are often dramatic. When writer Robert Heinlein underwent this operation, he awoke the next morning and said that he felt as though he'd just been awakened from a five-year sleep.

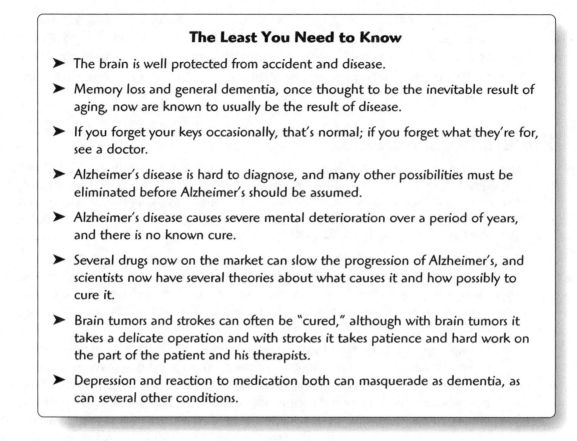

The Least You Need to Know

➤ The brain is well protected from accident and disease.

➤ Memory loss and general dementia, once thought to be the inevitable result of aging, now are known to usually be the result of disease.

➤ If you forget your keys occasionally, that's normal; if you forget what they're for, see a doctor.

➤ Alzheimer's disease is hard to diagnose, and many other possibilities must be eliminated before Alzheimer's should be assumed.

➤ Alzheimer's disease causes severe mental deterioration over a period of years, and there is no known cure.

➤ Several drugs now on the market can slow the progression of Alzheimer's, and scientists now have several theories about what causes it and how possibly to cure it.

➤ Brain tumors and strokes can often be "cured," although with brain tumors it takes a delicate operation and with strokes it takes patience and hard work on the part of the patient and his therapists.

➤ Depression and reaction to medication both can masquerade as dementia, as can several other conditions.

Short-Term to Long-Term

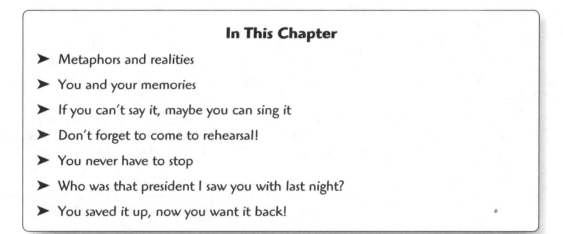

Chapter 8

In This Chapter

➤ Metaphors and realities

➤ You and your memories

➤ If you can't say it, maybe you can sing it

➤ Don't forget to come to rehearsal!

➤ You never have to stop

➤ Who was that president I saw you with last night?

➤ You saved it up, now you want it back!

You probably knew all along, intuitively, that you don't learn and remember every-thing, all at once, and all in the same way. You also know that there are many differ-ent ways to memorize any one thing. From earlier chapters in this book, you've learned a good deal about the human brain and how it works, and about human memory and how *it* works.

We've used a number of metaphors for memory, and each of them may be useful, and you're free to use whichever of them you find most plausible, or to devise one—or several—of your own if you prefer. We'll talk about these some more in a little while.

For now, though, it's important to remember that these metaphors are models. They help us understand the brain. But while the way the brain works may resemble the way a computer works, you must remember that the brain is not the same as a computer.

Your memory may be said to file information like a library, but it is not the same as a library.

One of the most important concepts we need to grasp, in order to understand memory is the difference between short-term and long-term memory. That distinction, as well as other ideas about your memory and the several *kinds* of memory that researchers believe you have, is what this chapter is about.

We also have a couple of little quizzes for you. Don't be scared. You can administer them yourself (with or without the help of a friend), and you'll probably enjoy doing it. They're designed to demonstrate something of the way your various "memories" work together. It will help if you have a few sheets of paper and a pen or pencil handy.

How Many Memories Do You Really Have?

Psychologists and memory researchers throw around a lot of terms for memory. How many types of memory does one person have? If you read extensively in the literature, you'll find more kinds of memory described and more names for them than you can shake a stick at.

There are different ways to look at memory. A very useful way is *sequential*. That is, when a bit of data hits one of your sensors (such as an image or part of an image impacting on your eye), the information passes through several "memories" one after another.

These are often referred to as *immediate memory*, *short-term memory*, and *long-term memory*. These are terms we'll use a lot in this chapter (and throughout this book), but there are a good many other terms. We'll make their meanings clear whenever we use them.

What's in a Name?

Here are some of the terms applied to different kinds of memory. You don't need to memorize this list, but you'll probably want to refer back to it from time to time.

➤ Event

➤ Fact

➤ Skill

➤ Body

➤ Kinesthetic

➤ Declarative

➤ Haptic

➤ Stimulus/response

➤ Abstract

These all fit in with the concept of "hard" and "soft" memories that we spoke about in Chapter 2, "To Live Is to Remember." We'll mostly talk about "soft" memories, however, because those are the memories we can do something useful about. Some deal with ideas; some deal with sensations or skills. But you don't need to worry about that right now.

This is quite a list of terms, and you'll probably come across mentions of still others. Do you really have this many different memories?

No, you don't. Not in the sense that you have 10 fingers. You don't actually have 8 or 10 or 20 separate and distinguishable memories, each one located in a different part of your brain and functioning independently of all the others. Rather, the many types of memories that researchers talk about are based more on function than on physiology.

What makes this topic so perplexing is that different memories and functions are, at least to some extent, associated with different parts of the brain. The case of "HM," whom you met in an earlier chapter, seems to have proven that pretty conclusively.

Lessons Learned from Damaged Brains

While HM's is the most famous and probably the most important case in medical history, at least as it relates to our understanding of memory, it represents only one of many such cases over the years. A physician acquaintance of ours reported an oddity that he learned from his work with stroke victims.

These men and women had suffered brain damage as a result of blood clots or broken blood vessels in the brain. This condition can be very serious and can cause profound, long-term, disabling effects or even death. Or it can cause only slight or short-term loss of function.

Our friend treated a number of patients who were unable to speak as a result of strokes. The patients indicated that they could understand speech and could formulate their responses mentally—as concepts—but they could not articulate them. On such occasions, they became frustrated and upset—not surprisingly.

Then the doctor had an idea. He asked his patients to sing familiar songs. In several cases, they were able to do so even though they still could not speak in a normal manner.

Somehow, the information and "programming," or neural instructions involved in everyday speech had been damaged by their strokes, but the information and software needed for singing remained intact.

What lesson can we draw from this phenomenon?

It seems quite clear that different parts of the brain store different categories of data (ordinary vocabulary, song lyrics, and melodies) and instructions or internal "commands" that control speaking or singing.

Words to Remember

Haptic: Pertaining to the sense of touch.

Haptic memory: Your memory of how something feels when you touch it.

Maybe we should add two more kinds of memory to the list you read a few paragraphs back:

➤ Speaking

➤ Singing

Actually, this is a pretty silly idea. If we started down this path, we'd have to add brushing-our-teeth memory, tying-our-shoelaces memory, blinking-our-eyes memory, and all the millions of other "memories" that represent everything we might ever know, or think, or do.

Three Is a Very Fine Number

Following is a useful model some researchers have developed for the flow of information as it is received and recorded.

You may or may not be a sports fan, but just for the moment let's assume you are. You run into a pal at the water cooler, and he says, "I just heard the score of today's game. It was Gallopers 5, Mockturtles 4."

Even as you hear the game score from your friend, it enters an information-holding area called *temporary storage* or *immediate memory*. Researchers suggest that this area has a very small capacity, perhaps just a single item. According to this model, you hold the score "Gallopers 5" only for a very brief period—perhaps as little as half a second, at most four seconds.

As soon as you hear "Mockturtles 4," the first piece of information is gone from temporary storage, replaced by the second piece of information. If the only memory you had was this immediate memory, you would be rendered helpless. You would be living in an ever-changing single moment, an "eternal now," with no past and no future. This would resemble poor HM's case, only it would be even worse.

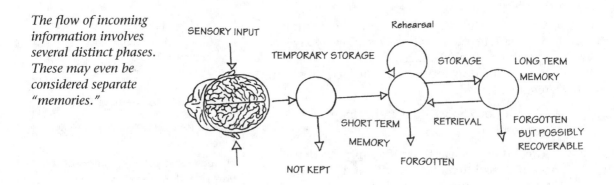

The flow of incoming information involves several distinct phases. These may even be considered separate "memories."

At this moment, your brain has a very important choice to make. Should the information be discarded when it is replaced? Or should it be passed along to the next level of memory, short-term memory? You make this decision countless times every day, taking in thousands or millions of sensory impressions, colors, sounds, faces, odors, fleeting images, and thoughts. The overwhelming majority of them are quickly discarded. This is for the best; otherwise you would be overwhelmed by a mass of data far too great to process effectively. You would be left confused and helpless, drowning in a sea of images and information!

You've trained yourself since early childhood to choose which information to keep and which to discard. Sometimes you need to rev up this ability. If you've ever been sitting in a classroom or a business meeting and let your attention wander, only to realize with a jolt that you've just missed something important, that important something almost certainly passed into your immediate memory and was then discarded!

What Do I Do with This Stuff?

With your immediate memory acting as a filter, you send any information your "filter" lets through to your short-term memory. Your short-term memory holds information for a little while. Experiments indicate that this period may be as short as 10 seconds or as long as 30 seconds—half a minute.

Short-term memory also has a modest holding capacity. It can retain 5 to 10 items as compared to the immediate memory's single-item capacity. Short-term memory is like immediate memory in another way. Newly arriving information tends to drive out information already in short-term memory and take its place.

Thus, if your friend goes on from the result of the Gallopers–Mockturtles game and gives you the score of the Archangels–Zoomers game and then that of the Rainbow Sox–Whizzers game, and so forth, your immediate memory will keep passing these scores along to your short-term memory, and your short-term memory will soon begin to lose track of the scores you've already heard.

Suppose one of the scores is really important to you, however, and you want to remember it and repeat it to another friend. You might find yourself repeating it mentally, over and over.

Archangels 11, Zoomers 9.

Archangels 11, Zoomers 9.

Archangels 11, Zoomers 9.

This is a common practice called *rehearsal*. This process of incessant repetition continuously refreshes the storage circuits. It reinforces the information, keeps your short-term memory busy, and prevents new incoming data from rushing in from your immediate memory and replacing the item you want to retain.

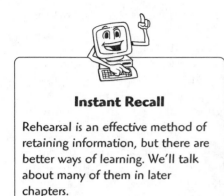

You probably used rehearsal when you were a child. If you were too young to read and write but you wanted to keep hold of a piece of information, say, a shopping list, you would repeat it to yourself.

"Loaf of bread, quart of milk, half a dozen eggs, four tomatoes," all the way to the store. If you stopped to watch an interesting frog jumping in a pond, to chat with a friend, or to admire someone's shiny new bike, you probably stopped repeating the shopping list and "lost" one or more items from it.

You also probably used this method of repetition or rehearsal to memorize lists of information for school exams. Other forms of repetition can be used later in the memory process. Terms such as *reverie*, *reliving*, or even *meditation* are applied to the practice of calmly and deliberately setting out to relive an earlier experience.

With practice, you can relive a past experience with remarkable vividness. Some people find this to be a useful technique not only for recalling information but for regaining the feeling or emotional state of a particular, earlier moment. Some actors use this method to create or re-create an emotional state, mentally returning to a moment of great joy, tragedy, happiness, or rage in order to project the right emotion in a scene.

I Really, Really Want to Remember This!

If you rehearsed the shopping list enough times (or was it the Archangels–Zoomers score that you cared about?), your short-term memory passed the information along to your long-term memory.

This is the biggie, the 900-pound gorilla of memories. This is the one with virtually limitless capacity. (There probably is a theoretical limit to how much you can store, but if so, no one has ever found it.) People just keep adding and adding and adding to their long-term memories. Even men and women who are well over 100 years old, if they are healthy and are not suffering from organic brain damage or brain-damaging diseases, can still recall incidents from their early childhood. They also can still learn new things! The famous American painter "Grandma Moses" (real name: Anna Mary Robertson) painted scenes based on memories of her childhood when she was well past 90 years of age.

Why Those Different Figures?

You may have noticed that some of the figures we give you seem to hop around. They're inconsistent or they cover a broad range. You might prefer more specific numbers, and that makes a lot of sense. There are reasons, however, for the different numbers we give.

For example: Does temporary storage last only half a second or as long as four seconds?

Memory research is going on at universities, hospitals, and laboratories all over the world. It isn't a very new field, but in recent years, new techniques and improved scientific methods have added hugely to what we know. Until things settle down a little, however, and scientists have time to assimilate all the findings, there's going to be little agreement among them. Different researchers get different results! Another reason for the range of results is simple human variation. Suppose a researcher asked, "How long does it take a person to run 100 yards?" There is no "right" answer to that question! Or, if you prefer, there are many "right" answers. The fastest athlete in the world, clad in light clothes, wearing spiked shoes, and running on a carefully groomed track, could cover 100 yards in less than 10 seconds. An average person, wearing jeans and ordinary shoes and running on a typical city sidewalk, would take between 30 seconds and a minute to run 100 yards. A person badly out of condition, wearing a heavy overcoat and trying to run down a crowded sidewalk in the middle of a blizzard, would be lucky to cover 100 yards in 10 minutes. So we ask again, "How long does it take a person to run 100 yards?" Ten seconds, 30 seconds, 10 minutes, or longer—take your pick!

Which Long-Term Memory Were You Talking About?

Let's get back to long-term memory. Even here, things are not always as simple as we might like. Do you have only one long-term memory? Or 2, or 3, or 20?

Some researchers have suggested that long-term memory is actually divided into three types, or *submemories*. There are a number of terms for these, including *stimulus/response memory*, *event memory*, and *abstract memory*.

Stimulus/Response Memory

Let's assume that, like many people, you have a night table beside your bed and you keep a telephone on it. If you are awakened by an early morning telephone call, chances are you'll automatically turn toward the night table and reach for the telephone. You didn't think about it. It was something you learned through multiple repetitions until it became an automatic act. Remember our old friend the conditioned reflex? This is one!

Other conditioned reflexes include acts such as moving your foot from the accelerator to the brake pedal when you come to a red light in your automobile or even something as mundane as tying your shoelaces when you get dressed in the morning. What a chore this is for small children just learning to do it! At first, it's an almost impossible task. Then they learn to do it, but they must concentrate all their attention on it. They repeat to themselves, "Take the laces in both hands, twist *this* one around *that* one..." and so on. After a while, however, it's mastered and becomes an automatic series of actions that requires little thought if any. This kind of memory also is sometimes called *procedural* or *skill memory*. Some people simply call it *body memory*.

Event Memory

Depending on your age, you almost certainly remember learning of certain world events: the death of a president, the beginning of a war, the performance of an outstanding athletic feat. It made such a strong impression on you that you remember where you were when you heard the news, what you were doing at that very moment, and how you felt when you heard the news: shock, grief, or joy.

You probably also remember certain key events in your own life: your first kiss, your first day on the job, your high school or college graduation, the day you won a gold medal at a swimming meet, and so on.

These are all events, and it's easy to see why your memory of them is called *event memory*. Some people also call it *declarative memory*.

Abstract Memory

Okay, quick: Who was the first president of the United States? What is the capitol of your state? And here's a zinger: What is your own first name? Chances are overwhelmingly high that you can answer all three questions with ease and certainty, but chances also are overwhelmingly high that you don't remember when or how you learned those things. You remember the *event* of winning that gold medal, but you remember the *abstract fact* of your own first name.

This brings us back to early childhood learning and the fact that you absorbed huge amounts of information in your first years. You retain that information to this day, but you don't remember learning it. Some of this information, such as how to walk, found its way into your skill memory (or stimulus/response memory), which we just discussed. Other information, including your own name, found its way into *abstract memory*.

One or the Other—Or Both!

Still other information has aspects of both a skill and abstract data. A prime example of this is language itself. Think about associating words such as "doggie" and "mommy" with your own pet and your own mother. Advocates of a linguistic theory called *general* semantics warn against association of the symbol ("mommy") with the referent (the actual person). They warn that, "the map is not the territory."

In this sense, learning language seems like an exercise of abstract memory. But you also use language, don't you? In fact, even if you don't remember learning to speak as a child (hardly anyone does), you might have tried to learn a second language at a later age or observed a child learning to speak. In either case, you're aware that this is very much a skill and not just a pack of information.

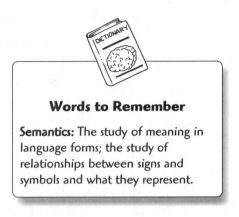

Words to Remember

Semantics: The study of meaning in language forms; the study of relationships between signs and symbols and what they represent.

So language is both fact and skill memory. And if you happen to remember the occasion when you learned a particular word, it can even be an example of event memory!

A Slice of Pingerberry Pie

Here's a little story about an imaginary friend of ours. We'll refer to her simply by her initials, AB. We'd like you to read the story and note how many ways the nature and name of pingerberry pie were recorded in AB's memory. Remember that each time a piece of information about pingerberry pie impacts on AB's senses, the message goes to her immediate memory. From there, it may or may not move on to her short-term memory and then to her long-term memory. AB and her friend, whom we'll call CD, agreed to meet for lunch one day. AB left her office, where she was senior vice president of a major television network, and met CD as planned at a posh midtown restaurant.

They shared a beverage and then a superb meal. At the end of the main course, the waiter approached AB and CD's table and asked if they'd like to see the desert cart. They agreed. On the cart, they observed a variety of mouthwatering pastries, frozen confections, and fruits.

AB noticed what was obviously a slice of pie with a golden crust, carefully scalloped edges, and filling of a particular blue-green shade she had never seen before.

"What's that?" she asked the waiter.

"That, Madame, is pingerberry pie."

"I've never heard of pingerberry pie."

"Pingerberries are extremely rare, Madame. They grow only in a secret valley in Antarctica, warmed by underground springs, and they are imported expressly for this restaurant. Further, they are only available during a very short period of time, and the supply is so limited that we only serve pingerberry pie once a year on the birthday of Priscilla P. Pinger, the discoverer of the pingerberry. You are very fortunate, as today happens to be that day!"

"CD, did you ever hear of pingerberries?" AB asked her companion.

"Oh, yes, they're delicious and they make a splendid pie. I had a slice of it a year ago, and I'll never forget the experience."

"Then I'll try a slice," AB told the waiter.

When the waiter placed the slice of pie before AB, she cut into it with her fork and tasted the pie. She found that pingerberries have a firm, meaty consistency. They tasted sweet at first and then left a pleasantly refreshing, tart aftertaste. There was even, AB noticed, a faint but pleasant, flower-like odor.

"I don't want to forget this," AB told CD. "Pingerberries, eh?" She took a small electronic device from her pocket, carefully wrote the word "pingerberries" with a stylus, and then read what she had written to make sure she had it right. "This gadget is my memory," she said to her friend CD, laughing.

"I wouldn't worry about that," CD replied. "I'm sure you'll remember pingerberries."

How Many?

Did you keep count? Want to go back over the story and see how many times—and how many ways!—AB imprinted pingerberries on her memory? We're talking about her own memory, by the way, and not the electronic gadget.

We counted at least 13 imprintings of pingerberries on AB's memory and at least eight different forms of imprinting. Consider this:

- ➤ She saw the pingerberries in the pie.
- ➤ She heard the waiter tell her what they were.
- ➤ She said the word "pingerberries" several times herself.
- ➤ She felt the texture of the pingerberries in the pie.
- ➤ She tasted the pingerberries.
- ➤ She smelled the flower-like aroma of the pingerberries.
- ➤ She wrote the word "pingerberries" on her electronic gadget.
- ➤ She read the word "pingerberries" after she wrote it.

Each time AB saw the pingerberries, heard the word, tasted them, or received a sensory impression of pingerberries (the referent) or the word "pingerberries" (the symbol), her memory traces were reinforced. She may or may not have rehearsed the word or image in her mind; she didn't have to.

AB will not soon forget those berries!

Get Out Your Exam Books, Students!

Not really. This is just for fun, but you might want to jot down your answers to the following questions on a separate sheet of paper. Go ahead, we'll sit here exchanging witty repartee until you get back.

Ready? Good! Here we go:

1. What color are pingerberries?

2. Where do pingerberries grow?

3. How did pingerberries get their name?

4. How often is pingerberry pie available?

5. Do you believe any of this?

We're not going to tell you the answers to these questions, but feel free to reread the story and score your own paper. Anyone who scores 100 percent wins a pingerberry pie—if you can find the right restaurant!

Chances are, however, if you have a good verbal memory, you remembered the story in words. When you took the test, you recalled the words you had read and got the answers to the questions. If your memory is primarily visual, you more likely translated the story into a series of pictures or a little movie as you read it and then reran the movie in your mind when you took the test.

Remembering What's Important

There are many cases of people with odd memories—people who remember only certain things, people who remember too much. Such a wild talent can be a blessing or a burden. We'll meet a number of individuals who have unusual memories in Chapter 13, "Very Special Memories."

But for the great majority of people, there is a desirable balance between remembering too much and remembering too little. When you were a child, did your parents ever chide you for "cluttering up your mind" with such trivia as the names of all the members of your favorite bands, the batting averages of dozens of baseball players, or the secret identities and special powers of a hundred superheroes—while forgetting where you left your house key?

Instant Recall

One of the lessons involved in having a good memory is using your memory effectively. Decide what matters to you and devote your attention to learning and remembering what's important, useful, or amusing, while letting the rest of the daily information flood wash over you.

These facts weren't trivial to you. They were part of your everyday life, they mattered, and they were important. Anybody can lose keys. Hey, it happened to us. In fact, it happens to most people.

Here's another little test. You won't even need a pencil and paper for this one. You can administer it to yourself, but it's better if you have a friend help you with it.

Read the following paragraph just once. Better yet, ask your friend to read it to you. You're on your honor until after you've answered the questions that follow.

> James Knox Polk, the eleventh president of the United States, is probably the least remembered and most overlooked of our truly important presidents. He believed it was the "manifest destiny" of the United States to span the continent, and in a peaceful dispute with Great Britain, he obtained the Oregon Territory for the United States. He led the United States into war with Mexico, adding Texas and much more of the southwestern region to the nation. He was accused of deliberately provoking the Mexican War in order to gain territory. He and his running mate, George M. Dallas, had been elected in 1844, narrowly defeating the ticket of Henry Clay and Theodore Frelinghuysen. Polk declined to run for a second term. He left office with the comment, "The presidency is not a bed of roses," and he died three months later.

Without looking at the paragraph again (and without getting any help from your friend), see if you can answer the following questions:

➤ What territories did President Polk add to the United States?

➤ What war was fought under his leadership?

➤ Who was Polk's opponent in the presidential election?

➤ In what year did Polk become president?

➤ Who was Polk's vice president?

➤ Who was Polk's opponent's running mate?

Remember This!

What does this test prove? That you already are making choices, remembering the facts that are important to you, and ignoring others that don't really matter much.

Of all the people who take this little quiz, the greatest number get the first answer right (Oregon, Texas, and the Southwest). Most also remember which war he led the nation in (the Mexican War).

The deeper people get into the list of questions, the less likely they are to remember the answers. This is because these facts are less important than the answers to the first two questions. (By the way, the answers to the other questions are: Henry Clay, 1845, George M. Dallas, and Theodore Frelinghuysen. The year Polk became president is the only trick question in the quiz. Polk and Dallas defeated Clay and Frelinghuysen in the election of 1844, but they did not take office until 1845!)

This brings us to the final point of this chapter, and it's a very important one.

How Do You Get It Back?

Until now, we've concentrated on obtaining and retaining information. That information isn't any good to you, however, unless you can recall it. When you do this, you send a message or a command (another computer-like "software" function) to your memory to give back a piece of information.

It may be something you learned and stored just seconds ago. ("Uh-oh, I just met this truly wonderful person, and I didn't pay enough attention as we were being introduced. Now I can't remember her name!") It may be something you learned and stored many years ago. ("Oh, gosh! I sang this song when I was in first grade. Now how does it go?")

Or it may be something in between. The answer to a test question that you *know* is going to get you an "A" in American history if you can remember it. You learned this back at the beginning of the semester, and you just *know* that it's buried somewhere in your memory—if you could just find it! ("Oh, blast it, I know I know the names of the original 13 United States!")

The process of recalling information you already have stored opens a huge new topic, and we will pay a good deal of attention to it as we proceed. For now, keep in mind that some researchers would add a fourth circle to the model we showed you earlier in this chapter. Their idea is that short-term memory "talks to" long-term memory. The information is then transferred (or, more accurately, copied) from long-term memory to short-term memory, which now acts as a new kind of "working memory."

Once the information is available to you, you can use it for whatever purpose you had in mind. "Ah yes, Angelica, wasn't it?" Or "The wheels on the bus go round and round." Or "The original 13 states were Massachusetts, New Hampshire, Connecticut, Rhode Island, New York, New Jersey, Pennsylvania, Delaware, Maryland, Virginia, North Carolina, South Carolina, and Georgia."

Memory experts have worked for thousands of years to devise methods for remembering and recalling information. The term most often used for these techniques is *mnemonic devices*, and we're going to learn a lot of them in later chapters.

The Least You Need to Know

➤ There are many metaphors for human memory, but the most common are computers and libraries. These models are very useful in learning to understand memory, but we must never mistake the model for the reality it represents.

➤ Each of us has many memories including immediate, short-term, and long-term. Some "brain-mappers" have found that these are located in separate parts of the brain. Other researchers, however, have found that information may be distributed or duplicated in many parts of the brain.

➤ A good way to retain information in short-term memory, where it usually fades out in a very short time, is through repetition or rehearsal. This also helps move the information to long-term memory.

➤ Immediate memory has a very small capacity, generally one item at a time. Short-term memory has a larger but still very limited capacity. Long-term memory has virtually unlimited capacity.

➤ Long-term memory usually is divided into three parts: skill, event, and abstract. (There are many different sets of terms for these.)

➤ It isn't necessary to remember everything. In fact, it's probably best that you don't. Instead, it's a great idea to select what you want to retain and concentrate your efforts on those things. The rest can slide.

➤ Once information is stored in long-term memory, it sometimes is difficult to retrieve it. Many methods have been invented for doing this. The common term for these methods is mnemonic devices.

Nutrition and Memory

In This Chapter

➤ Various supplements help memory

➤ Start with a healthy body

➤ Various B vitamins and vitamins C and E

➤ Choline and lecithin

➤ Ginkgo biloba, the Chinese wonder herb

➤ Other possible supplements

Most people in this country are living longer and are staying healthier as they age. We're sure you'll agree that this is basically a good thing. But more and more people now are reaching the time of life at which they become aware that their memories are slightly less dependable. They worry about this and are concerned because they cannot remember the name of their third-grade teacher—a name they haven't tried to think of for possibly 40 years. Every hesitation in remembering a name or a date, which would have been ignored at age 30, becomes a cause for alarm at age 60.

The natural question is, "Is there anything I can take to help me get my memory back?"

Yes. To start with, take a trip to your doctor's office. Next, remember that, as we told you in Chapter 7, "In Sickness and in Health," occasionally forgetting a name, an event, or whatever is normal at any age. This book will teach you how to remember what you want to remember. You'll learn enough techniques and little tricks of memory that you'll be able to show off how good your memory has become. Honest!

Instant Recall

Those of you who have passed what we kindly call "middle age" and have found things harder to recall than when you were 30, keep in mind that you've lived twice as long. Now you have twice as many things to remember. Of course it takes longer!

Remember This!

Beware of publications issued by the manufacturers or marketers of "health" products. They are not concerned with your health; they are out to sell their products.

There are some things you should know about how nutrition can affect your memory. Nutritional studies have shown that some specific dietary supplements can do good things for mind and memory. You should be aware that some of these studies are better conducted than others, and some have stronger and more consistent results. Contrariwise some of the studies, although exciting, have yet to be replicated or were done with too small a sample to be reliable. The history of science is full of exciting discoveries that were made in good faith by capable people but that didn't pan out in the long run. The problem is that sometimes it takes years to discover which studies are reliable and which are unreliable.

This is why doctors and experts in the public-health field are usually the last to recommend a new nutritional miracle; they want to wait until they are sure they're right.

We're going to take an in-between position in this chapter. We'll tell you about nutritional information that seems to be pretty sound, and we'll recommend a few ingestibles that might improve your memory and even your brain power. We suggest *strongly* that you do further research on this yourself before popping any pills because the information and recommendations change monthly. Ask your doctor or medical nutritionist for advice, or consult one of the many magazines and journals published by universities, medical societies, or other reputable institutions.

Before using any new dietary supplement, you should consult your doctor or dietitian and check the latest findings. With that advice firmly in mind...

Eat, Drink, and Remember

A variety of vitamins, foods, and food supplements are known or believed to enhance mental function and memory. A few of them are discussed in this chapter, but before we get into that, we'd like to pass on some more general notions about nutrition.

To start with, remember that mental health requires physical health. As the Roman writer Juvenal said 2,000 years ago, you should strive to have "*mens sana in corpore sano,*" a sound mind in a sound body. We know there's only a certain amount of control you have over how sound your body is, but most of us don't even exercise that much control. Most of us, as a matter of fact, don't even exercise.

A Sound Body

As a starting point, before considering what nutrients are specifically good for the memory, you should get in the habit of eating foods that are good for your body and avoiding those that are not. You should keep your weight close to what your ideal weight should be. You also should avoid animal fat, which will clog your arteries. Arteriosclerosis (clogged arteries), besides being very dangerous for the heart, also cuts down the blood supply to the brain. This is, as you read in Chapter 7, "In Sickness and in Health," one of the causes of dementia.

You also should exercise. A brisk half-hour walk each day is probably sufficient for most purposes (but check with your doctor), although a little weight training wouldn't hurt. Walking has immediate benefits. After a brisk walk, you will have increased blood flow to the brain, and you actually will be thinking better and be better able to concentrate. If you can manage to walk where there aren't too many distractions, the walk itself is a good place to do some thinking and planning for your next project. You might want to get one of those little pocket tape recorders to take down your thoughts because it's hard to walk briskly and make notes at the same time.

There are many places to find good advice about what to eat for good health and what's the best way to exercise, so we won't preach to you about that. This is an important starting place, however, for improving your mental sharpness and your memory. The mind and body are both cleverly designed to respond to the demands made of them and to improve with practice. If you exercise muscles—and your heart is a muscle—the master control somewhere in your brain will decide you need to strengthen those muscles and will improve the blood flow to them. If you don't, they will get weak and flabby.

Likewise, if you exercise your brain, using it for problem-solving and developing your memory, the neurons will branch out and will make new connections to help you think and memorize better. The blood flow in the brain also will improve (unless your body is in such bad shape that your arteries are too clogged). Exercise is even good for your immune system; it helps keep you free of disease.

Now you're thinking, "I know all this. I've heard it all before. It's elementary." Okay, Sherlock, but are you doing it?

Instant Recall

Researchers have found that keeping a rat on a diet of only about two-thirds the normal number of calories but sufficient vitamins and minerals not only extends the rat's life but improves the rat's memory and prevents or delays ratty senility. How well a similar regime would work on people is not yet known.

Now a Few Don'ts

Here we're going to tell you about the possible benefits of some vitamins, drugs (prescription and nonprescription), and herbs. The key word here is "possible." All people are different, and what might be of great benefit to Herbert might just give you a headache or something worse. So follow these simple rules:

Refresh Your Memory

"Dis-moi ce que tu manges, je te dirai ce que tu es." (Tell me what you eat and I will tell you what you are.)

—Anthelme Brillat-Savarin (1755–1826), master chef

(This is often misquoted as "You are what you eat," which is quite another thought.)

Remember This!

Many people who call themselves nutritionists, herbalists, or dietitians have little or no formal training. More than half of the states have no licensing requirements for these titles. Try to find out the background of anyone whose advice you're relying on.

➤ If you think there's something wrong with your memory, your concentration, or for that matter anything else medical, do us and yourself a favor and see a doctor to find out just what it is before you start treating it.

➤ If you're on any medication, check with your doctor or pharmacist before adding anything to the mix—this includes elixirs, potions, powders, blossoms, berries, roots, herb teas, and anything in pill form (even if it's called an herbal remedy or a nutritional supplement rather than a medicine).

➤ If you are pregnant or think you might get pregnant, check with a doctor before taking *any* medication.

➤ Don't take something just because it's recommended to you by someone who works in a health food store, by someone who says it helped his Uncle Max, or by your own Uncle Max, or because you read in a book that it would be good for you—even this book. Do more research and find out what the experts say.

➤ Don't be fooled by the word "natural" on the label of a health product. Just because something is natural doesn't mean it's good for you or even safe. *Amanita phalloides* is completely natural—and very deadly. It's better known as the death's cap mushroom.

➤ Don't decide that, if 500 mg a day of a medication is good for you, 1,000 mg will be even better. Get advice you trust (again, from a doctor) and stick with it.

➤ Many doctors don't know much about nutrition. If you find a nutritionist, an internist, or a family practice doctor who has studied nutrition, so much the better. On the other hand, most doctors, if they err, will do so on the side of caution. So the advice of any doctor is certainly safer than the advice of the guy at the health food store.

Why all these caveats? Because we care about you! We plan to write other books, and we want you to be around to read them.

Basic Brain Food

The brain needs many vitamins and minerals to maintain its health. Luckily, most of these can be found in adequate amounts in a normal, healthy diet. Recently, however, nutritionists have decided that a few, such as vitamin E, might need to be supplemented.

The Vitamin Story

Vitamins got their name because they were believed to be substances essential to life that are not manufactured by the body. Some of them, such as thiamin (vitamin B1) and vitamin C, are just that—if you are deprived of them long enough, it will kill you. The others certainly are essential for good health. A well-balanced diet of meat, milk, eggs, green vegetables, and fruit will supply the minimum daily requirements of all vitamins. There are several reasons why someone might want to take supplements of some vitamins. For one thing, many people are avoiding eating as much meat and eggs as they used to. For another, some studies suggest that some vitamins, if taken in amounts substantially larger than you get from a normal diet, can have unexpected beneficial effects.

Some Memorable Facts

In 1747, British doctor James Lind discovered that scurvy—a debilitating and eventually deadly disease effecting mainly sailors on long sea voyages—could be prevented by adding fresh fruit or vegetables to the men's diets. In 1896, Christiaan Eijkman, a Dutch physician working in the East Indies, discovered that beriberi, a disease marked by extreme fatigue and eventual death, was the result of a diet deficient in nutrients accidentally removed in the processing of the polished rice the people were eating. Based on these findings, British biochemist Frederick Gowland Hopkins proposed in 1906 that certain trace compounds were vital to good health. These substances, called "vitamins," were discovered over the next few decades. Hopkins and Eijkman shared the Nobel Prize in medicine and physiology in 1929.

The B Vitamins

Here is a list of those B vitamins that have been shown to affect intelligence or memory.

➤ Vitamin B1, also known as thiamin, is needed to efficiently convert carbohydrates (starches and sugars) to brain food. If you don't have enough in your diet, it can cause depression, fatigue, and insomnia. Thiamin is found in whole-grain cereals, dried peas, peanuts, and some meat.

➤ Niacin, or vitamin B3, helps improve memory. It also can help prevent strokes by lowering blood cholesterol. Some people experience skin flushes and itching when taking moderate doses. Large doses over time can cause liver damage. Niacin is found naturally in salmon, swordfish, trout, and a few other fish as well as in peanuts, chicken, and liver.

➤ Vitamin B6, also known as pyridoxine, is needed for the brain to produce *neurotransmitters*. It is found in whole grains, sunflower seeds, brewer's yeast, some meats, and most vegetables. Taking supplemental B6 has helped some women relieve their symptoms of PMS.

➤ Vitamin B12 aids in the production of acetylcholine, which is needed for improved memory. It is found in dairy products, meat, and fish.

➤ Folic acid (folate) helps in the production of catecholamines, which are a specific class of neurotransmitters. Anxiety, depression, and trouble concentrating can be results of insufficient catecholamines. Folic acid also can help lessen memory loss and fuzzy thinking. It is found in whole grains, black-eyed peas, beans, and broccoli.

Folic acid should be taken by women who plan to get pregnant to help prevent brain and spinal cord defects in the baby.

Words to Remember

Neurotransmitters: The chemicals that neurons use to transmit information from one to the next. Examples include acetylcholine, serotonin, dopamine, and norepinephrine.

Some Memorable Facts

Mental illnesses such as depression and schizophrenia were once thought to be the result of childhood trauma and were treated as such by psychiatrists. Now there's a consensus that many mental illnesses are due to chemical imbalances. Many drugs have become available in the past couple decades (and more are on the way) to treat these conditions.

Vitamin C

Although there's some dispute about how effective vitamin C (ascorbic acid) is in curing colds, there's no question that it's an effective *antioxidant*. Lack of sufficient vitamin C can cause memory problems, inattention, and fatigue, although there's no proof that increased amounts of the vitamin can improve memory. Many months of being deprived of vitamin C can cause scurvy, which eventually can kill you. Curiously, all mammals except primates (monkeys, apes, and us) and guinea pigs make their own vitamin C internally. Vitamin C is found in most vegetables and especially in citrus fruits and red and green peppers. One glass of orange juice supplies the minimum daily requirement of vitamin C, but many nutritionists now feel that the vitamin is so important to the brain and the body that a supplement of 200 to 500 mg a day is recommended.

Vitamin E

Like vitamin C, vitamin E (tocopherol) is a powerful antioxidant. It is believed to be helpful in warding off heart disease, and there's evidence that it is useful in some 40 other diseases. Recent experiments indicate that large doses of vitamin E can slow the progression of Alzheimer's disease by about six months. The best sources of vitamin E are green vegetables, vegetable oils, and eggs.

Words to Remember

Oxygen: An element needed in the body to burn nutrients and produce energy. An oversupply of oxygen can combine with other chemicals to form molecules called free radicals, which damage cells. There is some belief that, over time, this cell damage can cause aging and, in the brain, symptoms of dementia.

Antioxidant: A substance that scrounges up and neutralizes free-radical molecules before they can cause harm.

107

Antioxidants

The importance of antioxidants in removing free radicals from the system is unquestioned. Many investigators even believe that a daily dose of antioxidants can help prevent heart disease, strokes, and dementia. Antioxidants also are proving to be of value in enhancing memory retention. In one study, old rats who were given antioxidants did better on memory tests than a control group of rats whose diet was not so enhanced. This gives us a wonderful image of a group of experimenters gathered around an aged rat, possibly with a cane, with one of the experimenters asking: "On what date was the Declaration of Independence signed?" Actually, we think they probably tested the rats' ability to remember how to run a maze.

An all-around antioxidant pill would include vitamin A, vitamin C, vitamin E, and the minerals selenium and zinc.

The suggested dosage of one popular antioxidant supplement is two pills per day. The following table gives the active ingredient list for these two pills.

Active Ingredients for Two Pills (the Recommended Daily Dosage) of a Popular Antioxidant Formulation

Active Ingredients	Amount	%RDI[1]
Vitamin A (beta carotene)	5000 IU[2]	100
Vitamin C	500 mg[3]	833
Calcium ascorbate	50 mg	34
Magnesium ascorbate	25 mg	2
Vitamin E	400 IU	1333
Zinc (chelate)	15 mg	100
Selenium (chelate)	50 mcg[4]	72
Chromium (chelate)	30 mcg	25
Citrus bioflavonoids	50 mg	**[5]
Grape skin extract	5 mg	**
Green tea extract	5 mg	**
Grape seed extract	100 mcg	**

[1] RDI = Recommended Daily Intake for adults and children four years of age

[2] IU = International Units: an internationally agreed-upon standard of dosage strength

[3] mg = milligrams

[4] mcg = micrograms

[5] ** = no recommended daily intake established

Other Nutrients

Most of the nutritional supplements sold mainly in health food stores were, until recently, considered by the scientific community to be of no particular health value. In some cases, this was because they were naturally made by the body, and it was assumed that the body made enough that no supplementation was necessary. In other cases, this was because the stories told of their benefits were classified as folklore, and their use was considered folk medicine.

Many of these supplements still remain in disrepute. Although they may be touted by ads in health magazines, they are of unproved merit. It appears, however, that some might be of value in combating a variety of ailments.

Choline and Lecithin

Lecithin is a type of lipid, which is a fat found in all living cells, particularly in red blood cells and in neurons. It is made up partly of the B vitamin choline, which is used in the body to make the neurotransmitter acetylcholine. As you will remember, a reduction in the amount of acetylcholine in the brain is one of the signs, and possibly one of the causes, of Alzheimer's disease. Animal studies also have shown that supplementing a normal diet with lecithin and choline enhances learning and memory. When pregnant rats were fed a lecithin-laced diet, their pups were able to learn and remember how to run mazes faster than pups whose mothers' dinners lacked the extra lecithin.

Instant Recall

Most nutritionists classify choline as one of the B vitamins, but others deny it that honor because it can be made in the body from serine, which is an amino acid. Vitamins usually are considered to be substances that the body needs in small amounts but cannot manufacture for itself.

In one human study, a group of adults who took a hefty dose of lecithin daily for three weeks showed a significant improvement in their short-term memory. In a five-week study, a group of 61 healthy adults between 50 and 80 years old were fed either two tablespoons of lecithin or a placebo. The lecithin-takers reported a hefty decrease in memory lapses—almost 50 percent. The placebo takers did not. The experimenters wrote that "the cost of lecithin is so low, the negative side effects so minimal, and the potential benefits so positive that we would recommend ... all persons experiencing memory problems ... [try] lecithin granules as food supplements."

The Enhancers

Now we'll move on to ginkgo biloba, DHEA, and other herbal remedies and nutritional supplements that have proven to be useful memory enhancers and aids to clear thinking. Other herbs, such as kava kava and St. John's Wort, seem to reduce depression, which certainly is a condition that affects memory and rational thought. The latter products are ever so slightly beyond the scope of this book, however, so look elsewhere for information on them.

Ginkgo Biloba

The ginkgo biloba tree comes from China, where its leaves have been used by Chinese herbalists to treat failing memory for more than 4,000 years. Recent controlled experiments by Western investigators have shown that these ancient herbalists knew what they were doing. The herb's effects seem to be due to chemicals called *bioflavonoids* found in the leaves. Tests have shown that ginkgo biloba extract has a wide variety of effects on the body's functions, including:

➤ Powerful antioxidant action

➤ Improving blood circulation, particularly to the brain

➤ Making blood vessels more elastic

➤ Preventing platelets in the blood from clumping together, which helps prevent blood clots

➤ Treating Alzheimer's disease

➤ Improving the ability of nerve cells to utilize oxygen

➤ Improving memory and learning ability

Several different experiments over the past 20 years have shown that ginkgo biloba extract helps in the treatment of several types of dementia including Alzheimer's disease. The improvement in mental function started to show up after the patients were on the pills for a month, and it continued for the duration of the tests, which ran from three to six months. There is no reason to assume the benefits would not continue indefinitely.

Dosage

The recommended dose for a person whose memory loss or other signs of dementia are not too severe, but who is trying to enhance mental function, is 120 mg a day (usually as two 60 mg pills, one in the morning and one in the evening). The dose for Alzheimer's patients and others with mild or moderate dementia is 240 mg (usually four pills taken in two or three doses throughout the day). Results should be noticeable after about a month. After six months, the dosage can be reduced to 120 mg a day.

Some Memorable Facts

Several studies have tested whether there are any immediate results from taking ginkgo biloba. The studies show that a dose of 120 to 240 mg taken all at once increases alpha-wave activity in the brain and depresses theta-wave activity. These usually are recognized as signs of improved brain function. The improvement begins about 30 minutes after taking the pills and peaks two to three hours later, but it continues on for a day or two. We would not want to suggest that taking ginkgo biloba before the big test, the big job interview, or even the big chess match will make the difference, but as one of our grandmothers used to say, "It couldn't hurt!"

Side Effects

The side effects reported when taking ginkgo biloba in the recommended dosages are few. Mild stomach upset occurred in less than 1 percent of those reporting. People with poor blood flow to the brain may get a mild headache for the first day or two, but it goes away after that. People on anticoagulant medication should consult their doctor before taking ginkgo biloba.

DHEA

DHEA (dehydroepiandrosterone) is a hormone naturally produced in the body, mostly in the adrenal glands and to some extent in the gonads. The amount of DHEA produced increases through childhood, peaks between ages 20 and 25, and then decreases until, by old age, very little is being produced. No one knows why this is, but some people think that, if old people have very little DHEA and young people have a lot of it, maybe having a lot of it will, well, not make you young again, but at least ward off some of the ill effects of aging.

Most ideas like this, no matter how reasonable they sound, turn out to be of limited, if any, value. The workings of the body are too complex to allow for any simplistic solutions to the problems of aging. For a while in the 1920s, it was thought that the secret of aging was in the glands. People spent fortunes to get injected with extracts of youthful glands from various animals. The only thing this accomplished was enriching the suppliers of the various glands.

In DHEA, however, youth-hunters might have really found something. In tests, the hormone has been shown to:

➤ Serve as an antioxidant

➤ Reduce fatigue

➤ Improve the ability to exercise

➤ Aid in losing weight

➤ Protect against heart attacks

Of particular interest to us, it also can:

➤ Improve cognitive response (the ability to think clearly)

Dosage

The suggested diet supplement of DHEA is 25 mg per day. The natural levels of DHEA in the blood are highest in the morning, so it's probably a good idea to listen to the wisdom of the body and take the supplement in the morning. It is not known whether taking more than this amount is safe over the long term, so we strongly suggest you don't go over that dosage.

Remember This!

A class of supplements called **nootropics** are slowly entering the market. Some are available in health food stores; some are available only by mail order from exotic locations. As combinations of various supplements, herbs, and drugs, they claim to be memory enhancers or to increase your powers of concentration—but be cautious! The only ability most of them probably share is the ability to remove $30 or $40 from your pocket.

Some Others We've Seen

In India, doctors have been prescribing an herb called brahmi (Bacopa monniera) for thousands of years to improve thinking and memory. Brahmi tea is given to babies to give them a head start in learning ability. At religious schools, the students use brahmi to aid them in memorizing the thousands of lines of ancient religious hymns they have to learn. In recent testing on rats, brahmi was shown to improve both short-term and long-term memory. The herb is believed to be very safe, even at high doses, but no optimum dosage has yet been determined. Our guess is that the herb will be appearing shortly at health food stores, along with more information about dosage.

A new entry in the field of antidementia drugs is DMAE (2-Dimethylaminoethanol). There have been a few studies of using this drug to treat Alzheimer's, and so far the results are mixed.

Other substances that have been touted as brain food, with varying evidence, include ginseng, glutathione, arginine, taurine, germanium, N-acetyl-L-carnitine (ALC), GABA, and inositol. Many of these are used as the active ingredients in the various "smart pills" and "power drinks" that are the latest fads of the diet drug companies. In most cases, the amounts of these ingredients in the pills or drinks is not enough to hurt you, but it's also not enough to do you any good.

No Cures Yet

None of these pills, herbs, or whatnot will cure Alzheimer's disease, prevent strokes, or reverse the inevitable aging process. None of them on their own is as good at keeping you young and your memory intact as a healthy diet and regular exercise. When added to a healthy diet and exercise, however, some of the supplements might well improve your memory, aid the clarity of your thought, and help keep your mind youthful and supple well into your ninth or tenth decade of living. The techniques discussed later in this book will enable you to make the best use of your youthful, powerful brain.

Good luck, eat right, exercise, and stay healthy!

The Least You Need to Know

➤ Slight memory loss over the years is natural, but anything more might indicate a medical problem.

➤ A healthy diet and exercise are the starting points in supplying proper nutrition to your brain.

➤ Be cautious when anyone recommends strange herbs or drugs.

➤ Supplementing your diet with additional B vitamins as well as vitamins C and E might help keep the brain healthy.

➤ Antioxidants may help prevent aging and improve brain function.

➤ Choline and lecithin have been shown to improve memory.

➤ Ginkgo biloba, a Chinese herb, has an impressive variety of positive effects on cognition and memory.

➤ DHEA, a natural hormone, seems to help clear thinking and improves many body functions.

➤ Keep an eye out for other supplements that will be available in the near future.

Part 3
Of Truth and Memory

Two people see the same event and give completely different versions of it when they are questioned. Six people make positive identifications of a suspect in a crime. He's convicted. Years later, new evidence proves that he couldn't possibly have committed the crime. Dozens of toddlers come home from preschool and tell their parents horrifying tales of sexual abuse, satanic rituals, and animal sacrifices. Is it possible? Is it true? If not, why are the children making these dreadful reports? We'll look into false memories, distorted memories, implanted memories—and also some very special memories. The story of the man who forgot everything he knew. The man who remembered everything. The woman who couldn't learn to dress herself but could read music and became a concert musician—the wonders of memory are endless!

Chapter 10

I Saw the Whole Thing

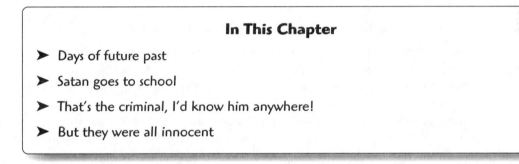

In This Chapter

➤ Days of future past

➤ Satan goes to school

➤ That's the criminal, I'd know him anywhere!

➤ But they were all innocent

In 1948, British novelist George Orwell sat down to write a novel warning of the horrors of dictatorship. Orwell got the title for his book by simply reversing the last two digits of the then-current year. The book was called *1984*, and it instantly became a classic. Possibly the most frightening aspect of *1984* was the way Orwell's imaginary dictator, known only as Big Brother, exercised power. It wasn't enough that everyone had to obey the commands of the government; their minds were controlled by the government as well.

Everything had to agree with Big Brother's ideas; everyone had to believe what Big Brother wanted them to believe. Even history had to conform to Big Brother's wishes. That's where Orwell's hero, Winston Smith, came in. Winston Smith wrote for the *Times* newspaper. What is curious, however, is that he didn't write for today's (or tomorrow's) editions of the newspaper. He wrote for past editions that were constantly revised to make them agree with the present policies of Big Brother.

Some Memorable Facts

George Orwell was the nom de plume of Indian-born Englishman Eric Arthur Blair. His experiences as an officer in Burma in the Indian Imperial Police (1922–1927) made him acutely aware of the injustices of imperial rule and led him to write his early novel, *Burmese Days*, in 1934. His first success, the autobiographical *Down and Out in Paris and London* (1933) recounted what it was like to live like a beggar in these two wealthy capitals. His experiences with communism, which he concluded was even more soul-destroying than capitalism as a system for humans to live under, led to the two classic books *Animal Farm* (1946) and *1984* (1948).

Here's the way George Orwell described Winston Smith at work:

> "For example, it appeared from the *Times* of the seventeenth of March that Big Brother, in his speech of the previous day, had predicted that the South Indian front would remain quiet but that a Eurasian offensive would shortly be launched in North Africa. As it happened, the Eurasian Higher Command had launched its offensive in South India and left North Africa alone. It was therefore necessary to rewrite a paragraph of Big Brother's speech in such a way as to make him predict the thing that had actually happened."

In other words, Winston Smith's job was to change the record of history to make it say what Big Brother wanted it to say. Of course, Winston Smith was only working with printed pages. Could Big Brother actually change people's memories so they would remember exactly what he wanted them to remember? If so, the past would become plastic, pliable, and shaped into any form Big Brother wished. People would lose their mental bearings and would have to rely on the all-powerful State to tell them what to believe.

Does this kind of thing actually happen to individuals? Do we change the past in our own minds? We tend to think otherwise. "I saw the whole thing!" "I remember it in vivid detail!" "I couldn't possibly be wrong about this!" And yet, time after time, we are wrong about the past. We manufacture or distort recollections, we unconsciously fill in the blanks when we have only limited data, and under the right circumstances, our memories can be amazingly subject to suggestion and manipulation.

In this chapter, we'll examine these odd and frightening phenomena and look into some actual cases in which false, distorted, or implanted memories may have led to tragic consequences. We'll discover some of the mechanisms investi-gators use that create these false memories, perhaps unintentionally and even unknowingly. We'll also take a look at some research that may point the way toward a means of separating these false memories from authentic ones.

The Tragedy of the McMartin School

Manhattan Beach, California, is a thriving suburban town located on the Pacific Ocean a few miles southwest of Los Angeles. Prior to 1984, it was little known to the rest of the world. In that year, Manhattan Beach and its residents became the center of a legal controversy and a vast media circus. The events affected the lives of many individuals, cost millions of dollars, and brought terrible harm to everyone concerned.

A central figure in the tragic story was Virginia McMartin, a wheelchair-bound, 77-year-old grandmother. She wasn't the type of person you would expect to be high priestess of a satanic cult of child molesters.

Instant Recall

The leaders of the former Soviet Union believed in re-creating the past. As party members fell out of favor and were executed or sent to Siberian labor camps, their images would be carefully excised from old photographs. Sometimes, other people's images were even inserted. Of course, the Soviet leaders never went so far as to try to rewrite newspapers already printed, but they did issue the *Soviet Encyclopedia* in loose-leaf format so it could be constantly updated with the latest version of the "truth."

Yet, in 1984, a district attorney in southern California brought an indictment against Mrs. McMartin; her daughter, Peggy McMartin Buckey; her grandchildren, Peggy Ann Buckey and Raymond Buckey; and three teachers at the preschool they operated in Manhattan Beach. The charges against the school operators and teachers were enough to make anyone cringe in horror and to make any parent of a small child panic.

The district attorney alleged that children at the McMartin Preschool were subjected to sexual abuse and molestation and that the McMartins and their employees were members of a satanic cult that conducted rituals at the school involving young children and animal sacrifices.

The case had been brought to the attention of the authorities by the mother of a two-and-a-half-year-old boy enrolled at the McMartin Preschool. The child's mother suspected that her son was being sexually abused and reported her suspicions to the local police.

Police and District Attorney's investigators and trained psychologists interviewed the young child and other children who attended the McMartin Preschool. They encouraged the children to describe the activities at the school, furnished them with anatomically correct dolls, and asked them to demonstrate on the dolls the acts that the teachers performed or forced the children to perform.

When they heard the stories told by these children, prompted by the "trained investigators," the appalled authorities swooped down on the suspects. The preschool was closed, Virginia McMartin, the Buckeys, and their employees were placed under arrest, and the wheels of justice began to turn. Some 52 counts were brought against the defendants. The nation was rocked by the horrors of the alleged crimes, and suddenly similar stories began emerging elsewhere around the country. Reports of satanic cults and mass child-abuse rings echoed from big cities and small towns across the land. Whole communities were torn apart as accusations were brought against teachers and caregivers. Had a network of satanic cults cast its frightening web over a continent?

As the McMartin case progressed, the longer and harder the prosecution worked to prove their charges, the more difficulty they had. There were lurid stories, but there was not an iota of physical evidence. And since the witnesses, who also were the victims of the alleged crimes, were small children whose memories had been prodded by adult interviewers, there were serious questions about how reliable they might be.

Some Memorable Facts

One of the accusations of the children was that there was a network of tunnels running under the school, leading to a secret room where many horrible things were done. For some reason, this was not checked during the trial. After the trial, the grounds around the school were dug up, and the walls and floors of the school building were tested. There were no tunnels.

By 1986, all charges were dropped against the elder Mrs. McMartin; her granddaughter, Peggy Ann Buckey; and the unrelated teachers at the preschool. Still, the state persisted in its case against Peggy McMartin Buckey and her son, Raymond Buckey. They were charged with multiple counts of molestation against children over a period of five years.

In 1990, Peggy McMartin Buckey was acquitted of all charges. Her son was acquitted of 40 counts, although the jury was deadlocked on several other counts against him. A second jury was assembled and another trial was conducted, at the end of which the jury was still deadlocked on eight counts. These were finally dropped.

The case had lasted seven years. The County of Los Angeles had spent $13 million on it, with an end result of no convictions whatsoever. The process had all but destroyed the defendants. The McMartin Preschool was closed, never to reopen. The defendants were financially ruined, and their careers were ended. They had nothing left but to live out their days, forever under a cloud. Once horrendous charges like these were brought, they could never be totally dispelled.

After all, there was no proof that these people did the terrible things they were charged with, but there also was no proof that they didn't do them either, was there? Of course, it's almost impossible to prove a negative.

What about the children who told those horrifying stories? They'll go through life remembering the case if not the supposed events themselves. They may find themselves wondering, years or even decades later, what really happened at that little school near the ocean.

It's almost certain that nothing happened.

Remember This!

The wave of unsubstantiated accusations against preschools and others responsible for the care of small children, brought on by untrained investigators, overzealous prosecutors, and public fear, is only now beginning to abate. Tests show that children's memories are malleable, as you can read in this chapter and in Chapter 13, "Very Special Memories."

Some Memorable Facts

In 1997, Mark Pendergast compared the rash of allegations of satanic cults to the medieval witch burnings in Europe. He pointed out, "Many 'witches' confessed to the most ridiculous charges ... They had developed very coherent, detailed memories of the orgies in which they had taken part, the babies they had roasted and eaten. Young girls would describe in gory detail how they had been deflowered by the Devil, though examination proved them to be virgins."

How could a sequence of events as terrible as those that took place in Manhattan Beach come about? We'll go into that shortly. For one more moment, let's return to the origins of the McMartin case. Remember the mother of the toddler that first approached the Manhattan Beach police in 1983? Whatever became of her? And why did she have the suspicions that she first brought to their attention? Well, it later came to light that the poor woman had a long history of mental illness. The entire matter almost certainly had its genesis in this woman's disturbed brain.

Dr. Varendonck

As long ago as 1911, a Belgian physician by the name of Julian Varendonck was consulted by a court in his home country and was asked to evaluate the testimony of children in a criminal trial. Dr. Varendonck interviewed the children and reported back to the court that their testimony should not be given credence because they could be manipulated by the interviewer to give answers of his own choosing.

Dr. Varendonck entered a Belgian classroom and asked the teacher to leave. There were 19 seven-year-old students in the room. Dr. Varendonck asked the students the color of their teacher's beard. Sixteen of the students said the teacher's beard was black. Varendonck repeated the experiment with a class of 20 eight-year-old children. This time, 19 of the students reported a variety of colors for the teacher's beard.

A total of 35 students out of 39 told Varendonck what color the teacher's beard was. In fact, the teacher had no beard! What was going on? We can't be certain, but in all likelihood, the children were not deliberately inventing a beard and placing it on their teacher's face just to please Dr. Varendonck. The most likely explanation is this:

Dr. Varendonck didn't ask whether the teacher had a beard; he asked what color the beard was. Therefore, obviously, the teacher much have a beard. What color was it? Most Belgians tend to have dark hair and beards. If the teacher had a beard, it almost certainly would have been black.

The children must really have believed that their teacher had a black beard. What a droll surprise when he strode back into the room, smooth-shaven as an egg, *n'est-ce pas*? If Dr. Varendonck had asked "Does your teacher have a beard?" the results probably would have been different. Better yet, if he had simply asked "What does your teacher look like?" he would not have led the children to a specific answer.

How does Dr. Varendonck's work relate to the tragic case of the McMartin Preschool more than 70 years later? Critics and researchers have been studying the McMartin case ever since it hit the headlines, trying to figure out what went wrong. It looks as if the same kind of "leading" that Dr. Varendonck used with his beard question caused the children of Manhattan Beach to furnish their interviewers with startling and horrible reports. It is possible to ask sensitive, important questions without leading witnesses. Judges often try to require attorneys to ask their questions in nonleading ways, and lawyers often jump up and object to "leading questions." In an assault case, for example, a witness might be asked essentially the

Instant Recall

The better part of a century later, a growing body of evidence tells us that Dr. Varendonck was right. The leading researcher in our own era is Dr. Elizabeth Loftus, a professor of psychology who frequently is consulted as an expert witness on the subject of memory. Dr. Loftus's work includes such controversial subjects as false memory, lost (or repressed) and recovered memory, and implanted memory.

same question in several different ways, and the nonleading way is the one a good judge would insist on.

Let's look at a hypothetical case.

Charlene and Marty are standing in a room. Estelle walks in and—according to a lawsuit later filed by Marty—punches him. The case comes to trial and Charlene, a witness, is questioned by Marty's lawyer.

Marty's lawyer: Did Estelle punch Marty very hard?

Estelle's lawyer: Objection. Leading the witness.

Judge: Sustained.

Marty's lawyer: Very well, how hard did Estelle punch Marty?

Estelle's lawyer: Objection. Still leading the witness.

Judge: Sustained.

Marty's lawyer: All right, did you see Estelle punch Marty?

Estelle's lawyer: Objection. Still leading.

Judge: Sustained.

Marty's lawyer: Okay, what did you see?

Judge: Good, the witness may answer the question.

Do you see what happened here? If the lawyer managed to get in the question "How hard?" Charlene (the witness) likely would think, at least subconsciously, "Hmm, did she punch him very hard? Pretty hard? Not so hard?"

The question "Did you see Estelle punch Marty?" is much better. It allows for the possibility that Estelle did not punch Marty. "What did you see?" is best of all, however, because it makes no assumptions, and it influences the witness to make no assumptions. She'll just tell the court what she saw, which might or might not have included the famous punch.

Detectives investigating a case like the McMartin case do not operate in a courtroom and are not challenged by an opposing attorney. They are not supervised by a judge whose job is to keep them in line and discourage them from leading the witness. Sometimes they'll try to influence a witness to get the answers they want or expect. More often, they're acting in good faith, trying to get the truth. But they do have certain expectations, and there are answers they hope to get.

Witnesses often want to please the detectives, either for their own reasons (such as favorable disposition of unrelated charges) or simply because, unconsciously, people generally want to give answers that will please the people asking the questions. This especially is true when dealing with authority figures such as police officers, detectives, or district attorneys.

123

We learn this conduct from our parents when we're small children. The reward for giving the "right" answer is a hug, a kiss, or a cookie. The lesson is reinforced by our teachers. The reward then becomes a good grade, a word of praise, or a place on the honor roll. The lesson often is further reinforced in the workplace or in social situations.

By the time the detective asks "What color is your teacher's beard?" most of us would answer that it's black—and we'd really believe it!

"Number Four, Step Forward and Sneer"

We've all seen police lineups. They appear regularly on TV cop shows and in movies. We even hear about them (although they're not shown on TV—yet!) on the news when witnesses or victims of crime are called on to identify bad guys.

The previous situation involving Marty, Estelle, and Charlene did not involve identification. The identities of the participants in the event were not questioned; it was the event itself to which Charlene was asked to testify.

What if Estelle had said, "Hey, I don't know what these people are talking about. I wasn't even there!" The police would have had to find out who really came through that doorway and did (or did not) punch Marty.

How would they go about this?

First, they would separate Marty and Charlene to prevent cross-contamination of their memories. Otherwise, Marty and Charlene might discuss the event. Their dialog might go something like this:

Detective: "That was a tall, slim woman, wasn't it?"

Charlene: "Was she? Hmm. Yes, now that you mention it, she was tall, very tall. And slim, very slim. Ah yes, I remember it well!"

Detective: "What else did you notice about her? Hair, eyes, clothes...?"

Charlene: "Hmm, her hair—you know, I don't remember what color her hair was."

Marty: "I noticed that. Honey blonde. Medium length. Combed back from her face and worked into a chignon."

Charlene: "A chignon, a chignon. Ah yes, I remember it well. And her eyes, those blazing, hazel-colored eyes."

Detective: "Blazing, were they? And hazel-colored?"

Charlene: "Very much so."

Marty: "Ah yes, I remember it well."

Within minutes, prompted by the detective, the two witnesses have reached a consensus description of the person they saw. But how much does Marty really remember? How much does Charlene really remember? They're not trying to work in collusion, nor is the detective really trying to influence their testimony. They're all working in good faith, but the effect is a combined image of the mystery woman that might have little or no connection to the truth.

For this reason, the police should escort Marty and Charlene into different rooms and question them separately. They may ask each to work with a police sketch artist or an Identi-Kit technician to combine facial features, hair styles, age indicators, moles, scars, and other descriptors to get a picture of the suspect.

Remember This!

Remember Mommy and Daddy and the cookie. Remember the teacher and the honor roll. If the "right" answer is "Oh, yes, I'd know that face anywhere," that's the answer likely to emerge, eventually if not right away.

Another method frequently used by police is to ask the witness or victim to look through a "mug book" containing photographs of hundreds of known criminals in hopes of recognizing the right face. Alternately, they may show the witness a photo lineup of up to 20 individuals who fit the witness's general description of the criminal.

Suppose the witness picks out a photograph and says, "I think that's the person." The police investigator is likely to follow up by asking, "Are you sure? Is that definitely the person?" The witness is likely to answer affirmatively, moving in stages from a vague resemblance to a probable identification to moral certainty. The police aren't trying to lead the witness (or maybe they are, but that's another can of worms). The witness is trying to be honest and helpful. But she knows the police are hoping for a positive ID, and...

After an ID is made, things move another step. The person identified in the photograph is picked up by the police and is placed in a "live" lineup with half a dozen others. The witness is asked to survey the individuals in the lineup. Lo and behold, she picks out the "right" suspect.

Now she really does recognize him. But why? Does she recognize him from the original event? Or from the photo lineup? "I know that face." Indeed she does!

Suppose the police and the District Attorney do their customary superb work, the case reaches Criminal Court, and the State calls its star witness.

She ascends the stand and is sworn in. In response to the District Attorney's inquiries, she describes the events of the night in question. Finally, the District Attorney peers into the witness's eyes and asks, "If the person you saw commit these horrendous deeds is presently in the courtroom, please point him out."

The witness scans the courtroom, her gaze finally settling on a well-dressed individual sitting at the defense table. The witness raises one hand and points dramatically. "That's the man. I would know him anywhere. I could never forget that face!" Right! It's the same face the witness saw in the live lineup and, before that, in the photo lineup or the mug book. Sure, she remembers that face. But is it the same face she saw at the scene of the crime? It's hard to tell. It's very, very hard to tell.

"Prosecutors Hid Evidence, Sending 67 to Death Row"

This is an actual newspaper headline, and it isn't from some scandal-ridden time like the Prohibition Era of the 1920s or the McCarthy-driven Red Scare of the 1950s. The dateline is January 1999, and it refers to a survey conducted by the *Chicago Tribune* and reported by one of today's ace journalists, Ken Armstrong. Between 1963, when a Supreme Court ruling designed to curb prosecutorial misconduct was issued, and 1998, no fewer than 381 homicide convictions were thrown out, returned to lower courts for retrial, or dismissed. Of the 381 persons improperly convicted, 67 had been sentenced to death. Of the 67, at least 28 were subsequently freed, although the survey points out that nearly all the persons involved served at least five years in prison. And remember, these were only the faulty homicide convictions. How many faulty convictions for assault, robbery, burglary, rape, and other offenses took place? Surely the number is in the thousands, possibly in the tens of thousands.

Let's note that the *Chicago Tribune* survey refers to misconduct by police, investigators, and prosecutors. The number of good-faith errors is unknown, but it almost certainly is at least as great as the number of misconduct cases.

The Least You Need to Know

➤ Memory is malleable. The past is not firmly fixed in our minds; it can be shaped and altered by later events.

➤ Fear and hysteria can travel through a community like a virus. The McMartin Preschool case is a glaring example.

➤ Eyewitness identification is dramatic and often convincing, but in fact, it really is very unreliable.

➤ Information-sharing can lead to the creation of a conveniently agreed-upon "memory," but this memory is dangerously unreliable.

➤ Identification is subject to suggestion and distortion. The process of moving from a photo lineup to a live lineup to a courtroom confrontation can change a vague and uncertain sense of familiarity into a firm—but mistaken—conviction.

➤ Many innocent people have been convicted of very serious crimes and have been sentenced to long prison terms and even death. Some of these cases have been uncovered and reversed—but only some.

Chapter 11

Tune in Tomorrow!

In This Chapter

➤ Conviction of the innocent...

➤ ...and one who may not be innocent

➤ Sulthoids, Gorkoids, and Floobers

➤ Six missteps for witnesses

➤ Tune in tomorrow—or maybe not

➤ Conflation and confusion

Consider the following wrongfully convicted individuals in notable cases from recent years. We'll then describe just a handful of cases out of thousands that have taken place.

Kirk Bloodsworth was convicted in 1985 of raping and murdering a nine-year-old Maryland girl. Bloodsworth was sentenced to death. After 18 months, his conviction was overturned for technical reasons. The district attorney chose to try the case again. Bloodsworth was convicted a second time, with the case resting on the testimony of five eyewitnesses. Bloodsworth was sentenced to life imprisonment.

Bloodsworth remained in prison, protesting his innocence, for nine years. At that time, a DNA fingerprint test was applied to evidence in the case that, fortunately, had been preserved. This test proved that Bloodsworth could not possibly have been the guilty party. He was freed and the State of Maryland paid him $300,000 as restitution for his years in prison.

Some Memorable Facts

DNA testing has only been available since about 1994, and it did not come into general use until a few years after that. It didn't even exist at the time of Bloodsworth's original trial. More than 100 people have been released from prison in the past few years because DNA testing, unavailable at the time of their conviction, has proven their innocence. It's interesting to consider, in light of this statistic, how many people are in prison—some of them on death row—for crimes they did not commit. Unfortunately, in the overwhelming majority of these cases, DNA evidence either did not exist or was not preserved.

Most law enforcement professionals agree that objective, scientific evidence like DNA testing is more reliable than the uncertain memories of eye witnesses.

Timothy Hennis was convicted in 1986 of the horrendous rape and murder of a North Carolina woman and her three-year-old child. Hennis, a career Army noncommissioned officer, had answered a newspaper advertisement placed by the victim, offering a dog for adoption. Hennis took the dog and shortly thereafter wrote a letter expressing his pleasure at how well the dog was getting along with another pet he already owned.

He then allegedly returned to the house where he had received the dog and committed his grisly deeds.

When the crime was discovered, the local sheriff's department issued a bulletin asking the man who had taken the dog to contact them. Hennis learned of this from a television news bulletin and immediately contacted the sheriff. Hennis was identified by a local maintenance worker who claimed to have seen a man walking down the driveway of the victims' home in the middle of the night.

The maintenance worker very tentatively picked Hennis's image out of a photo lineup. A detective asked, "Are you sure?" The witness replied, "Naw, I can't answer that." Still, the maintenance man also described the car that the man he had seen climbed into—and the description matched Hennis's car!

As the investigation progressed, it became clear that the state's case would rest almost entirely on the eyewitness testimony of the maintenance worker. The scene of the crime was dusted for fingerprints and plenty turned up—but none of them belonged to Timothy Hennis.

When Hennis's defense lawyers interviewed the eyewitness prior to the trial, he backed away from his identification once more. He signed a statement saying, "I thought that I was positive that the person I picked out in the lineup was the person I had seen.

However, after thinking about the matter, I have doubts as to whether or not I picked out the right person."

Yet, after further consultations with the prosecution, he changed his mind again and returned to his "firm" identification of Hennis. And at the trial, the prosecution produced a second eyewitness— a woman who testified she had seen Hennis using a stolen ATM card to withdraw money from the victim's bank account shortly after the murders.

Hennis was convicted and sentenced to death.

Then private investigators hired by Hennis's defense team scored a major breakthrough. They learned that a neighborhood character known as "the walker" had been known to wander the streets of the neighborhood where the crimes took place, late at night. He had moved away from the town, but they were able to track him down and establish that he was the man the maintenance worker had seen walking down the driveway of the victims' home. The identification of the witness who saw someone using the victim's ATM card proved similarly unreliable.

Instant Recall

In a macabre twist of fate, a self-identified "Mr. X" wrote letters both to Hennis and to the police stating that he was the criminal. Who was the murderer? Was it Mr. X? Or was Mr. X a harmless crackpot? No one knows. The real murderer is almost certainly still out there and may well strike again.

The witnesses who had testified against Hennis were not acting from malice (they didn't even know him) or in hopes of personal gain. We can only assume that they really believed they had seen him at the times and places they claimed. Somehow, in the process of recording, retaining, and retrieving information, they had come inadvertently to give false testimony. They weren't really lying, they were just mistaken. But they nearly cost Hennis his life.

Sergeant Hennis was eventually exonerated. Neither he nor "the walker," who was also cleared, could possibly have committed the crimes.

Ivan the Terrible

In 1987, one John Demjanjuk was brought to trial in the State of Israel on a variety of charges including war crimes, crimes against humanity, crimes against a persecuted people, and crimes against the Jewish people. Specifically, it was charged that Demjanjuk had worked for the Nazis at the Treblinka death camp during World War II.

Of all the sadistic agents of Hitler's regime, Ivan Grozny, a guard at Treblinka who became known as Ivan the Terrible, was one of the most monstrous. He tortured prisoners, taking obvious glee in his work as he whipped, beat, and tormented them. On at least one occasion, he plunged a prisoner's head into a bucket of water and held the prisoner's head submerged until he drowned. He herded prisoners into mass death chambers, and when that chore was not sufficient for his monstrous appetite, he would personally kill selected individuals, crushing their skulls with blows from massive iron pipes.

There was no question as to the horrors of Ivan's crimes. The defense put up by Demjanjuk's lawyers was one of mistaken identity. The prosecution maintained that John Demjanjuk was Ivan the Terrible. The defense insisted that he was not.

The prosecution relied on two forms of evidence. One was a document; the other was eyewitness identification.

The document presented was an ID card bearing a photo of the youthful Demjanjuk and his personal information. It had been issued by a Nazi training camp in Poland in 1942. Even after half a century, Demjanjuk's facial features resembled those of the young man in the photograph.

Indeed, Demjanjuk had been a Nazi—of sorts—at that time. Born in Ukraine, which was then part of the Soviet Union, he had been inducted into the Soviet Army and was sent to fight against the Germans in the early days of World War II. Along with many of his comrades, he switched sides and joined an all-Ukrainian unit created by the Nazis and used against the Soviets.

After the war, Demjanjuk made his way to the United States. He covered up his highly irregular past, became a citizen, and worked in an automobile factory until his retirement. At that late time, his duplicity was uncovered. He was stripped of his American citizenship and was extradited to Israel to stand trial.

Ivan the Terrible certainly had committed terrible crimes. But was John Demjanjuk really Ivan the Terrible?

No fewer than five survivors of the Treblinka camp pointed to Demjanjuk and identified him as Ivan the Terrible. But half a dozen other survivors looked at Demjanjuk and denied that he was Ivan. The memories were old, nearly half a century old. The witnesses were aged men and women.

Could these witnesses positively identify Ivan the Terrible after the passage of so many years? They believed that they could. But old memories decay. They fade, they lose definition, and they become *conflated*, contaminated by intervening events, and distorted.

It was up to the court to decide whether to accept the identification of Demjanjuk as Ivan.

But what about that damning ID card?

Remember This!

Under our system of law, you cannot be tried and convicted of simply being a bad person. You must be accused of committing specific crimes, and it must be proved beyond a reasonable doubt that you did commit those crimes. The framers of the Constitution understood that people must be protected from the state being able to lock them up just because it doesn't like them. Most modern countries have adopted similar restrictions on the police power of government.

The Soviet KGB (secret police) furnished the court with a photocopy of the card but refused to relinquish the card itself. Documentation experts, studying the photocopy, found a number of highly suspicious elements. Information was missing, the form itself contained misspellings, seals were misaligned, and the photograph of Demjanjuk appeared to have been removed from another document and reattached to the card.

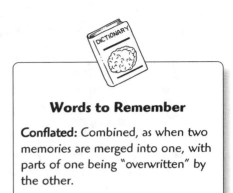

Words to Remember

Conflated: Combined, as when two memories are merged into one, with parts of one being "overwritten" by the other.

In the photo, Demjanjuk was wearing a Soviet-style military tunic—hardly the outfit one would expect him to wear for a German military ID card. But why would the KGB bother to create such a document? Demjanjuk, a Ukrainian, had served first with the Soviet army, then switched to the German side. He was regarded as a Soviet traitor, and the KGB had a long memory. If they couldn't get their hands on him and try him for treason, they would help to convict him in another country on other charges!

Despite the wobbliness of the evidence against Demjanjuk, his case had stirred up such emotional memories of horrible events and the court was convinced of his guilt. Demjanjuk was convicted. The verdict was rendered in April 1988, and Demjanjuk was sentenced to death.

But execution was stayed while the case was appealed, and the Israeli Supreme Court threw out the conviction. By this time, the Soviet Union had dissolved and Ukraine was an independent nation. Demjanjuk was freed and returned to Ukraine.

Was he really Ivan the Terrible? Or was the whole case a terrible mistake? Only John Demjanjuk knows.

Now Just a Minute!

Let's emphasize something. We're not saying that most criminal convictions are the result of either trumped-up evidence or honest errors. Most of them are legitimate, and we certainly don't advocate opening the prison gates and letting a flood of criminals back onto the street.

Child molestation cases, in particular, are very hard to handle. They are especially tragic in that their victims are so young and so vulnerable. The victims are likely to carry the scars and suffer the pain of their victimization for the rest of their lives.

But even one innocent man or woman convicted by error or fraud is one too many. And the execution of even one innocent person is itself a monstrous crime. We need to take a close look at our criminal justice system and do everything possible to clear out corrupt or overzealous prosecutors. We also need to re-examine our procedures to make sure that innocent people aren't mistakenly convicted.

Whatta Ya Know for Sure?

You've just seen examples of at least two people who were unjustly convicted on the basis of faulty eyewitness identifications. One of them actually was sentenced to death. Fortunately, the errors were discovered and the innocent persons were freed.

Instant Recall

"It is better to risk saving a guilty person than to condemn an innocent one."

—Voltaire (Francois Marie Arouet) (1694–1778)

In the third case, however, that of John Demjanjuk, we're still not certain. Was he Ivan Grozny, Ivan the Terrible, or wasn't he? There was no question of Ivan's terrible crimes, but there were very serious questions about Demjanjuk's identity. At first, an Israeli trial court ruled that Demjanjuk and Ivan the Terrible were one and the same man. Then the Israeli Supreme Court ruled that it wasn't certain that he was Ivan. Let's call it the equivalent of the American notion of reasonable doubt. Demjanjuk was freed.

We've talked about how a tentative and uncertain eye-witness identification can turn into a moral certainty. The progression from photo lineup to live lineup to courtroom confrontation can make a weak witness into a very strong one. Alas, while this might contribute to a high rate of convictions for an ambitious prosecutor, it does not always contribute to the cause of justice.

Other mechanisms also come into play that tend to make eyewitness testimony just about the least reliable kind of evidence. We're going to ask you to role-play now. You won't have to put on a costume or stand in front of an audience. This is just mental role-playing, but it can be highly illuminating.

"He Came Straight at Me, I'll Never Forget That Moment"

You've probably never been the victim of a serious crime, but if you have, you almost certainly recall the event vividly. Whether you've been a victim or not, we're going to ask you to imagine yourself in such a situation.

Don't be afraid. This is only make-believe.

Let's say you're five feet tall, 19 years old, and an ethnic Sulthoid. You're rather slim. You weigh, let's say, 88 pounds soaking wet.

The Sulthoids, by the way, are a green-skinned people from a tiny island in the Sulthian Ocean. It's a very tiny island. There are very few Sulthoids around. Trust us.

You've put in a hard day's work, have had a pleasant dinner with your favorite dinner companion, are relaxed and listening to Mozart (or Barry Manilow or—well, you get the idea), and are starting to think about getting a good night's rest. You take a stroll to the kitchen, contemplating a bedtime snack, and open the refrigerator. You discover that you're all out of orange juice and milk for your morning coffee. Even though it's raining hard tonight, you put on your hat and make your way to the local convenience store to stock up on comestibles.

The street leading from your home to the store is dark. There are heavy shade trees overhead, and it's a dark and stormy night. The store itself is brightly lit.

Just as you reach the store, the door is shattered with a burst of deafening noise from inside the establishment. You hear gunfire in the store, and a heavy figure staggers out, a blazing gun in his hand. He almost tramples you as he turns away. You catch a momentary glimpse of his face and then he's gone into the darkness.

Inside the store, you can see a blood-spattered clerk reaching for the telephone to call for assistance. Almost before you know it, sirens wail, lights flash, and the local police force's rapid-response unit is rolling into the parking lot. You turn back and see that the clerk has fallen to floor, bleeding profusely. There also is blood on the jagged glass edges of the door.

"I saw him," you tell a police officer. "I was this close to him. I could almost touch him. I'd know that man anywhere!"

"Are you certain?" the officer asks.

"He came straight at me," you shudder. "I'll never forget that moment."

Less than an hour later, you're sitting in police headquarters face to face with a sketch artist, trying to describe the person you encountered leaving the store.

He was huge. He must have been 6'8" tall and weighed 300 pounds. He was wearing a slouch hat and a raincoat, and he was a Gorkian.

The Gorkians, by the way, are a race of purple-and-blue mottled people from the Gork Archipelago, which is located near the Islands of Langerhans. There are very few Gorkians in your town, but obviously there was at least one.

The artist asks you for details about the robber. His hair? It was hidden by his hat. His face? Well, er, he was a Gorkian, you know. Purple and blue skin. He looked like, well, like a Gorkian.

How old was he?

It was hard to tell, but he was old. He must have been at least 60.

The artist asks you some more questions, but you aren't able to give him much more information. You do, however, remember the gun he was carrying. The thing was huge. You don't know much about guns, but this thing must have been two-feet long. It was dull black with a long curved thingamajig sticking down underneath. When he fired it, there were greenish-bluish flashes. It made a sound like *whammity-whammity-whammity-whammity.*

Will any of that help?

Well, the police thank you for your assistance, take your address and telephone number, and tell you that they'll be in touch.

Two days later, they ask you to come in for a lineup.

They've got a row of Gorkians, and the first thing that springs to your mind is that you're acting like a bigot. After all, you know that the great majority of Gorkians (like the great majority of Sulthoids) are decent, law-abiding citizens. Was it unfair and racist of you even to mention that the person you saw leaving the convenience store was a Gorkian?

Well, no, it wasn't racist. Unless you think Gorkians are intrinsically dishonest and unreliable, it wasn't bigoted of you to mention that the person leaving the store was a Gorkian. It's just a fact, like saying that he was tall, or short, or bearded.

You look at the Gorkians standing on the platform and you realize, to your horror, that all Gorkians look alike to you. This is another racist stereotype, and you're more upset than ever. Furthermore, in this light, you can see the subjects in the lineup ever so much better than you did outside the convenience store, and you realize that you can't identify the person you saw at all.

But wait a minute. The Gorkian you saw coming from the store cut himself on the broken glass. You take one more peek only to realize that every person in the lineup has a heavily bandaged hand. Good police work, of course. Keeps you from jumping to the conclusion that any Gorkian with a cut on his hand must be the crook. But it makes it harder to identify the culprit.

Well, don't feel too bad. It's unfortunate that you can't pick the bad guy out of the lineup, but it's better to admit as much than to pick one when you're not really certain and possibly perpetrate a terrible injustice. Just a few pages ago, you saw a number of cases in which people were put through terrible experiences as a result of mistaken eyewitness testimony.

In fact, when you encountered that gun-toting individual coming out of the convenience store, you were subject to at least four of the six most significant problems that effect eyewitness identifications. Let's take a look at these:

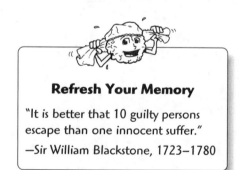

Refresh Your Memory

"It is better that 10 guilty persons escape than one innocent suffer."

—Sir William Blackstone, 1723–1780

1. **Lighting and ambient conditions.** Remember, it was a dark night and it was raining hard. Your eyes were accustomed to the darkness, and the person coming out of the store came from brightly lit surroundings. These circumstances are bad for seeing anything, especially making a certain identification of a total stranger.

2. **Emotion, excitement, and distraction.** Evidence is mixed on this subject. Some experiments suggest that we actually remember better in moments of excitement and intense emotion. At the same time, the noise, flashing lights, action, and excitement of the moment almost certainly distracted you.

3. **Weapon fixation.** This is a commonsense phenomenon that is supported by experiments. When somebody comes at you with a weapon in his hand, your attention fixes on the weapon, whether it's a gun, a knife, a hand grenade, or a fireplace poker. This makes sense—you have to decide in an instant whether to dodge, flee, try to knock the weapon aside, or try to talk the attacker out of using it. You're going to think about that Uzi, not whether the person carrying it has green eyes or brown eyes.

4. **Race.** Do not—we repeat, do *not*—beat yourself up over this. Sure, to Sulthoids, all Gorkians look alike. It's a fact. To Gorkians, all Sulthoids look alike. When we see other people, one of the first things we do is identify them by type, group, or race: male or female, old or young, black or white. Many experiments have shown that, to African Americans, all white people look alike. To European Americans, all black people look alike. The same holds true for Asians, Native Americans, Pacific Islanders, and so on.

But—when you are within a group—black looking at black, white looking at white, Asian looking at Asian—that identity becomes meaningless, and you focus on other characteristics.

It's not race but proximity and experience that determines this. If you live among Gorkians, you will soon be able to see beyond their general Gorkian appearance and note their distinctive characteristics—even if you, yourself, are a Sulthoid.

Another factor that might have affected your description of the robber is the tendency to exaggerate differences from ourselves. Experiments show that, when we meet someone taller than ourselves, we tend to think he or she is even taller than is actually the case. When we meet someone shorter, thinner, fatter, and so on, the same principle applies.

When a young person meets an older person, he or she almost always thinks the person is older than he or she truly is. Similarly, to someone over age 90, a 20-year-old and a 30-year-old might look about the same age—and that age might very well look like 15!

Well, never mind. The holdup artist will doubtless try again. Sooner or later, he'll get caught. Most of them do, eventually.

Here are the remaining two problems with eyewitness identification:

5. **Contamination.** Remember our story in the preceding chapter about contamination of recollections? Fortunately, in your case, no one was there saying, "Now wait a minute, I could have sworn it was a woman. And she wasn't a Gorkian. I'm pretty sure she was a Floober. You know those Floobers! And..."

6. **Time.** Old memories become cluttered with intervening thoughts, experiences, and feelings. You think you remember the night of your senior prom in its every glowing, gorgeous detail. But we'll bet a nickel that you could poll 10 of your classmates and get 10 different versions of what that night was like!

By the way, the criminal at the convenience store was later identified by a DNA fingerprint. His genetic tags were a perfect match with the DNA in the blood on the broken glass in the doorway. So your testimony was not needed after all, and the bad guy was convicted.

The Case of the Flying Man

Captain Marvel was one of the greatest superheroes of the Golden Age of Comics. He was a worthy newsstand rival of Superman, Batman, Wonder Woman, Captain America, and the Human Torch. Millions of kids thrilled to his adventures every month and shouted his magic word along with him:

SHAZAM!

Shazam was an *acronym*, by the way. The letters stood for Solomon, Hercules, Atlas, Zeus, Achilles, and Mercury. They furnished Cap with their wisdom, strength, stamina, power, courage, and speed, respectively.

A great many of the adventure heroes of that era (mainly the 1940s and '50s) were featured in several media— movies, radio series, books, comics, and pulp magazines. If you were a kid back then, you might see your favorite character on the movie screen on a Saturday afternoon, then read about him in the funny pages on Sunday, and finally listen to his exploits on the radio until Mom called you for dinner.

And thereby hangs a tale.

Words to Remember

Acronym: A word formed from the initial letters of a name, or by combining initial letters or parts of a series of words, such as NASA (National Aeronautics and Space Administration) or DefCon (Defense Condition).

Golden Age radio shows brought adventure heroes into the homes of millions of children.

Richard:

When my buddy Michael and I aren't collaborating on nonfiction books (like this one), we both write novels. A couple of years ago, I was planning a murder mystery set in a radio station. One of my characters was a broadcaster whose avocation was collecting Golden Age radio shows. To get authentic details, I started researching the subject.

It turns out that many, many radio shows were adapted from other media (or were adapted from radio *to* other media). Some examples of characters who were featured both on the airwaves and in comic books are Superman, Batman and Robin, Captain Midnight, the Green Hornet, Buck Rogers, Flash Gordon, Tarzan, Little Orphan Annie, Doc Savage, and the Shadow.

Conspicuously missing from that list is Captain Marvel, a childhood favorite of my own. Cap appeared in comic books, in at least one pocket-size illustrated novel, and in a wonderful Saturday afternoon movie serial—but no radio show.

Or so I thought until I came across a reference to a Captain Marvel radio series in a book called *Radio & TV Premiums* by Jim Harmon, one of the world's leading authorities on popular culture. Harmon didn't give any cast or production credits or other details about the show, but even so—was I ever excited!

Refresh Your Memory

"In the early '40s, Captain Marvel was heard on the air; newspaper radio listings and the fading memories of a few people can attest to the fact. No recordings or scripts are known to have survived."

—Jim Harmon, 1997

Refresh Your Memory

"I grew up in San Francisco and remember listening to Captain Marvel on the radio, probably in the early 1940s ... The names of Billy Batson, the crippled newsboy (Captain Marvel's Robin??), and Mary Marvel come to mind, and the image that they could somehow fly a *la* Superman. I know Captain Marvel was a popular comic book character and may even have been syndicated for newspaper distribution at some point, but those radio memories persist. Maybe those folks who speculate about a West Coast–only version of this character are correct."

—Michael Berger, 1998

I wrote to Harmon and asked if he could furnish any specific information about the show or any documen-tation to prove it really existed. He wrote back stating that, alas, he had no personal memories of the program but that he'd had a friend who remembered it very clearly. Unfortu-nately, the friend was now deceased. Harmon said he would look for those old program sched-ules and would let me know what he turned up.

So far, no luck.

Another radio historian, Michael Berger, offered his own recollection. Berger had heard the show, he said, and this would seem to prove the point.

Or would it?

Okay, what's going on here? Are Jim Harmon and Michael Berger on to something? Is there really a "lost" Captain Marvel radio show still floating around up there in the ether? Certainly this isn't a hoax. But is it a mistake?

It's entirely possible that Harmon and Berger, inde-pendently of each other, have conflated a set of remembered audio images and have thereby created a false memory of a radio show that never existed! How could this be? Consider the following:

➤ They both were youngsters in the 1940s.

➤ They read about Captain Marvel in the comic books of the era and entertained vivid fantasies of the wonderful flying man in their childish imaginations.

➤ They might well have seen the Captain Marvel movie serial and, in the darkened movie theater, actually have seen and heard Billy Batson say the magic word that transformed him into the great hero.

➤ They almost certainly heard the adventures of both Superman (a flying hero) and Captain Midnight (an intrepid aviator) on the radio.

If you put together bits and pieces of the Captain Marvel comic book and movie serial and the Superman and Captain Midnight radio shows, you have a perfect example of conflation to create a false recollection of a radio show that never existed!

What about those newspaper listings? So far, they're unfound. But even if they ever turn up, might not some linotype operator half a century ago have let his mind wander from the typewritten copy that read *Captain Midnight* and inadvertently set the type that read *Captain Marvel*?

Will we ever know for certain? Who knows? Tune in tomorrow!

The Least You Need to Know

➤ Eyewitness testimony is dramatic and convincing, but forensic evidence such as DNA fingerprinting actually is far more reliable.

➤ Most criminal prosecutors act in good faith; deliberate frame-ups do occur, but they are relatively rare. Still, the end result of a good-faith error might be indistinguishable from that of deliberate prosecutorial misconduct.

➤ Among the major problems with eyewitness identification and other eyewitness testimony are lighting and ambient conditions; emotion, excitement, and distraction; weapon fixation; race and other stereotypes; contamination; and passage of time.

➤ The conflation of several actual memories, further distorted by imagination, can lead to the creation of highly convincing but nonetheless false memories.

Chapter 12

When You Wake Up You Will Remember...

In This Chapter

➤ False memories in adults and children

➤ Fooling the experts

➤ Hypnotism and false memories

➤ Little green men, shining blonde ladies, and other aliens

➤ "Recovered memories" of rape and incest

It should come as no great shock to learn that everyone forgets things. Some things like names and telephone numbers are difficult to remember in the first place. But does this work in reverse? Is it possible to remember something that really didn't happen? That's a frightening thought.

The last couple of chapters showed that memory can be distorted, conflated, rearranged, and changed in subtle ways so that eyewitness testimony isn't always reliable. A defendant in a criminal trial may be falsely identified by an eyewitness because of the witness's different ethnic background, the witness's memory being altered by group pressure, badly conducted police photo spreads or lineups, or merely the passage of time.

But can a person be induced to remember an event that never happened at all?

It's not easy to believe, and it's not at all self-evident, that totally false memories exist. After all, you know what you know, and you remember what you remember, don't you?

Well, it appears that sometimes you do and sometimes you don't.

Created Memories

Many things influence the creation of the traces and connections among the neurons of your brain that make up your long-term memory. One influence is events, of course, as recorded by your senses and gathered for analysis by your forebrain. If the event is deemed important enough because of its emotional content or because of repetition—replaying it in your mind, thinking it over, musing about it—it goes into long-term storage.

This is not the only way a memory can be created. There are ways that an event that didn't really happen at all can sneak—or be inserted—into your memory. You might recall it as vividly as a memory created by a real event and believe just as strongly that it is true. Let's look at a few examples of memory creation.

Michael:

> When I was very young, I met President Eisenhower. I can tell you where it was (a golf course in Florida) and what happened (the President showed me how to putt), but do I really remember it? Or only remember being told about it? I think it must be the latter because I remember nothing else whatever about the trip—I don't even remember where the golf course was.

Childhood's Golden Memories

Many people have detailed memories of childhood experiences. Although the events remembered may be true, the memories themselves are actually secondhand. We don't really remember going to the World's Fair or being at Woodstock when we were four years old. We remember being told about it. We were told about it so often and in such detail, however, that the story of the event shifted in our memory into the event itself.

Some Memorable Facts

"One of my first memories would date, if it were true, from my second year. I can still see, most clearly, the following scene, in which I believed until I was about 15. I was sitting in my pram, which my nurse was pushing in the Champs Elysées, when a man tried to kidnap me. I was held in by the strap fastened round me while my nurse bravely tried to stand between me and the thief. She received various scratches, and I can still vaguely see those on her face, then a crowd gathered, a policeman with a short cloak and a white baton came up, and the man took to his heels. I can still see the whole scene, and can even place it near the tube station. When I was about 15, my parents received a letter from my former nurse saying that she had been converted to the Salvation Army. She wanted to confess her past faults, and in particular to return the watch she had been given as a reward on this occasion. She had made up the whole story, faking the scratches. I therefore must have heard, as a child, the account of this story, which my parents believed, and projected it into the past in the form of a visual memory, but false. Many real memories are doubtless of the same order."

—Jean Piaget, *Play, Dreams, and Imitation in Childhood*

Even small events and places from your childhood can be subtly, or even grossly, changed in your memory over time: the park where you played, the first school you attended, the house or apartment you lived in until your were seven years old. When you go back to visit these places, you will probably find that they have changed considerably. Well, perhaps they *have* changed, or perhaps it's just your memory of them that has changed.

Just as interesting to students of memory, our memory of past events can shift subtly as our opinions change. Let's say, for example, that John W. suddenly discovers, at age 30, that his beloved father has had a drinking problem all his (John's) life, but it was kept secret from John. John now realizes that the reason the family moved around so much was because his father kept getting fired from jobs when he went off the wagon.

As John reinterprets his past in light of this new knowledge, his memory of the events in his life will subtly shift. He will remember times his father was away on a "business trip" and will think that, even back then, he could sense that there was something wrong. Long-past arguments between his mother and father will take on a new significance in his memory. He is, in a sense, rewriting the facts of his own history, and his memory will henceforth follow the new script.

Dr. Loftus Remembers

Dr. Elizabeth Loftus, a psychologist who is one of the leading experts on the phenomena of repressed and recovered memory, believes that most such memories are false. But even she, armored as she is in her knowledge of the possibility of falsifying memories, has come close to "recovering" a childhood memory that proved to be false.

Instant Recall

You might be saying to yourself, "Well, I wouldn't do that," but the odds are that you already have. Some scenes from your life have been subtly rewritten already. Embarrassing moments have been recast as less embarrassing, or perhaps they seem even more embarrassing than they really were. Moments of total indecision are now remembered as moments in which you cleverly picked just the right path. Honest. Trust us on this.

When Dr. Loftus was 14 years old, her mother died in a tragic accident. Thirty years later at a family gathering, an uncle told her that she had been the one who found her mother's body. Memories, unbidden, came to her of the horrors of finding the body. "I remember," she recorded in her book, *The Myth of Repressed Memory*, "the police cars, their lights flashing, and the stretcher with the clean, white blanket tucked in around the edges of the body."

But her uncle had remembered incorrectly, as was soon proven by other members of the family. Her Aunt Pearl had found the body, and Loftus had never seen her mother's body after the accident. When she was told that she had been present, her mind created the whole scene as she imagined it must have been.

If Dr. Loftus, who understands the whole process of memory creation far better than you or we, can be fooled into fabulating a false memory, then surely none of us are immune.

Memorable Facts

At Cornell University a few years ago, psychologist Stephen Ceci headed an experiment in which a group of children were asked whether they remembered five different things that had happened to them. For each child, four of the things—a trip or a birthday party, for example—actually had happened, but the fifth was made up. In each case, the made-up event was that the child had gotten a finger caught in a mousetrap and had to go to the hospital to be treated. The memory test was repeated once a week, and by the eleventh week, fully a third of the children "remembered" the mousetrap incident, often with a wealth of corroborative detail that their "memories" had supplied without prompting by the experimenters.

Get Off the Bus

In 1973, psychologists George Goethals and Richard Reckman performed a classic series of experiments at a Massachusetts high school. They began by giving students a preference test to determine the students' attitudes about busing to achieve school integration—a hot topic of the day.

Then they divided the students into two groups: the 42 percent in favor of busing in one group and the 53 percent against it in the other. (The remaining 5 percent were presumably wishy-washy on the subject and were eliminated.) Each group was then forcefully fed a variety of propaganda designed to make them reverse their opinion. The anti-busing group saw pro-busing material and vice versa, and each side was aided by a "plant," a student leader primed to espouse the appropriate view.

It is not surprising that, when subjected to this barrage of artful arguments, many of the students changed their minds on the subject of busing. What *is* surprising is that, when asked to fill out questionnaires restating their original opinions, most remembered themselves as being much closer to their new opinions than they actually had been. When shown the original test results, they were all astonished that they hadn't correctly remembered their opinions of only a few weeks before.

Sleep ... Sleep ... Sleep

One of the most insidious despoilers of memory is hypnotism. Hypnotic induction can produce memories that are so complete and so complex that it's difficult to believe the events remembered never happened, but in many cases they never did.

Some Memorable Facts

Hypnotism properly applied is a powerful tool that can be useful for many things. It has been successfully used as an anesthetic in operations ranging from dental surgery to childbirth. It also has proven useful for controlling chronic pain and even reducing bleeding during surgery. Posthypnotic techniques have been used to help people suffering from panic disorder and other psychological problems. Some people have even found that it helped them quit smoking.

By its very nature, hypnotism's usefulness in recovering memories is full of problems. Hypnotism is the ultimate example of the power of suggestion. Once hypnotized, a subject normally is eager to do what the hypnotist wants done and will seize upon clues that even the hypnotist is not aware he is sending, to discover what that might be.

145

Hypnotism doesn't really put the subject under the hypnotist's "control." That's the stuff of bad horror movies. The hypnotist cannot tell his subject to commit murder or jump off a building and expect to be obeyed. But hypnotism does relax inhibitions, and stage hypnotists have induced some pretty average people to do some pretty silly things—act like a chicken, take most of their clothes off, think and behave as though they were on a sinking ship—in front of an audience of strangers.

Someone going to a therapist for help with a serious personal problem—a deep depression or a failing marriage, for instance—is going to try very hard to trust the therapist and to believe what he or she says. If the therapist believes—as some apparently do—that hundreds of thousands of North Americans have been visited by interstellar aliens, then the therapist might seek evidence of alien visitation in his hypnotized patients. If the therapist believes—as some apparently do—that most women and many men were sexually molested or subjected to satanic ritual abuse as small children, the therapist might induce "evidence" of that.

Instant Recall

If a therapist believes in past lives, age regression of the patient may well take her (such patients are usually female) beyond the moment of her birth and into "remembering" being tried for witchcraft in seventeenth century Salem, being Nero's favorite slave girl, or being Cleopatra, complete with a vivid memory of the pain when the poisonous asp sank its fangs into her bosom.

It is the patient's unconscious eagerness to follow the therapist's suggestions, no matter how subtly presented, that has created whole industries—and several successful TV shows—around the idea that aliens in flying saucers are abducting, experimenting on, and impregnating humans by the hundreds. It is similar unconscious collusion between therapist and patient that has created a surfeit of books about past lives and, unfortunately, many unfounded criminal cases of "remembered" sexual molestation, satanic ritual abuse, or even murder.

Grayish-Colored Beings

In September 1961, Betty and Barney Hill were visited by interstellar beings. It was evening, and they were on their way from Canada back to their home in Vermont when they saw in the air ahead of them a circular disk "as wide in diameter as the distance between three telephone poles." They stopped the car, and Barney got out to take a look at the strange craft, which was hovering over a nearby field. When a door in the craft opened, Barney became frightened and ran back to the car, and the Hills drove home.

After they got home, they realized it was two hours later than it should have been. Two hours of their evening had mysteriously disappeared. This episode bothered them more and more until finally they sought counseling from a psychiatrist. Under hypnosis, they remembered a bizarre and much more complex series of events than they had been consciously aware of.

The story that emerged when they were hypnotized went like this:

Barney, who was driving the car, felt compelled to leave the main road and take a side road that led deep into the woods. Six odd-looking men stepped in front of the car, and Barney stopped. The men were small, grayish-colored, and hairless and had great big eyes set in large heads. Three of these beings came to take him out of the car, and three came to take Betty. Barney felt a compulsion to keep his eyes closed during most of what followed, and he did so with some relief. It was somehow less scary with his eyes closed. He did not attempt to speak with his abductors. Betty, however, kept her eyes open and conversed with her captors.

They were taken inside the ship, which was saucer-shaped, and were led to different rooms where each of them was examined. The aliens put Betty on an examining table and took her shoes off to look at her feet. They also examined the skin of her arm, behind her neck, and in her ear. At one point, they had her take off her dress and stuck a needle into her navel—the only part of the procedure that was actually painful.

She asked the alien boss, who was larger than the rest, where they were from. He pulled a star map from a drawer and showed it to her, but the pattern made no sense to her. After the Hills left the spacecraft, the memory of their visit was somehow erased until it was brought back under hypnotism.

After the publication of John Fuller's book, *Interrupted Journey*, which detailed the Hills' experience, many other people realized, suddenly or gradually, that they also had been abducted by aliens. Most of their stories paralleled the Hills', some with the addition of more graphically sexual details. Some people even believed that this had happened to them many times since they were children and that the aliens were somehow keeping tabs on them and taking them away regularly for examination.

Refresh Your Memory

"There is a tendency, sometimes called role expectancy, on the part of many hypnotic subjects to comply with what they perceive as the expectations of the hypnotist. This can occur even when the hypnotist has no conscious investment in the outcome, and is of course even more likely to occur when the hypnotist does have such an investment. This is more the rule than the exception in hypnosis."

—Michael B. Conant, Ph.D., Director of The Institute for Bioenergetics and Gestalt, Berkeley, California

Instant Recall

Excluded from this discussion are those people, if any, who really have contacted, spoken with, or otherwise interacted with interstellar beings. There may be some of these people out there, and if so, they may be among those we are categorizing as self-deluded. If so, we apologize.

Close Encounters of Two Distinct Kinds

People who claim to have had really close encounters with aliens come in two distinct categories: the truly phony and the self-deluded.

Among the truly phony we include George Adamski, who claimed to have talked with Venusian saucer men in the desert in 1952. They supposedly told him that the first Venusians to land on Earth arrived in the year 18,617,841 B.C. Another true phony is George King, a London cabbie who first spoke with the "Cosmic Masters" in 1954. They told him that he "was to become the voice of Interplanetary Parliament." Adamski wrote a book and King started a cult.

Words to Remember

Dirigible: An airship (balloon) capable of being controlled, directed, or steered. Most often, of a long, cylindrical shape, pointed at both ends, and powered by propellers.

The Self-Deluded

For all we've learned about the mind in the past half-century, in many ways it's still as great a mystery as any hidden in the outer reaches of the universe. Through the ages, a great number of people have believed that they've seen, heard, touched, or been touched by beings or objects that later generations have become convinced were hallucinatory. Science does not yet know why all or most of the people so afflicted at the same historic time had the same or impressively similar false memories of these events. But the afflictions were real, even if the remembered events were not.

In the 1300s, a great many people throughout Europe saw flying dragons. Many others saw and spoke to the devil, who gave them the answers to many theological questions and explained to them the difference between heaven and hell. Of course, he was the Prince of Lies and was not to be believed. In the seventeenth century, people in Europe and America saw witches flying about on their broomsticks. In the nineteenth century, many people in America saw men—and a few women—in *dirigibles* flying by. Some flew so low that they were able to converse with the passengers. This might not strike you as strange until we tell you that, although its general appearance had been predicted by the scientific press, the dirigible would not be invented for half a century.

Refresh Your Memory

There also are people who do their best to delude others, such as Marshall Herff Applewhite, a troubled man who founded a cult called Heaven's Gate. He committed suicide in March 1997 with 38 of his followers. They believed that a spaceship following the Hale-Bopp comet would come for their souls after they left their bodies, which Applewhite called their "earthly vehicles."

Secret Life

We can't prove that all cases of alien abduction discovered by hypnotic induction are false, but we can show logically that most of them almost certainly are.

An ever-increasing number of therapists of varying degrees of training and competence endeavor to use hypnotic regression to relieve their patients' (or "clients'" if they are not doctors) anxiety, sleeplessness, depression, and other symptoms. These therapists often have their own notions of what must be causing the symptoms. Each of these therapists usually finds his or her patients to have repressed memories of just the experience the therapist expected to find, whether it's being abducted by aliens or being sexually molested by a satanic cult as a small child.

Doesn't it strike you as being strange that the "alien abduction" therapists only get clients who have been abducted by aliens, and the "sexual molestation" therapists only get clients who have been sexually molested? There is even a small group of therapists who seem to get only clients who have been sexually molested by aliens. This is not a joke!

We should point out that we don't think most of the "abductees" are consciously creating a fraud. We think they honestly remember what they claim to remember. A memory created by hypnotic induction seems just as real as a memory of a real event. The wealth of supporting detail is supplied by the patient's own subconscious mind.

Remember This!

Not all practicing therapists are trained or licensed. Check the certification of any therapist you visit.

Refresh Your Memory

"He awoke to the taste of ammonia and cinnamon and his limbs pinioned upon a table. Around him he saw familiar, albino, bug-eyed faces. Again they were speaking cosmic gibberish at him. Again the hum of a moving craft. Again the blinking lights. Again the thing approaching with the—*oh God, not that again.*"

—Christopher Buckley, *Little Green Men*, 1999

We also don't think the therapists are perpetrating a deliberate fraud in most cases. If you believe something strongly and if everything you do—in this case, everyone you hypnotize—tends to confirm this belief, you have to be almost superhumanly dedicated to the pursuit of truth to question these confirmations of your beliefs.

Among the "alien abduction" therapists are John E. Mack, M.D., a Harvard professor of psychiatry whose best-selling book *Abduction* relates the case histories of 13 of his patients. These patients discovered they had been abducted by aliens after he hypnotized them and led them through regression to "remember" these experiences.

Some Memorable Facts

"When an abduction begins during the night, or, as is common, during the early hours of the morning, the experiencer may at first call what is happening a dream. But careful questioning will reveal that the experiencer had not fallen asleep at all, or that the experience began in a conscious state after awakening."

—John E. Mack, M.D., *Abduction*

Another "alien abduction" therapist is David M. Jacobs, Ph.D. His book *Secret Life* records more than 325 hypnosis sessions conducted with more than 60 abductees. Another is Bud Hopkins, the author of *Missing Time* and *Intruders: The Incredible Visitations at Copley Woods*. (*Intruders* was made into a two-part miniseries aired by CBS in 1992.) There are dozens of others.

But We Regress

Why, in the face of all this evidence, do we think we're dealing with false memories? Both the overwhelming similarities of the stories and the small differences lead to this conclusion, as do those parts of the stories that violate the laws of physics as we understand them. These parts more properly belong in a dream.

In an average story, the experiencer is removed from his (or her) bedroom or a moving car. Sometimes the experiencer claims to have passed through the wall and floated to the saucer. In the saucer, the experiencer may be undressed and examined by odd medical instruments, often piercing the body through the navel.

The experiencers who visit one therapist will see short, gray aliens with big eyes set in big faces. Another therapist's clients will mostly see aliens that look like reptiles wearing robes. One therapist's patients will experience sexual activities including insemination and pregnancy; another's patients will not.

This seems to us to be a strong indication that the ideas of the therapists have an overwhelming influence on the memories of their clients.

There also is the problem with the statistics. If the people who have abduction memories are a reasonable sample of the people who actually have been abducted but whose memories haven't yet been recovered by hypnosis, these alien abductions have been going on at the rate of at least 10 a day, and perhaps as many as 100 a day, for the past 30 years.

Now I Remember—My Daddy Raped Me

A much more frightening problem with hypnotically induced false memories are the "recovered" memories of women—and some men—that they were raped or sexually abused in their youth and that they've repressed the memory of it for 20 or 30 years. What makes this especially scary is that many children really are sexually abused, although most of them remember it without resorting to hypnotism.

The biases of the therapist sometimes effect the results of the therapy. One prominent hypnotherapist has stated her belief that all girl children were raped by their fathers, often with the help of the mother. With a mindset like this, is it any surprise that many of her clients "remember" that they were abused? The people who go to these therapists for help are often depressed or confused and are especially vulnerable to suggestions of an exterior cause for their depression or confusion, even if it means accusing a formerly loved parent of sexual abuse, completely without evidence other than the memory "recovered" (or induced!) with the aid of the therapist.

The psychological problems here are immense. A false accusation of incest can ruin a family and can even send an innocent parent to jail. Women with "recovered" memories of having been raped by their fathers, sometimes with satanic ritual abuse thrown in, believe these memories whether or not they are true. Sometimes even after the memory has been proven false—on occasion getting a parent who has been wrongly convicted released from prison—the child refuses to believe the evidence showing that the memory was false. The child might continue to believe—and remember—the story of abuse that was *confabulated* from the mind of the hypnotist.

Refresh Your Memory

"The first stage of hypnosis is one of suggestibility. It is supposed to be useful to have a person lose weight, or help them cut down on smoking, or something like that. But if you say to a person, 'You murdered someone!' in the first stage of hypnosis, they're going to spend the rest of their lives looking for the body."

—Betty Hill, in an interview with the *Fortean Times*

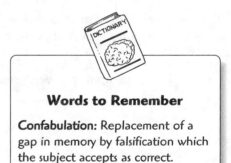

Words to Remember

Confabulation: Replacement of a gap in memory by falsification which the subject accepts as correct.

Ah Yes, I Remember It Well

False memories are possible, making the memory mechanism of the human mind fallible in both directions. It can forget events that it should remember, and it can create memories of events that never happened. Interestingly, however, there is some evidence that the mind knows, at some deep level, which is which. Tests have shown that, when remembering an event that actually happened, the memory centers of the brain show activity, as do the areas regulating the senses involved—sight, hearing, smell, and the like.

In false memories, however, the memory center is activated but the sense areas are not. Since the memory never went through the sense area when it was created, there is no neuron trace connecting it back to the senses.

Although the conscious mind does not know that your memory of being abducted by aliens and being forced to play cribbage at a dollar a point is a hypnotic hallucination, somewhere buried deep in your subconscious is the fact that you don't know how to play cribbage.

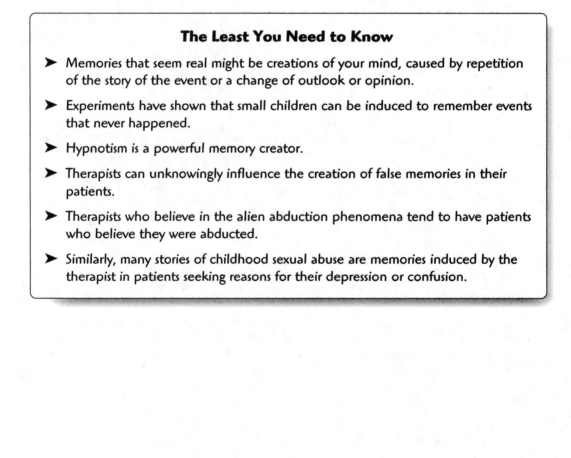

The Least You Need to Know

➤ Memories that seem real might be creations of your mind, caused by repetition of the story of the event or a change of outlook or opinion.

➤ Experiments have shown that small children can be induced to remember events that never happened.

➤ Hypnotism is a powerful memory creator.

➤ Therapists can unknowingly influence the creation of false memories in their patients.

➤ Therapists who believe in the alien abduction phenomena tend to have patients who believe they were abducted.

➤ Similarly, many stories of childhood sexual abuse are memories induced by the therapist in patients seeking reasons for their depression or confusion.

Very Special Memories

Being the clever and discerning reader that you are, you've no doubt noticed the way we mix things up in this book. We sometimes refer to memory in hardware terms. That is, we speak of the brain, the parts of the brain, neurons, and neural networks. At other times, we speak of memory as if it were software. We may speak of files, word searches, and association of ideas, all of which sound a lot like computer software hyperlinks.

The reason for this is that memory is both hardware and software. It's both your brain and the way you use your brain.

In this chapter, you'll learn about several people who had very special, very unusual memories. In some cases, the reason for this was clearly physical—it was due to unusual hardware. Other people we talk about started out no better at remembering things than you are, but they trained themselves to remember what they had to remember and ended up with exceptional memories.

A Bullet in the Brain

We already told you about the famous HM, whose hippocampus was surgically removed. Thereafter, HM was unable to form new "fact" or "event" memories, but he retained those he had formed before his surgery. Remarkably, he was still able to form new "skill" memories. Now you'll learn about a man whose brain was altered by a war wound and how he compensated for the loss.

Volya Zasetsky was a bright young engineering student when Nazi troops invaded his country in 1941. He had completed three years of engineering studies and was proficient in the Russian, German, and English languages. Zasetsky had to leave school and enter military service. By 1943, he had risen to the rank of a junior officer. There's no exact equivalent in our own army for Zasetsky's rank in the Soviet army; his title translates as sublieutenant.

On March 2, 1943, during the battle of Smolensk, Zasetsky was wounded. Bullet fragments lodged in his brain, destroying parts of the occipital lobe (toward the rear of the brain). Zasetsky lost consciousness when he was wounded and awakened in a Soviet army field hospital.

His first memory after awakening was of doctors leaning over him. He didn't know who he was, where he was, or what had happened. His survival was little short of miraculous, and his physical healing was rapid and very nearly complete.

But his mind was profoundly affected.

The right side of his vision was replaced by a gray blur; however, he had not been blinded in his right eye. Both eyes were undamaged. It was the receptors of the nerve messages from his eyes that were damaged and in a very peculiar way. He could see everything from the center-point of his vision to his left with both eyes, but he could only see the gray fog to the right of the center point.

He had lost much of his vocabulary. He lost not merely the words but his grasp of the concepts as well. He also lost his left-right orientation. He lost his knowledge of his body parts and what they were for. He lost much of his "fact memory" and even more of his "skill memory."

When he tried to read, he couldn't recognize the letters of the Cyrillic (Russian) alphabet. Working with his therapists, he managed to relearn each letter, but amnesia was only one of his problems. Major circuits in his brain had been destroyed by his wound (which he later came to refer to as either his injury or his illness). Other brain circuits were damaged or destroyed by scar tissue.

He had not, however, lost all his memories. He still remembered how to recite the Cyrillic alphabet. When a therapist pointed to a letter, let's say, "M," Zasetsky was unable to remember its name. But he could recite the alphabet, and when he came to "M," something in his mind would click into place and he would say, "That is M."

He was released and returned to his family home. When his mother gave him a hammer and nails and asked him to fix a broken door, he couldn't figure out how to do it. When he finally got the idea, he missed the nail and pounded his fingers because his vision was distorted.

When he tried to read, he found that he had lost the ability to transfer items in short-term memory to long-term memory. At first he could retain only one letter at a time. Eventually, he was able to remember as many as three letters at a time but not more. This intelligent, educated man had become effectively illiterate.

And yet, his basic intelligence remained intact, and his awareness and understanding of his plight were remarkable. He decided to write his memoirs. The first time he picked up a pencil, he didn't know which end to write with or how to use it. Once he mastered this "trick," he faced a new dilemma.

With his drastically shortened attention span and his defective short-term memory, he could only remember one word at a time. When he tried to write even this one word, he would have to "draw" each letter, laboriously, the way a small child does when first learning to write.

By the time Zasetsky had "drawn" the first letter of a word, he would have forgotten what word he'd intended to write—and the sentence it was part of!

What could he do?

At this point, Zasetsky had a wonderful idea. Perhaps his "skill" memory hadn't been completely destroyed. Prior to his injury, he hadn't had to draw each letter laboriously. His brain just issued a command to his hand to write a word, and the hand would do it.

If Zasetsky wanted to write "cow," instead of laboriously drawing a c, an o, and finally a w, he would try to relax, just tell his hand to write "cow," and let it do the work. And it did!

In time, he was able to write coherent sentences in this fashion, and he started to work on his memoirs. Over a period of nearly 30 years, he was able to write 3,000 pages. He worked from dawn until dusk, struggling to fill a single sheet of his notebook with words.

Instant Recall

You might want to try an experiment of this nature yourself, either with a pencil and paper, a typewriter, or a computer keyboard. Just think of what you want to write and start writing it. Try not to be conscious of the individual letters but of the words as a whole. If you can do it, it actually speeds up the writing process considerably.

He could not back up and review what he had previously written. He was never able to read effectively. But he continued his work, finally completing one of the most remarkable autobiographies ever written.

Some Memorable Facts

Zasetsky's work became invaluable source material for his chief therapist, Aleksandr Romanovich Luria (1902–1977), who was one of the world's greatest researchers in the field of memory. Extensive excerpts from Zasetsky's tragic, heroic, and ultimately triumphant memoirs are interpolated into Luria's book, *The Man with a Shattered World*.

It's not easy to say what lesson can be drawn from Zasetsky's experience, but perhaps it is this: Even following a profoundly disabling injury, human ingenuity and will can achieve an astonishing degree of recovery.

The Nearsighted Conductor

No, we're not talking about the fellow who collects your fare on the train. We're talking about a fellow who led orchestras in Italy and in the United States. Arturo Toscanini (1867–1957) was perhaps the world's most brilliant interpreter and conductor of great symphonies and operas. Almost half a century after Toscanini's death, and despite all the advances in recording technology, many of his records are still regarded as the definitive interpretations of important musical works.

Toscanini was so nearsighted, however, that he couldn't read a musical score while standing at a podium and leading an orchestra.

So what did he do?

Toscanini was able to read the scores of the symphonies he was conducting if he held them close to his face, and he found that he could memorize an entire score after a few readings. He could hear the music in his head and see what was supposed to be on the paper. The amazing part is that he memorized not only the conductor's score but every note of every musician's part. Think of that. An hour-long symphony, an orchestra of 60 to 100 musicians, and Toscanini was able to memorize every part.

On one occasion, or so the story goes, the program was fully rehearsed, the orchestra was in place, and the audience had filled a great auditorium. The concert was about to begin when a violinist rushed to the podium, panic-stricken.

"Maestro, Maestro, we have to delay the performance. I was tuning my instrument and a string broke. I'll need a few minutes to replace the string."

Toscanini, famous for his angry glare at such moments, stared at the violinist (who must have been little more than a blur to the maestro's weak eyes). "Which string broke?" he demanded.

"Uh—the D string, Maestro."

Toscanini paused for a moment, going over the score in his head. "Return to your place and don't worry about it," he commanded finally. "At no time in tonight's concert do you need to play any note on that string."

Haydn, Sousa, and Buddy Bolden

The Toscanini story may be true or it may be legend. The following story we know is true because we witnessed it ourselves. It concerns a person whose privacy we will protect by using only a set of initials (YX). We'll also change a few other details, but the story itself is true and the person is real.

From early childhood, YX seemed to be a slow and very limited learner. She (or he—we're not telling) had trouble with many of the things children learn at an early age, and her parents were deeply concerned about her development. But she loved music. She would listen to music tirelessly, would sing spontaneously, and seemed to have an instinct for playing almost any musical instrument placed before her.

As YX grew to adulthood, she remained small and physically undeveloped. She learned to speak and to read but lacked other skills. Even now that she's an adult, she must be assisted when dressing and undressing and must be taken to and from appointments.

But she is a brilliant musician. She's a member of a municipal band in her home city, and she leads a Dixieland group. She also is first-chair trumpet in a classical orchestra.

At a concert by this orchestra that we both attended, we saw YX sitting quietly with her mother until it was time for the performance to begin. Her mother led YX to her place in the orchestra and left her there.

The evening's concert was devoted to the works of Franz Joseph Haydn. YX not only performed her part flawlessly, she stood and played Haydn's trumpet concerto brilliantly.

Is YX deficient? Or gifted? Or both?

Her condition is sometimes known as *savantism*. At one time, such persons were called idiot savants, but this is an inaccurate term. They are not idiots (a nasty but medically meaningless term). They are just very unusual people with very unusual talents and limitations.

Words to Remember

Savant (sometimes **idiot savant**): A mentally defective person with a highly developed special talent, as an ability to play music, to solve complex mathematical problems at great speed, etc.

I Really Need This Job!

James Augustus Henry Murray (1837–1915) was the son of a poor Scots family. Although his parents gave him as good an education as they could afford, he was forced to drop out of school at the age of 14.

He continued to study independently, and he managed to scrape a meager living teaching other youngsters the things he managed to learn on his own.

By the age of 20, he had been married, widowed, and married a second time, and he was struggling to support his children (there would eventually be 11 in all). In 1856, he applied for a job with the British Museum. His letter of application remains one of the greatest exercises in modesty we've ever come across. You really need to read it for yourself.

Instant Recall

James Augustus Henry Murray was an eccentric individual. On one occasion, he designed a pair of water wings and decided to try them out himself. They worked too well. They flipped Murray upside down and floated very nicely while he very nearly drowned.

"I have to state that Philology, both comparative and special, has been my favorite pursuit during the whole of my life, and that I possess a general acquaintance with the languages & literature of the Aryan and Syro-Arabic classes—not indeed to say that I am familiar with all or nearly all of these, but that I possess that general lexical and structural knowledge which makes the intimate only a matter of a little application. With several I have a more intimate acquaintance as with the Romance tongues, Italian, French, Catalan, Spanish, Latin & in less degree Portuguese, Vaudois, Provencal, and various dialects. In the Teutonic branch, I am tolerably familiar with Dutch (having at my place of business correspondence to read in Dutch, German, French & occasionally other languages), Flemish, German, Danish. In Anglo-Saxon and Moeso-Gothic my studies have been much closer; I have prepared some works for publication upon these languages. I know a little of the Celtic, and am at present engaged with the Slavonic, having obtained a useful knowledge of the Russian. In the Persian, Achaemenian Cuneiform, & Sanskrit branches, I know for the purposes of Comparative Philology. I have sufficient knowledge of Hebrew and Syriac to read at sight the Old Testament and Peshito; to a less degree I know Aramaic Arabic, Coptic and Phoenician to the point where it was left by Genesius."

—James Augustus Henry Murray

Murray wasn't bragging and wasn't inventing credentials just to get a job. In time, he became not the first but the most influential editor of *The Oxford English Dictionary*, the most complete and authoritative dictionary of the English language and one of the world's greatest scholarly achievements.

How did he learn all those languages? No one knows. Surviving photographs of Murray show a tall, gangly person, but he was not so odd as to appear abnormal. He lived a full family life, received recognition and great honors for his work, and died at the age of 78.

Was there something about his brain, some extra circuits or special wiring that made him able to learn all those languages? It is clear that he was a man of great intelligence, and we also know that he was a dedicated and diligent worker. But there is no indication that he was a true genius. He did not contribute great original thoughts to the world. He was no Albert Einstein or Stephen Hawking.

But he *was* a man with a very special memory.

Get It Now, While the Getting's Good!

James Murray was unusual in his apparent ability to keep learning languages. For most of us, the "language window" opens at an early age and closes again a few years later.

Generally, if you haven't learned a language by the age of five, you will never learn to speak it like a native. You can study to your heart's content, like millions of high school students who struggle with Spanish, French, German, or other languages.

You can memorize the rules of grammar and study vocabulary lists until your eyes are weaker than Toscanini's. It is possible to get very good at a language. But if you didn't learn the language as a young child, you'll never quite get the accent, the rhythm, the lilt, and the intonation quite the way a person who has spoken that language from childhood gets it.

Refresh Your Memory

Harvard professor Howard Gardner has proposed that the intelligence measured in IQ tests—the ability to manipulate words and symbols—is only one of the many sorts of intelligence that should be considered when evaluating a person's intellectual capacity. So far he has come up with (at last count) eight different sorts of intelligence, which he lists as:

➤ Visual / Spatial Intelligence

➤ Musical Intelligence

➤ Verbal Intelligence

➤ Logical / Mathematical Intelligence

➤ Interpersonal Intelligence

➤ Intrapersonal Intelligence

➤ Bodily / Kinesthetic Intelligence

➤ Naturalistic Intelligence

So far this is merely Professor Gardner's theory, and whether his ideas will become generally accepted remains to be seen.

Refresh Your Memory

"Twenty-six letters! Boy, if the alphabet wasn't in alphabetical order, I don't know how I'd ever remember it!"

—Bob Thaves, cartoonist and creator of "Frank and Ernest," 1999

Words to Remember

Feral: Existing in a wild or untamed state; having returned to an untamed state from domestication; of or suggestive of a wild animal; savage.

No one knows why, but we do know our brains change throughout our lives. One study found that a newborn baby's brain develops new connections almost from birth. By age 2, you have as many connections as an adult. By age 14, you have far more connections than an adult.

Then the connections begin to fade away, and you are back to normal adult level by the time you reach age 20. So the old notion that "kids are know-it-alls" and the complaint that "my parents don't have the faintest clue" actually are closer to the mark than we might think.

One attempt to shed light on the language-window phenomenon is the study of so-called *feral* children. Folklore and fiction abound with babies lost, stolen, or abandoned by their parents and raised by wolves (Romulus and Remus in Roman legend, Mowgli in Kipling's *Jungle Book*), apes (Edgar Rice Burroughs' *Tarzan*), or other animals.

Such occurrences are extremely rare, but they do occur.

When feral children are found and returned to human society, they never learn to speak very well. It isn't a matter of accent, vocabulary, or grammar, either. There's something about the very concept of language that they don't quite get. They learn a few words and can express very simple ideas but never more than that.

Linguist and sometime social activist Noam Chomsky argues that language is a basic part of being human. To return to our earlier images of hard-wired and soft-wired intelligence, it would seem, based on Chomsky's ideas, that language skills are hard-wired. Something about the experience of being exposed to speech from our earliest days somehow activates the speech circuits in our brains.

If they aren't activated at an early age, they degrade. They'll never work very well, if at all.

Note that these circuits (if Chomsky is right) permit us to learn and use language. They do not contain coding for any specific language. Thus, a Chinese child is not "pre-coded" to learn and speak Chinese, nor is a Greek child "pre-coded" to learn and speak Greek. A resolution to this latter, absurd effect, was adopted by the school board of Oakland, California, a few years ago. It provoked a raging controversy and made the Oakland school board, for a time at least, the laughing stock of the nation.

Chomsky's ideas are not unchallenged. A person might argue that learning to use language is no more natural than learning to drive a car. Each is a skill, and each is acquired through a process of observation and practice. We don't have driving-a-car circuits hard-wired in our brains, Chomsky's critics argue, and we don't have language circuits. We just have a general mental capacity and we learn ... well, whatever we learn.

In any case, the mystery of the language window remains one of our more baffling puzzles. But it is clearly absurd to suggest that a knowledge of, or even a predisposition to learn, any particular language is genetically transmitted.

Now consider this question: Are there other learning windows? Is there a mathematics window? Is there a geography window? Is there a sports window?

Refresh Your Memory

I have no mother tongue, nor a father tongue either. My language has its roots in the Yiddish of my eldest brother, Mordechai, overlaid with the Babel–babble of an assortment of children's barracks in the Nazis' death camps in Poland.

It was a small vocabulary; it reduced itself to the bare essentials required to say and to understand whatever would ensure survival. At some point during this time, speech left me altogether and it was a long time before I found it again. So it was no great loss that I more or less forgot this gibberish which lost its usefulness with the end of the war.

But the languages I learned later on were never mine, at bottom. They were only imitations of other people's speech.

—Binjamin Wilkomirski, *Fragments*, 1996

Could a person fairly say that, if you don't learn to play baseball by the time you're eight years old, you'll never be very good at it?

No one knows for sure. Think about it. The language window seems to be a very real phenomenon. We don't know about the others.

Some Memorable Facts

Many great performers and creators start preparing for their careers very early in life. Whether a musical genius like Mozart or Bach (or Stevie Wonder!) or an athlete like Tiger Woods, they exhibit talent even as young children and flower as time passes. Perhaps this is another aspect of the "window" phenomenon, or perhaps it's just a question of getting an early start, being exposed to good influences, and having extra years to study and practice.

On the other hand, there are "late bloomers" like Einstein, who was a rather poor student as a child, or Grandma Moses who took up painting in her 90s and became world famous before her death.

We're not sure what all this means, but if in doubt, we'd rather go with the notion that it's never too late to learn!

"I Thought Everybody Could Do That"

Earlier in this chapter, we mentioned the great Russian psychologist Aleksandr Romanovich Luria and his work with the man who had bullet fragments in his brain. This poor man had forgotten most of what he'd ever learned. He waged a monumental struggle to regain even a part of what he'd lost and to live a life that even remotely resembled the normal.

Sublieutenant Zasetsky was one of Luria's two most famous cases. The other case was a man referred to in the literature only as "S." His real name was Shereshevsky. He was born in a Russian town and studied violin, hoping to become a professional musician. An ear infection suffered at an early age ruined Shereshevsky's perfect pitch (although he could hear well enough for ordinary purposes), and instead he became a journalist.

One day, as Shereshevsky sat in an editorial meeting, the editor fixed him with an angry stare. "Why aren't you taking notes?" he demanded. "Everybody else is taking notes. Get out your notebook."

"Why?" Shereshevsky responded. "I know everything you said."

"Oh, really?" the editor shot back. "What have I said?"

Shereshevsky recited back every word the editor had uttered during the entire meeting. Astonished, the editor asked how Shereshevsky could perform such a trick. "I don't know," Shereshevsky replied. "I thought everybody could do that."

Eventually, Shereshevsky abandoned journalism and took up a career on the stage performing amazing feats of memory. In later years, he encountered Aleksandr Romanovich Luria, the same Dr. Luria who later treated Sublieutenant Zasetsky. In Shereshevsky's case, however, the relationship was not that of therapist and patient but of researcher and subject because Shereshevsky was neither injured nor ill. On the contrary, he was, to put it melodramatically, the man with the super memory.

One of the first things Luria learned from Shereshevsky was that Shereshevsky had always had a remarkable memory. We've already mentioned that normal memories stretch back no farther than an uncertain realm between the ages of three and five. For some reason, even though everyone certainly has experiences from birth onward (and there is some evidence that we have at least some experiences even before birth), and even though we learn immense amounts in those earliest months and years, and even though we retain the skills and facts we learn, we all seem to have forgotten just about every actual experience of those early years.

Luria theorized that memory is associated with language. Before we learn language, we cannot manipulate the mental traces of experience. They are simply lost to us, are never recorded in the first place, or—and this is most intriguing—are stored but "lost" because our software/hardware "search engines" cannot locate them! (Luria worked and wrote in an era before such terminology was used, but the concepts were there.)

Shereshevsky told Luria that he had memories dating from his infancy. He remembered his crib, he remembered being rocked and handled by his parents, and he remembered his diaper being changed. All of these are common, practically universal experiences, and we don't remember them—but Shereshevsky did!

What does this mean?

Our guess—and it's only a guess, but at least it's an educated one—is that Shereshevsky's brain was wired a little differently than other people's brains. There does seem to be a genetic component in play. Shereshevsky told Luria that several members of his family, including both his parents, siblings, and

Refresh Your Memory

"The human brain has about 100 billion neurons. With an estimated average of 1,000 connections between each neuron and its neighbors, we have about 100 trillion connections, each capable of simultaneous calculation. That's rather massive parallel processing and one key to the strength of human thinking. A profound weakness, however, is the excruciatingly slow speed of neural circuitry—only 200 calculations per second. For problems that benefit from massive parallelism, such as neural-net–based pattern recognition, the human brain does a great job. For problems that require extensive sequential thinking, the human brain is only mediocre."

—Ray Kurzweil, *The Age of Spiritual Machines*, 1999

cousins, had unusually good memories—although not as outstanding as his own. Luria tried to measure the capacity of Shereshevsky's memory by giving him more and more things to remember, but he soon gave up. There seemed to be no limit to Shereshevsky's memory, so Luria switched to a series of experiments attempting to learn *how* Shereshevsky's astonishing memory worked.

One of Luria's experiments involved tables of essentially meaningless numbers. He asked Shereshevsky to look at the following table:

6	9	8	0
5	4	3	2
1	6	8	4
7	9	3	5
4	2	3	7
3	8	9	1
1	0	0	2
3	4	5	1
2	7	6	8
1	9	2	6
2	9	6	7
5	5	2	0
0	1		

Shereshevsky studied the numbers for three minutes and then told Luria that he had "impressed them on his mind." He was able to recite them back to Luria in any sequence Luria requested: top to bottom, across the rows, diagonally, bottom to top. He finally converted the table into a single, 50-digit number and recited it to Luria without missing a single digit.

Luria repeated the experiment with Shereshevsky using different tables of numbers, and Shereshevsky "impressed" and recalled each table to perfection. Several months later, he still was able to recall and recite each table. Luria asked Shereshevsky 10 years later and again 16 years later to recall and recite the numbers. On these later occasions, Luria reported, it took Shereshevsky a little longer to recall the tables—but he was still able to do it to perfection!

The Least You Need to Know

➤ We've said it before and we'll say it again: Memory functions can be seen in terms of hardware or software. In fact, your memory isn't either of these—it's both, inextricably linked.

➤ Medical ethics prevent us from performing experiments on people's brains, but doctors can study persons who suffer brain damage in accidents and war. The case of Sublieutenant Zasetsky, as brought to the world by Dr. Luria, proved both enlightening and inspiring.

➤ Some people have very special memories. Toscanini could memorize entire symphonic scores. YX cannot even dress herself unassisted, but she has become a successful and versatile musician. James Murray attended school only through age 14, but he became one of the world's great linguists.

➤ Speaking of linguists—there is a childhood window of opportunity for learning to use languages naturally and without accent. Why this is true and what other learning windows exist remain fertile areas for research.

Chapter 14

Let's Look at Your Memory

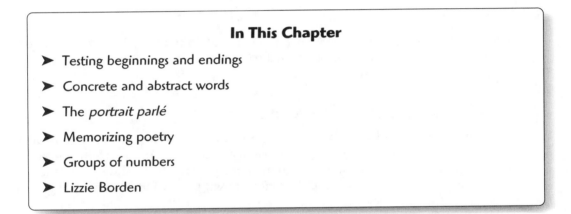

In This Chapter

➤ Testing beginnings and endings

➤ Concrete and abstract words

➤ The *portrait parlé*

➤ Memorizing poetry

➤ Groups of numbers

➤ Lizzie Borden

Before we get down to the nitty and the gritty of enhancing your memory, let's get an idea of what shape it's in. This chapter is devoted to some memory tests you can take by yourself or, preferably, with the help of a friend to determine how well you're processing your short-term and long-term memory right now.

We'll do this in two parts. The first set of questions, which we'll call Test A, is designed to demonstrate how memory goes about its job, not just in you but in everybody. Of course, as you've seen in earlier chapters, the process of storing memory in the brain is very complex. Different bits are scattered throughout the cerebrum and the other neural structures and are reassembled on demand by a process we don't yet fully understand. Here we'll treat the process of remembering as a whole and just be concerned with results.

Instant Recall

When you lace your fingers together, does your left or right thumb end up on top? People tend to do this the same way every time. See if you remember which way you do it, and then try it and see if you were right.

The test will touch on a few of the more easily demonstrable highlights of memory processing that affect you from day to day. We all process incoming information and store it for retrieval in just about the same way. These first questions will illustrate some of the memory crotchets that everybody shares.

The second set of questions, Test B, will take a look at how well your memory is doing with ordinary tasks such as memorizing phone numbers and your boss's wife's name. Keep in mind that there's a wide variance in what is considered normal. Difficulty in calling to mind, say, the names of movie stars or what type of wine goes well with a hamburger might be your personal quirk, while someone else might not do well with yesterday's lunch or relatives' birthdays.

Test A

Remember, there's no right or wrong or good or bad in this test. Everyone's memory is imperfect. Some work better at one thing; some work better at another. At the end, we'll discuss what the various items show.

1. Name That Thing—Beginnings

You can either do this by yourself, reading each item and saying the answer aloud, or you can have someone read it to you one item at a time and respond with the answer. If you draw an absolute blank on any item after trying for 20 seconds or so, take a deep breath and go on. Time yourself and see how long it takes you to complete this. Write the time in the space below.

Name an animal that BEGINS with the letter	C	_____
A fish	S	_____
A bird	E	_____
A vegetable	P	_____
A profession	D	_____
An article of clothing	T	_____
A country	I	_____
A city	N	_____
A state	P	_____
A planet	M	_____

Time: _____

2. Name That Thing—Endings

Again, you can either do this by yourself, reading each item and saying the answer aloud, or you can have someone read it to you one item at a time and respond with the answer. If you draw an absolute blank on any item after trying for 20 seconds or so, take a deep breath and go on. Time yourself and see how long it takes you to complete this. Write the time in the space provided.

Name an animal that ENDS with the letter	E	_____
A fish	A	_____
A bird	W	_____
A vegetable	H	_____
A profession	Y	_____
An article of clothing	T	_____
A country	D	_____
A city	O	_____
A state	S	_____
A planet	H	_____

Time: _____

Okay, what have we learned from these two exercises? It probably took you much longer to complete the list when you had to work from the last letter of the word than from the first letter. This is a demonstration of the way nouns—or at least the spellings of nouns—are stored in the brain. Other lists also are usually stored in a particular order, and knowing the order can aid in retrieving the wanted fact.

3. Words, Words, Words

Here's a list of 10 words. Spend three minutes doing your best to memorize them. Then close the book and write down as many as you can remember.

1. Stove
2. Library
3. Orange
4. Wristwatch
5. Peanut
6. Flower

Instant Recall

If you have trouble recalling someone's name, try going slowly through the letters of the alphabet in your mind: A—Anne, Alice, Astrid; B—Betty, Beatrice, Blondie; and so on. This often works to help you pull that stubborn name from your subconscious. The last name usually will pop up along with the first name.

7. Door

8. Television set

9. Bed

10. Bridge

How many? _____

4. And Yet More Words

Here are another 10 items. As in the preceding exercise, spend three minutes trying to memorize them. Then close the book and write down as many as you can remember.

1. Love

2. Happiness

3. Joy

4. Enthusiasm

5. Delight

6. Bliss

7. Zeal

8. Fervor

9. Cheer

10. Gladness

How many? _____

What have we here? Most of us have a far easier time remembering concrete words like stove, peanut, or television set than abstracts like joy, bliss, or gladness. To further stack the deck against you, we made the words in this exercise all similar, happy words. There was little contrast to aid your memory. We're betting you did a lot better in the preceding exercise than you did in this one.

5. We've Got a Little List

Read over the following list carefully two times. Then close the book and write down as many of the items as you can remember.

Dog, gown, deer, strawberry, horse, golf, pasture, tie, hill, bicycle, cow, potato, sled, apple, elevator, tennis, lake, archery, tomato, hat, chess, island, shoes, bus

How many? _____

6. The Same Sort of List Rearranged

Now we have some new items for you, and we've arranged them into six categories: animals, articles of clothing, geographical features, food, transportation, and games. See if this makes it any easier. Go over the following list twice, slowly and carefully. Then close the book and write down as many of the items as you can remember.

> Cat, sheep, pig, goat, dress, shirt, pants, socks, mountain, meadow, ocean, valley, orange, lemon, cabbage, peanut, car, trolley, boat, plane, baseball, basketball, volleyball, Ping-Pong

> How many? _____

You should have done better in this exercise than in the preceding one. The same types of items were in both lists—clothing, animals, and so on—but arranging them more logically makes them easier to remember.

7. What Do We Know About Those We Love?

Many police forces use a system called the *portrait parlé* (spoken picture) for describing suspects or other people they want to find if they don't have a picture. Following are some of the most basic questions from the *portrait parlé*.

Some Memorable Facts

A French criminalist named Alphonse Bertillon developed the *portrait parlé* for the Paris police over a century ago. He also developed a method of identifying people by careful measurement of their bodies—the exact distance from the left elbow to the tip of the left ring finger, for example. This didn't work very well, but the *portrait parlé* was a great success. It originally was very specific, asking for four classes of information: the color of the left eye, hair, beard, and skin; a detailed description of the right ear; body shape, dress, voice, and "social standing"; and scars, birthmarks, and tattoos. In a more general form, the *portrait parlé* has been used by most major police forces ever since.

Do you have a wife or a husband, a significant other, or perhaps a best friend you see almost every day? Pick the most significant person in your life and see if you can answer the following questions about him or her:

Color of hair? _____

    Hair long or short? _____

    Thick or thin? _____

    Bald or partly bald? Which part? _____

Color of eyes? _____

    Eyes close together or far apart? _____

Height? _____

Weight? _____

Describe his/her face:

    Long, round, oval, square, or flat-top? _____

    Chin small or large? _____

    Square _____ dimpled _____ double _____ flat _____ arched _____

Ears small or large? _____

    Close to head or projecting out? _____

    Pierced? If so, which ear and how many times? _____

Describe any beard, mustache, or other facial hair:

_____

_____

_____

Here are a few things not on the list that you might be surprised to discover that you don't know about a friend or loved one:

    Age? _____

    Birthday? _____

    Middle name? _____

If you're like most people, you didn't do as well on the *portrait parlé* as you thought you would. It's not merely a question of memory; it's also a question of observation. Most of us, as Sherlock Holmes would put it, *see* but do not *observe*. One of the best ways to aid your memory is to make it a practice to carefully observe what you see. Are there steps leading up to your house? How many and what are they made of? How many houses are there from your house to the corner on the left? On the right? You'll be amazed at how much you can remember once you get into the habit of loading your brain with the proper information.

8. Visual or Auditory

Some people do better when they see and study what they're trying to learn, and some do better when hearing it. Finding out which type of learning suits you best might help you learn or memorize something quickly for a big test or job interview.

Here are the first few verses of "The Walrus and the Carpenter" from Lewis Carroll's *Through the Looking Glass*. They should not be tough to memorize. The object of this is to determine whether you do better memorizing by eye or by ear. Read over the first two verses a couple times, close the book, and see how well you know them. Then go back to them for two more readings and see how you've progressed. Do this for as many readings as it takes.

When you've got them down to your satisfaction, have a friend read the next two verses aloud, slowly and clearly, two times. See how well you can recite them back. Then have your friend recite them two more times and so on until you know them well.

Compare the length of time and the number of repetitions it took you to remember the verses by reading them and by hearing them. If there's a significant difference, you have a better idea of how best to study for that big test or how to memorize that speech you have to give.

Use the technique that works better for you to memorize the fifth verse. See how fast it goes now that you've had some practice.

> The sun was shining on the sea,
> Shining with all his might:
> He did his very best to make
> The billows smooth and bright—
> And this was odd, because it was
> The middle of the night.
>
> The moon was shining sulkily,
> Because she thought the sun
> Had got no business to be there
> After the day was done—
> "It's very rude of him," she said,
> "To come and spoil the fun!"

The sea was wet as wet could be,
The sands were dry as dry.
You could not see a cloud, because
No cloud was in the sky:
No birds were flying overhead—
There were no birds to fly.

The Walrus and the Carpenter
Were walking close at hand:
They wept like anything to see
Such quantities of sand:
"If this were only cleared away,"
They said, "it *would* be grand!"

If seven maids with seven mops
Swept it for half a year,
Do you suppose, the Walrus said,
"That they could get it clear?"
"I doubt it," said the Carpenter,
And shed a bitter tear.

Test B

In this test, you'll see just how well your memory is doing and what areas might need a bit of shaping up.

Some Memorable Facts

"Everyone experiences lapses in memory. Whether these lapses are bothersome depends on how frequently these lapses happen, and whether they concern matters important or less important to the individual. As we age, memory lapses tend to occur more often. However, it is extremely important not to ascribe increasingly frequent and bothersome memory lapses to aging and ignore them. Because memory disturbances can be (but not always are) signs that something might be going wrong in the brain, it is best to have a neuropsychologist evaluate whether: a) there really are memory problems, b) if there are, how severe these problems are, and c) what might be causing these problems. In this way, one can get help early on if something is wrong, or feel reassured that one's memory is quite comparable to that of other persons of similar age. Remember that memory problems can be due to fatigue, depression, disinterest, medications, and so on. There is no need to torture yourself with fears of the worst!"

—Alex Troster, Ph.D., *Remembering Made Easier*

There's always the temptation to do as well as possible on a test by anticipating the question or by looking down the page for the answers. Because this test is designed for you to judge yourself, however, you will resist these temptations. Read the instructions carefully and do the best you can.

Explanations of these tests and what they mean will follow the last test.

1. Numbers, Numbers, Numbers

Have someone read these groups to you one group at a time, slowly and clearly. Recite each group back after you hear it. Have your helper keep a record of how well you do. When you reach the point where you just can't remember the whole group, stop there and see how far you got.

Five-Number Groups

16579

23173

67806

19867

86147

Six-Number Groups

692783

486027

951274

068357

719842

Seven-Number Groups

1462652

6309183

2944132

8595918

9782163

Eight-Number Groups

43259948

76905827

84402538

18212439

41079265

continues

continued

Nine-Number Groups

439579526

294582067

382375296

740951853

815979375

Ten-Number Groups

8473201936

5362307814

4085714967

2100357483

6026856714

Eleven-Number Groups

34263128347

87125182649

50958387328

14091278963

05475449276

Twelve-Number Groups

912507381647

897116814631

248542499173

463925770878

274530588546

Number of mistakes: _____

Highest group managed: _____

2. SrebmuN, SrebmuN, SrebmuN

This is pretty much the same as the first test. This time, when your helper reads the numbers aloud to you, you recite them back to him or her backward—in reverse order. In other words, if he or she reads 3456, you would recite 6543 back to him or her. As in the preceding exercise, when you reach the point where you can't reverse the numbers in your head, stop there and see how far you got.

Number of mistakes: _____

Highest group managed: _____

3. The Lady with the Axe

Read the following story once carefully. Then cover it with a piece of paper and answer the questions that follow.

Lizzie Borden

Lizzie Borden took an axe
And gave her mother forty whacks.
When she saw what she had done,
She gave her father forty-one.

Refresh Your Memory

Over the past century, Lizzie has been the subject of innumerable magazine articles and books as well as a couple of plays, an opera, a ballet, several movies and television shows, and a musical comedy sketch that included the memorable song, "You Can't Chop Your Poppa Up in Massachusetts."

One of the most famous women in American crime—and the subject of what is certainly the most famous stanza in American crime verse—Lizzie Borden was tried for the murder of her father and stepmother, a murder that occurred on Thursday, August 4, 1892, in Fall River, Massachusetts.

Lizzie lived with her father Andrew, her stepmother Abby, and her sister Emma in a two-story house in Fall River. On the morning of the murders, her father went out early, her stepmother and Bridget, the maid, commenced the day's housework, and Lizzie went to the barn to find some lead sinkers for fishing. Or so she claimed. Why she would go into a closed, hot barn on a sweltering August day has never been satisfactorily explained. Sister Emma was away visiting a friend.

Mr. Borden came home at around 10 and was never seen alive again. Shortly after 11, the bodies of Mr. and Mrs. Borden were found. She had been killed in an upstairs bedroom, and he was killed about an hour later in the downstairs sitting room. They both had been hacked to death presumably by an axe, although the weapon was never found. Lizzie was indicted and was tried for the murders. Against her was the fact that she disliked her stepmother, that she had had fights with her father, and that it was hard to see how any stranger could have snuck into the house to kill Mrs. Borden and then hidden for an hour until Mr. Borden came home.

In her favor was the fact that there was no blood on her clothes even though the killings must have been bloody deeds and that no one could believe that the church-going, Sunday-school teaching, proper young lady could have murdered both her parents. Indeed, nobody could believe it; Lizzie was acquitted of the murders. No one else was ever tried for the crimes or even seriously suspected.

Questions

Have you read the Lizzie Borden story carefully? Good! Now cover the story and answer these questions.

1. How many whacks did Lizzie give her mother in the rhyme? _____
2. Her father? _____
3. What city did the murders take place in? _____
4. What state? _____
5. What was the year? _____
6. The date? _____
7. The day of the week? _____
8. What was Lizzie doing in the barn? _____
9. What was Lizzie's sister's name? _____
10. What was the maid's name? _____
11. Lizzie was convicted _____ acquitted _____ for the killings.
12. What was the relationship of the woman killed to Lizzie? _____
13. Where was she killed? _____
14. Where was Lizzie's father killed? _____

4. What Does It Mean?

On a separate piece of paper, define the following words:

1. Modem
2. Iatrogenic
3. CD-ROM
4. Neuron
5. Euro
6. Megamerger
7. Medulla oblongata
8. Ginkgo biloba
9. Clone
10. Internet

Don't look at the definitions until you've tried to define the words yourself!

5. The Little List

Read this list of words or have someone read them to you, slowly and clearly. Go over the list twice if you like and try to remember them in order.

1. Merry-go-round
2. Bookstore
3. Shoe
4. Fire engine
5. Christmas
6. Apple tree
7. Swordfish
8. Bottle of beer
9. Space ship
10. Chocolate-chip cookie
11. Overcoat
12. The river Nile
13. Peanut butter
14. George Washington
15. Kitchen stove
16. Squirrel
17. The state of Nebraska
18. Barber's chair
19. The right eye
20. Wristwatch

Remember them all? Good! Now cover up the list. Have someone test you on the words. If no one is around, try writing down the answers to these questions:

What's number 6? _____

What's number 2? _____

What's number 14? _____

Now name them all in order.

Great! Now name them all in order backward.

Tomorrow over breakfast (or lunch if you don't eat breakfast), get a pencil and paper and write down as many of the words on the list as you can remember.

Pencils Down!

Okay, that's the test. Now let's talk about the answers and what your results may mean.

1. Numbers, Numbers, Numbers

Most people can remember and repeat between seven and nine numbers in a sequence. If you do better than nine, your brain is nimble; if you do worse than seven, your brain is getting sluggish. You should reread the nutrition chapter (Chapter 9, "Nutrition and Memory") and practice some of the mental exercises you'll find later in the book.

If you want to make the test more difficult for yourself, take the highest group you can comfortably do and try waiting five minutes before repeating the numbers aloud. You'll probably only be able to do this by constantly repeating the numbers to yourself until the five minutes are up.

2. SrebmuN, SrebmuN, SrebmuN

Adding an element of mental manipulation to the process makes it more difficult. In this exercise, you probably went down a notch or two in the number of consecutive numbers you could handle. In Chapter 17, "I've Got Your Number," we'll show you techniques for memorizing long strings of numbers, if that's something you're desperately eager to do.

3. The Lady with the Axe

Of the 14 questions, you should have gotten at least seven correct. If you didn't, reread the section and try again.

4. What Does It Mean?

In this exercise, we're testing your attention to the world around you. These are words that have come into use recently (or that you should have learned reading earlier chapters of this book). One common cause of poor memory is inattention. If the facts don't make it into your memory, there's no way you can ever get them out. If your definitions are not the same as ours but are basically right, that's fine. We're not strict here.

The definitions are:

1. **Modem:** Stands for *mo*dulator-*dem*odulator. A modem is the device that allows your computer to connect to other computers or to the Internet over the telephone lines.

2. **Iatrogenic:** An illness caused by or related to medical treatment. If you get an infection while in the hospital that is not related to the illness that brought you in, and if it's one that other patients in the hospital are getting, it is an iatrogenic illness.

3. **CD-ROM:** Compact Disk-Read Only Memory. A compact disc that contains a program or an information file for a computer.

4. **Neuron:** One of the cells in the brain that carries or stores information (see Chapter 5, "The Brain and Why You Have One").

5. **Euro:** The new currency being used jointly by most European countries.

6. **Megamerger:** A merger of two giant corporations involving billions of dollars and tens of thousands of jobs.

7. **Medulla oblongata:** Located between the main part of the brain and the spinal cord, the medulla controls basic functions like breathing and heart beat.

8. **Ginkgo biloba:** The Chinese herb now being tested as an aid to memory and other mental abilities (see Chapter 9).

9. **Clone:** An exact genetic duplicate of an organism created from that organism's own genetic material.

10. **Internet:** The network that has been created from various cable, optical, satellite, and standard telephone connections to allow computers worldwide to communicate and share information.

5. The Little List

If you didn't use a mnemonic system to memorize the words, you're doing well if you remembered 10 of the 20. One simple mnemonic you might have used is creating a story like this:

> I got off the *merry-go-round* to go to the *bookstore*, where I traded in my *shoe* for a pop-up book about *fire engines*. It was *Christmas*, and we put the lights on our *apple tree* so we wouldn't have to chop down an evergreen. My Christmas presents were a *swordfish* and a *bottle of beer*. I was disappointed because what I wanted was a *space ship* and a *chocolate-chip cookie* to keep in my *overcoat* while I floated down *the river Nile* spreading *peanut butter* (over the cookie). And that's no lie. Like *George Washington*, I can't tell a lie. I did use the *kitchen stove* to cook a *squirrel* that I caught in *the state of Nebraska*. I was sitting in a *barber's chair* keeping *my (the) right eye* on my *wristwatch* when the unfortunate squirrel ran by.

We'll teach you even better systems later in this book, but the story method, silly as it might sound, works very well. This is partly because it *is* silly. Silly images stick in the mind better.

We hope you did well on this test. We know you'll do even better after you finish this book and learn to apply the systems we teach you. Try the tests again at that time. You'll be pleasantly surprised at how much better your memory has become.

The Least You Need to Know

➤ It's a good idea to have someone help you with some of the test questions.

➤ Test A gives you an idea of the memory problems we all share.

➤ Test B shows how your own individual memory is working.

➤ After learning the techniques in the later chapters of this book, you'll do even better on the test questions.

Part 4
Try to Remember

Some people are gifted by nature with exceptionally good memories. Learning and retention just seem to come easy to them. But even the most ordinary people, with no special talent or outstanding intelligence, can learn to remember. There's a huge array of techniques for memorizing lists, numbers, and facts, for remembering names and faces, and even—this might be the toughest of all—for remembering where you left your keys. Number codes, chain links, key words, mnemonic devices—anyone can learn them. All it takes is concentration, commitment, and the will to do it. Entertain your friends and be the life of the party. Impress your boss and advance your career. Make your sweetie happy by remembering his or her birthday, favorite movie, and secret guilty pleasure. You can remember anything!

Chapter 15

Hear It, Say It, Write It, Remember It

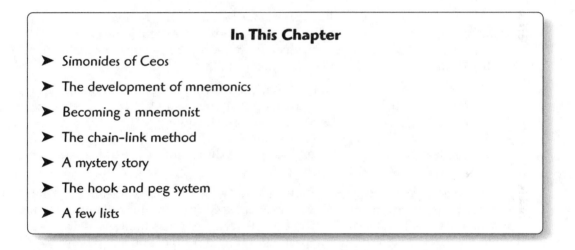

In This Chapter

➤ Simonides of Ceos

➤ The development of mnemonics

➤ Becoming a mnemonist

➤ The chain-link method

➤ A mystery story

➤ The hook and peg system

➤ A few lists

This chapter begins our discussion of actual memory systems you can use. It's clear that we are not the first people to have trouble remembering things. The idea of memory systems is over 2,500 years old. Systems were developed by the ancient Greeks as well as the Chinese and the Hindus.

The first time anyone is known to have given a thought to how memory works was in the sixth century B.C. The poet Simonides of Ceos was hired to compose a lyric poem and to recite it at a banquet in honor of a nobleman named Scopas. Simonides recited the poem, had an argument with Scopas over payment for his literary work, and then left the banquet hall. Shortly afterward, the roof of the hall collapsed, killing the diners

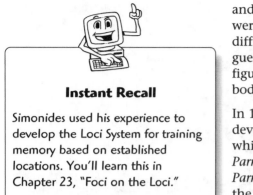

Instant Recall

Simonides used his experience to develop the Loci System for training memory based on established locations. You'll learn this in Chapter 23, "Foci on the Loci."

and burying them in the rubble. By the time the bodies were recovered, identification of the remains was difficult. Simonides was able to remember where all the guests had been sitting, which made it much easier to figure out who was where and to return the proper bodies to grieving relatives.

In 1648, the German Stanislaus Mink von Wenusheim developed a "most fertile secret" of memory recall, which he described in his book *Relatio Novissima ex Parnasso de Arte Meminiscentiae* (*New Material from Parnassus* [a magazine] *on the Art of Remembering*). This is the earliest of the mnemonic systems in which numbers are turned into letters that are then used to create words. His system was quickly taken up and improved upon. G. W. Leibniz, for example, devised "a secret how numbers, especially those of chronology, etc., can be conveyed to the memory so as never to be forgotten."

In 1730, Dr. Richard Grey published *Memorial Technical* (*The Technique of Memory*), which taught how to form words to represent numbers. A 1 could be either a or b, 2 could be d or e, and so on. Unfortunately, the words created by Grey's system were artificial and were themselves hard to remember.

The first truly practical system was the one proposed by Gregor von Feinaigle in 1812. In his system, numbers were represented only by consonant sounds. Vowels were used for fillers, making it much easier to create words. His system had 1 = T; 2 = N; 3 = M; 4 = R; 5 = L; 6 = D; 7 = C, K, G or Q; 8 = B, H, V or W; 9 = P or F, and 0 = S, X, or Z. In his system, the date 1776, for example, could be turned into the words TACK GUIDE or TAG GOOD. 1812 might be TUB TON.

The number alphabet most commonly used today, which you will learn in a later chapter, is an improvement on the von Feinaigle system, but it is only one of many mnemonic systems in use today. Some are better than others for a specific purpose. Then again, some are just more appealing to certain people. You will discover which ones fit you best and use them, and you will be rewarded with a fine memory that is up to whatever tasks you require of it.

All of this sounds great, but does it really work? We're here to tell you that it does, indeed, work. The mnemonic methods that you're going to learn are time-tested and proven. Uncounted people over the past several thousand years have contributed to their development. Literally millions of people have used them and have bettered their performance in school, in their professions, and in their personal lives.

Some Memorable Facts

The ancient Hindu system called **Katapayadi** was remarkably similar to the one devised by von Feinaigle. The Sanskrit alphabet is quite different from ours, but as closely as we can approximate it, the sound values for the different numbers in Katapayadi were as follows:

1: K, T, P, Y   6: Ch, T, Ph
2: Kh, Th, Ph, R   7: Chh, Th, S
3: G, Dz, B, L   8: J, D, H
4: Gh, Dzh, Bh, V   9: Jh, Dh, Lh
5: Ng, N, M, Sz   0: Ñ, N, Ksh

But don't take our word for it. This chapter describes several simple systems. You should try one of them out. For that matter, if you'd prefer, you can skip ahead to them right now. Take one out for a test drive. See how it handles. You're in for a pleasant surprise. Just don't forget to come back here after you're done with the experiment.

You don't have to memorize any part of the system at this point. The trial will work. It works best with the help of a friend, but you can do it yourself if no one else is handy. You'll see that the system works—as a matter of fact, you'll probably be surprised at how well it works!

Keep in mind that this is just one of many systems and techniques that we'll give you. You can even devise more of your own, now that you're learning the principles that these systems rely on.

All right, now this is important. To derive maximum benefit from the methods we're going to explain, you have to practice them. You remember how much we yammered at you about skill memory, fact memory, and event memory. You'll want to get these methods and techniques into your skill memory.

Up until now, this book has been devoted chiefly to background information, theories on the structure of the brain, and the way information is stored and retrieved. It's important for you to know all this. Learning that's based purely on "what," when it's not accompanied by "how" and "why," is, well, not worthless, but is of limited value.

Some Memorable Facts

"Non-literate societies depend heavily on oral tradition, enshrining important or significant information in some form of verse or song which is passed down from father to son. Such societies often have a specific person who is responsible for remembering such information. The Rwanda of Central Africa, for example, have four specialized remembrancers [people whose job it is to remember]. The task of the first (Abacurabwenge) is to remember the lists of kings and queen mothers; the second (Abateekerezi) is required to remember the most important events in the various reigns; the third (Abasizi) celebrates the deeds and qualities of the kings, and the fourth (Abiiru) must preserve the secrets of the dynasty."

—Alan Baddeley, *Your Memory: A User's Guide*

You'll find it useful and helpful to understand theories of the physiology and psychology, the hardware and the software, of memory. But now comes the "operating manual."

Just as practice without theory is limited in value, theory without practice is also of little, if any, use. So we urge you to practice the techniques offered to you.

One principle of learning that has been proven by laboratory experiments is that of spaced repetition. You understand now that impressing a sensory experience on your mind literally changes your brain by creating a new neural link. Repeating that experience reinforces the link. Re-creating that experience in different manners creates other links to the same element of stored information.

As early as 1944, Dr. Bruno Furst, one of the great pioneers of our field, reported on university research on learning through repetition. Furst reported a group of studies that showed that a given bit of information could be learned by 68 consecutive repetitions.

Sounds pretty dull, but it's effective.

Suppose, however, the repetitions were not consecutive. Suppose the student volunteers took a break after a while. Suppose they took a walk, took a nap, stopped to chat with friends, or stopped to have a snack or a sip of liquid refreshment before resuming their study.

In these cases, the average number of repetitions needed to learn the item in question (and what that item was doesn't really matter right now) was just 38.

Remember This!

The old saying that "You can catch more bees with honey than with vinegar" applies to most aspects of life. It certainly applies to learning.

Think of that. Just 38 repetitions instead of 68. An increase in efficiency of more than 33 percent!

Another point, and this is very important.

Hey, you in the corner, shape up or ship out!

Whoops. Just kidding, folks.

The exercises we're about to suggest (and this whole book, for that matter) should be fun for you. The experience should not be a source of stress. We most emphatically do not subscribe to the "no pain/no gain" philosophy of pedagogy. On the contrary, we are firmly convinced that learning and self-improvement can and should be pleasant and not painful.

The Chain-Link Method

Suppose you want to remember a list of items without writing them down and carrying the scrap of paper with you. If you're going to the grocery store and simply need to remember milk, broccoli, oranges, and cottage cheese, but you're in a hurry and don't want to stop and write out the list, you can just remember those items. You can, can't you?

Hey, if you're like either of us, you'll get to the store, remember three of the four items, and stand there scratching your head.

If you want to remember a longer list, it becomes more and more difficult. Sometimes you just don't want to bother with a sheet of paper; sometimes you're not allowed to bring a sheet of paper with you (during an academic exam, for example).

There's a method for retaining such a list, and it's known by several names including the chain-link method or the connected picture method. Our late friend T.A. Waters was an expert at this, and in earlier years, the great Shereshevsky (you remember him, of course) used an "imaging" method that rather resembled this.

Here's how it works. Using any list of objects, visualize the first two and forge a link between them using a visual image or event. To remember milk and broccoli, for example, you might visualize a bathtub full of milk. Suddenly, a huge head of broccoli crashes through the roof and falls into the milk with a terrific splash. Sounds silly, doesn't it? But you'll find that it works. You've created a link from milk to broccoli. What's next on your shopping list?

Oh yeah, it was oranges. Okay. As you stand contemplating the odd sight of a giant head of broccoli floating in a bathtub full of milk, the door opens and four giant oranges come marching into the room, singing lustily at the top of their lungs (yes, these amazing oranges have lungs). The oranges halt, staring aghast at the broccoli floating in the milk and—what's the next item on the list? Oh yeah: cottage cheese— these oranges reach into their backpacks, pull out containers of cottage cheese, and start pelting the poor battered broccoli with them.

Run that story through your mind a few times and you'll remember your shopping list!

The Game of Tell-a-Story

There's a wonderful old parlor game that we just made up called the tell-a-story game. Note that it's a cooperative game and not a competitive one. Everybody works together on this. The players shouldn't try to outdo one another. You can play the game with a theme or a specific type of story such as a medieval adventure, a western, a swash-buckling romance, or a horror tale. Or you can make it completely open-ended and random.

To play the game, each participant writes a word or a short phrase on a slip of paper and places it in a hat or a bowl. Each player in turn draws one of the scraps of paper and uses the word or phrase to continue the story, forging a link with the previous player's image.

Our Game

Because both of us are mystery writers (in our other lives), we decided to create a sample game using many of the standard props of murder mysteries. To make it tougher on ourselves, we wrote our clue words on separate scraps of paper, threw them into the air (literally), and wrote them down again in a random sequence. Hmm, perhaps we could have made a better story if we'd put them in a more logical sequence, but that would have been cheating. We wound up with the following list. There are only a dozen items on it, but when you get good at this, you'll be able to forge a chain of remarkable length. For really dedicated players, there's hardly any upper limit.

1. Voluptuous redhead
2. Secret message
3. Piercing scream
4. Handcuffs
5. Professor Stoopnagle
6. Sliding panel
7. Diamond mine
8. Shattering glass
9. Wisp of smoke
10. Country house
11. Gun
12. Blood

The Case with a Dozen Clues

Links 1 and 2: The woman was a *voluptuous redhead*. Throughout her life, she had drawn the attention, admiration, and envy of everyone who knew her. She was famous for her beauty, her curvaceous figure, and her spectacular, flaming tresses. And yet, for some reason unknown to her, someone had sent her a *secret message*. She stood with the paper in her hand and stared at it, trying to make out its meaning.

Links 2 and 3: The letters of the *secret message* seemed almost to writhe and twist with a life of their own. Their meaning seemed tantalizingly clear, so close, so very, very close. Just as they were about to reveal that meaning, there was a *piercing scream*. It smote the redhead's eardrums like razor-sharp knives. Never before in her life had she heard such a sound as the piercing scream.

Links 3 and 4: Even before the *piercing scream* could fade away, the redhead felt something cold and metallic on both her wrists. She looked down and found that, more rapidly than she could even react, someone had clasped a pair of icy, unyielding *handcuffs* on her wrists.

Links 4 and 5: Her eyes popped as she beheld the person who had clapped the pair of *handcuffs* on her. It was a sinister, all-too-familiar, and frightening face. It was the dreadful face of *Professor Stoopnagle.*

Links 5 and 6: Where had the evil *Professor Stoopnagle* come from? She looked around and, behind him, saw a previously unknown and cleverly concealed *sliding panel.*

Links 6 and 7: A *sliding panel*? What could lie behind it? Perhaps, the redhead thought, it was the legendary lost *diamond mine* she had been searching for since her childhood! As she concentrated on penetrating the darkness, she realized that she was, in fact, peering into the depths of a lost diamond mine.

Links 7 and 8: Even as she stared into the *diamond mine,* her attention again was drawn away by the frightening, unmistakable sound of *shattering glass.*

Links 8 and 9: *Shattering glass*? She whirled and saw shards of glass lying on the floor. Through the broken window drifted a *wisp of smoke.*

Links 9 and 10: The redhead wondered, "What is a *wisp of smoke* doing here in this secluded, mysterious, *country house*?"

Links 10 and 11: Then she saw what had shattered the peace in the *country house.* Through the broken window someone—some mysterious intruder—had thrown a *gun.*

Links 11 and 12: Acting more rapidly than her captor could imagine, the redhead dived onto the carpet and grabbed the *gun.* As Professor Stoopnagle lunged at her, she pulled the trigger. The evil Professor collapsed in a pool of his own *blood.*

We'll stop here. After all, we're out of words.

Let's do a quick review. The *voluptuous redhead* is looking at a *secret message* when she hears a *piercing scream*. Before she can react to it, a pair of *handcuffs* are clapped on her wrists by the evil *Professor Stoopnagle,* who appeared from a *sliding panel* behind which is a *diamond mine* (and why not?). The redhead hears *shattering glass* and sees a *wisp of smoke* in the *country house*. It is coming from the muzzle of a *gun,* which she uses to shoot the evil Professor Stoopnagle, who falls in a pool of his own *blood*.

There!

Well, all right, "The Case with a Dozen Clues" won't win any Pulitzer Prizes, but it links each of the dozen items on our list into a story. For many people, the tell-a-story or chain-link method can be enhanced by visualizing the linked events as if they were a miniature movie. If you were playing this game and you kept your mind on the developing story, visualizing each link vividly, you would be able to recite the dozen clues after the first or, at worst, the second recitation.

Not 68 repetitions, not even 38—but the very first (or second) time.

The Hook and Peg Systems

The hook and peg systems are the ones in which you have a previously memorized set of pegs on which you can hook the words or phrases you need to remember. These systems are great for lists, especially when you might have to recall item seven (for example) out of order. With the chain-link method, you would have to mentally go through "voluptuous redhead-secret message-piercing scream-handcuffs-Professor Stoopnagle-sliding panel-diamond mine" before you could announce that item number seven was the diamond mine.

Instant Recall

The rhyming system was developed around 1879 by an Englishman named John Sambrook. One version of it looks like this:

one: gun	six: sticks
two: shoe	seven: heaven
three: tree	eight: gate
four: door	nine: wine
five: hive	ten: hen

and so on.

Do It with Rhymes

In one of the simplest hook and peg variants each number is pegged to a word that rhymes with it. Here's an example: Number one is a gun, number two is a shoe, number three is a tree, number four is a door, number five is a hive, number six is a pile of sticks, and so on.

Suppose your spouse calls you at work and says, "Don't forget, dear, to bring home a lamp, a toothbrush, a horse, a mirror, and a kangaroo." You have nothing handy to write the list down on.

You can hook each item onto its place in the list with a strong image. A silly image or one that provokes an emotional response works best. For this example, we'll stick to silly.

Number one, a gun, is to be hooked with a lamp: GUN = LAMP

What sort of strong, silly image can we think of in a couple of moments that will make the hook? We don't want to spend too much time on each item.

A sharpshooter takes his GUN and shoots the LAMP out of his assistant's mouth.

Number two, a shoe, is to be hooked with a toothbrush: SHOE = TOOTHBRUSH

My son just polished his SHOE with my TOOTHBRUSH—no wonder the toothpaste tastes funny!

Number three, a tree, is to be hooked to a horse: TREE = HORSE

Look at the top of that TREE—isn't that a HORSE dangling from the top branch?

Number four, a door, is to be hooked to a mirror: DOOR = MIRROR

I open the DOOR, and all I see is myself—a giant MIRROR fills the doorway!

Number five, a hive, is to be hooked to a kangaroo: HIVE = KANGAROO

The bees are buzzing out of the HIVE because a giant KANGAROO has just hopped, hopped, hopped, and batted the hive with his kangaroo head as he passed.

Try this with your own list. You'll be surprised how quickly and easily you can remember the items. Stick to nouns when you start; they're easier to make funny images with.

Finally, a Use for the Alphabet

One nice way to create a peg list is to take a subject you're familiar with—say a hobby or something associated with your job—and create an alphabetical list of items associated with that subject. This will give you, if you use the whole alphabet, numbers from one to 26. Here are a couple of sample lists for which we'll provide the first 10 items:

➤ If you're a car fan, this list of past and present automobile marques might stick in your mind:

1: Austin, 2: Buick, 3: Cadillac, 4: DeSoto, 5: Essex, 6: Franklin, 7: Graham-Paige, 8: Hudson (or Hispano-Suiza if that suits you better), 9: Isotta, 10: Jeep

➤ Zoologists can try this list:

1: Anteater, 2: Bull, 3: Cow, 4: Dog, 5: Elephant, 6: Fox, 7: Gorilla, 8: Horse, 9: Ibex, 10: Jackrabbit

➤ For all the chefs out there:

1: Artichoke, 2: Beet, 3: Carrot, 4: Date, 5: Eggplant, 6: Fig, 7: Grapes, 8: Honey, 9: Ice cream, 10: Jam

➤ If geography is your passion, here's a list of American cities and towns:

1: Atlanta, 2: Boston, 3: Chicago, 4: Denver, 5: Elkhart, 6: Freeport, 7: Groton, 8: Houston, 9: Indianapolis, 10: Jacksonville

You get the idea. In Chapter 18, "He's Making a List," and later chapters, we'll show you how having multiple lists like this can be of great use.

In these lists, you should replace any items you are unfamiliar with—or just don't like—with something that suits you better. That holds for all future systems we show you. The more you can adapt these to yourself and your own needs, the better they will work.

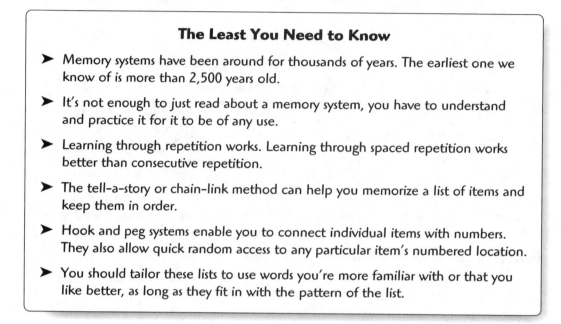

The Least You Need to Know

➤ Memory systems have been around for thousands of years. The earliest one we know of is more than 2,500 years old.

➤ It's not enough to just read about a memory system, you have to understand and practice it for it to be of any use.

➤ Learning through repetition works. Learning through spaced repetition works better than consecutive repetition.

➤ The tell-a-story or chain-link method can help you memorize a list of items and keep them in order.

➤ Hook and peg systems enable you to connect individual items with numbers. They also allow quick random access to any particular item's numbered location.

➤ You should tailor these lists to use words you're more familiar with or that you like better, as long as they fit in with the pattern of the list.

Chapter 16

A Face in the Crowd

> ### In This Chapter
>
> ➤ Name, rank, and serial number
>
> ➤ Tell 'em, tell 'em again, and tell 'em still again
>
> ➤ Mr. Fish, Ms. Carr, Dr. Sharpe, and Rev. St. John
>
> ➤ As plain as the nose on your face, Mr. Schnozzola
>
> ➤ Even if it doesn't work, it works!

If you stay up late enough surfing the movie channels, you're sure to run across this scene. A heroic American flyer (you can tell by the bomber jacket and the military cap with 50-mission crush) sits in a hard wooden chair, a spotlight blazing on his face.

Opposite him, a man wearing a World War II German or Japanese officer's uniform sits smoking a cigarette. Every so often, he demands of the American, "What is your unit? What was your mission? You might as well tell us now; we have ways to make you talk!"

And the American, with sweat running down his handsome face, gathers his strength and responds, "Jones, Walter W., Captain, 04063066."

"We already know that, Captain Jones," the interrogator purrs. "Now you must tell us more. Wouldn't you like a drink of water? Wouldn't you like a cigarette?"

Captain Jones grits his teeth and says, "Jones, Walter W., Captain, 04063066. Name, rank, and serial number. That's all I have to tell you."

The interrogation goes on for a while. It really gets nasty, in fact, before the cruel interrogator's boss shows up. The boss says, "Back to the compound with this one. He won't crack. The next one will have to talk."

Right.

That name, rank, and serial number routine was drilled into millions of American servicemen (and women) over the years. It's part of an international agreement called the Geneva Convention, and it's still in effect.

In the military everyone is expected to learn the "chain of command," from the President of the United States down to his or her immediate commander. Every military post has a rogues' gallery (they don't call it that!) with photos of every person in that chain of command. And woe to the soldier who fails to recognize and salute the commanding officer—even if that officer is wearing civilian garb.

In the business world the same principle applies. And in social relationships connecting names and faces can be highly useful, too.

Say, Haven't We Met Before?

One of the biggest memory problems people have is recognizing individuals they've met only once or a few times and connecting the name with the face. At a cocktail party, this can be a minor embarrassment, although getting a person's name right has led to more than one happy relationship.

Refresh Your Memory

"I never forget a face—but in your case I'll make an exception!"

—Groucho Marx

In the business world, it's beneficial to your career to get to know people, to know things about them, and to let them know that you see them as individuals and that you care about them. If you're a traveling sales representative and you can call the buyer at every account by his or her first name, you're already on your way to success. If you can ask a question like, "How did your daughter make out in the statewide finals?" or say with concern in your voice, "I hope your husband's surgery came out well and he's back on his feet," the buyer feels you know her and care about her as a human being and not as just a business contact. Your success will increase accordingly, and your association will be all the more pleasant and rewarding for both parties.

Aside from these crass commercial considerations, it should feel good to remember the names of people you meet. It eliminates that moment of panic as the person walks toward you and you wonder how you're going to address her or introduce her to your husband (now what was her name?).

Richard:

> When I was in the computer business, I was part of a task force engaged in an important project. The company's chief engineer was scheduled to come to an early morning meeting and brief me and my colleagues. When he arrived, there was silence. This was a man who could make or break a career with a word. Then one person spoke up. "Dr. Blitzen," he said, "have you lost weight?"
>
> Dr. Blitzen turned to me and said, "Richard, I've been dieting for weeks. It's the hardest thing I've ever done, and you are the first person who's noticed. Thank you!"
>
> Yes, it was I who had spoken. Dr. Blitzen knew that I knew he wasn't just an engineer. He was a human being. And to my astonishment, he knew my name! It was a lesson I've always remembered.

What's in a Name?

Everyone wants to remember other people's names, and there are any number of "systems" to help you accomplish this. For decades, Harry Lorayne has been one of the world's most famous memory experts. He isn't a university-trained psychologist, and he'd be the first to tell you that. He isn't a researcher or a theorist. We're sure he has a good natural memory, but he's no Shereshevsky. He has just spent a lifetime applying himself to ways of using his memory to the greatest possible effect.

One of his favorite demonstrations is to address a luncheon or a dinner meeting of hundreds of people. He tries to arrive early to meet and chat with every person in the room. When his turn comes to speak to the crowd, he's able to single out every person there and call him or her by name.

Lorayne has always denied that there's any magic or trickery involved in his appearances. He has never claimed to have an exceptional memory. He simply developed methods that he used in his lectures and books.

Instant Recall

Among Lorayne's favorite stories is the occasion on which he appeared before a group including more than 30 Smiths. Rather than just calling each of them Mr. or Ms. Smith, Lorayne addressed every one of them by his or her first and last name.

Keep in mind that Lorayne wasn't the first such memory maven. In fact, most of his techniques were already in common use when he came onto the scene. Some of them are even hundreds or thousands of years old. We're not going to hitchhike on Lorayne's methods, although we certainly tip our hats to him. We're simply going to teach you some of the methods that memory mavens have been polishing since the days of classical Greece!

The Lesson in Triplicate

Tell 'em what you're gonna tell 'em, tell 'em, tell 'em what you told 'em!

An old teaching theory is summed up in these 15 words. According to this theory, the instructor starts each class session by telling the students what they'll learn in today's lesson. He "tells 'em what he's gonna tell 'em." This primes the students as to what salient points to look for in the day's class.

Then the instructor "tells 'em." He presents the day's lesson in full detail, emphasizing the major points and supporting them with as much detail and background information as appropriate.

Finally, the instructor "tells 'em what he told 'em." By reviewing the major points of the day's lesson, he reinforces what the students need to take away from the class.

This is a method of teaching used in the best institutions of higher learning. It's also one used by the military, where getting the lesson right can lead to victory and life and getting it wrong can lead to defeat and death.

You may even have noticed that it's the method used in this book. Every chapter begins with a sketch of important points and ends with a review of the vital information the reader has just been given.

It might surprise you—or then again, maybe not—that the same three-step process can be hugely useful in learning people's names and faces. This isn't the only technique we're going to give you, but it's a fine place to start.

Words to Remember

"Unfortunately, I never had the opportunity to receive a formal education. I didn't complete the first year of high school. My grades, during that short time, were among the highest in my class. Why was this so? My IQ was average, and my "Natural" memory was no better or worse than most people's. As a matter of fact, I originally was one of those many people who think they have the worst memory in the world.

I received good grades for one reason—I applied memory systems to my schoolwork. It's as simple as that."

—Harry Lorayne, *The Memory Book* (Lorayne & Lucas)

Repeating the Name

"Bon Soir, Madame Schumann-Heink. Enchanté, Madame Schumann-Heink. Au Revoir, Madame Schumann-Heink."

The first time you're introduced to someone, whether it's at a job interview, a business meeting, or a cocktail party, the first thing you're likely to hear is the person's name. You'll want to impress that name on your mind, and a good way to start is to repeat it.

"A pleasure to meet you, Madame Schumann-Heink."

There, that wasn't difficult. You've already begun to impress that name on your memory. At the same time, you've impressed Madame Schumann-Heink with the fact that you care enough about her to get her name right. You might even go out of your way to ask her the spelling of her name. (Schumann-Heink isn't exactly a name you come across every day.) She won't be offended. Would you be offended if someone asked you how your name was spelled?

You might want to ask her about her name. It is indeed an unusual and noteworthy name. Is she related to the famous composer, Robert Schumann? Perhaps descended from the famous soprano, Ernestine Schumann-Heink? She is? How wonderful! And she has the same first name, has she?

Ernestine Schumann-Heink, indeed.

By the time you've chatted with Madame Schumann-Heink for 10 minutes, perhaps sipping cocktails and nibbling hors d'oeuvres, you'll find yourself being dragged away by your hostess to shake hands with someone else who's just been dying to meet you all evening.

You don't want to just walk away from your new friend, however. You agree to call her next week, you shake her hand once again, and you tell her, "It has been a great pleasure to meet you, Madame Schumann-Heink."

Take it from us, you'll never forget Madame Schumann-Heink's name. When you phone her next week, she will surely remember you with the greatest of pleasure.

Instant Recall

Paying attention is the first step in remembering anything. When you are introduced to someone, make a point of paying attention to his name. Say it aloud, say it again, and say it to yourself as you walk away. If you have a chance, write it down in a little notebook. When you leave, open the notebook and go over the names. This alone is as valuable as all the rest of the hints in this chapter.

Tying It In

If you're trying to remember a grocery list, you start with the advantage that each item on the list probably is something you're already familiar with. If you have to buy milk, eggs, matches, and bleach, you could tie the items together in a little mental chain. To get started, remind yourself that you're not cowed by going to the store. "*Milk!*" you cry. And into this milk you throw some—*eggs*. Will they break? A-ha, an omelet! To cook the omelet, you need *matches* to light the stove. Look how stained the stove top is. Perhaps some *bleach* will help.

Okay, it's dumb. But that's part of the reason it works.

Instant Recall

Dumb, or funny, or melodramatic, or frightening, or naughty images work better in mnemonic systems because their very dumbness (or funniness or whatever) makes them different from your usual run-of-the-brain thoughts, and thus causes them to stick out—and to stick in your memory.

It really works because you already have an image of each of the items. You can do something silly with eggs because you know what eggs are.

If you're introduced to a Mr. Gumleighter, however, his name doesn't come with a built-in image. He himself might look quite memorable—after all, how could you forget a man with tufts of multicolored hair all over his face and a nose that would make an aardvark proud? But unless you've met another Gumleighter, there are no built-in associations to which you can tie the name.

So you have to create your own.

Look at his nose—that unforgettable Gumleighter nose. Now imagine it with a black spot on the end. That's where he burned himself when he forgot that he had given up smoking, you tell yourself, and tried to light a stick of gum. Why, the man really is a gum-lighter.

Here are some images you might try with some more common names pulled at random right from our phone book. Yes, some of the connections are really silly, but that will makes them even easier to remember.

You might already have a connection with one or more of these names—perhaps a relative, or a friend, or a movie star. That would be even better. But if you don't, perhaps these will suffice:

➤ **Boyington:** The superhero BOY who can control his own weight. When he sits on the bad guys, he turns into an INGot weighing a TON.

➤ **Lindsay:** Can you dance the LINDy when you SAY hello to Mr. Lindsay? Or, for you fans of New York politics, recall Mayor John Lindsay, and his unsuccessful campaign for the presidency of the United States.

➤ **Farquharson:** You and your little boy are standing on a hill, and off in the distance is a quaint old church. And, remembering to create a strong, funny image, picture Mr. Farquharson standing outside that church in his bridal gown. Next to him outside the church, the choir is practicing—what a lovely sight it is. Your little boy asks what you are looking at. "It's the FAR CHOIR, SON," you tell him.

➤ **McIver:** Picture a delicate model of a MACK truck carved out of IVORy. Or if you are a television fan, and remember the *MacGyver* show, picture this McIver lighting the fuse to one of the contraptions jury-rigged by Angus MacGyver, the show's hero (he was played by Richard Dean Anderson, you TV trivia buffs!).

➤ **Butler:** If you're a mystery fan, he's obviously the one who did it. If not, picture him in a dress suit, standing at respectful attention, awaiting your instructions for dinner.

➤ **Rocco:** Several religious possibilities spring to mind. "Thy name is Peter-oh, and upon this ROCK-OH I will build my church-oh" might do it for you. If not, just sing "ROCK O' Ages" when Mr. Rocco comes into view. (Attention again, TV trivia lovers: Versatile character actor Alex Rocco may come to mind.)

➤ **Douglas:** When dis guy drinks he drains DUH GLASS. Or, if you're a fan of military history, picture Mr. Douglas with a corncob pipe in his mouth, and sunglasses, proclaiming "I shall return," like his first namesake, General Douglas MacArthur.

➤ **Wadsworth:** Look at the wad of money he just took out of his pocket! Why that WAD'S WORTH thousands! Or sandwich him in between Henry and Longfellow, for an unforgettable image.

➤ **Adair:** Look at him! He's just (or he definitely is not) the sort of man who would live dangerously, who would take A DARE just for the fun of it.

➤ **Hopkins:** You can't trust him at a party. He'd HOP on the napKINS. Picture him doing just that. Or, for you movie fans, picture him in a cell strapped to a board, wearing a weird hockey mask, like Anthony Hopkins in the movie *Silence of the Lambs*.

Of Course I Remember You, How Could I Forget That Face?

Now let's get down to the nitty and the gritty of remembering faces. Here is a group of people you might meet at a party or at work. The descriptions contain the sort of information you might learn about them in a brief social situation. Your assignment is to remember their names.

Start by looking them straight in the face and saying their name aloud, as you would if you met them at a party. "Glad to meet you, Mr. Towers. Have you been here long, Mr. Towers?"

Then read the information about them as though you were hearing it. The more you know about someone, the easier it is to get them fixed in your mind.

Al Berman

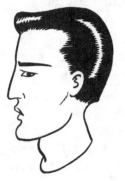

Al is the manager of a local Digital Delite Computer superstore. He thinks he's a killer with the ladies, but poor Al seems to have a slight drinking problem. He's never gotten over his successes in high school football, and he still tends to dress as if the bell for third-period class will ring any second.

TO REMEMBER HIS NAME: When you look at him, think about how cold he looks. He sends shivers right through you. All BRRR, man! Don't forget to picture his face as you create the mental image!

Estelle Parker

Estelle is new at your company in the accounting department. A graduate of Wharton Business School and very bright, she is destined to go places despite her high, squeaky voice. The word "perky" was invented for her.

TO REMEMBER HER NAME: Estelle is going to be a star—she is a stellar performer at her job and will do well wherever you park her. Don't forget to picture her face as you create the mental image!

W.A. Towers

To look at him, you would never suspect that 22-year-old W.A. Towers is the head of the multimillion-dollar Digital Delite Computer superstore chain that has stores in more than 200 locations nationwide. He started the business out of his father's garage when he was 12. When you ask him what he likes to be called (you can't call him "W.A."), he says, "Just call me Wally." A nice kid, for a multimillionaire.

TO REMEMBER HIS NAME: Use his youth as a peg. With acne or without, the kid towers over the competition. Well, he does! Don't forget to picture his face as you create the mental image!

Frances Hilton

She looks like a sweet, innocent young girl, but Frances Hilton is a detective on the local police force. She's been assigned to the Major Crimes Task Force for the past two years and has two citations for valor. An interestingly eclectic woman, she's crazy about baseball and has season tickets to the opera.

TO REMEMBER HER NAME: Here is a woman you could have a good time traveling with to Paris. You could stay together at France's Hilton hotel. Don't forget to picture her face as you create the mental image!

Shigeo Takagi

This young Japanese scholar spends his spare time scuba diving for rare coral-reef fish when he's not working on his thesis on "Quantum Subparticle Changes in the Thermal Variance of X-ray Illumination of Crystal Lattice Structures." His other passions are computer pinball and long-distance bike riding.

TO REMEMBER HIS NAME: Shigeo is a shy Joe; when you take your mental picture of him, you can tack it to the bulletin board. How often do you tack a guy on your bulletin board? If you happen to know Japanese, you will note that Takagi means "tall tree," and can add the image of young scholar Takagi atop a six-story birch. Don't forget to picture his face as you create the mental image!

Harmony Hummingbird

She looks thoroughly punked-out with her glossy black hair and purple highlights, midnight-blue lipstick, and multiple piercings. In fact, you find her a little off-putting until you chat with her for a few minutes. Turns out she's a "poor little rich girl" who ran away from home at age 14, lived on the street, and got into big trouble. She spent time in rehab, cleaned up her act, and now works as a youth counselor, helping kids avoid the mistakes she made. And she has a terrific record of success!

TO REMEMBER HER NAME: This one is easy! Here's a person whose life was a complete mess until she straightened herself out and got into harmony with herself. She also has the grace, the beauty, and the flitting, darting movements of a hummingbird. Don't forget to picture her face as you create the mental image!

Francis Xavier McCabe

When he was a young fellow, Mr. McCabe fought for the Irish Republican Army and then spent 20 years in a British jail. He was accused of manufacturing high explosives. When he was released, he came to the United States and became, wouldn't you know it, a chemist. Retired now, he remains a staunch supporter of the Irish cause, but he's also a strong advocate of peaceful solutions to political problems.

TO REMEMBER HIS NAME: Anyone who works with chemicals could easily have been an FX technician in the movies. "FX" is Hollywood lingo for special effects, and Mr. McCabe fits right in. Can't you just see him during his career as a fugitive, hiding out in a cave? Don't forget to picture his face as you create the mental image!

A.W. Sanders

What a striking person! A.W. Sanders is a Native American activist and lobbyist. She divides her efforts between her tribal home in New Mexico and Washington, D.C., where she wields amazing influence. Senators, cabinet officers, and bureaucrats ask for her views on important issues. She served 20 years in the United States Army, rising to the rank of lieutenant colonel, and commanded a tank unit in Operation Desert Storm. She still holds a commission in the reserves.

TO REMEMBER HER NAME: With all the politicians chasing her, you can almost hear the disappointed complaints of those who don't catch her eye. "Awww," they whine. You also can see her whipping across the desert sands of Kuwait in her fighting tank. Don't forget to picture her face as you create the mental image!

Claude Lincoln

Once a graffiti artist and tagger (one of those youths who writes large on the sides of buildings, buses, etc.), Claude won a scholarship to art school where he majored in cartooning and animation. He showed terrific talent and, upon graduation, was snapped up by the top animation studio in Hollywood. He is now the chief inker on the Panther-Girl show, the most popular animated adventure series on TV.

TO REMEMBER HIS NAME: Can't you just see this talented young man, hard at work on his animation drawings? His specialty is that clawed heroine, Panther-Girl. Although he leaves penciling duties to others, he keeps close control of all inkin' himself. Don't forget to picture his face as you create the mental image!

Maria diMarco

Maria is proud of her mixed-ethnic heritage. Her mother is a Filipina; her father is half African American and half Italian. She speaks perfect English, Tagalog, Spanish, Italian, and Kiswahili—and she can sing everything from traditional lullabies to grand opera in any of those languages.

TO REMEMBER HER NAME: She can sing a folk song, a rock 'n' roll anthem, or some aria. That's the mark o' ("di marco") this amazingly versatile woman. Don't forget to picture her face as you create the mental image!

Willem van der Zee

Willem is an exchange student completing his doctorate in historical influences of the Dutch colonial administration of New Amsterdam (now New York). His long-term goal is to have New Amsterdam's transfer of administration from the Netherlands to England declared illegal and become the greatest Dutch governor of the city since Peter Stuyvesant. (You think this is a wee bit unrealistic, but Willem makes a fascinating companion once he gets rolling.)

TO REMEMBER HIS NAME: Here's a new technique. We're going to suggest an image that you'll describe in rhyme. You've noticed that Willem loves snacks. Here at the party, you can create a mental image of him balancing a paper plate of messy, red sauce–drenched noodles on his nose—while standing on an expensive white carpet. Say to yourself, "If Willem should spill 'em the hostess will kill 'im!" If she does, you'll have to get him to the hospital by van. As a matter of fact, you decide, he's rather a pest. It might be a good idea to send him back across der sea to his homeland. (By, the way, if you happen to know the Dutch language—or even if you don't—"van der zee" means "of the ocean"—picture Willem floating over the waves.) Don't forget to picture his face as you create the mental image!

Kinesha Foster

Kinesha Foster is one of the movers and shakers in your city's social circles. She's always on the go, and despite her slightly excessive bulk, nobody's ever been able to keep up with her for more than a few months. That includes her three ex-husbands and uncounted suitors.

TO REMEMBER HER NAME: Kinesha moves so fast, she's a ball of kinetic energy. No matter how fast you try to go, it seems that she can always go a little bit faster. ("Kinetic Faster" is a close phonetic equivalent of "Kinesha Foster." If you can remember the image and the phonetic equivalent of her name, your mind will bridge the gap.) Don't forget to picture her face as you create the mental image!

The Sillier the Better

Now you see how this is done. Some of the images and wordplay can get silly at times. Some of the puns and homonyms are admittedly far-fetched. Admittedly? Heck, we're proud of 'em. Let's face it, we have no shame.

In fact, the more far-fetched the story and imagery you concoct to help you remember a name and associate that name with a face, the more likely you are to succeed. A drab and commonplace story won't make much of an impression. A lurid, absurd, memorable one will be ... well, yes, memorable.

Remember This!

If you create a mnemonic "reminder image" that is phonetically close to the name you want to remember but is not a perfect match, that's okay. Your mind will bridge the gap between, for example, "AWww SANDS" and "A.W. SANDERS."

Next we'd like you to go back over the drawings you've just seen. Refresh your memory by looking at the images and by rereading the names. If you found the little bits of wordplay that we offered to help you remember each name, run through them again, striving to make the imagery as vivid as possible in your mind. Make more of those "little movies," remember?

If our clues and wordplay don't work for you, make up some of your own. In fact, since you're going to be devising clues and reminders on your own in the real world, it would be good practice to start on our 12 faces.

When you feel ready, continue with the following exercise. You'll see the 12 faces again. Try to remember the wordplay that will bring their names back to you. Write the names under the pictures and then turn back to the descriptions earlier in the chapter to see if you're right.

Good luck! And remember—have fun!

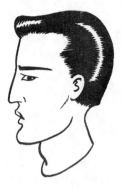

_____

_____

_____

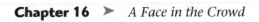

_____

_____

_____

_____

_____

_____

209

The Least You Need to Know

➤ Remembering people's names and a few salient facts about them can be helpful.

➤ The principle of repetition applies to learning names. When you meet someone, make it a point to repeat their name several times.

➤ Some people's names carry ready-made imagery with them. Others require some complicated wordplay to turn them into memorable images, but with a little work any name can be made memorable.

➤ Connecting people's faces not only with their names but with facts about them makes them all the more memorable.

➤ This one is really, really important: No matter what trick or technique you use to help you remember someone's name, the very fact that you are making an effort will help you concentrate on remembering the person's name. That in itself will help you remember!

Chapter 17

I've Got Your Number

In This Chapter

➤ Clumping large numbers

➤ Remembering the clumps

➤ Weekdays for the year

➤ The number alphabet

➤ Phone numbers

Numbers, numbers, numbers. Our civilization today is plagued with numbers. Everyone's got more than they can handle—or remember—or would ever want to remember. You're just about born with a Social Security number these days. Then there are your credit-card numbers (and their PIN numbers), your department store account numbers, your health-plan number, your phone number (with area code), and the phone numbers of your doctor, your lawyer, your bank, your Internet account (which probably has its own number), your police and fire departments (increasingly, but not always, 911), your office, your clients, and all your friends (and cell-phone numbers and pager numbers to an increasing number of them). And you wouldn't want to forget your street address and nine-digit zip code, not to mention various appointments, birthdays, and anniversaries.

When you go on a trip, you have flight numbers, baggage claim-check numbers, car-rental numbers, route numbers, street numbers, hotel room numbers...

And on and on.

Well, we can't get rid of the number clutter for you. It seems to be here to stay and to be getting worse year by year. Wouldn't you think the government would just give everyone a number at birth and that would be it? Your phone number, Social Security number, credit-card number, and so on would all the same. Some day it will come to that, and then people will complain that it's a violation of their personal privacy—and they're probably right.

Wouldn't you like to be able to remember at least the most important of these numbers? You don't want to feel like you're stranded on a desert island just because you left your address book at home or because the batteries for your pocket information manager went dead.

Remembering Numbers

Tests have shown that the average person can remember a number that has between five and 12 digits. A person can at least keep the number in short-term memory for a couple minutes—long enough to make a phone call or to recite it to an interested party. To transfer the number to long-term memory requires more time and a lot of repetition, but it also can be done.

Suppose the number contains more digits than you normally can hold in short-term memory or you need to retain it longer than a couple of minutes? Can you remember it then?

You can and we'll show you how. Later in this chapter we'll show you an even more useful way, but it's a way that requires more work at the beginning to be able to use it.

Take a Number

Let's take the following 12-digit number and examine it.

265274263153

Let's see, that's two-six-five-two-seven-four-two-six-three-one-five-three. Yeah, that's it.

Got it? No? Well, it's pretty long. Maybe we should divide it up in some way to make it easier.

Clump It Up

Experiments have shown that most people can remember only seven items in a list without working at it. But there's something tricky about this fact. When dealing with numbers, the "items" don't have to be single digits. They could be, for example, clumps of three or even four digits. If each of the number clumps has some sort of meaning for you—say it's your house number or your birthday—all the better. For example, look over this number:

5017761314920

It doesn't jump out at you and say "Remember me!" does it? If we were to point out to you that there are 50 states, but that in 1776 there were only 13 states, and that back when Columbus got here in 1492 there were 0 states, you probably could remember 50-1776-13-1492-0 with very little trouble. If you can find some way to give the number clumps meaning, they'll stick in your memory much more easily.

If It Were Only That Easy

Unfortunately, most long numbers don't set themselves up to be remembered quite that conveniently. With a little thought, however, you usually can get a handle on them. Let's take another look at the number we started with:

265274263153

Let's divide it into clumps of three.

265-274-263-153

It helps to examine the numbers and see their relationship. Let's see: 265 starts with 2. A-ha! It's a second-place number. And it goes on to 6, which is 2 + 4.

2 (+4) = 6

Drop back one from the 6 to get the 5. 265.

The next group starts with 2 again, then adds one to the middle digit, and then subtracts one from the final digit, for 274.

So now we have 265 and 274. What can we do to fix the next group, 263, in our memory? Well, it

Instant Recall

This is harder to read than it is to do. If you go through it once or twice to see the pattern, you'll see what we're talking about and be able to do it with any number. Honest. Did we mention that we have a fun reward for you for working along with us? Really, we do.

starts with 2 again, as a matter of fact. It starts with 26 just like the first group. And the last number, 3, is one less than the last number in the previous group—which, come to think of it, is one less than the last number in the first group: 5-4-3. See what we mean? 265, 274, 263.

And the last group? 153. Well, it doesn't start with a 2 like the other three groups do. A 1, you will notice, is one less than a 2. And, curiously, a 5 is one less than a 6. So the first two numbers are each one less than the first two numbers in the third group (and group one as well). The last number is the same as the last number in group three. 3 = 3.

Now we have 265, 274, 263, 153.

Now for Your Reward

In doing this exercise you've probably ended up memorizing 265, 274, 263, 153. We know we have.

Luckily, you can put this number to use. What we have here are the dates on which the first Sunday in each month falls in the year 2000.

The First Sunday in:	Falls on the:
January	2nd
February	6th
March	5th
April	2nd
May	7th
June	4th
July	2nd
August	6th
September	3rd
October	1st
November	5th
December	3rd

"Oh, goody!" you are probably saying. "So what?"

Well, if you know the date of the first Sunday, you can quickly compute what day of the week any date falls on. Let's take some dates at random and test this out: February 19, August 3, October 22, and Christmas, December 25.

Instant Recall

You can make a "First Sundays" list for any year and can memorize it just as easily as you did this one—or even more easily, now that you've had the practice.

The first Sunday in February falls on the 6th. The next Sunday would be seven days later, the 13th, and the next would be the 20th. So the 19th would be a Saturday.

The first Sunday in August is the 6th. So August 3rd would be three days earlier, a Thursday.

The first Sunday in October falls on the 1st. The 22nd would be—hey—the fourth Sunday (1st, 8th, 15th, 22nd).

The first Sunday in December is the 3rd. The third Sunday is the 24th ($7 \times 3 + 3$) so December 25, Christmas, is on a Monday.

The Number Alphabet

Now we're going to give you a truly splendid method for memorizing numbers. Well, "give" may not be quite the right word for it. You'll have to pay for this, and the currency in which you pay is effort. Effort, concentration, mental elbow grease (bet you haven't come across that expression in a dog's age), and plain hard work.

But if you're willing to put a little work into it up front, and if you'll exert the effort necessary to learn the number alphabet, you'll acquire a mental tool that will enable you to remember any number you ever need to memorize. In other words, the long-term dividends will far exceed the short-term investment.

Remember This!

If you only want to memorize one or two numbers, we'll be honest with you. It's probably less work to just memorize those numbers using what is sometimes referred to as the brute force method.

Sounds like a good deal to us.

The number alphabet originally was devised several hundred years ago. It has been revised and refined over the centuries, and in its current form, it is used by virtually every "memory maven" around, whether as a show-business stunt or as a practical, everyday tool.

Here's how it works:

For starters, each number from 1 to 9 plus 0 is assigned an alphabetical value. Some people see deep, almost mystical meanings in these values. Others maintain there is no meaning at all and the values are completely arbitrary. We take a middle course. If you think you see reasons for the assigned alphabetical equivalents, that's fine. They may help you remember the values. If you don't see any reasons, that's okay, too. Just remember them.

- ➤ 1 = t or d
- ➤ 2 = n
- ➤ 3 = m
- ➤ 4 = r
- ➤ 5 = l
- ➤ 6 = sh, ch, or j
- ➤ 7 = k, hard g (as in "go"), or q
- ➤ 8 = f (or ph) or v
- ➤ 9 = b or p
- ➤ 0 = s or z

But What Does It All Mean?

Okay, here are some cues that you can use (if you choose) to help you remember the letter/number equivalents in this code. If you don't want to bother with them—if you'd rather just memorize the codes flat out—that's okay, too. Just skip the explanations. But if you like having reasons for things (or if you think it will help you to remember the codes), here they are:

➤ **1 = t or d.** When you make the letter "t," it has a single downstroke just like the number 1. And "d" is a close phonetic equivalent of "t."

➤ **2 = n.** The letter "n" has two downstrokes. Also, if you turn the number 2 on its side, it looks like an "n." Well, sort of.

➤ **3 = m.** The letter "m"—right!—has three downstrokes. If you turn a 3 on its side, it looks a little like an "m."

➤ **4 = r.** Yes, 4 sounds like an "r" and ends with an "r." If you're as cockeyed as some-body whose name we won't mention at the moment, and if you turn an uppercase "R" around and get a little fuzzy about it, it even looks a little bit like a 4.

➤ **5 = l.** Here's an amusing one! Hold your left hand at arm's length palm away from you, fingers joined but thumb pointing to your right. What do you see? Right! It's the letter "L."

➤ **6 = ch, sh, or j.** Flop the "j" left-for-right and it suggests a 6. A little bit. The "ch" and "sh" are related sounds.

➤ **7 = k, q, or hard g.** Again, there's a slight resemblance in shape for the "k." Also, two 7s, back-to-back, will look like a capital K. And the sounds for "k" and hard "g" are formed in the same way in your mouth (well, in most people's mouths). Q can also be used, since its sound usually is a "k" sound.

➤ **8 = f or v.** A hand-written lowercase "f" looks a lot like an 8. This one is also a sound code. 8 = fate. Hence the "f." In many languages, "v" is the phonetic equivalent of "f." Ask any German how to pronounce "Vvvvvvvvvvolkswagen" and the answer will be "Ffffffffffolksvahgen." Remember, it's the sound that counts. So "ph," as in "phone" also counts as an "f."

➤ **9 = b or p.** Another shape connection here. Revolve a 9 and get a "b." Mirror-flop a 9 and get a "p." Or pretty darn close, anyhow.

➤ **0 = s or z.** A mathematical purist might suggest that the code should begin with 0 rather than end with it, but traditionally it has ended with 0, and we're staying with tradition. Think of "z" for "zero." And "s" is a close phonetic equivalent of "z."

Instant Recall

"Volk" is "folk" and means "people." "Wagen" sounds like "wagon" and means "car." "Volkswagen" is a nice word meaning "people's car," but unfortunately it was Hitler's idea. So why did the hippies like it? Well, it *was* one of the cheapest cars around...

You'll notice that there are no values assigned for the unvoiced consonants "w," "y," or "h." There also are no vowels in the code, and the letter "h" is used only in "sh," or "ch." When you apply this code, you have free use of a-e-i-o-u as well as the unused consonants to fill out words. These letters have no number equivalents in this code. You may use them as you wish. Think of them as helpers.

Double letters that sound together don't count. "Bill," for example, is the number 95 not 955. For 955, we might use "pill wall" (picture a wall of pills, not a bad image) or "Bailleul" (which, as we're sure you know, is a city in Belgium).

"Kiss" is not 700, but 70. 700 would be "kisses." Incidentally, "x" can be thought of as "ks" (which is how it usually sounds), if you find that helpful. Its number therefore would be 70—but a single letter with a double-digit meaning might be confusing, and many persons simply avoid "x."

Some Memorable Facts

Experts in using the number alphabet often add a refinement to enable them to handle double or triple numbers. If the number, for example, is 888, it's hard to think of a word using three Vs and no other consonants. What these experts do is use a W preceding the voiced consonant or a Y after the voiced consonant to indicate that the number is doubled, or both to triple it. "Wit," for example, would be 11, and "witty" would be 111. "Wavy" would be that 888 we mentioned above.

This is rather complicated, and prevents you from using a leading W or a trailing Y except when the number is doubled or tripled, so even many experts choose not to use this refinement to the system, and you certainly shouldn't try it unless you are an expert. But we just thought you'd want to know.

So Let's See How It Works, Already!

Let's take a numberscommon class of numbers such as telephone area codes. They're only three digits long, and most of us have no trouble remembering the ones we use frequently. The others we can look up when we need them. But just for demonstration purposes:

New York City (well, most of Manhattan anyway) has an area code of 212. If we try to convert this to alphabetics, we get n-t-n. This doesn't mean anything, so we might as well just remember 212. But remember, vowels are free in this little game. And here's another point we should emphasize: In using this code, the actual sound of the letters is what matters. This is phonetic. "Tough," for example, could be used for 18 because it's the sound that matters. It's as if it is spelled "tuf" in the number alphabet.

Back to 212. Think of messy old Manhattan. Wouldn't you like to *NEATEN* the streets? Or, since it's the Big Apple, wouldn't it be loved by Sir Isaac *NEWTON*? And then again, remember when the island was bought for some trinkets from an *INDIAN* (who was actually conning the Dutch settlers, since he didn't even own it). Here are a few other area codes of major cities:

Los Angeles = 213 (again, one of several area codes). 213 becomes n-t-m or n-d-m. Can we add vowels and turn either of these into memorable words? Easily. How about, since no real people live in Los Angeles, *NOT HOME*? And, if you're planning to become a Hollywood (also 213) star, there's *NO TIME* like the present. Hey, so what if it's silly. Silly is good. It helps to create code words or mnemonics that are meaningful and memorable to you. If you're from Massachusetts, you're probably familiar with the town of *NEEDHAM*. This isn't as silly, it will do nicely.

Miami = 305 = m-s-l or m-z-l. Miami is a good town for having a *MUSSEL* dinner. Remember, the double "s" only counts as one, and the vowels don't count at all. Or, if you take your dog to Miami, you may have to *MUZZLE* it.

Salt Lake City = 801 = v-s-t or f-s-t = vast or vast.

Washington, D.C. = 202 = n-s-n = no sun.

St. Louis = 304 = m-s-r = mouser or miser. Hey, a cheapskate or his cat!

You see how it works? You can make up your own key words for area codes or any other numbers. If the numbers get long and you want to break the numerical equivalents into brief sentences, that's okay, too. The spaces between the words also are free like vowels.

Now let's try some longer numbers. They're actually more interesting, and they're not really any more complicated than the area codes. Once you've worked with this system for a while, you'll become remarkably adept at it!

Four Naked Acrobats Jumped Out of a Cake

What do you think of the number 842717491063911877? Hard to remember? Give it a try for a minute:

842717491063911877

You could memorize it, but it wouldn't be fun. On the other hand, suppose we told you that four naked acrobats jumped out of a cake? That image might stay with you for a while.

Well, the naked acrobats will take you by the hand and will lead you to this number. Like this:

Four naked acrobats jumped out of a cake.
8   4 2 7 1 74 9 106 39 1   1 8   7 7

There you have it. We'll be the first to admit that not every number you need to memorize will work out to a memorable sentence. With a little effort, however, you usually can come up with something easier to remember than the naked number.

Michael:

> When I first learned this system many years ago, I used it to memorize my girl-friend Mary's phone number. The mnemonic I came up with was so wonderful that I remember it to this day, even though I haven't seen Mary in 20 years. (How are you Mary? I hope you're doing well.) Her number (long since changed and I won't tell you the city) was 982-4219. It works out to "bovine roundup." Even though there was nothing bovine about tall, slender, elegant Mary, "bovine roundup" is not the sort of phrase you (or at least I) can ever forget.

A Number or Two

Let's try the system on a couple real phone numbers so you can see that this works in real life and not just on numbers we make up. We'll pick some government numbers. We both live in the San Francisco Bay area, so let's start with the phone number for San Francisco's City Hall.

The San Francisco area code is 415, which we will make into *RETAIL*.

The City Hall phone number is 554-6141.

5 5 4 6 1 4 1
l, l, r, ch, t, r, t

After a little effort, we come up with "Hallelujah! Rich treat."

So San Francisco's City Hall phone number, including area code, is RETAIL—HALLELUJAH! RICH TREAT.

The United States government has a number you can call to get the weather in northern California. Located in Monterey, the number is 650-364-7974. One possibility for this is "Shelley, some shy rag picker."

Instant Recall

We can use "hallelujah" for 5–5 despite the "j," which usually is a 6, because in "hallelujah" the "j" is pronounced as a "y"—one of our unvoiced consonants. Remember, it's the sound that counts.

Here's one more. The United States government's general information number is 800-688-9889. This isn't easy because of all the repeated digits. 800 is not a memorization problem because many numbers are referred to as "800 numbers." If you want a mnemonic, however, how about "heavy sauce" or "wave's ace." For 688-9889 (a tough one), you might try "chief of beefy VIP."

Maybe that mnemonic just doesn't do it for you. Well, that's okay. The idea is for you to learn to create your own. One you devise yourself will be easier for you to remember. What's that? You like "Shove off, boy, if you have a hobby"?

Hmmm...

A Few to Practice On

Try turning a few of these numbers into words. See what you can come up with:

1. 583-1214
2. 147-8132
3. 758-5270
4. 384-9741
5. 194-2119
6. 468-4107
7. 703-3185
8. 330-9590
9. 702-1150
10. 943-5272

Some Possible Results

Any phrases you came up with, if they fit the numbers, are fine. Here are some you might have discovered in the preceding numbers:

1. Love me tender
2. Dark of the moon
3. Golf links
4. Humphrey Bogart
5. To be or not to be
6. Reach for the sky!
7. Kiss me, you mad fool!
8. Mom's apple pies
9. Guys and dolls
10. Abraham Lincoln (remember, the second l is not pronounced)

"First Sunday" List Revisited

Let's see if we can use this system for the first Sunday of the month list. As we're sure you remember, the numbers for the year 2000 are 265-274-263-153.

Well, perhaps the phrase explains why we stayed home instead of going fishing this winter:

"No chill, no gear, no chum (bait), a dream…"

In the next chapter, we'll show you how to use this number alphabet to memorize lists of items. You can use it on grocery lists, parts lists, lists of random objects—whatever types of lists you might use in your work or hobby.

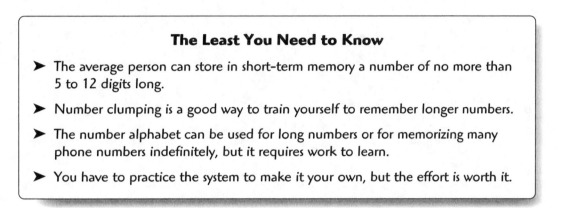

The Least You Need to Know

➤ The average person can store in short-term memory a number of no more than 5 to 12 digits long.

➤ Number clumping is a good way to train yourself to remember longer numbers.

➤ The number alphabet can be used for long numbers or for memorizing many phone numbers indefinitely, but it requires work to learn.

➤ You have to practice the system to make it your own, but the effort is worth it.

Chapter 18

He's Making a List

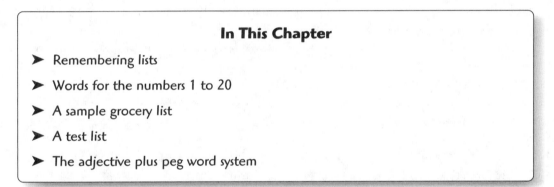

In This Chapter

➤ Remembering lists

➤ Words for the numbers 1 to 20

➤ A sample grocery list

➤ A test list

➤ The adjective plus peg word system

The number alphabet that you learned in the preceding chapter is useful for much more than just memorizing phone numbers. It can be used to memorize just about anything you might want to list.

Using it to remember things instead of numbers, however, requires a little more work on your part. You must make up a list of words based on the letter equivalents for the numbers we gave you in the last chapter.

Instant Recall

You will instantly recall, of course, that the letter equivalents are:

1 = t or d; 2 = n; 3 = m; 4 = r; 5 = l; 6 = sh, ch, or j; 7 = k, q, hard g, or hard c; 8 = f or v; 9 = p or b; 0 = s or z

Don't forget it's the sound that counts and not the actual letter. The word "tough," for example, would be equivalent to 18 because the "gh" sounds like an "f."

Instant Recall

One use for this system is to create a PIN number for your bank cards. Instead of converting numbers to letters, you reverse the process, converting words of your choice to their number equivalents. Thus the name MABEL JONES would become 395620. Nobody but Mabel would guess that number, but she could "re-create" it in an instant if she ever forgot it.

The List

The first step is to make a list of words using the letter equivalents for the numbers from 1 to as high as you'd care to go. Let's begin with 1 to 20, since there are a variety of ways to go for bigger lists. Remembering 20 items on a list in less than three minutes—which you will be able to do easily after you've mastered this—is pretty impressive all by itself.

For numbers 1 through 9 we've selected words that begin with the letter "h" to make them easier to remember. If you need a plain naked 0 (zero) in the "h" system, you might use "hose." For 10 through 19 we'll use words that begin with "t" or "d" because these are the letter equivalents of the number 1. You'll notice that when we reach 20, the first letter of the key word is "n." Why is this? Ah hah! Exactly as you remembered, "n" is the letter equivalent for 2.

The list of words we use for the numbers 1 to 20 is:

1 = hat	11 = dad
2 = hen	12 = den
3 = ham	13 = dome
4 = hair	14 = door
5 = hole	15 = tail
6 = hash	16 = dish
7 = hook	17 = dike
8 = hoof	18 = dove
9 = hoop	19 = tape
10 = toes	20 = nose

These are only suggestions. You should feel free to substitute any word you prefer (that fits the pattern) for any word on this list. The word should have a strong meaning for you so it's easy to recall, and after you pick a word you should stick with it. If you alternate with two or more words for the same number you may have trouble recalling just which word you used to remember the item you're trying to recall.

The number 5, for example, is hole on our list, but it could also be ale or well. 7 is hook on our list, but it could be key, wok, cow, or hookah. 11 could be tide, teat, to-do, or doodoo.

If you pick a silly word, or even what Michael's Aunt Zenobia used to call an "off-color" word, that's okay. It probably will create a stronger image for you. Remember, no one but yourself ever has to know what your peg words are.

When presented with a list of items you wish to memorize, go over them slowly and tie each item to its peg word with as silly or as powerful an image as you can create in 10 or 15 seconds. It doesn't take longer than that. When you've had some practice, you can cut the time down to three or four seconds for each item.

Shopping for Groceries

As an example, let's take a simple grocery list:

1. A half-gallon of milk
2. A dozen eggs
3. A loaf of whole-wheat bread
4. A three-pound chicken
5. An eggplant
6. Peanut butter
7. A six-pack of beer
8. Toilet paper
9. A sponge
10. 10 pounds of kitty litter

Now we'll memorize the list. We go in each case from the peg word to the item we're trying to memorize. Put the picture firmly in your mind—take 10 seconds or so—and then move on. You will find that when you go over the list, as you think of each peg word the item on the list will be recalled with it—if you have created a strong enough image. Here we go:

➤ Our first peg word is hat, and the first item on the list is a half-gallon of milk. We can picture a fedora turned upside-down. Into it we are pouring milk. How much milk? A HALF-GALLON OF MILK. Really picture it—get a good, firm image in your mind.

Got it? Good!

➤ Our second peg word is hen, and the second item is a dozen eggs. Hey, we walked into an easy one. We can picture the poor hen straining to lay the last of A DOZEN EGGS in its proper slot in the egg carton.

Got it? Good!

➤ Our third peg word is ham, and the third item on the list is a loaf of whole-wheat bread. Well, how about slicing that ham and putting it between two pieces of bread. What kind of bread? WHOLE-WHEAT BREAD. Add some lettuce and mayo, and you've got a nice little sandwich. Picture slicing the ham, and it will all come back to you.

Got it? Good!

➤ Our fourth peg word is hair, and the fourth item on the list is a three-pound chicken. Okay. Picture a clump of hair. Where is the hair coming from? Oh my gosh! It's sprouting out of the neck of a chicken. What sort of chicken? A THREE-POUND CHICKEN. A gross image? Good, it's all the more memorable.

Got it? Good!

➤ Our fifth peg word is hole, and the fifth item on the list is an eggplant. Okay. There is this hole—a round, black hole in your kitchen floor. But not as black as the giant EGGPLANT emerging from it!

Got it? Good!

➤ Our sixth peg word is hash, and the sixth item on the list is peanut butter. Let's go directly for it this time. What we have here is that famous peanut butter hash recipe that everyone is talking about. When you think of hash, how can you think of anything but PEANUT BUTTER?

Got it? Good!

Remember This!

You might be able to come up with stronger (funnier, more vivid, more disgusting, more off-color) images than the ones used here. If so, feel free to use them. The stronger the image, the more certain the recall. And remember—no one can tell what you're thinking.

➤ Our seventh peg word is hook, and the seventh item on the list is a six-pack of beer. Okay. Picture a large hook on your refrigerator (since these are all grocery items, we'll locate as many images as possible in the kitchen). From this hook is dangling A SIX-PACK OF BEER. See it held up by that plastic gizmo that holds the six-pack together.

Got it? Good!

➤ Our eighth peg word is hoof, and the eighth item on the list is toilet paper. Easy. Picture a cow's hoof with TOILET PAPER on it. What is the cow doing with the toilet paper? Well, what do you usually do with toilet paper? Now there's an image that will stay with you.

Got it? Good!

➤ Our ninth peg word is hoop, and the ninth item on the list is a sponge. Let's picture a hoop being trolled through the bottom of the ocean. What is it doing, it is being used to gather up A SPONGE from a bed of sponges. Or—now here's another thought—picture a hula hoop being twirled by a little girl sponge.

Got it? Good!

➤ Our tenth peg word is toes, and the tenth item on the list is 10 pounds of kitty litter. Imagine you are standing barefoot, wiggling your toes in 10 POUNDS OF KITTY LITTER. Thank goodness it's fresh and unused. There's a brief but powerful image.

Got it? Good!

If you've actually done the imaging as you read along here, now you can close the book and recite the grocery list. If you haven't memorized the peg words yet, read on. The peg words are listed for you in the following Instant Recall sidebar. If you've just been reading along, now is the time to go back over the list and actually create the images in your mind.

Try it.

Each item may take a moment or two to come to you, but they will come. Honest. Trust us—try it!

Still having doubts? You can prove to yourself that this system works even before you go to the trouble of memorizing the words. Write down the peg words for the numbers 1 to 10 or remove the number alphabet tear-out card from the front of this book. Have someone make up a list of 10 items and then read it to you.

An Indian Memory Expert

In India, memory experts called Ashtavadhinis are known for performing remarkable feats of recall. In 1886, *Theosophist Magazine* reported about a memory expert who gave an exhibition during which he did the following:

➤ Played a game of chess without seeing the board.

➤ Devised a poem (in Sanskrit) from a first line given to him by someone in the audience.

➤ Multiplied a five-digit number by a four-digit number.

➤ Added three columns of eight-digit numbers.

➤ Memorized a 16-word Sanskrit verse, with the words being given to him in random order over a period of time.

➤ Completed two different "magic squares," four-by-four squares filled in with 16 different numbers in which all the horizontal rows, vertical columns, and diagonals add up to the same number.

➤ Completed a "knight's square" tour of a chessboard—having a chess knight making its ordinary moves land on each of the squares of a chessboard once and only once until every square has been touched—starting from a square picked by an audience member.

➤ Memorized two different sentences in Spanish with the words being given to him out of order.

➤ Kept track of the ringing of a bell held by someone in the audience and gave the total at the end of the performance.

He did these things all at the same time. Afterward, he was able to go over each of the feats and recall all the moves of the chess game, all the numbers in the magic square, and so on.

A Moment to Review, Maestro!

Let's take another list and see how this system works out. Let's say we wish to remember the year William the Conqueror landed in Britain and conquered the island. We'll have it made if we can convince ourselves that William on the plains of Hastings (where his decisive battle was fought) was a lot like Joshua before the walls of Jericho. (That's a Bible story, in case you missed it. It inspired one of the great songs of all time, "Joshua Fit the Battle of Jericho." But we digress...)

Instant Recall

1 to 10 Number Alphabet:

1: Hat, 2: Hen, 3: Ham, 4: Hair, 5: Hole, 6: Hash, 7: Hook, 8: Hoof, 9: Hoop, 10: Toes

When did William the Conqueror land in Britain? 1066.

1 = t or d; 0 = s or z; 6 = j, ch, or sh; 6 = j, ch, or sh (again)

Remembering that vowels are free, we can convert 1066 into "It's Josh!" Poor King Harold might have muttered this to himself, remembering his Bible, when he caught sight of William's army.

The number alphabet that we've been working with in this chapter is based on a number-to-letter conversion, but the peg words used are arbitrary. Anyone using this system can make up his or her own set of peg words, but once you've got your list in place, it's a good idea to stick with it. If you keep making up new lists of peg words, even though they might work well enough, there's a risk of confusing them.

You might wind up wondering, "For the number 4, did I mean hair, oar, ear, ray, or..." See what we mean?

Another Example, Just for Practice

Let's make another list, this time without a unifying theme. We'll mix groceries with articles of clothing with movie stars' names and a few other surprises. Here's our list:

1. Sneakers
2. Moon rocks
3. Pingerberry pie
4. Marilyn Monroe
5. The *Titanic*
6. A hot fudge sundae
7. Buckingham Palace
8. A bikini bathing suit
9. "I Wanna Hold Your Hand"
10. Two giant pandas

How do we remember these 10 very disparate items? And not only them, but also the number assigned to each? Let's apply our number alphabet and see what happens.

➤ Our first peg word is hat. The first item on our new list is sneakers. So what sort of hat do we have this time? A top hat. And it's on the head of the famous, elegant dancer Fred Astaire. Indeed Fred is all spiffed up in his top hat, tails, and walking stick, dancing in his SNEAKERS.

Roll this image around in your mind for a few seconds, and you won't worry about forgetting it. You must remember, however, to concentrate on the sneakers and the hat. You might want to make the rest of Mr. Astaire fade out, while his hat and sneakers glow brilliantly on the screen of your mind.

➤ Our second peg word is hen. The second item on our list is moon rocks.

Whoa, that's easy for us but tough for the poor hen. Hasn't she been through enough today? Now she has to lay MOON ROCKS!

Think of that poor little hen laying moon rocks, and you won't easily forget it.

➤ Our third peg word is ham. The third item on our list is pingerberry pie. Oh, pingerberry pie again, remember that from Chapter 8? What a meal. A great big ham steak and a slice of mouth-watering PINGERBERRY PIE. Yum!

Once again, think about this picture. See the ham and the pingerberry pie. Imagine yourself slicing your dinner and eating it. Think of the textures and flavors involved.

Instant Recall

When you use peg words, you must "set your memory store" with the key words and work from them to the target objects—not the other way around. By doing this you will *always* be able to find the items on your list.

➤ Our fourth peg word is hair, and the fourth item on our list is Marilyn Monroe. So what sort of hair do we picture? Long, beautiful blonde hair? Whose hair? One of the most famous movie stars of all time, the beautiful and talented MARILYN MONROE.

We need only concentrate for a moment on Marilyn Monroe and her gorgeous, shimmering blonde hair. It's a lock!

➤ Our fifth peg word is hole, and the fifth item on our list is the *Titanic*. And where is this hole? It is in the hull of the famous floating city, "the unsinkable" ship that *did* sink when it hit an iceberg in the darkness of the North Atlantic— the *TITANIC*.

➤ Our sixth peg word is hash, and our sixth item is a hot fudge sundae. How are we going to combine hash with hot fudge sundae?

Where is this hash? It's sitting atop a HOT FUDGE SUNDAE, in place of the whipped cream. Well, there's no accounting for taste!

➤ The seventh peg word is hook. The seventh item on our list is Buckingham Palace.

There is a hook. Where? Why on the end of the arm of a captain in the Guards. Resplendent in his bright red uniform and high hat and shiny hook, the captain is in charge of the guard at BUCKINGHAM PALACE.

➤ Our eighth peg word is hoof. The eighth item is a bikini bathing suit.

What do we see hanging over the hoof? Why it's a BIKINI BATHING SUIT! And there you have it. If you think that isn't a strong enough image (actually, it is), try losing the image of a cow in a bikini waving its hoof at you.

➤ Our ninth peg word is hoop, and the ninth item on our list is "I Wanna Hold Your Hand." We threw this one in because it isn't a physical object or a person— it's a song! A number-one hit in its day, this is one of the most popular single songs of the past 50 years. It was the first huge hit for the Beatles.

Imagine a hoop being twirled by an attractive young lady—you can put her in the bikini bathing suit from the last image if you like—and gathered around her are the Beatles trying to grab her hand as she twirls away from them. They are, of course, singing, "I WANNA HOLD YOUR HAND."

➤ Our peg word for 10 is toes, and our tenth item is two giant pandas. Remember how we formed the word "toes" from the key letters for 1 and 0 (t and s).

When we hear "10" we think "toes." And this time they are not human toes. They are the toes of a giant panda, what are they doing? When a boy and girl panda meet and decide they really like each other, the first thing they do is "hold toes." So we see the toes of TWO GIANT PANDAS—a boy and a girl. This is a cheerful, vivid, and memorable image!

There you have it. Another exercise in the use of the number alphabet. Let's repeat an earlier point. Our list of 10 peg words is the one we recommend, but there is nothing sacred about it. You should use it until you're comfortable with the system, but if any of the words give you a problem feel free to alter them as you like, or even make up your own list of peg words. Whatever is best for you is what you should do.

Moving Beyond Ten!

Now that you know how to form peg words for two-digit numbers (10 and higher), you can construct your own peg word list and can make it any length you choose.

Let's try a few numbers beyond 10. In Appendix B we'll give you a table of these numbers up to 100. And there are published lists that go up to 1,000 and probably higher. You might have fun creating your own list of the higher numbers, and it will get you well acquainted with the system.

Multiple Lists

The basic list we've shown you—hat, hen, ham, and so on—works very well, as you've already discovered if you've experimented with it. One problem is that, when you remember a new list with it, it's liable to drive the already-memorized list back further in your mind or out altogether. Tests have shown that people who use the system don't tend to get the lists mixed up, but they do tend to forget the earlier lists and replace them with new ones.

This is not a problem for grocery lists or the like. Why bother remembering a list of items you've already purchased? But sometimes there may be lists that you want to keep in memory indefinitely. You need the ability to create multiple lists.

Many people have addressed this problem, and a variety of ingenious solutions have been devised.

Refresh Your Memory

"The antagonistic attitude of experimental psychologists toward mnemonic devices is even more violent than their attitude toward their subject's word associations. Mnemonic devices are immoral tricks suitable only for Gypsies and stage magicians..."

—Karl Pribam (as quoted in *Memory's Ghost* by Philip J. Hilts)

Remember This!

What should you do if you don't know anything at all about a state and you can't even make up some sort of image of it? If you can't think of anything special about an Alaska hat (perhaps the giant earmuffs?), for example, you'd better not use that state to create a list. With no image, there is no peg for memory.

One solution is the state list. Simply add the name of a state to each key word. For our first list of items, we would use such pegs as Alabama hat, Alabama hen, Alabama ham, and so on. For our second list (this involves taking the states in alphabetical order), we would use Alaska hat, Alaska hen, and Alaska ham, and so on. From there, we would move on to Arkansas hat, Arkansas hen, Arkansas ham, and so on.

Another system involves multiple sets of peg words. This is more complicated and requires more memorization, but it has its uses. This is the *adjective plus peg word system*. To use it, you need to create a set of key adjectives to put in front of the number alphabet words you already know (which, you will notice, are all nouns). For example, you could use "hot," "cold," "big," "little," "young," "old," "skinny," and "fat."

You can create eight different lists using these adjectives. The first list would be:

1 = hot hat

2 = hot hen

3 = hot ham

4 = hot hair

5 = hot hole

6 = hot hash

7 = hot hook

8 = hot hoof

9 = hot hoop

10 = hot toes

The images created with this system are vastly different from each other. A "hot ham" is not easily confused with a "skinny ham," for example. The lists you memorize using these different pegs will not easily be confused, and memorizing a new list with a new adjective modifer should not cause you to forget an earlier list using a different adjective modifer.

There's a variant of the adjective system that we call the color-peg system. We're particularly proud of this one because we invented it ourselves. Although we've recently discovered that memory experts like our friend Max Maven have used systems like this for years, we're still pleased at having reinvented it for ourselves.

To use the color-peg system, simply take a list of familiar colors and arrange them in order. They could be in alphabetical order or in the order of the colors of the rainbow, or an order of your own devising. As long as you'll remember the order you use, it doesn't matter. We use the colors of the rainbow spectrum, remembering them with the acronym ROY G BIV:

Red Orange Yellow Green Blue Indigo Violet

To apply this color-peg system, you can imagine yourself wearing a set of tinted goggles and seeing everything in that color as you're constructing the list. Or you can leave the goggles off and just see all the objects on the list in that color.

For the first list, you would have a red hat, a red hen, a red ham, and so on. For the second list, you would have an orange hat, an orange hen, an orange ham, and so on.

You've probably noticed by now that we encourage you to modify our methods and to create others of your own. You have an imagination, and you have creative abilities. When you apply them, you might very well come up with something truly wonderful that no one else has ever thought of before. We invite you into the club!

Here's another reason for the encouragement: When you create a system, the very act of working it through, testing it, modifying it, and perfecting it will impress it in your mind. You'll remember it better, and you'll enjoy using it!

The Least You Need to Know

➤ The number alphabet can be used to memorize lists of any sort and just about any length.

➤ Our peg word list is a good one, but you should feel free to modify it if you can substitute words that will make stronger images for you.

➤ Our first 20 peg words are 1 = hat, 2 = hen, 3 = ham, 4 = hair, 5 = hole, 6 = hash, 7 = hook, 8 = hoof, 9 = hoop, 10 = toes, 11 = dad, 12 = den, 13 = dome, 14 = door, 15 = tail, 16 = dish, 17 = dike, 18 = dove, 19 = tape, 20 = nose.

➤ You should be able to memorize a test grocery list with little trouble.

➤ A list of random items might be even easier.

➤ For lists you want to keep in memory, you might want to use an adjective-plus–peg-word system.

Chapter 19

Every Good Boy Deserves Favor

In This Chapter

➤ Different ways to look at memory

➤ Mnemonic techniques for *using* memory

➤ "Thirty Days Hath September"

➤ Mnemonic techniques as abstractions

➤ Commonly used mnemonics

You might recognize the title of this chapter, in which case we'll ask you to bear with us while we talk about other things. If, on the other hand, "Every good boy deserves favor" is puzzling to you, hang in there. We'll explain it later in the chapter. But first, as they used to say in the golden age of radio, a word from our sponsor.

You've no doubt noticed that the first half of this book was loaded with theoretical information about your memory, what it is, and how it works. In reviewing the literature on the topic of memory, we've found a dazzling array of approaches to the subject. Some authors treat memory as an electrochemical process that takes place within the brain.

As science reporter George Johnson put it:

> "Included in the neuroanatomist's palette is a dye that stains for an enzyme, acetylcholinesterase, that is always present in the cholinergic neurons; it is the chemical the neuron uses to break down excessive amounts of the neurotransmitter. Using the dye, (Gary) Lynch believed he could make the new sprouted neural connections show up as a dark band on a microscope slide."

A prize-winning science reporter like George Johnson, in writing about researcher Gary Lynch, could describe Lynch's work and the functioning of memory in such terms. Johnson has written several brilliant books. Although an understanding of memory on this level may be vitally important to a medical researcher, it is of little use to an ordinary person seeking to improve his or her memory.

Similarly, neuroscientists like Russian psychiatrist Aleksandr Romanovich Luria treat memory in the context of brain anatomy:

"A person works with his right hand, it plays a dominant role in his life. Yet it is the opposite, the left, hemisphere that controls this hand and the faculty for speech, one of the most complex human activities ... Is it any wonder, then, that destruction of the 'tertiary' sectors of the cortex of the left hemisphere produces more serious consequences than those we have just described? A person with such an injury finds his inner world fragmented, he cannot think of a particular word he needs to express an idea; he finds complex grammatical relationships unbelievably difficult; he forgets how to add or use any of the skills he learned in school. Whatever knowledge he once had is broken down into discrete, unrelated bits of information. On the surface his life may appear no different but it has changed radically; owing to an injury on a small part of his brain, his world has become an endless series of mazes."

Words to Remember

Brain-mapping: Discovering by means of direct stimulation by electrodes and Magnetic Resonance Imaging (MRI) and other subtle means where the various aspects of personality and memory are located in the brain.

Luria began his career as a classical psychiatrist. However, he began to feel that traditional psychiatry, which explains the workings of the mind in terms of life experience, was flawed. Instead, he came to believe that the mind is strongly affected by chemical imbalances and other physical influences. He felt that the workings of the mind can be explained physiologically, and he became an advocate of this *brain-mapping* approach to memory.

Some scientists use the computer analogy, metaphorically transforming sense organs into input devices, working memory into RAM, long-term memory into disk drives, and so on. They liken memory to directories, subdirectories, and files. Attempts to recall information are likened to word searches.

Others prefer the more old-fashioned metaphor of the library. A person's memory is like a great storehouse of information. There are rooms; and within the rooms, sections; and within the sections, shelves; and on the shelves, books; and in the books, pages. You can narrow your search until you come to the single statement of fact you were looking for in the first place.

All of these approaches have historically been regarded as legitimate and even scientific. There's another approach to memory, however, that has had a harder road to respectability. This is the approach of the memory aids that fall under the general heading of *mnemonics*.

Remember to Remember

We've already introduced several mnemonic techniques. If you've been reading this book as an active participant and not as a passive observer, you've probably already learned some of them. Keep using them and keep applying them in your daily life. You'll get so good at remembering things that you'll amaze yourself even more than you amaze your friends.

This mnemonics-based approach to memory fits in with the *behaviorist* school of psychology.

Instant Recall

When Richard Lupoff, one of the authors of this book, developed a course about memory for the United States Army, he avoided the whole hardware/software/biological/ chemical/physiological controversy and concentrated on practical methods that would help his students remember what they needed to remember. This is the mnemonics approach.

Behaviorists eschew most theories and focus on observable phenomena. Taken to an extreme, this means they don't even like to talk about the "mind." The brain, yes. We have brains. We can look inside our skulls with x-rays or CAT scans and can *see* our brains. But you can't *see* a mind.

We don't go that far, however. We believe in things that function (such as our minds) even if we can't see them.

Mind Magic with Professor Mento!

For a very long time, mentalists and magicians—sometimes elegantly dressed in formal clothes, sometimes dressed as swamis or in other exotic costumes—have stood before amazed audiences, performing brilliant feats of memory. Dr. Luria's famous patient Shereshevsky earned a handsome living doing stage acts.

But while this kind of exhibition has served to bring mnemonics to the attention of the public, it also has given mnemonics a slightly shady reputation. You may have heard these lines yourself:

"Oh, it's just a stunt."

"There's some kind of trick to this."

"It has to be phony."

"They're in cahoots."

Some practitioners of mnemonics have added to the public's suspicion and the scientific community's wariness. People who write books with titles like *Never Forget Anything Again!* or who sell courses such as *Magical Miracle Mind Magic Memory* (we're only exaggerating a little) may make a very tidy living, but they don't add much to the respectability of our field.

The fact is, mnemonic techniques *work*! You've already learned how to memorize a list of 10 items quickly and reliably, how to recall the information easily, and how to retain it longer and more accurately than if you had used *rote learning*—the brute force method.

What's the Matter with Mnemonics?

Some teachers, psychologists, and others have objections to the teaching and practice of mnemonics. Some of these objections are quite valid. Others are offered in good faith and may sound quite plausible, but in fact turn out to be needless apprehensions. Let's take a look at these objections.

"It Isn't Less to Learn, It's More to Learn!"

There's no question that you have to learn a mnemonic device if it's going to be much use to you. If you just wanted to remember your shopping list, you could have memorized your shopping list. Why bother with all that hat-hen-ham business?

If you're using rote memory you have to start from scratch and learn every list as if it were the first. On the other hand, once you've learned the number alphabet, learned 1 = t = hat, 2 = n = hen, and so forth, you can apply it to any list. Your initial investment of time and effort in learning the method soon pays dividends that far outweigh the cost.

"Memorizing Isn't the Same as Understanding"

This is absolutely true. Suppose you want to remember the names of the five Great Lakes. You can learn them by a combination of association and simple rote as Richard, the dull Memory Brother, did many years ago: "Lake Michigan, yes, I went to the beach on Lake Michigan when I was visiting my sweetheart in Evanston, Illinois. Lake Huron, yep, I don't know why I remember that one, I just do. Oh, and Lake Erie, I remember Lake Erie from that time I went to a convention in Cleveland. Um, and Lake Superior. Right, Lake Superior. And, uh, oh darn it, I can always remember four of them but I forget the fifth!"

Or you can learn a simple *acronym* mnemonic as Michael, the clever Memory Brother, did—HOMES.

> Huron
>
> Ontario
>
> Michigan
>
> Erie
>
> Superior

It's important to note that learning HOMES is not a substitute for learning the names of the five lakes. You still have to learn them—you can't *remember* them if you don't *know* them—but if you use HOMES, you'll be able to call them to mind more quickly and more easily than if you rely on rote memory.

"But It's Just a Trick"

This one doesn't cut much kindling. Consider this: We all know there are 12 months in a year. (How do we know this? Bet you don't remember learning it. It's just something you picked up as a small child. It's part of your "fact memory" and not your "event memory.") We know there are long months with 31 days and short months with 30 days (except for February, which has 28—29 in leap years).

You're right. It's always those weird exceptions that get you.

How can you remember which months are long and which are short? There's an old rhyme you may have learned somewhere along the way. "Thirty days hath September, April, June, and November..."

Is learning this little poem just a trick? Would you be better off staring at a calendar for hours on end, memorizing the months and the number of days in each? Of course not! The "Thirty Days" rhyme is a perfectly good way to learn and retain this information.

If you don't especially like memorizing poems (some people do, some people don't—there's no accounting for taste), there's another little trick for remembering the lengths of the months.

Make a fist and run a finger of your opposite hand along the ridge of clenched knuckles. The first knuckle represents January. The knuckle is raised, representing a long month (31 days). Next comes a little valley. It represents February, a short month. Next is up again for March (long), "down in the valley" for April (short), and so on for May (long), June (short), and July (long).

Instant Recall

Thirty days have September,
April, June, and November.
All the rest have thirty-one
Except the second month alone
To which we twenty-eight assign
'Til leap year gives it twenty-nine.

Now comes the part you just have to *remember*. Don't start back across your hand. That will throw you off by one month. Instead, continue on to the other hand, or go back to the beginning on the same hand and start over with the first raised knuckle. That represents August (long). Now continue again through the process for September (short), October (long), November (short), and December (long).

Hey, believe us. It takes longer to explain this than it does to do it. Try it out and you'll see. Is this just a trick? Does it mean you don't really understand the months? Nonsense!

"It Only Works for Lists of Things"

This is not quite true. In one of our exercises in the preceding chapter, we included a song, "I Wanna Hold Your Hand," in our second key word example. Remember the girl twirling the hula hoop surrounded by singing Beatles? What was the number? Do you remember?

9 = **p** or **b** = hoop. The song was number 9, right.

Instant Recall

We'll say it again. *Whatever works best for you is the method you should use!* There's not one right way to do this!

There are many mnemonic devices and many *kinds* of mnemonic devices. Different techniques work better for different applications. Some techniques also work better for certain *people* than others. Some people are good at visual imaging; others do better with mathematical or verbal methods.

"But What About Abstractions?"

One leading academic memory expert, Dr. Kenneth Higbee, has devoted great effort to this problem and has come up with some excellent solutions. Our colleague Harry Lorayne also has done the same. Lorayne likes to talk about "visualizable equivalents."

What are Higbee and Lorayne (and others) talking about? It takes some imagination, ingenuity, and effort to make their approach work, but it can certainly be done. Let's take an example. Suppose we're in training to be actors and we want to memorize a list of emotions. Let's think of a few. How about the following:

1. Kindness
2. Love
3. Injustice
4. Anger
5. Grief
6. Relief

Let's try our old friend the number alphabet and see what we can come up with.

1 = hat. All right, we see an aid worker in a drought-stricken land distributing food to hungry children. The sun is beating down, and the worker is wearing a huge hat that shades both herself and the children (= Kindness).

2 = hen. Let's make this one silly. A cartoon hen is love-smitten, and we see her surrounded by bright red hearts (= Love).

3 = ham. A criminal is swinging a ham at the famous statue of Blind Justice, knocking her famous balancing scales right out of her hand (= Injustice).

4 = hair. Two angry children are rolling around on the floor screaming as they pull each other's hair (= Anger).

5 = hole. A poor, sad individual is sitting at the edge of a large black hole, staring into its depth, and thinking of throwing himself over the edge because he is so unhappy (= Grief).

6 = hash. There's the bowl of hash, but where is that bunch of bananas? Don't tell me my spouse has cut them up into the hash! Oh, thank goodness! They're on top of the refrigerator—the hash is still pure (= Relief).

There is a danger here of remembering the wrong word from the right image. Instead of "kindness," one might mistakenly think of "generosity." "Anger" might become "rage" or "violence." This system doesn't work quite as well with abstractions as it does with physical objects, but it can be made to work.

Some Favorite Acronyms

Here are some acronyms that have been used by students and others for centuries as memory aids.

Some Memorable Facts

If you ever took a music appreciation class in high school, you probably remember such mnemonic lyrical aides for identifying composers and their compositions as "Poppa Haydn's dead and gone, but his music lingers on" for recognizing Franz Haydn's "Surprise" symphony. Another one is "This is the symphony that Schubert wrote and never finished" for realizing that you are listening to Franz Schubert's B minor (the "unfinished") symphony.

Look at a piece of sheet music for the piano. You will see a staff of 10 lines.

The lines of the treble clef (the upper five lines with the symbol that looks like this: 𝄞) represent the notes (going up from the center) E, G, B, D, F. This has been taught to generations of music students with this acronym:

➤ Every Good Boy Deserves Favor

Or sometimes:

➤ Every Good Boy Does Fine

The spaces between the lines are also notes. They are (once again going up) F, A, C, E. As you've already noticed, they form their own acronym. Nothing additional needs to be devised.

Instant Recall

You might have noticed that some of the woodwinds are not made of wood. The flute, for example, often is made of silver. It used to be made of wood, however, and traditions die hard. Traditions, after all, are a sort of institutional memory.

The sections of the orchestra usually are considered to be *strings* (violins, violas, and the like), *woodwinds* (oboes, clarinets, flutes, etc.), *brass* (trombones, tubas, and so on), and *percussion* (drums, cymbals, and others). They tend to be arranged sort of front-to-back, although there is no hard and fast rule. You can remember them more easily if you reflect that in an orchestra:

➤ Saints Will Be Praised

The Rainbow

The colors of every rainbow are the same, made from the white light of the sun refracted (bent) by raindrops. From the inside out, they are: red, orange, yellow, green, blue, indigo, and violet. You can remember them with the aid of the following sentence:

➤ Richard Of York Gave Battle In Vain

The first letters of each color, with nothing else added, also make up the name Roy G Biv.

The Atmosphere

From nearest to the earth's surface to farthest out, the atmosphere has been divided into the *troposphere*, the *stratosphere*, the *mesosphere*, the *ionosphere*, and way out at the edge of space, the *exosphere*. If for some reason you want to memorize this, you first should say the names aloud to make them part of your memory. That should make it easy.

To remember their order, just say to yourself:

➤ That Should Make It Easy

The Solar System

The planets in our solar system, going outward from the sun, are Mercury, Venus, Earth, Mars, Jupiter, Saturn, Uranus, Neptune, and Pluto. Often included in this list are the asteroids, a swarm of miniature planetoids between the orbits of Mars and Jupiter that might be the remains of a planet that might have once occupied that orbit. To remember the planets' order, repeat the following to yourself:

➤ Man, Vain Ethereal Man, Almighty Jove Shall Use No Pity

If that's too mystical for you, try the following:

➤ Mother Very Early Made a Jelly Sandwich Using No Peanutbutter

Note that in our solar system "peanutbutter" is one word.

If the asteroids have no thrill for you, leave them out. Then you can just remember the following romantic phrase:

➤ Mary's Violet Eyes Make John Stay Up Nights Pacing

Instant Recall

To remember which way to set your clock for daylight saving time, just repeat to yourself "Spring forward, fall back."

Zoology

Zoologists like things to be put in order, and the order is very specific. First, every living thing is classified by kingdom, either Animalia (animals), Plantae (plants), Fungi, Monera, or Protista. The Animalia are what interest zoologists, and they are further subdivided by Phylum, Class, Order, Family, Group, and Species.

Humans, for example, are in the Phylum *Chordata*, subphylum *Vertebrata*, Class *Mammalia*, Order *Primates*, Family *Hominidae*, Genus, *Homo*, and Species *Homo Sapiens*. If you want to memorize the order of these categories: Kingdom, Phylum, Class, Order, Family, Group, and Species, you might try to remember the following:

➤ Kindly Put Clothes On For Goodness Sake

British Nobility

The order of precedence, and thus importance, of the British nobility is as follows: Duke, Marquis, Earl, Viscount, Baron, Baronet. To remember this, just ask yourself the following:

➤ Did Mary Ever Visit Brighton Beach?

The Resistor Code

Electrical resistors, which are usually small ceramic tubes with a wire at each end, are too tiny to have their ohm values (electrical resistance is measured in ohms) printed on them at a readable size. Instead, they have bands of color surrounding them, and each color represents a number as follows:

1 = black

2 = brown

3 = red

4 = orange

5 = yellow

6 = green

7 = blue

8 = violet

9 = gray

0 = white

A 1,200-ohm resistor, therefore, would have four bands of color reading, from the band closest to the end, black-brown-white-white. To remember this color code, an electrician might say to himself:

➤ Bad Boys Ruin Our Young Grass, But Violets Grow Wild

There also might be gold or silver bands to represent the tolerance—how close the resistor is guaranteed to come to the assigned value—but you're on your own for remembering that gold is 5 percent and silver is 10 percent.

Instant Recall

Sailors forecast the weather with this age-old verse:

Gray sky at night, Sailors' delight, Gray sky at morning, Sailors take warning.

Pi

The relationship between the circumference of a circle and the diameter is represented by the Greek letter π, known as *pi* (pronounced "pie"). It also shows up in all sorts of scientific formulas that don't seem to have anything to do with circles, and it's a generally all-around useful number. Unfortunately, it's an "irrational" number, which means it's a fraction that keeps going without ending. Scientists and mathematicians like to memorize it to six decimal places, and that's enough accuracy for most uses. Some people who like to show off have memorized it to one or two hundred places. A good in-between, semi-show-off position is to memorize pi to 20 decimal places (3.14159265358979323846). To learn this, just memorize the following poem. The number of letters in each word is the digit for π at that place:

Pie: I wish I could determine pi
Eureka cried the great inventor
Christmas pudding Christmas pie
is the problem's very center

Cranial Nerves

Medical students have worked out many mnemonics for remembering the names of the various bones, nerves, muscle groups, and so on that they have to know. One example is the 11 nerves of the brain, known collectively as the cranial nerves. They are: optic, oculomotor, trochlear, trigeminal, abducens, facial, auditory, glossopharyngeal, vagus, accessory, and hypoglossal. After learning the names, medical students often use the following mnemonic as a refresher:

➤ On Old Olympia's Towering Top A Finn And German Vault And Hop

Onward!

As you can see, mnemonic systems have been used from music to medicine and at most points between. The next few chapters will show you some specialized uses for memory systems, and you will learn how to adapt them for your own special needs.

The Least You Need to Know

➤ Some researchers see the brain as an electrochemical device; others analogize it to a computer or to a library.

➤ Mnemonic systems work regardless of how you think of the brain using them.

➤ Some psychologists see mnemonics as just a trick. Our response is, "We don't think so, but if it is and if it works, so what?"

➤ With a little work, mnemonics can be used to remember abstractions.

➤ Mnemonics can be used in the fields of music, science, medicine, and many others. This chapter shows you some of the ways various mnemonic techniques are used.

Part 5

Using Memory to Improve Your Skills

Few people like numbers, but we all have to work with them. This section shows you some interesting facts about numbers, including how different civilizations used to count and the importance of zero. And for those of you who think the three numbers after 10 are Jack, Queen, and King, we'll show you how to remember all the cards played in your favorite card game. We'll then go from cards to the events of your day, and we'll talk about how to use your memory as a mental "to do" list for all the errands and chores you have to perform. It's still better to write them down; this not only gives you something to consult, but the very act of writing them helps you remember them. You'll also learn how to cope with the greatest fear of all—no, not the fear that you're losing your hair—the fear of public speaking. We'll then get into the Loci System, which is 2,500 years old and still one of the best. How many of us can say that? Finally, we finish off this very busy section with a chapter about how your new memory skills can help you get a job and can improve your performance while you're on the job.

Chapter 20

Something About Numbers

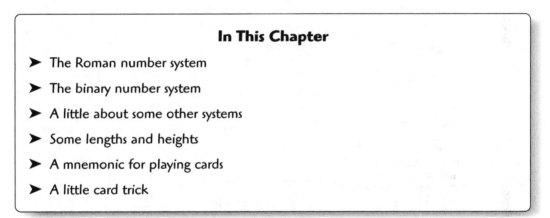

In This Chapter

➤ The Roman number system

➤ The binary number system

➤ A little about some other systems

➤ Some lengths and heights

➤ A mnemonic for playing cards

➤ A little card trick

Nobody knows who invented numbers. The idea probably was developed independently many times. Early peoples, we imagine, must have found practical value in counting, at least. Long before anyone thought of the concepts of "one," "two," and so forth, they must have wanted to keep track of how many ears of corn they had on hand and how many members of the family or the tribe were present to share them.

If there were as many ears of corn as there were people, everything was fine. If there were a couple of extra ears of corn, there might have been a problem about who would get them or how they would be divided. If they were one ear of corn short, there was real trouble. Would somebody get left out? Would Little Mug and Little Zug have to share? Would everybody chip in just a tiny bit to make up for the missing ear of corn?

So Who's Counting Anyway?

People who like to theorize about such things generally figure that our remote ancestors began by matching their fingers to actual objects. If there were as many members of the family as fingers on one hand, the person in charge of dinner could see to it that there was an ear of corn for each family member. No extras to fight over, no shortages to cause conflict.

It was an obvious step from keeping track on one's fingers to making scratch marks on the ground or the wall to represent the amount (not yet a number) that was meant. You could even add or subtract without having any concept of numbers (or of addition or subtraction) by scratching another mark on the ground or by rubbing out a mark.

Each scratch mark represented "one," of course, and its absence represented "zero," even if our ancestors didn't have these concepts yet. They didn't know it, but they were using a kind of primitive *binary system*.

Still, things got cumbersome when there were too many scratches. The next step (probably) was the devising of symbols to represent groups of scratches. We still use this technique, by the way. We're not so far beyond great-great-great-grandmother Ug and her husband, great-great-great-grandfather Gug. If you doubt this, think of the common counting method that involves marking simple vertical lines side by side to represent one, two, three, and four.

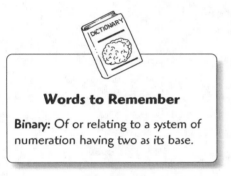

Words to Remember

Binary: Of or relating to a system of numeration having two as its base.

What comes next to represent five? Not another vertical line but a diagonal across the first four lines. That symbol might not look very important, but it *is* very important. It's a higher digit.

Different people over the ages developed different numbering systems. The one we're most familiar with is often called "Arabic" because the crude and superstitious medieval Europeans learned it from the cultured and civilized Arabs, who in turn had learned it from the sophisticated ancient civilizations of India. This system involves our familiar numbers 1, 2, 3, 4, 5, 6, 7, 8, and 9—plus 0 (or zero), the representation for a vacant position. This made positional notation possible, but we'll tell you all about that a little later.

Several hundred years later, when Europeans visited the Americas, they discovered that the Mayans had been ahead of them, too. They also had the zero. Bright folks!

Zero made math a whole lot easier. Before the Arabs taught the Europeans their system, the Europeans were still using the Roman system. That system, for all the ingenuity and brilliance of ancient Rome, is a nightmare for math.

Some Memorable Facts

No one knows why we are pentadigital (that is, why we have five fingers on each hand and five toes on each foot). Evolutionary scientists like to find a good reason for every aspect of our makeup, but there is no apparent benefit in having five fingers rather than, say, four or six. If we had four fingers on each hand we probably would use an octal (eight-base) numbering system. If we had six fingers on each hand we'd probably use a duodecimal (12-base) system.

A Quick Visit to Ancient Rome

Remember the Roman system? They would count, I, II, III, IV, V, VI, VII, VIII, IX, X. What the heck is that? One, two, and three are pretty obvious. Heck, even dear old Ug and her hubby Gug would nod their understanding.

Let's skip to V. A-ha! That's the Roman numeral for five, and it may come from the shape of an upright hand with all the fingers spread. Hmm, and the three middle ones left out. Well, it's just a guess.

By putting a I before the V, the Romans indicated "I less than V," or IV (four). By putting a I after the V, they indicated "V plus I," or VI (six). In this system, which as we're sure you've noticed is still used for dates when the user wants them to seem important, X is 10, L is 50, C is 100, D is 500, and M is 1,000.

To this day, "C-note" is gangster slang for a $100 bill. "C for century" is 100 years, while "M for millennium" is 1,000 years.

This system is really tough for addition and subtraction. If you want a complete nightmare, try multiplying MDCXXXIII by CXIV or dividing DCCIX by XXIV. Call us when you have the answers.

Instant Recall

It took the Romans a while to use IV for four. Originally four was IIII. Sometimes on the cornerstones of buildings, the date of construction is given in the older Roman form. So a building erected in, say, 1944 wouldn't have MCMXLIV on the cornerstone but MDCCCCXXXXIIII. It must have been hell remembering people's birthdays.

The Romans didn't try to multiply or divide using Roman numbers, but devised an instrument made up of a square wooden board with grooves cut in it and small round pebbles for markers. Its use greatly resembled what we think of as an abacus, although the pebbles were not on strings. As a matter of fact, the word "abacus" is Latin for "square board."

Some Memorable Facts

"Doc Savage had done one thing daily since childhood. He had devoted a two–hour period to exercise. Not merely a flexing and strengthening of the muscles, but a scientific system of actions designed to strengthen eyes, olfactory senses, vision, hearing, and the others. Perhaps the most unusual, and no doubt the more important, was the set of mental exercises which quickened his wits, strengthened his memory, and otherwise had equipped him with the amazing physical and mental powers he possessed ... The amazing brain took up an involved calculus, mental mathematics requiring the extreme of deductive analysis."

—Lester Dent (writing as Kenneth Robeson)

Other Number Systems

The Babylonians seemed very fond of the number 60, and their influence persists in our 60-minute hour and 60-second minute. The number 60 also worked very nicely into another terrific number, 360 (6 times 60). This is approximately the number of days in a year and was used in some primitive calendars (until calendars became more accurate). We still divide a circle into 360 degrees, each degree into 60 minutes, and each minute into 60 seconds.

The number 360 is wonderful because it is evenly divisible by so many smaller numbers. You can divide 360 evenly (or "rationally," as mathematicians like to say) by 1, 2, 3, 4, 5, 6, 8, 9, 10, 12, 15, 18, 20, 24, 30, 36, 40, 45, 60, 90, 120, and 180. Did we leave any out?

Don't think so.

Refresh Your Memory

"There are three types of people in this world ... those who can do math and those who can't."

—Art and Chip Sansom

Our familiar 10-base system (called the *decimal* system) is probably the result of our ancestors counting on their fingers. We understand that some peoples use a 20-base system, probably based on fingers and toes.

Obviously, this wouldn't work in too cold a climate in which shoes are necessary to protect the feet.

Some people want us to adopt a 12-base system, known as *duodecimal*. Other symbols would be substituted for 10 and 11; the "one-zero" number would be worth not 10 but 12. There's even a Duodecimal Society of America dedicated to the promotion of this system!

Some Memorable Facts

Octopuses, dolphins, and elephants are all pretty clever creatures. In fact, we don't know exactly how smart. If they were smart enough to do mathematics, the octopuses would probably use an octal (eight-base) numbering system because they have eight tentacles—their equivalent of fingers or hands. Dolphins, by contrast, use their snouts to manipulate objects. Elephants use their trunks for the same purpose. This suggests that their math (if any) might be based on a single digit. On or off, yes or no. In effect, they might use binary.

ENIAC and All That Again

In the twentieth century, with the development of the electronic computer, a new technology came on the scene that depended on vacuum tubes turning a current flow on and off. Poor old ENIAC, the early computer we talked about in Chapter 4, "Even Educated PCs Do It," didn't "know" any other "numbers." Just on and off. And even though we've now moved several generations beyond vacuum tubes, the basic concept of on and off is still the way our computers work.

If you have a single position, it can be worth either "1" (on) or "0" (off). That's great if you're only interested in one or zero, but how do you represent 2?

A-ha! Now we come to positional notation. Don't let the term scare you. In our ordinary decimal math, we can count up to nine with one digit. We then go back to zero, but we "carry the 1" to the next position to the left. In that position, the number is worth 10 times as

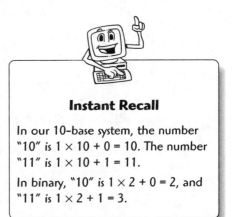

Instant Recall

In our 10-base system, the number "10" is $1 \times 10 + 0 = 10$. The number "11" is $1 \times 10 + 1 = 11$.

In binary, "10" is $1 \times 2 + 0 = 2$, and "11" is $1 \times 2 + 1 = 3$.

much, and we continue merrily along, counting 11, 12, and so on. This is what positional notation is all about. You do it all the time.

In binary, you do the same thing. You just add another position (to the left of the first) and "carry the 1." In that position, on means 2 and off means 0. To represent 3, you just turn the 2 position on *and* turn the 1 position on, and you get something that looks like "11" but really means "three." Each step to the left makes a number worth two times as much (in binary) instead of 10 times as much (as in decimal).

It goes on like this, but we're not going to lecture you about number theory. That's a subject for another book. We will mention, however, that there are other computer numbering systems. One is called *binary-coded decimal* (BCD). Another is known as *hexadecimal* or *hex* and is a 16-base system. The digits are 1 through 9 plus A, B, C, D, E, and F (and of course 0). The number that looks like "11" actually means 17. We'll show you what we mean about the hexadecimal system with a comparison list.

Decimal	Hexadecimal	Decimal	Hexadecimal
1	1	17	11
2	2	18	12
3	3	19	13
4	4	20	14
5	5	21	15
6	6	22	16
7	7	23	17
8	8	24	18
9	9	25	19
10	A	26	1A
11	B	27	1B
12	C	28	1C
13	D	29	1D
14	E	30	1E
15	F	31	1F
16	10	32	20

Back to Good Old Decimal

We're not going to drone on any more about different numbering systems. If you want to investigate them, however, or if you are of a mathematical turn of mind, there are many wonderful books on the subject.

The brief sketch we've given you is just designed to familiarize you with the idea that there are many ways of counting. Our familiar one is only one of the many!

For the rest of our little games, tricks, and demonstrations, we'll stick to the system you know best—the good ol' decimal system.

Name	Finger-Matching	Roman	Decimal	Binary
one	1	I	1	1
two	11	II	2	10
three	111	III	3	11
four	1111	IV	4	100
five	11111	V	5	101
six	11111 1	VI	6	110
seven	11111 11	VII	7	111
eight	11111 111	VIII	8	1000
nine	11111 1111	IX	9	1001
ten	11111 11111	X	10	1010
eleven	11111 11111 1	XI	11	1011
twelve	11111 11111 11	XII	12	1100
thirteen	11111 11111 111	XIII	13	1101
fourteen	11111 11111 1111	XIV	14	1110
fifteen	11111 11111 11111	XV	15	1111
sixteen	11111 11111 11111 1	XVI	16	10000
seventeen	11111 11111 11111 11	XVII	17	10001
eighteen	11111 11111 11111 111	XVIII	18	10010
nineteen	11111 11111 11111 1111	XIX	19	10011
twenty	11111 11111 11111 11111	XX	20	10100

Some Lengths and Heights

Way back in 1896, Professor A. Loisette wrote a book called *Assimilative Memory*, in which he formulates a number alphabet much like the one we've taught you in the last couple of chapters. In his book, he gives some phrases for remembering the lengths of great rivers and the heights of great mountains. In his system, the first voiced consonant in each word is the one that counts. Great Jumping Frog Contest, for example, would be merely 7687 instead of 741639284772101. The following sections contain some of his phrases.

Rivers

Mississippi—4,382 miles long—*R*ushing *M*ississippi's Wa*V*es E*N*croach

Nile—3,370 miles long—*M*ighty *M*editerranean's *G*reatest *S*tream

Volga—2,400 miles long—I*N* *R*ussia's *S*oil *S*uperior

Mountains

Popocatapetl—17,783 feet—*T*he *G*reatest *C*rater *OF* Mexico

Mt. Brown—16,000 feet—*T*his *CH*arming *W*estern *S*cenery *C*elebrated

Mt. Blanc—15,781 feet—*T*his *AL*pine *C*one *F*ascinates *T*ravelers

Note that Professor Loisette used "th" for 1, in addition to "t" and "d." Some number alphabet experts advocate this, but most find it too confusing. Also note the use of the "C" in "Celebrated" as an "s" because it is *sounded* like an "s."

The first-consonant-in-the-word system seems to be very useful for creating phrases to memorize long numbers. It is worth keeping in mind.

It's in the Cards

There are many card games in which it's useful to be able to remember what cards have been played. In some games, it's just necessary to remember the value of the cards—have all the threes been played? In others, it helps to remember the suit as well.

We've Got a System

Here's a mnemonic system based on the classic number alphabet (1 = t or d, 2 = n, and so on). Each card is represented by a word. To make things easy and logical, all the words for Spades start with the letter "s," the Hearts start with "h," the Clubs with "c," and the Diamonds with "d." The nine of Spades, for example, is coded as the word "soap" (S for Spade and P for nine). The face cards are treated as numbers: Jack = 11, Queen = 12, King = 13.

Here's the list:

	Spades	Hearts	Clubs	Diamonds
1	Suit	Hide	Coat	Dodo
2	Sun	Honey	Cone	Dawn
3	Seam	Home	Comb	Dam
4	Sore	Hero	Crow	Deer
5	Sail	Hail	Coal	Dial
6	Sash	Hash	Cash	Douche
7	Sock	Hook	Cook	Duck
8	Safe	Hoof	Calf	Dove
9	Soap	Hoop	Cop	Dope
10	Seeds	Hothouse	Cats	Dots
11	Statue	Hot tea	Cadet	Deadhead
12	Stone	Hoedown	Cotton	Dead hen
13	Steam	High dome	King	Daytime

Some of these words are not wonderful, but they're the best that could be devised in the system—and sticking to the system is important. Many of the words for Hearts duplicate words in your regular number alphabet, but that shouldn't present a problem since the uses won't overlap. Note that the key word for the King of Clubs is "King." This doesn't exactly fit with the system, but you won't forget it.

Let's see how this works. We'll randomly deal 20 cards and work at remembering them. (Honest, that's what we're doing at this very instant.) We get:

1. The Jack of Clubs
2. The 10 of Spades
3. The 2 of Diamonds
4. The 6 of Spades
5. The 10 of Diamonds
6. The 10 of Hearts
7. The Queen of Hearts
8. The 10 of Clubs
9. The Ace of Spades
10. The Queen of Spades
11. The 5 of Hearts
12. The 3 of Hearts
13. The 5 of Diamonds
14. The Queen of Clubs
15. The 3 of Diamonds
16. The 8 of Hearts
17. The 2 of Spades
18. The Ace of Hearts
19. The 3 of Clubs
20. The Queen of Diamonds

Now, what are our key words? We're sure you've memorized them already, but here they are again just in case:

1. The Jack of Clubs = Cadet
2. The 10 of Spades = Seeds
3. The 2 of Diamonds = Dawn
4. The 6 of Spades = Sash
5. The 10 of Diamonds = Dots

6. The 10 of Hearts = Hothouse
7. The Queen of Hearts = Hoedown
8. The 10 of Clubs = Cats
9. The Ace of Spades = Suit
10. The Queen of Spades = Stone
11. The 5 of Hearts = Hail
12. The 3 of Hearts = Home
13. The 5 of Diamonds = Dial
14. The Queen of Clubs = Cotton
15. The 3 of Diamonds = Dam
16. The 8 of Hearts = Hoof
17. The 2 of Spades = Sun
18. The Ace of Hearts = Hide
19. The 3 of Clubs = Comb
20. The Queen of Diamonds = Dead hen

Hat, Hen, Ham...

We can remember these key words with the numeric alphabet, using good old hat, hen, ham, hair, and so on. Therefore:

1. Our hat is a kapo, one of those tall, military ones worn by a CADET.
2. The hen is pecking at the ground, eating SEEDS.
3. A giant ham is rising over the Atlantic; it is DAWN.
4. Our hair is all tangled up in the window SASH, and we can't open the window.

For most card games, however, this would be unnecessary overkill. It is enough to construct a continuous story, adding each card as it appears.

The Story Line

Our story here might be:

The cadet is marching along (doing what?)—eating seeds.—(when?)—It's dawn—and his fancy sash—is full of sparkling dots. (Where is he?)—He is passing a hothouse (what's happening?)—where they're having a hoedown—of dancing cats—that are all wearing suits.—My gosh, the suits are made of stone. (Stone = hailstone = hail)—The hail threatens to crack the hothouse glass—so they run home—and dial the weather bureau—with their cotton telephone.—The dam (above the house) is cracking—and a great hoof is sticking out of the crack— illuminated by the bright sun.—There's nowhere to hide—so they take their comb—and start combing a dead hen...

As we've tried to indicate with the dashes between ideas in this story, this must be done as a sort of stream-of-consciousness creation. After all, you can't slow down the card game to memorize the cards. With a little practice, however, the stream will come up with images that will stick with you.

Usually the peg words are used as nouns, but when the image works (as in "there's nowhere to hide"), conversion to a verb is quite acceptable.

We've indicated in parentheses some of the thoughts that might help you make the connections.

The Whole Deck

There's a memory stunt you might like to try, but make sure you practice before doing it for your friends. You just need to have someone shuffle a standard deck of cards and then remove several cards from the deck. You then go through the remaining deck and identify the missing cards.

To do the trick, you don't build a memory chain story as you do for card games. You just slowly go through the cards and associate each card you see in some way with yourself. If it's the 6 of Hearts, for example, you mentally stuff some *hash* in your mouth. If it's the 9 of Spades, you *soap* up your face. If it's the 8 of Clubs, you're riding a *calf*.

Instant Recall

Magicians do tricks similar to this in many ways, but in a sense you are not really doing a trick because no trickery is involved. You really have memorized the deck! This means you can do it with any deck, any time, any place.

When you've gone through the pack, close it up and mentally inspect your memorized card codes, running down the list one at a time: suit, sun, seam, sore, and so on. Whenever you reach a word that has no association with it, it's a card you didn't see in the pack. That means it's one of the cards that was taken.

You can design the presentation of this trick to suit your own sensibilities about doing card tricks, but one possibility is to have several people pick cards. The more people, the harder the trick looks—but it's no harder for you. If anything, it's a little easier. This slows down the process and give you more time to prepare. You stand there slowly going through the remaining deck until you finally close the deck and say (for example), "The missing cards are the 3 of Hearts ... the 10 of Diamonds ... the 6 of Clubs ... and the 8 of Hearts!"

At this moment, each of the people who took a card will reveal that he or she is indeed holding the 3 of Hearts, and so on.

To make it even more dramatic, you could have everyone who picked a card stand up and then sit down when they hear their card called.

To speed things up—and not bore your audience—you might want to remove the picture cards or possibly the twos, threes, and fours.

You can devise many variations of greater or lesser complexity to practice your memorization and to amuse your friends.

The Least You Need to Know

➤ Early numbering systems were not very efficient for addition, subtraction, and other sorts of number manipulation.

➤ The Roman system (I = 1, V = 5, X = 10, L = 50, C = 100, D = 500, M = 1,000) looks good on the facades of buildings, but it's sheer torture when doing math.

➤ The 10-base system, which uses Arabic numerals, manipulates numbers efficiently and easily.

➤ Many other systems, such as the binary system (based on 2) and the hexadecimal system (based on 16), have specialized uses. The binary system, for example, is what computers use to crunch numbers.

➤ Professor Loisette's first-voiced-consonant-in-the-word mnemonic system is useful for medium-length numbers such as the height of mountains in feet or the length of rivers in miles.

➤ An adaptation of the number alphabet is designed for memorizing a deck of cards, which can be useful in card games or for card tricks.

Chapter 21

Puppy Biscuit

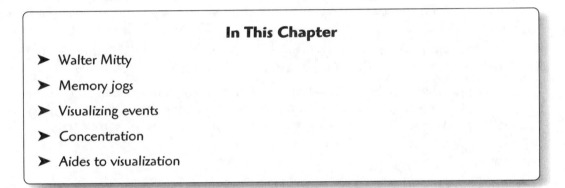

In This Chapter

➤ Walter Mitty

➤ Memory jogs

➤ Visualizing events

➤ Concentration

➤ Aides to visualization

In his short story "The Secret Life of Walter Mitty," James Thurber tells of Mitty walking down the street immersed in a daydream. In the daydream, Mitty, the hero, is on the witness stand in a murder trial when:

> "...A woman's scream rose above the bedlam and suddenly a lovely, dark-haired girl was in Walter Mitty's arms. The District Attorney struck at her savagely. Without rising from his chair, Mitty let the man have it on the point of the chin. 'You miserable cur!'"

Mitty snaps out of his dream. "Puppy biscuit!" he says aloud. Mitty's subconscious has jogged his memory.

This method worked for Mitty, albeit inadvertently, but it is not a system of recall we can recommend unless you do a lot of daydreaming. Even then, it may only work if you've forgotten the puppy biscuit. What daydream would remind you to get the orange juice or the pork chops, we don't know.

Dreams, day or night, may be full of inner significance, but they can't be depended on to help you remember the puppy biscuit. Remembering one item—something to do, buy, fix, or whatever—is in some ways harder than remembering a list of items. When you go to the grocery store, you know you're there to buy groceries. Your presence in the store prompts you to recall the list.

But what prompts you to go to the store?

Honey, I Forgot the Tickets

There you are, you've just arrived at the opera, you classical music lover you. You and your spouse are looking forward to a wonderful evening seeing *The Barber of Seville*, particularly hearing that acclaimed new baritone playing Figaro. How does that aria in the first act go? "Figaro si, Figaro sa, Figaro chi, Figaro..." Well, now—where did you put those tickets?

You frantically search through one pocket after another and reluctantly come to the horrible realization that you forgot them. Your spouse has a few choice words to say.

As you race home to get the tickets, which you now remember you left on the dining room table, you hope you get to see at least the last half of the opera. You also try to figure out why all the wonderful new mnemonic systems you've learned didn't prevent you from forgetting the tickets.

Simple.

You didn't use them. It never occurred to you that you might forget the tickets—after all, you left them in plain sight on the dining room table—so you didn't tie them in with a peg word or make them part of a list. The only thing you were doing this evening was going to the opera, so what good is a single-item list?

What could you have done?

Placing One Thing with Another

We have a friend, we'll call him Tom, who is a professional magician. He is always rushing off from his Los Angeles home to fly to Houston for a club date, to Seattle to host a corporate dinner, to Rio to catch a cruise ship, or hither and yon around the world. Each of these trips requires a different list of items he has to take with him. Forgetting any one of the items—his tickets, his passport, his list of contacts, the information packet from the cruise line, the various items needed for the stage or close-up act he is going to perform—could turn a pleasurable and profitable trip into a logistical nightmare.

What does he do?

The day before he has to leave, Tom begins making a pile of whatever he has to take with him on a table by the front door. The items themselves form the memory prompt for him not to forget them. When there are only one or two things to remember, say the tickets to a play he is going to see that evening or the written directions to a local job, he may place them on the floor in front of the door so he has to walk over them to leave.

The String Method

If there's something you have to remind yourself to do the next morning—such as finding some paperwork before you leave for the office, picking up the dry cleaning, or calling someone on the phone—you need to create a physical reminder that something needs to be done. You will probably recall whatever you must do when you spot the reminder.

If there are a number of things to be done, you can remember the list using the number alphabet system (stuff papers in a hat, hang the dry cleaning over a hen, telephone using a ham as the handset). The physical reminder will key in the memorized list, and you're off to a great start. But how do you jog the memory that reminds you there is something to remember?

There are several time-honored memory jogs. Tying a string around your finger is a recognized classic, as is turning a ring around so the stone faces inward or putting your wristwatch on the wrong wrist. All of these can work, but the flaw in them is that you might forget they're there. You'll be washing your hands after you get home from work, and you'll notice the string tied around your finger. "Oh my!" you'll say (or perhaps something stronger). "I was supposed to pick up the dry cleaning. Goodness but my spouse will be peeved."

Another potential problem with the "tie a string" system is that the string may remind you that you were supposed to do *something*—but you can't remember what it was!

Remember This!

Make sure you're actually going to see your prompt in the morning. Tying a knot in a random sock that isn't one of the pair you're going to wear won't help. You'll end up with many knots in your socks and lots of unclaimed dry cleaning.

The Knot Method

A better idea is to create a memory jog that works at the proper time. If there's something you want to remember to do in the morning, tie a knot in one of your socks the night before as you visualize picking up the dry cleaning. As you untie it, the words "pick up the dry cleaning" (or whatever) will come to you.

An even stronger method is to take the dry cleaning receipt and tape it to the inside of your front door at eye level.

The Visualization Method

Instant Recall

The imaging technique Shereshevsky used is his own "self-invented" version of a classical method called the Loci System. We'll tell you all about it in Chapter 23, "Foci on the Loci."

Remember Dr. Luria's friend Shereshevsky (from Chapter 13, "Very Special Memories"), the man with the amazing memory? One of Shereshevsky's techniques (and he was far from the only person to use it!) was something called *imaging* or *touring*. Wanting to remember a list of items, Shereshevsky would take an imaginary stroll through the village where he grew up.

He knew the village intimately and could re-create in his mind not only the locations but the physical descriptions of the tailor's shop, the grocery store, the elementary school, the Russian Orthodox church, the Jewish synagogue, the public square, and so on. He had a favorite route through the village, and he would review this route in his mind, placing each item he wished to remember in a prominent spot along the route.

When he wished to recall the list, he would mentally retrace his steps through the village. Ah, what's that in the window of the tailor's shop? Oh yes, a ball of yarn. And there in the doorway of the schoolhouse is the Tolstoy novel.

The visualization method of remembering things to do works something like Shereshevsky's imaging, but it isn't quite the same. Here's how it works. Let's say you want to:

➤ Pick up your friend Pete on the way to work

➤ Buy a bouquet for Mabel because it's her birthday

➤ Meet Harry and Gladys at La Cornucopie for lunch

➤ Drop Pete off on your way home from work

➤ Pick up a pepperoni and mushroom pizza for dinner

There are a number of ways to remember to do these things, including using the number alphabet method. How would that work? Well, imagine yourself in a strong-man suit lifting Pete above your head while he waves a Mexican sombrero to the crowd. Then imagine a hen holding a beautiful bouquet of flowers and giving them to a startled and delighted Mabel.

If you don't want to keep consulting a mental list all day, the visualization method is a better idea. Instead of hat-hen-ham, you can develop the following pictures in your mind as you foresee yourself making your way through the day:

➤ Mentally visualize yourself driving to work. You already know the route you'll take. At the point where you'll pull over to the curb and pick up Pete or alter your course to go to wherever Pete is waiting, see yourself doing just that. Make this a powerful mental image. Pick a landmark you can't help seeing as you reach the location and think about picking up Pete as you mentally stare at it. Add sound and kinetic sensation to your image. When you actually reach that location and reality matches anticipation, the act of picking up Pete will click into place.

➤ The next scene in your mental movie will be stopping at the florist's stand in the lobby of your office building. You already are friends with the florist, and you see and hear yourself saying to him, "Jim, it's Mabel's birthday. I want a lovely bouquet for her. What do you recommend?" In a little while, when you walk through the lobby and see the florist's stand, you'll remember this scene from your visualization.

➤ We know you're going to do your morning's work, so the next scene in your mental movie will feature you getting ready for lunch. As you picture doing some rote action you always do right before lunch—closing your desk drawer, getting your jacket, taking off your red fright wig and putty nose, or whatever—continue the image and imagine walking into La Cornucopie. You see Harry and Gladys seated at a table. They wave to you. You cross the restaurant and join them. When lunch time actually rolls around and you screen your mental movie, you'll see yourself joining Harry and Gladys.

Instant Recall

Don't forget the simplest, and one of the most powerful, methods of memory recall—write it down! Keep a pocket date book, write all your appointments in it, and check the book every morning. You'll seldom forget an appointment. And the process of writing the information down actually helps you memorize it.

Instant Recall

If the florist is not so conveniently located, you'll have to visit him during the day. Imagine a bouquet of flowers hanging over the door-knob of your office door as you enter. Every time you look at the door, you'll be reminded of the florist until you actually go get the flowers.

Instant Recall

Remember, if you're using the visual-ization method, you'll want to link it to anticipated events, locations, moments, and sensory impressions that will bring you up with a jolt. Ah, the little antique shop on the corner! That's where Pete always waits for me! When you see the antique shop, it should remind you of Pete. The same is true with the florist, the restaurant, and the pizza. Tie in the visualization of the event with some-thing you know you're going to do to key in the memory.

➤ Don't forget to include a scene in which you drop Pete off on your way home from work. You'll use the same technique, seeing yourself meet Pete on the way out of the office. At the end of your work day, you'll rerun your mental movie, see yourself meeting Pete at the exit, and make sure you match the reality to the visualization.

➤ Oh, that pizza! Imagine the joy when you get home tonight carrying that big cardboard box full of steaming, delicious pizza. What kind was it going to be? Oh yeah, pepperoni and mushroom! This is the happy climax of your mental movie. After you drop off Pete at his home, you'll rerun the movie and remember to pick up the pizza. What a hero you'll be!

But as the old farmer said, "If you want to make sure your jeans don't fall down, you better wear a belt and suspenders."

Build certain checkpoints into your day, specific moments or situations in which you pause and review your mental movie of the day's plans. This will help you remind yourself of the things you intended to do.

Taking Clues from Nature

Just the other day a friend of ours, let's call him Orville, left his home to attend a business meeting. He knew it was going to be pretty informal, so he didn't make any great fuss. He knew he'd want to make notes, however, so he grabbed his favorite clipboard as he was leaving the house.

No sooner had Orville stepped onto the porch than he realized it was raining hard, so he retreated into the house and picked up an umbrella.

He attended the meeting, which wound up taking all day. It took place at an associate's office where he felt comfortable and relaxed. At the end of the session, he shook hands all around, left the building, and went home.

Halfway home, Orville realized he'd left his clipboard behind.

As he walked up the steps of his home, he realized he'd also left his umbrella behind. Orville likes to claim that he's an expert on the subject of memory and that he has an excellent memory himself, so he was pretty embarrassed. But every experience is a potential lesson, and he took the time to analyze the lapse in memory. What had happened was this:

When Orville was preparing to leave his house, he knew he was headed for an important meeting. He looked forward to the event, and he imagined himself seated at a table and jotting notes as the meeting progressed. Perhaps consciously, perhaps otherwise, he visualized himself using the clipboard.

Thus, when he left the house, the clipboard was part of his image of his day, and he had no problem remembering to bring it with him. He didn't think about the umbrella, but as soon as he stepped outside and saw the rain falling, he realized he'd need one and stepped back into the house to get it.

By the end of the day, Orville was physically and mentally fatigued. All he could think about was the comfort of his home, the enjoyment of his dinner, and the companionship of his family. The clipboard was the farthest thing from his mind, so he forgot all about it.

Further, the rain had stopped. A pleasant, warm breeze was in the air when Orville left the meeting and headed for home. The sky was clear, the air and the streets were dry, and there was nothing to make him think of rain—or of his umbrella. So he didn't take it with him.

No harm was done, save for a little embarrassment, but Orville wondered what he might do to avoid a repetition. He knew he couldn't count on rain every morning and every evening to remind him to take his umbrella. He might want to create a mental checklist and run through it each morning as he left his house, the way aviators run through checklists prior to every flight. Clipboard, briefcase, notebook, umbrella...

He then could run through the same checklist at the end of each business day before heading home. After all, Orville was lucky. There were no confidential notes on his clipboard, and he left it at an associate's office where he was able to retrieve it the next day. If he'd been carrying the Naval Treaty and left it behind, an empire might have fallen!

It doesn't hurt to keep visual clues for the checklist in a place where you know you'll see them at the crucial moment. It wouldn't make sense for Orville to leave his umbrella in the upstairs bathroom where he would see it every morning as he shaved. He'd probably forget about it again by the time he went downstairs to leave the house.

But if he kept it by the front door, he'd have to see it as he was leaving the house. Better yet, he might keep his car keys and his umbrella together. He has to take his car keys with him every morning, and if they're with the umbrella—maybe even clipped to it with a little spring-clamp—he'd have a certain reminder.

The Power of Concentration

A point that keeps coming up in the context of memory is concentration. Some critics of memory systems have even charged that all the systems are worthless. All that happens when you apply a peg word, think of an acronym, tie a string to your finger, or create a mental movie of your plan for the day is that you force yourself to concentrate on whatever you're trying to remember—and that helps you remember it.

Our response to this charge is twofold. First, even if this were true—so what? As long as it works, isn't that what matters? If you're trying to learn the first 10 amendments to the Constitution that make up the Bill of Rights, what you want to do is remember the amendments. It doesn't matter whether you remember them by hook and peg or by number alphabet, whether you use imaging, visualization, or an acronym, or whether you make up a little rhyme or song to help you remember them.

Heck, you could even tie 10 strings to your fingers, one for each amendment. As long as it works, to paraphrase the famous Yogi Berra, it works.

Our second response to the concentration argument is that mnemonic techniques *do* work. University studies have proven as much. Time and again, volunteer students have been divided into test groups given material to learn and mnemonic devices to use and control groups given the same material but instructed to learn the material in the usual way— brute force repetition.

Remember This!

If you want to use rote memory, more power to you. But believe us, you're doing things the hard way unnecessarily.

After a brief study period, the volunteers were tested on what they could remember of the study material. At a later date, they were tested to show how much they had retained.

Consistently, the test groups scored higher than the control groups in both initial learning and long-term retention and recall.

Wait a Minute, Fellas!

If you read the previous heading, "The Power of Concentration," and the section of information that followed, you might well be saying to yourself, "Wait a minute, fellas! Hadn't you better get your story straight? Are you pushing for concentration or are you arguing against it? Make up your minds!"

The fact is that mnemonic devices do work, but they only work if you concentrate on them. Remember when we mentioned a couple of acronyms? There are a zillion acronyms out there, but two we noted were HOMES and ROY G BIV.

HOMES can help you remember the names of the five Great Lakes. ROY G BIV can help you remember the colors of the rainbow.

You still have to learn the names of the lakes (Huron, Ontario, Michigan, Erie, and Superior) if you want to use HOMES. You can learn the lakes by brute force memorization if you wish, but even then you'll find you can recall them more quickly and easily if you use HOMES than if you try to remember them by brute force recall.

Similarly, ROY G BIV (or its long form, "Richard of York gave battle in vain") is only useful to you if you know the rainbow's colors are red, orange, yellow, green, blue, indigo, and violet. But, once you know them, ROY G BIV will absolutely help you to remember their sequence.

So where do we stand on the subject of concentration? The answer is that we're in favor of it. Concentration is vital in developing and applying a good memory. Conversely, using mnemonic techniques will also help you to concentrate. Concentration works hand-in-hand with mnemonic techniques!

A Good, Hard Hit on the Head

Have you ever awakened in the middle of the night with a valuable and important thought in your mind? "I really have to remember this," you tell yourself. "Maybe I should turn on the light and jot it down. But I'm so sleepy, and my sweetie pie here beside me is dozing so peacefully. I don't want to disturb the little dear. Besides, this is such a great idea, there's no way I'll forget it by morning."

In the morning, as you and your sweetheart share a strong cup of coffee you say, "You know, I woke up in the middle of the night with a really, really great idea!"

And your sweetheart says, "Yes? What is it?"

You can feel the muscles in your face go slack as you lapse into an expression of blank despair. "I can't remember," you finally mutter.

Our friend Hildegarde, a superb short-story writer, told us recently that she'd had exactly this problem. "I'm always certain that I'm going to remember my midnight thoughts, and I always forget them."

We nodded sympathetically.

"Except for once," Hildegarde brightened.

"Yes?" we encouraged.

"One night I woke up with a great idea for a short story. I was so excited that I started to climb out of bed. I had decided to write down the idea. I wasn't going to let this one get away!"

We nodded eagerly and asked, "What did you do?"

"I started to climb out of bed. I slipped on the edge of the mattress and hit my head on the night table. Wham! I fell back onto the bed and lay there, stunned, with my eyes open. There on the ceiling, I saw my whole short story unfold like a stage play. Then I fell asleep."

"Oh," we murmured sympathetically. "And in the morning it was gone, eh?"

"No," said Hildegarde happily. "At first I couldn't remember the story, but I certainly remembered hitting my head on the night table. I had a lump the size of a tennis ball!"

When I ran my fingers over it, I relived the clout on the head, falling back into my bed, seeing the story like a stage play—and I could see it all over again! I ran to my typewriter, typed out the story, dropped it in the mail, and sold it on the first attempt!"

You Needn't Hit Your Own Head

We're not suggesting that you use Hildegarde's method. For one thing, you might not be as lucky as she was; a hard clout on the head can do serious harm. For another, there *has* to be an easier way!

You might just keep a notepad, a pencil, and a flashlight on your night table. You can also use various mnemonic devices—tricks, if you will—to help you remember these flashes of inspiration. You might, for example, try a variation of the number alphabet or maybe one that involves visualization.

Suppose Hildegarde's short story had dealt with an American journalist finding the lost crown jewels of the last Tsarina of Russia. (We don't really know whether this was the case. We didn't want to ask, and Hildegarde wasn't about to volunteer the information.)

She could have concentrated on her night lamp and seen it festooned in glittering emeralds, diamonds, and rubies. What a sight! She could have impressed this on her mind with such vividness that, when she awakened the next morning and saw the lamp beside her bed, she also would have seen the crown jewels and recovered the imagery of her story.

She also might have formed a vivid mental image of herself wearing the jewels. A glittering platinum-and-diamond necklace, a gorgeous gem-encrusted gold tiara, and a ring on every finger, each one more fabulous than the next. It's a good bet that when she looked in her mirror the next morning, she would have retained that image and remembered her story.

More Help for Hildegarde

There's one more thing Hildegarde might have done to give herself a tangible clue about her inspiration. If she feared she would forget the Tsarina's jewels, she might have hooked them in a visualization to something out of the ordinary. She might, for example, have mentally wrapped them around her alarm clock and moved it from the night table to the floor beside her bed.

Better yet, she might have stuffed them into a bedroom slipper she normally kept on the floor and put it on her night table. When she awakened in the morning, a bedroom slipper full of shimmering jewels (!) would be standing on her night table. Not something she would overlook!

And it's a lot easier on the noggin than a hard wallop.

Is It Magic?

Many magical remedies are touted to increase your mind powers, to improve your concentration, to help you use more of your brain, to revitalize your memory, and to perform other such miracles of mental gymnastics. There are potions, lotions, herbs, electrical devices, home-study courses, seminars, and even religions.

They all have one thing in common—the results can't be measured. Is your memory really better? Or do you just think it's better? Are you really thinking more clearly? Or are you just filling your mind with buzz words that substitute for clarity?

The wonderful thing about the mnemonic techniques we're showing you in this book is that they work whether you believe in them or not. When you remember that list of 10 items and can recall it in any order a week later—and you know darn well you couldn't do that before we showed you how—that's a tangible result. Your memory is now working better than it did before.

What we're doing is showing you how to give it structure, like the framework of a building as it's being erected. With that framework—the mnemonic pegs or one of the other systems—you can nail up whatever you need to remember, and it will be there when you need to recall it. When you've tried these methods and have discovered that they do work, you'll have the enthusiasm to learn them and practice them. You'll turn into a real memory expert. The more you practice, the more solid the framework gets, and the better, faster, and more accurate your memory becomes.

The Least You Need to Know

➤ Remembering single items can be difficult because there's no list.

➤ Provide yourself with a visual cue, like hanging something you have to take with you over the front door knob.

➤ You can remember a list of things to do by using visualization and creating a mental movie of the coming day.

➤ Concentration is not a substitute for mnemonic techniques, but it's an invaluable tool that makes mnemonics work better.

➤ These techniques do work whether you believe in them or not. And with practice, you get faster and more accurate.

Chapter 22

I'd Like to Thank the Committee

In This Chapter

➤ The fear of speaking

➤ Who needs to make a speech anyhow?

➤ Four ways to do this, all of them wrong

➤ The great and the not so great

➤ A room full of enemies

➤ Everybody stumbles sometimes

You stand behind a speaker's podium looking out over a sea of faces. Signs and banners are scattered around the huge auditorium. Delegates in funny hats gaze adoringly at you. Thousands of red, white, and blue balloons are suspended overhead, ready to be released. The glassy eyes of television cameras are trained on you, carrying your image into the homes of millions of watchers.

You gaze to the left and then to the right. Above the hall are booths crowded with journalists from around the world.

Your hands are shaking. Your knees are like water. You pull a handkerchief from your pocket and wipe your face, but it doesn't help.

"Unh ... uh ... I, uh, I just can't do this."

You turn your back on the podium and the audience, make your way through throngs of concerned functionaries and admirers, and collapse in the Green Room.

Instant Recall

A psychologist friend tells us that fear of public speaking is one of the biggies—right up there with fear of heights and fear of crowds. A comparatively new fear that has worked its way up the charts in the past few years—and is now some-where near the top—is fear of driving on freeways.

Your bid for the presidency of the United States has come to an untimely end.

This may sound like a politician's worst nightmare, but in fact, it's only a slight exaggeration of an all but universal fear. We're not sure why people who have no trouble chatting one-on-one with friends, family members, schoolmates, or business associates become terror-stricken when they face a room full of people, but it's true. Most people do. If you're not one of them, congratulations. Maybe you can share your secret with the rest of us.

The chances are pretty good that you'll never receive the presidential nomination of a major political party (although, who's to say?). But the chances are also pretty good that at some point you'll have to stand in front of a room full of people and give a talk.

Most people in the business world have to face groups of co-workers from time to time and explain their jobs, technical processes, or administrative procedures. Sometimes you might have to stand in front of your boss and deliver a progress report. A speech to an audience of one still can be stressful.

If you have ever asked anyone to marry you, you surely know the feeling of tightness in the stomach, the pounding heart, and the cold hands. Most of us get through it somehow, but—wow!—what an experience!

Well, cheer up. You can be an effective public speaker whether you know it or not. Like so many things in life, it has a lot to do with your mental preparation. You may still feel the momentary butterflies-in-the-belly sensation that even the greatest actors and musicians tell us they experience before going on stage, but you'll get past that moment. Once you get rolling, you'll feel an astonishing energy and exhilaration.

Hey, you may even get addicted to that adrenaline rush, "the roar of the greasepaint and the smell of the crowd." You might discover that, hidden inside your shrinking-violet soul, a real ham has lurked all your life.

And, come to think of it, the world is full of children who love to perform. Most young-sters positively bask in the attention of their elders. They'll sing, dance, recite, ride their bikes, stand on their heads, and put on shows complete with hand-me-down costumes and homemade sets. Anything for an audience. Anything for that wonderful applause.

What happens? As we grow up, we develop stage-fright, mike-fright, and shyness. It comes from somewhere, and you can send it right back with some preparation and practice. If you take the time to prepare and practice your speech using some of the suggestions you'll learn here, the next time you have to make a corporate presentation, guest-lecture in a classroom, plead with a jury, or stand up and entertain at a banquet, you'll bring it off with aplomb.

Possibly you'll even enjoy it!

Some Memorable Facts

"Being able to make a speech or being forced to refuse because you are not accustomed to public speaking and to thinking on your feet may spell the difference between success and failure in life. If you have to retire to a dark corner because you cannot face the limelight, hardly anybody will be enough interested in you to get you out of it. You may know a lot in your own particular field; you may have made some discovery which could save labor or money or both if you could only carry it through against hoary custom and red tape ... Your success then depends just as much upon the way you express yourself and the way you convey your thoughts to others as on your discovery itself. As long as human beings do not change, as long as we have competition in this world, success means fighting; and the weapons for this fight are not pistol and sword but thoughts and speech."

—Dr. Bruno Furst, *Stop Forgetting*

Pick, Gather, Sort, Order, Expand

When the convention committee informs you that you are the keynote speaker or the head of your section says it's time to justify to the Projects Committee just what you've been doing with the company's time, personnel, and all that expensive equipment, you'll realize you're going to have to give a speech. Most experts agree that you should follow the following five steps to prepare your speech, and yourself, for the occasion.

1. **Pick a topic.** Many times the topic is picked for you, but when it's not, make sure the subject is one that will interest and be understood by your audience. In addition, you must care enough about the topic to sound competent and enthusiastic when you deliver the speech.

2. **Gather your material.** Make sure you know enough about the subject to sound thorough, knowledgeable, and up-to-date. Check for the latest information. Make sure you have your dates and facts right. If what you're talking about is controversial, also collect the information for the opposing viewpoint.

3. **Sort your material.** Figure out what bits of information go together. Put them in order. Then stand back (metaphorically) and stare at what you've got.

4. **Order your material.** Find the most logical order for the material. If there is no logical order, create one. Try to figure out a sensible beginning, middle, and end.

5. **Expand on your material.** Flesh your material out with connections from one bit of information to the next and some interesting asides. Illustrative anecdotes, dates, and statistics can buttress your argument, but do not overload your audience with fine detail. You'll do better to stick with principles and leave the details for supporting documents. (You may want to furnish these yourself in the form of duplicated handouts.)

Give the other side's point of view if there is one, if only to show why it's wrong. If you feel the need to include humor in your speech, and you probably should, try to make the humor organic to the material.

When you've done all this, you'll be ready to give one heck of a speech. You can feel fairly confident that the audience will react favorably and that few rotten vegetables will be thrown at you while you talk.

Four Ways to Make a Speech

Thousands of speeches are made every year, from impassioned orations in the United States Senate to informal presentations about industrial processes. You can divide speeches into the following four categories:

1. Speeches delivered from memorized texts

2. Speeches read directly from prepared texts

3. Speeches delivered from notes

4. Speeches delivered extemporaneously

There's something to be said for each of these speech types. Each has its advantages; each has its drawbacks. We both happen to be fairly experienced at public speaking, and we can talk with some authority on all four.

"You Caught Me By Surprise, But..."

Just to keep things lively, let's deal with the fourth speech type first. What is an extemporaneous speech? And who is going to have to make one? If you're a brilliant performer with a lightning-fast mind and a vast store of experience, you can jump up at any moment and orate on any assigned topic. You can move an audience to tears, have them rolling in the aisles with laughter, or bring them to their feet cheering.

This kind of talent is rare, and unless you're born with it, you are unlikely to develop it. On the other hand, you can train yourself to deliver at least a brief, effective speech on only a few moments' notice.

Doubt us? Not to worry. Try this out:

You're attending a meeting of your local political discussion group and the presiding officer says, "How do you feel about the space program? Should we invest billions of dollars to send astronauts to Mars?"

Fortunately, you know at least a little about the subject. You're not an aerospace engineer yourself, and you're far from an authority on the subject, but you consider yourself a reasonably well-informed lay person. At least you've read a few articles on the subject in the morning newspaper or the Sunday supplement, and you've seen TV documentaries discussing the space program and a possible mission to Mars.

In the time it takes you to leave your seat, walk to the front of the room, and turn to face the group, you will be prepared. If you remember to pick, gather, sort, order, and expand, you can organize your thoughts.

You might organize them like this:

➤ We should definitely go to Mars.

➤ The universe is infinite, and this is the next logical step for humankind.

➤ We can learn about the solar system and about ourselves.

➤ We will develop technology as we prepare for such a project. This technology will pay us many times over in applications right here on earth for every dollar we invest in it.

➤ The sense of purpose and commitment by our nation and by the international community will raise spirits around the world and will benefit all of civilization.

Or...

➤ Travel to other planets is a foolish dream. We should face the terrible problems that exist right here on earth.

➤ We need to stop polluting our planet and clean up our environment before we destroy our home.

➤ We need to control population growth.

➤ We need to feed the hungry billions of people in third-world countries.

➤ We need to invest in universal education.

➤ We need to devote more resources to medical research.

➤ We already have a full agenda of problems on this planet.

➤ Let's concentrate our efforts and solve these problems first. Then, perhaps in three or four generations, it may be time to think about traveling to other worlds.

That wasn't so tough, was it? The subject was picked for you, and you gathered the information before you arrived. Sorting and ordering took but a moment as you walked forward. You could have taken either side of the question and offered cogent arguments as support. Expanding either of these outlines to a 5- or even 10-minute talk shouldn't be too difficult.

Could you have done that? If you haven't given any thought to the question of interplanetary exploration, perhaps not. But surely there are subjects on which you could give such a talk with only seconds to prepare. Try it sometime. You'll be delighted with your own ability, and you'll develop comfort and confidence at the prospect of delivering longer, more demanding talks.

"I Prepared a Speech Tonight..."

A speech delivered from a prepared text is the opposite of an extemporaneous speech. To the inexperienced speaker, it might seem like a good idea to have everything written out in advance. After all, then you need only stand up and read it. Much easier than extemporizing, wouldn't you think?

In fact, the opposite is more likely to be the case. Reading from a prepared text—we've done this so we know what we're talking about—actually is the most difficult format because so many things can go wrong.

You can stumble over a word, skip a line or a paragraph, or lose your place in the text. When you turn the page, you might inadvertently turn two pages at once—it's happened!—and lose your train of thought. The greatest peril, however, of making a speech from a prepared text is that it's almost impossible to make the speech sound natural.

Experienced politicians and trained actors can do it but hardly anybody else. Even these people have a three-part formula for preparing such speeches:

1. Rehearse
2. Rehearse
3. Rehearse

Prepared addresses of this type usually are read off sheets of paper. Abraham Lincoln wrote one of the most famous speeches of all time, the Gettysburg Address, on the back of an envelope while riding the train to Gettysburg to give the speech.

Instant Recall

Make sure you can say what you mean to say. Unintended tongue-twisters, hard-to-pronounce words or combinations of words, and sentences that are hard to understand on first hearing are all pitfalls you can avoid by rehearsing. Remember, members of the audience cannot go back and reread anything that was not understood.

It was just three paragraphs in length, fewer than 300 words, and it has echoed down the corridors of history as an example of eloquence and sincerity:

> "Four score and seven years ago our fathers brought forth on this continent, a new nation, conceived in Liberty, and dedicated to the proposition that all men are created equal.
>
> Now we are engaged in a great civil war, testing whether that nation or any nation so conceived and so dedicated, can long endure. We are met on a great battle-field of that war. We have come to dedicate a portion of that field, as a final resting place for those who here gave their lives that that nation might live. It is altogether fitting and proper that we should do this.
>
> But in a larger sense we can not dedicate—we can not consecrate—we can not hallow—this ground. The brave men, living and dead, who struggled here, have consecrated it, far above our poor power to add or detract. The world will little note, nor long remember what we say here, but it can never forget what they did here. It is for us the living, rather, to be dedicated here to the unfinished work which they who fought here have thus far so nobly advanced. It is rather for us to be here dedicated to the great task remaining before us—that from these honored dead we take increased devotion to that cause for which they gave the last full measure of devotion—that we here highly resolve that these dead shall not have died in vain—that this nation, under God, shall have a new birth of freedom—and that government of the people, by the people, for the people, shall not perish from the earth."
>
> —Abraham Lincoln, the Gettysburg Address, November 19, 1863

One argument in favor of the prepared text. is that if you're discussing a very important, very sensitive issue, the exact wording of your speech is crucial. If you are speaking about a controversial matter with legal implications, you need to be sure you say precisely the right thing in precisely the right words. If you're making a promise or a commitment, you want to make sure you're promising exactly what you meant to promise and nothing more. If you're criticizing someone, you'd better be very certain of your ground. Don't get sued for slander!

The Eyes Have It

A serious problem with reading a prepared speech is that it will sound like you are reading a prepared speech. It will lack spontaneity, and it most likely will be devoid of warmth and eye contact.

One of the best pieces of advice given to people who must make a speech is to find one person in the audience and address your remarks to that person. As the speech continues, switch from that person to another person in another part of the room. Continue switching until you cover the entire room and the entire audience gets the feeling you are speaking directly to them. This is hard to do, however, when you are reading word-for-word from a prepared text.

Keeping eye contact with the audience also makes you more aware of when they are not following what you are saying and when it might be a good idea to backtrack slightly and repeat what you just said in a different, perhaps more simple and direct, form.

Speaking from Notes

The method of speechifying that most people find most successful is giving a talk that is neither memorized nor written word-for-word; instead, it is worked out in general and then delivered from notes to cue in the different sections and subtopics. This keeps the speech sounding spontaneous, enables you to keep eye contact with your audience, and gives you the flexibility to expand upon, alter, or clarify sections of the speech depending on the audience's response.

This also is where a cleverly applied mnemonic system can come to your aid.

Remember This!

The cue words should be written on 4 × 5- or even 5 × 8-inch card stock. It should be thick enough that the cards can be easily handled. The words should be printed in large letters with dark ink for easy reading at arm's length.

May I Have the Next Card Please?

The secret is to go through your speech and find the places where a new topic is introduced or where you look at the subject from a fresh viewpoint. Make a cue card for each of these locations. If one word won't serve as a cue, use a sentence or even a short paragraph. The cue words must serve not only to describe the upcoming subject but to recall it to your mind.

Go through the cards several times, delivering the speech from the cues provided. When you feel comfortable with the speech and feel certain that the cues will work, go through the cards again and link the cues together in your mind.

Read the following speech, which is Hamlet's speech in Shakespeare's *Hamlet*, Act III, scene ii. Many commentators read this as Shakespeare's instructions to all actors. As with any advice, judge it for yourself.

Speak the speech, I pray you, as I pronounced it to you, trippingly on the tongue; but if you mouth it, as many of your players do, I had as lief the town crier spoke my lines. Nor do not saw the air too much with your hand, thus; but use all gently: for in the very torrent, tempest, and—as I may say—whirlwind of passion, you must acquire and beget a temperance, that may give it smoothness. O! it offends me to the soul to hear a robustious periwig-pated fellow tear a passion to tatters, to very rags, to split the ears of the groundlings, who for the most part are capable of nothing but inexplicable dumb-shows and noise: I would have such a fellow whipped for o'erdoing Termagant; it out-herods Herod.

Go to Mars

Let's take our brief "Let's Go to Mars" speech as an example. Here's another look at the full text:

➤ We should definitely go to Mars.

➤ The universe is infinite, and this is the next logical step for humankind.

➤ We can learn about the solar system and about ourselves.

➤ We will develop technology as we prepare for such a project. This technology will pay us many times over in applications right here on earth for every dollar we invest in it.

➤ The sense of purpose and commitment by our nation and by the international community will raise spirits around the world and will benefit all of civilization.

What should the cue cards say? How about:

1. Should go
2. Next logical step
3. Learn solar system
4. New technology
5. Benefit civilization

Now, how to link them together?

Use connective questions to lead from one cue to the next and to form a very brief running narrative, like this:

> We should go to Mars. Why? Because it's the next logical step. So what? We can learn from it. What good will that do? It will enable us to create new technology. To what effect? To benefit civilization.

There we have the cues for a 20-minute speech, or our name isn't Rumpelstiltskin.

Of course, you can keep the cue cards with you when you give the speech to give yourself the

Instant Recall

If you can, visit the hall where you are to give a speech beforehand, take your notes with you, and stand at the lectern (without an audience). Look around the room and associate each major speech point with an object—an exit door, a sound booth, a pillar or pilaster. When you return later to deliver your speech, each of your key objects will remind you of a key point in your notes, and you'll be able to give the speech without once consulting your cue cards.

feeling of security one can only achieve by wearing both a belt and suspenders. But if you practice a bit, and know your material, you should have no trouble delivering the longest speech anyone is likely to ask you to give without pausing for meals.

And you'll find that you're able to add material as the need strikes you, to wander off onto a related subject you hadn't intended to bring up, to answer a question from the audience (even an unexpected one), and to pause to explain more fully some obscure point. Yet you can still find your way back to the material when you're ready to return.

Lenny Bruce's Chinese Box

One of the most remarkable speeches we've ever heard wasn't really a speech at all—it was a monologue delivered in a Greenwich Village nightclub more years ago than we care to remember. The speaker was Lenny Bruce, a controversial comedian and social critic of the era.

His nightclub act was the soul of simplicity. Lenny Bruce simply walked onto a bare stage, hoisted himself onto a tall stool, and spoke to the audience in a conversational tone. He started with a joke but, before reaching the punch line, digressed to another topic. That topic seemed to be headed toward a dramatic conclusion, but once again, Bruce digressed before he got there.

In this fashion, he made his way through layer after layer of digressions. His seemingly spontaneous chat resembled the famous Chinese box puzzle, in which each box is opened only to reveal another box. After 20 or 25 minutes, he told a little story that *did* have a conclusion. This led him back to the previous story, which he wrapped up in a manner that led him to the one before that, and so on, until he finished his monologue some 45 minutes later by delivering the punch line to his original joke!

We're not saying you'll reach this level of performance just by following our rules. This took a rare combination of natural talent and years of hard work and experience. But we predict you'll do such a good job that you'll even surprise yourself. You just need to prepare, prepare, prepare, and practice, practice, practice.

"I Dreamt I Went to Carnegie Hall in My..."

A famous manufacturer of foundation garments once ran an ad campaign featuring beautiful models wearing just their underwear in unlikely places. In each ad the model would say, "I dreamt I went shopping in my Maidenform bra..." or "I dreamt I went to the opera in my Maidenform bra..." or some such line.

That incongruous and embarrassing image must have stuck in the minds of millions of readers. It's also something you can use to get over the flutters when you make a speech. Various people have suggested solutions. Look over this list and see which ones appeals to you.

➤ Remember that the audience members are your friends. They want you to succeed. Draw on their attention for support.

➤ If you're still daunted by the prospect of addressing a room full of listeners, choose a friendly face in the middle of the audience and talk to that person one-to-one. Let the others just eavesdrop.

➤ If all those business suits or fancy dress outfits are scary, remember this: Underneath those fancy clothes, each person is sitting there in his or her underwear.

➤ If that doesn't do the trick, take it one step further. Remember this: Your audience may be dressed to the nines on the outside, but underneath their expensive suits, every last one of them is absolutely stark naked.

The Least You Need to Know

➤ Almost everyone experiences some fear of public speaking. You are not alone!

➤ Almost everyone finds him- or herself in the position of making a speech (or at least an informal presentation) from time to time.

➤ The four major formats for speeches are: reading from a text, memorizing a text, speaking from notes, and speaking extemporaneously. Of these, speaking from notes generally is the most desirable method.

➤ The secret of successful public speaking is twofold: prepare, prepare, prepare, and rehearse, rehearse, rehearse.

➤ Working from cue cards can give you an air of spontaneity that makes you look knowledgeable and confident.

➤ If the cues are tied together by a brief question-and-answer dialog with yourself, you have effectively memorized the whole speech while maintaining the advantages of the working-from-notes format.

Chapter 23

Foci on the Loci

In This Chapter

➤ The Loci Mnemonic System

➤ A set of locations: your home, your car, the solar system

➤ Or even a baseball team

➤ Multiple lists

➤ Multiple items at each location

➤ A mental note pad

Now that you've seen the power of the linking system and the numeric alphabet, and now that you know this stuff really works, we'll show you what is perhaps the most powerful system of all. It can be used to memorize any type of information, and it can be used to create multiple lists without forgetting the lists that came before. You can even retrieve information from it in any order—although it takes slightly longer to pull a specific number, say item number 17, from the list than it does with the numeric alphabet.

Curiously, this system is the oldest of them all, originating somewhere around the year 500 B.C. Remember the story about Simonides we told you back in Chapter 15, "Hear It, Say It, Write It, Remember It"? (With a great memory like yours? Of course you do!)

Some Memorable Facts

The Greek poet Simonides had been hired to compose and recite a poem at a banquet given by a nobleman named Scopa. After delivering the poem (which he delivered from memory—poets in those days had to have really good memories) and having an argument with Scopa about payment, Simonides left the hall. While he was outside the roof of the hall collapsed, killing all the diners inside and crushing their bodies beyond recognition. At the request of the families of the victims, Simonides was able to reconstruct in his memory where each of the guests had been sitting around the great banquet table by mentally walking around the room and locating each guest. This enabled each family to reclaim the correct body for burial.

Simonides thought over his experience in the banquet hall (as described in the preceding Some Memorable Facts box) and developed what we now call the *Loci Mnemonic System*, a memory system that is elegantly simple and very powerful. Five hundred years later, the Roman orator Cicero used it to prepare the speeches he delivered before the Roman Senate and at the various criminal trials where he served as defense attorney. Cicero's speeches were delivered without notes and are studied today as models of powerful and effective oratory.

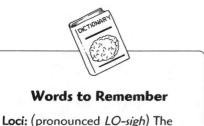

Words to Remember

Loci: (pronounced *LO-sigh*) The plural form of the Latin word "locus," meaning location.

Location, Location, Location

The idea behind the Loci System is deceptively simple. Unlike more complex systems, it involves only these two steps:

1. Prepare in your mind a list of sequentially related locations.

2. Assign each item you are trying to remember to one of these locations.

Sounds too easy, doesn't it? Well, if it's done properly, and if attention is paid to picking the locations and memorizing them, you'll find that it works very well.

The rules for picking the locations to memorize are as follows:

1. The locations must be familiar to you.
2. The locations should be logically related and in some sort of natural order.
3. Each location must be properly placed in relation to the one before it and the one after it.
4. Each location must be unique and distinct from all the other locations.
5. The locations may be close together in space if they are sufficiently different from each other so you won't confuse them.

What does this mean?

Let's say the locations you pick are places around your house—your living room, bedroom, kitchen, and so on. You should list them in the order you would walk through them from a natural starting point, say your front door. Your Loci list might look like this: front door, entrance hall, living room (to the left of the hall), dining room (next on the left), kitchen (in the back of the house), pantry (where you keep the canned goods), downstairs bathroom (on the right of the hall, in the rear), downstairs bedroom (next on the right), family room (right front). You then can mentally go upstairs and add the upstairs bedrooms, bathrooms, and so on.

If you live in a two-room apartment, you can use smaller divisions to create your locations: front door, entranceway, closet by front door, bathroom, and then close in on objects such as (in the bathroom) bathtub, sink, toilet, (now leaving the bathroom) living area, couch, bookcase, audio system, television set, armchair, dining table, and so on.

The same subdivisions can be made in a large house if you want a longer list of locations. The important thing is to create the list and formalize it so you know the locations you're going to use. Write them down in order, make sure you can visualize them, and make sure none of the visions overlap.

To use the Loci System, simply place each item you want to remember in one of the locations on your list (go sequentially, starting from the first location). As with the numeric alphabet, it helps to make the associations powerful. If you want to remember a dozen eggs and your location is the hallway, scatter the eggs around the hallway so you'd have to walk gingerly to avoid breaking an egg.

Where Am I?

The locations don't have to be in your house, of course. They can be almost anything that creates an image in your mind. If you drive a regular route everyday, they can be landmarks along your route. They can be places on your (or someone else's) body: hair, eyes, nose, mouth, neck, shoulders, left arm, left hand, right arm ... and so on. They can be locations on your car: front bumper right side, front bumper left side, right headlight ... and so on to the rear bumper.

Instant Recall

Recently, there was a movement to strip Pluto of its status as a planet because of its small size and its strangely un-planet-like orbit. But all you Pluto-lovers will be relieved to hear that the movement failed. Astronomers have agreed that henceforth and forever Pluto will remain the ninth planet.

Let's create a sample location list and see how it works. For our locations, we'll pick something simple, yet grandiose, and easy to remember—the solar system. After all, it's where we all live. (If any ETs are reading this book, feel free to use your own star system.) Our location list, from the center outward, would be: the sun, Mercury, Venus, Earth, Mars, the Asteroid Belt, Jupiter, Saturn, Uranus, Neptune, and Pluto.

The list could be made much larger, if necessary, by adding the major moons, the Oort belt, and the like, but the present list will do for illustrative purposes.

What do we have to remember? By accosting random strangers on the street and demanding that they name something—anything—we have come up with the following list (after eliminating a few names they came up with to describe us): a camel, an apple pie, a fiddle, the Eiffel Tower, a bathrobe, God, a German Shepherd, Santa Claus, a cup of coffee, a storm at sea, and a book of poetry by Ogden Nash.

There, we have gathered 11 items for our Loci list. Now let's match them so they'll be ours forever or for as long as we need them—whichever comes first.

Instant Recall

If you have somehow avoided learning the names of the planets, feel free to use a cheat sheet.

1. The sun—a camel
2. Mercury—an apple pie
3. Venus—a fiddle
4. Earth—the Eiffel Tower
5. Mars—a bathrobe
6. The Asteroid Belt—God
7. Jupiter—a German Shepherd
8. Saturn—Santa Claus
9. Uranus—a cup of coffee
10. Neptune—a storm at sea
11. Pluto—a book of poetry by Ogden Nash

Now to work:

➤ You can picture the blazing face of the sun with a camel laden with goods, stoically plodding along and occasionally spitting (as camels are famous for doing). The spit is instantly vaporized by the sun's burning gases.

➤ Mercury rotates very slowly. (It used to be thought that it didn't rotate at all.) We can picture an uncooked apple pie being inserted onto the surface of Mercury just as it rotates to face the sun. Being so close to the sun, the pie cooks as the planet rotates. It then reaches the night side and freezes, so we have a cooked, frozen apple pie to take away.

➤ Venus is next, the planet of love! As lovers sit gazing at Venus, a fiddle, played by a romantic fiddler, adds to the enchantment of the evening.

➤ As we stand on Earth, we can gaze at the moon just rising over the Eiffel Tower.

➤ Mars is named after a great warrior god, who is wearing a bathrobe over his bright red armor.

➤ The Asteroid Belt is made up of little rocks and pebbles, which God watches over, just as She does every fallen sparrow.

➤ Jupiter is known for its great red spot. This immediately makes us think of *Spot*, our dog—a great red German Shepherd.

➤ When we think of Saturn we think it is famous for its beautiful rings. Where did it get them? They were a Christmas present from Santa Claus.

➤ As you stand on the surface of distant Uranus, the planet named for the Greek god who was considered to be "the personification of the sky," you stare up at that dark sky. Uranus is so far from the sun, however, that when you try to drink a cup of coffee, you discover that the surface of Uranus is so cold that the coffee has frozen solid in the cup.

➤ Sometimes you just get lucky. The planet Neptune is angry. Imagine a storm at sea on the world named for the Roman god of the sea. Too easy!

➤ Pluto, the god of the underworld, tries to keep from laughing as he reads a book of poetry by Ogden Nash. (If that won't do it for you, picture the famous Walt Disney dog, Pluto, with his ears flying and his tail wagging merrily as he delivers the book to Mickey Mouse!)

Refresh Your Memory

Ogden Nash's most famous poem is titled "Ice Breakers." It is just seven words long, and it goes as follows:

"Candy is dandy,

But liquor is quicker."

For All You Sports Fans Out There

Some people love sports; some couldn't care less. If you fall into the latter category, this Loci list won't mean much to you. But if you're a dedicated sports fan—specifically, if you love baseball—it will be easy and fun and will carry you back to the balmy days of summer every time you use it.

Recalling a pleasant experience every time you use this list is just a bonus.

Playing By the Numbers

Baseball has long been a game of numbers—numbers and statistics: pitchers' won-lost records, ERAs, and strikeout-versus-walk percentages; hitters' batting averages, home runs, and RBIs; stolen-base totals; successful pickoff attempt percentages; and hundreds more.

If you've ever kept score using an official baseball score book, you know that the players' field positions all have numbers as well. These numbers have nothing to do with batting-order position or uniform numbers—they're just a convention that goes back many years.

Anybody who doesn't know baseball very well may be mystified to hear an announcer say, "The Goobers brought off an inning-ending four-six-three double play." But any knowledgeable baseball fan will know that the situation was one out with a runner on first base (and maybe other runners we don't care about).

The batter hit a ground ball to the second baseman who tossed the ball to the shortstop. The shortstop stepped on second base, making the runner from first base a force-out, and then threw to the first baseman, making the batter the third out and ending the inning.

We'll bet a nickel that some brilliant student of the rules of baseball will send us a cranky letter detailing another possible explanation, but let's let it be.

Here are the position numbers on a baseball team:

1. Pitcher
2. Catcher
3. First base
4. Second base
5. Third base
6. Shortstop
7. Left field
8. Center field
9. Right field

The American League also has a designated hitter (DH). DHs aren't used, however, in the more traditional National League. For our purposes, let's include the DH. And every baseball team has to have a manager. We'll include him, too. (The DH and manager don't have "scorebook numbers" in baseball tradition, but we'll assign them numbers for our own purposes.)

10. Designated hitter
11. Manager

Our Baseball List

This completes our version of the baseball numbering system. Now let's take that same list of 11 items we associated with the solar system and see if we can use a baseball team as our Loci list.

1. Pitcher—a camel

2. Catcher—an apple pie

3. First base—a fiddle

4. Second base—the Eiffel Tower

5. Third base—a bathrobe

6. Shortstop—God

7. Left field—a German Shepherd

8. Center field—Santa Claus

9. Right field—a cup of coffee

10. Designated hitter—a storm at sea

11. Manager—a book of poetry by Ogden Nash

Instant Recall

If any of the subjects we use as "hooks" are meaningless to you (whether it's numbers and you hate numbers, or sports and you're not interested in sports), use something else! Never use a hook you don't like.

Let's see how well we can make this work.

1. What's that on the pitcher's mound at your favorite ballpark? It seems to be a camel—staring down at the catcher to get his sign, winding up those long, knobby limbs of his, and unleashing a weird dipsy-doodle delivery.

2. You know the peculiar mask-and-helmet gadgets that major league catchers have been experimenting with in recent years? Suddenly the batter gets angry with the catcher, turns around, and smacks him right in the mask with an apple pie!

3. There's an agonizing delay in the game as the umpire demands to look at the ball and make sure the camel, er, the pitcher, isn't throwing a spitball. Meanwhile, the first baseman passes the time by standing on the sack playing a fiddle.

Instant Recall

You chess players can use the beginning positions of the chess men for 32 instant Loci. If you're an advanced player, and good at visualization, you can use the whole board to remember 64 different positions with an item in each. For example, to use the list we're working with, you could start with the white king's rook riding a camel.

4. The second baseman, during all this, has become impatient and has pulled some popsicle sticks out of his pocket. He sits in the base path like a child and begins to build a replica of the Eiffel Tower.

5. The third baseman is feeling chilly. Although everybody else on the field is wearing a regular baseball uniform, this fellow is keeping warm by wearing a bathrobe over his.

6. The shortstop (as you'll know if you're a real baseball fan) is probably the best all-around athlete on the field. There's a great one on our team. His only fault is his oversized ego. He seems to think he's God, and when we look at him, we can almost see a golden halo glowing all around him!

7. The left fielder is another great player and is renowned for his ability as a hitter. But he's also notoriously lazy in the field. The baseball term for his performance out there is "dogging it," and you can picture him as a German Shepherd in a baseball suit.

8. The center fielder, by contrast, is having trouble fielding his position because he's wearing a Santa Claus outfit and carrying a huge sack of toys.

9. The right fielder is very young and has spent most of the season playing in the minor leagues. The boss called him up for a few games at the end of the season, though, just to show what he can do. The baseball term for this practice is "up for a cup of coffee," but if the kid does a good job, his future is bright!

10. The designated hitter is another problem athlete. He's a powerful slugger, but he has a tempestuous temperament—he's a regular storm at sea.

11. The team's manager is one of those baseball lawyers who likes to quote obscure provisions in the rule book whenever he gets the chance. In fact, he carries a battered old copy of the rules in his back pocket during every game. When he ran onto the field to argue with the umpire today, he pulled out the book, waved it around, and was humiliated to discover that someone has switched it for a book of poetry by Ogden Nash.

Wow!

As Many Lists As You Need

What's your hobby? Stamp collecting? Tropical fish? Teddy bears? Rare books and manuscripts?

Whatever it may be, you can easily construct a Loci list based on your interest. Every item has a place in your mental imagery, every item has a position on the list, and every item will work when you have another list to remember.

Double, Double, Toil and Trouble

We've offered two sample Loci lists. You can make one of your own or as many as you wish. Suppose, however, that you want to extend the list beyond the 11 items we've used. There's nothing special about the number 11; it was arbitrary.

You can extend the planets Loci list, as we previously suggested, by adding more astronomical objects.

What about the baseball list? For starters, you can add an umpire (or several), a hot dog vendor, a broadcast announcer, or your neighbors in your season seat. You can "place" objects from your list around the stadium. One could go in the box seats behind first base, one in the upper deck behind home plate, one in the bleachers behind center field, and one on top of the scoreboard. Just remember to use the same locations in the same sequence every time you use the baseball list.

As for the players ... again, the average citizen on the street might not know this, but any dedicated baseball fan will tell you that, traditionally, the home team wears white uniforms and the visiting team wears gray uniforms. By adding the uniform colors to your images, you can double the number of Loci on your list from 11 (nine position players, a designated hitter, and a manager) to 22!

Some Memorable Facts

The Loci method is one that different people keep inventing and reinventing independently of one another. We mentioned that it is often attributed to the Greek orator Simonides, but it has been re-invented by several people since Simonides. A sixteenth century Jesuit priest named Matteo Ricci is known to have traveled to China, allegedly spreading the message of God but also disseminating the Loci method as a way for converts to remember his message. And in the twentieth century, the Russian mnemonist Shereshevsky "invented" the method all over again for his own use!

Each of these three used a different set of Loci. Simonides distributed his items around the interior of a great room. Matteo Ricci constructed "palaces of memory" and placed each item in a different room. Shereshevsky took an imaginary stroll through his home town and distributed the items in various doorways and buildings. But they all had the same idea!

Home Again, Home Again, Joggity-Jig!

We've offered you these contrasting Loci lists—baseball and the solar system—to show you how great the options are for this sort of list-making. A basic list based on your home, however, is almost certainly the strongest list you can devise because your familiarity with the locations will enable you to create memorable images for each spot on the list. You also can mentally walk through your house and examine each location to see what you have stored there.

You can create other great walk-through lists in addition to your house. Use your office, your school, or a local museum if you go there often enough to be able to picture the layout.

Talk Begins at Home

Remember that Cicero used this system for memorizing the important points in his speeches. This is one of the more powerful uses of the Loci System. The way to do it is to take your cue cards (remember the cue cards from the last chapter?) and go over each element of your speech while mentally standing in a specific location in your house. Then, as you give the speech, just imagine yourself walking from one spot to the next in your house. You will recall what part of the speech you are to give from each location.

Four at a Time

One interesting feature of the Loci System is that you can put more than one item in each location in the house. If you put four items in each location, a 10-location Loci list can hold 40 items. How does this work? Well, let's take it from the top. Remember the list of items we used the solar system and the baseball team to recall? Here's a method that will permit you to "compress" the Loci list, yet remember the full list of items.

Instant Recall

Remember, as you mentally walk through your Loci house, you can use furniture or other items from the various rooms to add to the number of locations available to you.

➤ Your Loci list begins with your front door. You arrive at the front door and what do you see? There tethered to the doorknob is a camel. On the welcome mat rests a bakery box holding an apple pie, which the camel is being very careful not to step on. The pie is from a French bakery, so there is a large picture of the Eiffel Tower on the box, which you suddenly notice is in the shape of a fiddle.

➤ Your next position is the front hall. You enter the front hall and immediately have to put out the fire on the burning bush, which has just been left there by God. (It's a Biblical reference, honest.) You do this by throwing the bathrobe from the coat rack over it. Your German Shepherd almost knocks you over when greeting you, pushing you into the no-longer-burning bush, which you now realize is a Christmas tree with a stuffed Santa Claus sitting amidst the branches.

Walking Through the House

The Loci System can be used as a mental notepad for remembering random facts that occur to you during the day: things to do, ideas to work on, or whatever. Think of all the times you're somewhere that you can't make a note. You don't have a pen with you, you're in your car in traffic, or you're at a meeting where you're supposed to be paying attention to the speaker. Maybe you're on a jury, and you're not supposed to be writing anything down.

All you have to do is associate the idea, thing to do, or whatever with one of your Loci locations. Say you want to remember to pick up the dry cleaning. Picture it hanging over your doorknob or, if you want to put the item in your mental kitchen, hooked to the refrigerator. If you want to remember to add soup to your shopping list, picture a bowl of it dumped onto the couch in the living room.

All you have to do later is mentally run through the various locations on your Loci list and see what's there.

If you decide to use the Loci System for this type of mental note-taking, you have to get in the habit of mentally running through it at regular intervals. You might want to do it when you get home from work or when you get up in the morning (in case you've added anything to it the night before), whenever it seems appropriate to you.

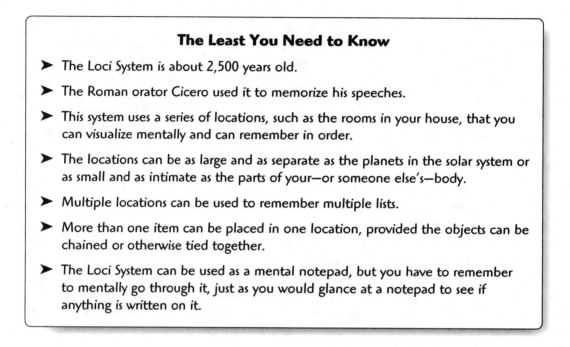

The Least You Need to Know

➤ The Loci System is about 2,500 years old.

➤ The Roman orator Cicero used it to memorize his speeches.

➤ This system uses a series of locations, such as the rooms in your house, that you can visualize mentally and can remember in order.

➤ The locations can be as large and as separate as the planets in the solar system or as small and as intimate as the parts of your—or someone else's—body.

➤ Multiple locations can be used to remember multiple lists.

➤ More than one item can be placed in one location, provided the objects can be chained or otherwise tied together.

➤ The Loci System can be used as a mental notepad, but you have to remember to mentally go through it, just as you would glance at a notepad to see if anything is written on it.

Chapter 24

On the Job

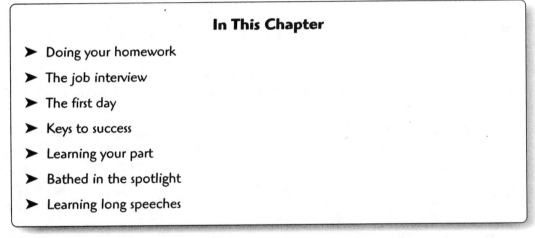

In This Chapter

➤ Doing your homework

➤ The job interview

➤ The first day

➤ Keys to success

➤ Learning your part

➤ Bathed in the spotlight

➤ Learning long speeches

Life seems to be an artful combination of moments of pleasure and joy intermixed with moments of pain, stress, and—for some of us—utter panic. As our sainted granny used to say, you have to take the good with the bad. In our experience, one of life's most stressful moments, sometimes approaching sheer terror in its intensity, is that common experience known as the job interview.

Everyone from your parents to your middle-school guidance counselor to your older siblings will be full of advice on this subject, and you really don't need us to chime in—except to remind you that your memory can be a highly effective tool in getting a job. We won't remind you to show up on time for your appointment, to make sure your fingernails are clean and your hair is combed, to dress appropriately, or to be polite. You know all these things. So where does memory come in?

To Whom Am I Speaking, Please?

For starters, remember that your dialog with the interviewer is a personal relationship. It may be a very brief relationship, or it may last for years. If you're aiming for a job with a giant corporation or another institution with a large staff and complex organization, you may see the interviewer only once. She might be a corporate bureaucrat sitting in a bullpen interviewing scores of applicants everyday. If you're applying for a job at a small company where an operating manager does the hiring, however, you may be talking with someone you'll see every day for the next decade.

In either case, you'll want to make a positive impression. Part of this process—in fact, something that goes on almost from the first moment—is connecting names with faces. Hey, remember the chapter that covered this exact subject? Remember your pals A.W. Sanders, Francis Xavier McCabe, and the rest of the gang?

You may have an appointment with a specific interviewer. If so, it's a good idea to confirm that person's name at the outset. "Hello, I'm Waldo Warmerdam, and you are Ms. Kladstrupp, I believe."

Ms. Kladstrupp will either confirm that this is indeed her name or she'll tell you that, no, she is not Ms. Kladstrupp. Ms. Kladstrupp is vacationing on the French Riviera this week; she is Ms. Browning. Either way, you're ahead of the game.

Of course, the interviewer's name may appear on her door or her desk. Even if it does, it's still a good idea to work it into the conversation several times and to do so early on. This isn't a social conversation, however, so it probably would be inappropriate to get into a cocktail-party-type conversation about the origin of her name. But do use it.

Shoes? I Wear Shoes!

It's a good idea to learn something about the organization to which you're applying before the interview takes place. You'll want to know at least a little bit about its history, its products, and its policies before the interview. You needn't memorize lots of details in this regard, but you don't want to tell an interviewer at the Hilton Shoe Company that you just love those darling little evening pumps, only to learn that Hilton makes brake shoes for steam locomotives and diesel trucks.

Some Memorable Facts

Learning about the company before you apply for the job might also save you time by alerting you to companies for which you wouldn't want to work. You might find that the way they treat their employees, although perfectly fine for some people, simply wouldn't suit you. Or you might find something about their product line or their customer base offensive. Here are some obvious and unsubtle examples: If you're a vegetarian, you wouldn't want to work for a meat packer; if you're unwilling to leave town, you wouldn't want to work for a company that routinely moves its middle managers around the country to give them experience.

You might also want to memorize the name of the president or CEO of the company and a little of his or her history. It's a plus to be able to tell the interviewer, "I've admired President Lapplung ever since I read the wonderful interview about the use of cheap labor in third-world countries that appeared in *Fortune* last year." Being able to quote some of the pithier passages is an A+.

If the job you're applying for is technical in nature, and especially if the interviewer is a technical employee or manager, be ready to talk her language. Be prepared to ask and answer questions about multilayer thin-film polymer deposition or inverse matrix program testing or whatever is appropriate for the particular job for which you're interviewing.

Be especially prepared to answer questions about anything you've claimed knowledge of or skills in on your application or your resumé. If your resumé states that you are able to pilot an Alpha-class interplanetary runabout, you'd better have your certification ready. If it's a skill you haven't used in the past few years, it's be a good idea to check for any recent changes in law and technology before the interview.

If you're looking for a job as a teacher, be ready to talk about both pedagogy and the specific subject you're qualified to teach, whether it's Medieval Castillian Irregular Verbs, the Taxonomy of Arachnoid Species Unique to New Zealand, or the Dynastic History of the Grand Duchy of Luxembourg.

Take mental notes of what the interviewer tells you. On the face of it, you're there to provide information. You may be surprised to discover, however, that you also can get information that proves useful either in the interview itself or later.

Remember This!

One underrated secret of highly successful people is that they are able to say "I don't know." If your interviewer asks you a question to which you don't know the answer, say so immediately. Then add, "I'll find out right away and get back to you." And do so.

When the interview ends, make sure you reinforce that person-to-person, name-to-name relationship. "Thank you, Ms. Browning. And please tell Ms. Kladstrupp that I hope she had a pleasant time on the Riviera."

"Welcome Aboard, Happy to Have You on the Team!"

If searching for a job is one of life's more stressful experiences, starting work can't be far behind. It's a rare worker who doesn't have first-day-on-the-job jitters, and for good reason—you're entering an unfamiliar environment, taking on new tasks, and meeting new colleagues. You know that all eyes will be on you (or at least you suspect as much), and you want very much to create a positive first impression. If you do, you're off and running. If you don't, you've got a deficit to make up before you ever score any points.

Here are a few suggestions for dos and don'ts—especially dos—to bear in mind that first week on the job:

➤ Get to know your co-workers by name and face as quickly as possible.

➤ Get to know the chain of command stretching from the head of the company to your immediate boss to yourself.

➤ Get to know your company's history (if you didn't learn it before your job interview), the way it's organized, and the way it works.

➤ Get to know your company's product line. If you're working in a service industry (including education or government) learn about your organization's services.

➤ Learn your company's policies and procedures.

➤ Learn as much as you can about other organizations and individuals you'll be dealing with, including customers, clients, and suppliers.

➤ Get to know the "little people" in your company. This can be anybody from the receptionists to the security guards to the cafeteria help to the cleaning crew that comes in at night after everybody else goes home. (And how would you know those late-night people? You can never tell. You might be working late one night yourself!) The folks in the mail room can be especially useful friends.

That's quite a list. Let's take a little closer look at it.

➤ **Get to know your co-workers.** Why is this important? If you need to borrow a lug-wrench, all you have to say is, "Hey, lend me a lug-wrench, will ya, chum?" Right? No, that's wrong!

The fact is—and this is based on the experiences of literally millions of workers in every industry from computer labs to hot dog stands—the sooner you get to know your fellow workers, start calling them by name, and know at least a little about them, the sooner you will be accepted as a member of the team. You will be valued and assisted in the workplace. You also will be included in off-hours social events, and the networking and career opportunities in this acceptance are invaluable.

So apply the name-and-face rules you already know. Get to know people and call them by their names!

➤ **Know the chain of command.** What do you care who the president, vice president, chief of operations, and so on down to section head of Gigantor Megaglom International are when you're just a file clerk in the Podunk Township Regional Office? Why should you waste your precious time and energy on these strangers?

That's the right attitude—if your intention is to stay a file clerk for the rest of your days. If you intend to rise in the company, however, you'd better start using your intelligence and abilities as soon as possible. Learning about people in positions of authority in the company is not a sign of sycophancy. It's an attempt to learn the policies and goals of the company by understanding the people who formulate those policies and goals.

➤ **Get to know your company's history.** The past is a window to the future. Knowing the history of your company, its successes, and its failures might well give you a good idea of where the company is headed. Being able to cite a past event from the company's history—"Yes, we tried that back in '67; it didn't work then, either"—might be useful.

➤ **Get to know your company's product line.** If the products have inventory code numbers and your job is in sales, delivery, or service, it might not be a bad idea to memorize those numbers. There's probably no need to memorize whole catalogs, but you should at least familiarize yourself with them. If people in your shop frequently refer to 709s, 2313s, or 22lbs, you'll help yourself fit in by finding out what these things are and by learning to use the vocabulary of the "in group."

➤ **Learn your company's policies and procedures.** If there are written policy statements or regulations, it wouldn't hurt to memorize them. After all, if the company has gone to the trouble of formulating regulations and writing them down, it probably wants you to take them seriously.

Instant Recall

One of the first things you're required to do when you join the military is learn—and memorize—the **General Orders** for guard duty. Both of us served in the military more than 30 years ago, and we both still remember those darn General Orders.

Remember This!

For concern to seem real, it has to be real. If you really don't care about the people you speak to, they will be able to tell.

➤ **Learn as much as you can about other organizations and individuals you'll be dealing with.** Your skills with the Loci System might come in handy. Put each organization in a different room in your house of memory, and use the chain system to memorize the important people and products of each company. While we're at it, it's also a good idea to be familiar with your company's competitors. That way, if somebody asks you, "What's the difference between your company's positronic veeblefetzers and Zilcho Corp's positronic veeblefetzers?" you'll be ready with an answer. You'll look good and your company will look good.

➤ **Get to know the "little people" in your company.** As you rise through the ranks, it never hurts to have the loyalty of the people around you, even the "little people." A kind word and remembering a few details about a person goes a long way toward showing you care. Remember the stories about Napoleon and Franklin Delano Roosevelt from Chapter 1, "28 Chapters to a Better Memory"? Napoleon remembered the names of the privates in his army and gained the loyalty of his troops, and FDR impressed those around him by remembering details of their lives. If it worked for them, it can work for you.

Just One More Thing

Assume that you achieve all the success you deserve. Before long, you'll not only be a valued member of the corporate team, you'll be busily climbing the ladder of success, bursting through the glass ceiling, escaping the pink- or white- or blue-collar ghetto, rocketing upward into the rarified atmosphere of the management class, and surveying the world from your own personal mountaintop.

Now that we've mixed every metaphor we can think of, it's a good idea to remember not to forget. Loyalty is a two-way street (hey, there's another metaphor!). If you want the loyalty of the people who work for you, you should remember them. Learn their names and take note of important events in their lives (such as weddings, births, kids in school plays, or little league games). You'll find, as did Napoleon and Franklin Delano Roosevelt, that when you care about people, they will care about you as well. They'll make the extra effort, give the extra loyalty, and pay you well for what you have done by remembering them.

Remember This!

As the old saying goes, you should be kind to the people you pass on the way up. They're the same people you'll pass on the way down.

The Curtain Rises

Remember the chapter about making speeches? Sure you do. Here again are the four types of speeches we described:

➤ The speech read from a prepared text

➤ The speech delivered from a memorized text

➤ The speech delivered from notes

➤ The impromptu speech

You'll recall that we advised against using a fully prepared text, whether you plan to read it to your audience or to deliver it from memory. Sometimes, however, you need to deliver material from memory, and you need to deliver it exactly as written.

An example of this is a dramatic (or musical) play. Most of us take part in amateur productions when we're youngsters, and we come away from the experience with memories that last a lifetime. Some people even continue as members of amateur troupes. Community theater can be great fun for all concerned. And, of course, there are the chosen few who go on to professional careers on the stage (or the screen).

A dramatic script isn't exactly a speech; it's more like a series of speeches. Some of them may be quite lengthy. Others can be very short.

> **Detective:** And so, having studied all the clues and having questioned every witness to the events in question and every suspect in the case, I have reached the unshakable conclusion that the guilty party could only be one person. Yes, one person and one person alone could have the means, the motive, and the opportunity to carry out this heinous deed. One person and one person alone had access to the poisonous mushrooms, to the box of holiday chocolates, to the hypodermic needle used to inject the extract of death's-head mushroom into the chocolates, and to induce the victim to eat a full five pounds of the poisonous sweets. That person is...

> **Zenobia:** No!

Remember This!

The first job of an actor is to memorize his part. (Well, the first job is to get the part, but that's another story for another book.) Everything else—staging, blocking, characterization, and the myriad details that go into creating a character and interacting with the other characters to create the play—cannot be accomplished until the actor knows his lines.

...well, in fact, Zenobia yes. The talented young lady playing Zenobia would have had little trouble learning her lines, at least as applied in this brief exchange. But what about the grizzled veteran actor who's playing the detective? How would he have gone about learning his lines?

Born in a Trunk

It's possible for an actor to memorize his lines without knowing any more of the play than those lines. Indeed, it is common practice in the theater to give an actor "sides"—excerpted sections of the play containing only his lines—to work from. This is sufficient for very short parts. After all, how many ways can a butler say, "Dinner is served, madam"? But it is not a good idea for longer parts. In addition to adding to the actor's understanding of his character, knowledge of the play actually makes it easier to memorize lines.

The Play's the Thing

If you are an actor—professional or amateur—and get a part in a play, the first thing you should do is read through the play. The second thing you should do is read through the play again. The third thing is—yes, you guessed it—to read the play one more time. By now, you should be very familiar with the outline and theme of the play, who the characters are, and how they function in the play.

Go through the play a fourth time, looking for places where you don't understand the dialog or the action. If there are any words you don't understand, look them up. (If the words occur in your own part, really study and learn their meaning and make sure of their pronunciation.) If you don't understand the action or the motivation, ask the director.

Now that you understand what the play means, at least to some extent, you're ready to memorize the lines. With each speech, you start, of course, from your cue. In most cases, your character is responding to something that has been said. Be aware of what provokes the response so that the response—your lines—fits naturally in that place. This makes them that much easier to remember.

Some Memorable Facts

There is a story about a young actor who had but one line in a play. After a pistol was fired in the second act, he was to say, "Hark! I hear a pistol shot!" He practiced the line off-stage all through the first act, striking various poses and declaiming, "Hark!" and then striking a new pose and continuing, "I hear a pistol shot!"

When his big moment came, he strode on stage and, after the off-stage shot, struck a pose and announced, "Hark! I hear a shistol pot—a shostel pit—a postel shit—damn it, I didn't want to be an actor anyway!"

(A variant ending has the actor looking startled after the shot and yelling, "What the hell was that?")

Long Speeches

When memorizing a long speech, begin by making sure you understand it. The better you understand something, the easier it is to remember.

Next you should read through the speech a couple times, then put it aside and go do something else for a while. Later, come back to it and read through it once or twice again. This time, you might want to close the script and see how much of it you remember. Then check your memory against the lines.

Don't try to memorize long speeches in sections (unless they're pages and pages long). It has been shown that you will actually remember the speech more quickly and more accurately if you go over the whole thing. Although you still learn it piece by piece, the pieces will come together more quickly.

For long speeches, chain the important points together and memorize them, making a sort of "spine" of the essential parts of the speech. Then go back and fill in the gaps, surrounding the spine with the rest of the body.

Pygmalion

Here is one of Doolittle's speeches in George Bernard Shaw's *Pygmalion*. Let's look at it and see how we can chain the ideas together.

Doolittle's daughter Liza has just moved into Henry Higgins' house to be taught how to speak properly. Doolittle, one of the "undeserving poor," suspects the worst. He has come to see if he can get £5 from Liza's new connections. Higgins says he thinks it's immoral to give Doolittle any money. Doolittle responds as follows:

> **Doolittle:** Don't say that, Governor. Don't look at it that way. What am I, Governors both? I ask you, what am I? I'm one of the undeserving poor: that's what I am. Think of what it means to a man. It means that he's up agen middle class morality all the time. If there's anything going, and I put in for a bit of it, it's always the same story: "You're undeserving; so you can't have it." But my needs is as great as the most deserving widow that ever got money out of six different charities in one week for the death of the same husband. I don't need less than a deserving man: I need more. I don't eat less hearty than him, and I drink a lot more. I want a bit of amusement, 'cause I'm a thinking man. I want cheerfulness and a song and a band when I feel low. Well, they charge me just the same for everything as they charge the deserving. What is middle class morality? Just an excuse for never giving me anything. Therefore, I ask you, as two gentlemen, not to play that game on me, I'm playing straight with you. I ain't pretending to be deserving. I'm undeserving; and I mean to go on being undeserving. I like it; and that's the truth. Will you take advantage of a man's nature to do him out of the price of his own daughter what he's brought up and fed and clothed by the sweat of his brow until she's growed big enough to be interesting to you two gentlemen? Is five pounds unreasonable? I put it to you; and I leave it to you.

If you string the ideas together, you might get:

I'm undeserving poor ... up agen middle class morality ... can't have it ... needs as great ... widow got money out of six charities ... need more ... eat as much, drink more ... a thinking man ... want cheerfulness ... charge the same ... what is morality? ... don't play that game ... undeserving and will go on ... take advantage ... his own daughter ... five pounds ...

We won't claim this is a substitute for the speech, but it's a good spine to hang the rest of the speech on. This should make it easier to learn the whole thing.

Remember the discussion of "clumping" in terms of memorizing long numbers earlier in this book? The same principle applies in learning speeches. In the case of speeches, we use "word clusters" in the same manner.

If an actor has to learn a long speech—say, 200 words—that actor doesn't sit down and memorize 200 separate units, each of them one word in length. What she does, even without planning to do so, is memorize short sections of the speech. Each of these, once learned, is a unit. You yourself are already familiar with many such "word clusters"— "To be or not to be, that is the question," "Ask not what your country can do for you, ask what you can do for your country," "In the beginning, God created the heavens and the earth..."

In learning a long speech, the actor divides the speech up into concept units or word clusters. Thus, a 200-word speech may contain four major concepts, each of which can be divided into two word clusters. The actor learns each word cluster, strings them together along the "spine" of major concepts, and is ultimately able to memorize the speech in terms of four concepts or eight word clusters, rather than 200 separate words.

Even while learning the speech, however, you'll probably find that it works best to study the whole speech rather than the separate word clusters. The clustering or clumping takes place as a natural by-product of the studying process.

Whatever the Speech

We've been talking about actors and plays, but these techniques can be used by anyone who needs to remember anything to be presented to a group, whether you wrote it yourself or it is the creation of another. Simply stated, the techniques come down to this:

➤ Read it.

➤ Read it again.

➤ Read it again.

➤ Understand what you're reading.

➤ Ask questions if you don't understand.

➤ If it's long, make a "spine" and memorize that.

➤ Go back and fill in the body around the spine.

As I Look Around This Great Hall

You'll also find that, when trying to remember your lines (whether you're delivering a monologue or portraying a character in a drama), it helps to have as many cues going for you as possible. In addition to the cue lines provided by other characters, there also are cues of place and position.

As our friend mentioned to us many chapters ago, the familiar rhythm of the play, the presence of the other actors, the costumes and props, and the action of the play all add to the gestalt in which you will participate.

Instant Recall

If the play is a musical, you'll probably find that the songs are easier to remember than the dramatic lines. This is because they are accompanied by music, and they have melodies, rhythm, and (in most cases) rhyme. Each of these elements provides additional cues to aid your memory.

You may also find yourself applying a version of the Loci System to help you recall your speech or your part in a play. You may do it consciously or even unconsciously. You may reach a point such as this: All right, I'm leaning against the fireplace, gazing into the flames, when the door flies open and Clarence stamps into the room, waving his arms angrily and shouting, "Where is that scoundrel Millipede! I'm going to teach him a lesson he'll never forget!"

Before you even know it, you whirl toward Clarence, extend your hands placatingly, and reply, "Now calm down, Clarence. Millipede has gone for the turkey and won't be back for hours."

By this time, the character has become part of you and you have become part of the character. The lines flow naturally and without effort on your part.

You're going to be a star!

The Least You Need to Know

➤ Using memory techniques can be of great help in a job interview.

➤ You can learn in advance about the company, the product, and the boss, and bring this information to the interview.

➤ Be ready to demonstrate your knowledge of any skills you put on your resumé by practicing and updating them before the interview.

➤ Once you have the job, the learning and memorizing continues.

➤ Begin learning and remembering the company's products, personnel, and procedures from the first day on the job.

➤ You can use mnemonic techniques to learn speeches or lines for a part in a play.

➤ When memorizing long speeches, begin by making sure you understand the speech. Use the link system to tie together the important elements of the speech into a "spine," and fill in the body of the speech as you learn it.

Part 6
Remembering and Forgetting

Can you look into a room full of furniture and the detritus of daily living, look away after a minute, and then list everything—well, almost everything—that you saw in the room? French magician Robert-Houdin could. He taught his son how to do it, and we're going to teach you. And once you've mastered this, you'll move on to the seven dwarfs and the seven wonders of the ancient world, which are just a warm-up to the main event—the Bill of Rights. Then a few words about forgetting, a few more lists and tricks, a little test to see how well you've been doing, some good advice, and finally, our best wishes.

Remember to keep this book with you and to go over the chapters that teach you the kinds of mnemonics most useful to you. There's no wrong way to do any of this stuff if it works for you. And, as you've already found out, it works surprisingly well and without much effort. Imagine how well it will work if you put your mind to it and really memorize the key words and special techniques.

A TEDDY BEAR, A MUSIC BOX, A COAT, A DRESSER...

Chapter 25

Trina's Room

> ## In This Chapter
>
> ➤ A living room full of objects
>
> ➤ How many can you remember?
>
> ➤ The MOMA method
>
> ➤ Major objects first
>
> ➤ Cluster the minor objects

Most of the memory techniques presented in the earlier chapters concentrated on helping you remember verbal or written material. This makes sense because most of what you need to remember involves verbal or written lists, prepared speeches, phone numbers, names, and the like. The exception, of course, was the method we showed you in Chapter 16, "A Face in the Crowd," for remembering the names of people you meet.

It also might be useful, however, to be able to remember items that make up the passing scene, to look around you and impress the vision of all the objects in sight into your memory so you can recall them at a later time when needed.

Trina's Room

So we went to our good friend Trina Robbins, a talented artist, writer, cartoon maven, and all-around nice person, and asked her to create a room for us. You already are familiar with her work. She created the people whose names you practiced learning in Chapter 16.

This is her room:

Trina's room.

As you can see, it's a lovely living room full of everyday, familiar objects. It's the sort of room you might walk into in any house.

What we'd like you to do now is look at the room for two or three minutes and mentally make a list of everything you can see in it.

When you're done, close the book, take a pad of paper, and write down everything you remember. Then open the book and come right back here.

HERE

How many items did you remember?

There are between 40 and 50 different things in the picture, depending on how finely you want to divide some of them up.

If you got more than 40, you are phenomenal, and our hats are off to you. Both Michael's dusty fedora and Richard's sweaty baseball cap.

If you got 30 or more, you're doing exceptionally well.

If you broke 20, you're above average.

If you managed 10 or more, you have a good but untrained memory.

If you didn't get at least 10, you need to practice your concentration and use some techniques for retention.

If you got *more than 60* you have an over-active imagination and we think you should try writing scripts for *The X Files* or *Futurama*.

The MOMA Method

We call our system for remembering objects you have seen the MOMA method.

MOMA stands for:

➤ Major

➤ Order

➤ Minor

➤ Attach

Well, that was easy. Surely you understand it all now, and we don't even have to explain what we mean. But just to make sure, we'll go over it.

Instant Recall

Some people with eidetic (or photographic) memories can look at a picture such as this one and recall it perfectly in their minds as a picture; so without even consciously noting any of the different objects when they looked, they can then name everything they saw. Many children possess this ability, but almost all of them lose it by the age of six. No one knows why.

Some Memorable Facts

The real world is full of distractions. If Trina's room were a real-life place and you were trying to memorize its contents, there'd probably be music playing, a dog barking, and someone downstairs shouting instructions to someone upstairs, and a neighbor who has decided that now is the perfect time to pound out the dent in the G below middle C pipe in his pipe organ.

So you must practice the ancient art of concentration. Breathe slowly and evenly and allow your mind to be filled by the task at hand—memorizing objects.

Major

If we tried to remember everything in the room by going from left to right or from top to bottom, we'd get hopelessly bogged down. We're going to use a chaining system here, but we're going to do it in two parts: major and minor. The major items in Trina's room are the big pieces of furniture. If you're looking at another scene to memorize, the major items would depend on the scene and on what you see as major; after all, you're the one doing the memorizing.

If you're looking at a shop window full of small merchandise—jewelry, for example— you could use the trays the jewelry rests in as your major items. You also could mentally divide the display into sections like a tic-tac-toe board, using each section as a major item. Use whatever works best for you.

Order

Next you have to decide the order in which you will remember these major items. In Trina's room, we'll go from left to right in several sweeps from back to front. There is no special reason for this; if something else works better for you, by all means do it your way.

So now we have MO—the major items in order:

➤ **Back row:**

China cabinet (or breakfront if you prefer)

Fireplace

Window

➤ **Middle row:**

Wing chair with end table

Couch

Coffee table

Easy chair with three-drawer table

➤ **Front row:**

Dog

Hassock or ottoman

Note the arbitrary placement of the coffee table with the couch. As long as you remember where it is, that's fine.

Now you should mentally go over the major-items list a couple times to fix it in your memory: china cabinet-fireplace-window-wing chair-couch-coffee table-easy chair-dog-hassock.

The attached objects, like the end table with the wing chair, should stick in your mind without too much effort. If you like, you can chain them together with silly images, as discussed in earlier chapters. Stick the china cabinet in the fireplace, right in front of a window in the fireplace's brick wall, for example. Often, because the images are visual—you're looking at them after all—that won't even be necessary.

Now on to MA.

Minor

Now that you have the major objects firmly in mind, attach all the minor objects that they are related to.

➤ **China cabinet:**

Sleeping cat

Two oval plates

Cup

➤ **Fireplace:**

Mantle

Picture of a woman

Doll

Another oval plate

➤ **In front:**

Christmas tree

Christmas tree ornaments

Star

➤ **Window:**

Valence across the top

Drapes tied to the right

Trees outside (Okay, we didn't ask you for what was outside, but if you saw it you should have noted it.)

Refresh Your Memory

"Once I had recognized the taste of the crumb of madeleine soaked in her decoction of lime flowers which my aunt used to give me—immediately the old gray house upon the street, where her room was, rose up like the scenery of a theater."

—Marcel Proust, *Remembrance of Things Past*

Refresh Your Memory

"You see, but you do not observe."

—Sherlock Holmes, *A Study in Scarlet*

➤ **Wing chair and end table:**

(Chair)

Large teddy bear

Cushion

(Table)

Eyeglasses

Letter-size envelope

➤ **Couch:**

Newspaper draped over the arm

Doily (or antimacassar if you like) on the back of the couch

➤ **Coffee table:**

Open drawer

Banana

Pear

Pipe with smoke rising

Cup and saucer with steam rising

Scarf with fringed end partially in the drawer

➤ **Easy chair with three-drawer table:**

Umbrella leaning against the chair

Vase with flowers placed on the table

Two books lying on the table

➤ **Slippers on the floor**

➤ **Dog:**

Dog collar

Bone

➤ **Hassock:**

Woman's summer hat with ribbons

How Many Was That?

As we mentioned, the number of items in the picture is subject to discussion. In fact, even the nature of some of the items may be ambiguous. Take another look at the picture.

On the mantle above the fireplace is a rectangular frame with a picture of a smiling woman, a wonderful doll wearing an old-fashioned hoop skirt, and ... what's that other

316

thing? We're calling it a plate because that's what the artist told us it is, but it could be a picture frame. If you can't tell—and in real life, you often can't tell—perhaps because of the angle, the shadows, or because you've never seen anything like it before, what are you to call it? And how are you to count it?

There are two books on the table. Should "books on the table" be one item or two? There are three cushions on the sofa. Do they count as separate items (making a total of four)? Or are they included in the sofa?

Actually, we counted some 45 items in the picture of Trina's room, but some of the items can be separated (the books, for example) to get more or combined (the Christmas tree and its ornaments, for example) to get less.

Instant Recall

Note that we stuck the slippers in between the easy chair and the dog because they weren't really associated with either. That's okay. (Well, we just did it, so of course it's okay!) An occasional random, unrelated minor item like that can easily be remembered.

Try it again and see how many you get using the MOMA system. You should get most of them, but don't worry if you still miss some. Like all the methods we've taught you, MOMA takes practice—and practice pays off!

What's This Good for, Anyhow?

Ah-hah! We thought you'd never ask! Actually, we'd have been disappointed if you hadn't. The MOMA exercise you've just performed (and we'll have another for you shortly) has practical value in many situations. Even in this age of ubiquitous video camcorders, we still need to be able to observe and retain. We don't want to let the machines do everything for us until we shrivel away into weak-eyed, spindly limbed, living brains like the futuristic monsters portrayed by some science-fiction writers.

This is a general reason for learning to observe and retain. Forgive us for waxing philosophical, but life on this planet can be wonderfully varied, colorful, and rich. It also can be dreadfully monotonous, drab, and impoverished. Learning to experience and enjoy our surroundings is one way of assuring ourselves of an enriched experience.

One person who observes a natural scene might say, "Right, some trees, yeah, and I guess those are birds up there. Let's go." Another person, a trained observer, can identify a hundred varieties of trees and can tell just from looking at them their age, the season, and recent weather conditions. She can look at the birds flying above and have an instant understanding of the local ecosystem: Where there are hawks there must be smaller birds or wildlife such as rabbits for them to prey on. Or perhaps they live on fish. Is there a stream nearby, even if we cannot see it from our particular vantage point?

From the angles of shadows, an acute observer can tell the time of day and perhaps even the time of year. Are there traces of snow on the ground? Are the trees in full leaf? Or are their limbs stripped?

One observer might see the universe in a drop of water. Another might see only the drop of water.

Some Memorable Facts

Unfortunately, training your memory and using mnemonic systems has not been shown to lead to any dramatic improvement in general memory function. Memory, unlike muscle, is not strengthened with use. Being able to remember a list of 20 items or to recall everything in a shop window does not automatically make it easier for you to remember where you put your keys. But the memory systems we are teaching you do work, and they become easier to use—and work better and faster—the more you use them. If you use the Loci System to memorize where your keys are or just practice being aware of what you're doing when you put them down, you'll be able to find them when you need them. If you practice memorizing what you see, the process will become automatic. If you ever need to use it, it will be there for you.

But What Is It Good For?

We already spoke about the general enrichment of life that comes with improving your powers of observation and retention. In some specific professions and situations, however, these powers have a direct and practical value.

If you are or plan to become a police officer or a private investigator, you will have to observe and remember things every day. In this situation, there's no shame in making a sketch, writing notes, or recording your observations on a portable tape recorder.

If you are or plan to become a journalist, you will need to observe and report on what you see. It isn't enough to say, "There's a scene of terrible carnage in the village where the guerrilla forces attacked the local residents." That may do for a start, but a good reporter trains him- or herself to observe and report on the details.

Some Memorable Facts

Nineteenth century French magician Jean Eugène Robert-Houdin, the court magician to King Louis XVIII, trained himself to glance at a room full of objects and remember the identity and location of every object in the room. His son said that, when he walked down the street with his father, Robert-Houdin would have him look at a display for 10 seconds and then turn away and name everything he could remember seeing in the window. After a while, the son could remember dozens of items after a short glance. The Hungarian-born American showman Erich Weiss, when he decided to become a magician, changed his name in honor of Robert-Houdin and called himself "Houdini."

How many victims were killed? How were they killed? Were they shot in the head, execution-style? Mowed down with automatic weapons? Hacked with machetes? Blown up by explosives?

Were there any survivors? What did they report of the incident?

Did the guerrillas take prisoners away with them?

Did they kill everyone they saw? Or did they spare women, children, and old people?

Did they destroy the villagers' homes? If so, how? Did they burn them? Blow them up with explosives? Crush them with heavy bulldozers or tanks?

How were the attackers dressed (assuming there were survivors to tell you)? Did they deliver any message? What language did they speak? Did they threaten to return and kill the survivors of their attack? Did they withdraw in an orderly manner? Or were they chased out by counter-attacking government forces?

There are 101 questions a good journalist will ask, and each one is an opportunity to observe and report.

How about becoming a novelist? The difference between success and failure in that profession is often the difference between creating characters or events that are bland and generic; and creating characters and events that are detailed and specific.

One wannabe novelist might write, "A woman entered the room and looked around at the people standing there."

Another might write, "A tall woman clad from head to foot in black leather strode confidently to the center of the room, paused between the alabaster pillars that framed the obscene altar, and glared at the flock of people cowering there."

Between the two of us, we've sold more than 50 novels. We can tell you right now that the second writer has a better chance of success. The first had better not quit her day job.

An Eye for Detail

Now we're going to try another quiz. You've already studied Trina's room at least twice. Before you read the following questions, go back and take still another look at it. If you have eidetic powers (or are trying to attain them), try to take a mental photograph of the picture.

If you prefer, you can use the MOMA method again. Scan the picture from side to side, mentally cataloging the major objects in the furthermost row, then the center row, then the nearest row. Link the objects and then cluster the minor objects around them.

Now put the picture away and answer the following questions:

➤ Was the cat awake or asleep?

➤ Was the cat striped, spotted, or solid-colored? Was she light or dark?

➤ Was her tail curled around her? If not, what was she doing with her tail?

➤ Was the woman in the picture on the mantelpiece wearing a dress or a T-shirt and jeans?

➤ Which of the teddy bear's eyes was closed, the left or the right?

➤ What was the headline on the newspaper lying on the sofa?

➤ Were the cup in the china cabinet and the cup on the coffee table part of a matching set?

➤ How many flowers were in the vase? How many leaves?

➤ Did the dog have "floppy down" ears or were they standing up?

➤ Was the umbrella open or furled?

➤ Was that a man or a woman peering in the window?

Refresh Your Memory

"Constantinople, the city of a hundred races and a thousand vices, was split in half by that thumb of the Bosporus known throughout recorded history as the Golden Horn. On one side, Stamboul, outpost of Asia; on the other Galata and Pera, terminus of Europe. A floating bridge connected Galata and Stamboul. The Galata side was European and nineteenth century. The men wore top hats and gaiters, and the ladies favored French bonnets and French perfumes; the hotels had gaslight and indoor plumbing.

"Stamboul was Roman and Byzantine and Turk and Arab; ancient and timeless. It smelled of Levant. The men wore turbans and fezzes and the women were veiled. Caravan drivers from Baghdad spread their goods in the Covered Bazaar, and one ate only with one's right hand."

—Michael Kurland, *The Infernal Device*

How many of these questions did you get right? Go ahead and look at the picture again to check your results. Oh, some of the questions were trick questions? Yes, they were. So clever of you to notice!

The More Details the Better

An interesting, but not obvious, fact about memorization is that the more (and more varied) details you pile on each item when memorizing a list, the easier the item is to remember. Likewise, if you observe the little details when you're trying to remember a scene in front of you, like all the items in Trina's room, the better your visualization will be and the easier the recall will be.

Don't just see a teddy bear on the wing chair; see a teddy bear with wide, staring eyes. Don't just see a dog on the floor; see a long-haired, medium-size dog with a studded collar, perky ears, a flat muzzle, and a big nose.

The Distant Sound of Silvery Horns

A well-publicized experiment not long ago showed that listening to music before taking an intelligence test actually raised the scores of a group of volunteers compared to the scores of a control group who did not listen to the music.

Further, and this we find fascinating, it wasn't just any music that produced this effect—it was Mozart.

We haven't tried to reproduce this experiment ourselves to see whether we could obtain the same results, but we are intrigued. Why Mozart? Why not Bach or Locatelli or Vivaldi or Hildegarde von Bingen? Why not Beethoven or Brahms? What about Gershwin, Cole Porter, or Miles Davis?

At this point, pending further experiments, we can only offer some advice. If you want to "tune up" your brain and help yourself concentrate, music may help. Certainly, it will help you close out the rest of the distracting world and focus your mental powers on the task at hand.

It's best to avoid vocal music. If you're trying to memorize, "Twas brillig and the slithy toves did gyre and gimbal in the wabe," while Ella Fitzgerald is singing, "A foggy day in

Refresh Your Memory

"You know my method. It is founded upon the observation of trifles."

—Sherlock Holmes, *A Case of Identity*

Refresh Your Memory

"A verbal art like poetry is reflective; it stops to think. Music is immediate; it goes on to become ... Music is the best means we have of digesting time."

—W. H. Auden (1907–1973)

London town," or Frank Sinatra is inviting you to "Come fly with me," or Mick Jagger is informing you, "I can't get no satisfaction," you are almost certain to become distracted or confused.

Stick with chamber music, cool jazz, or Gregorian chants.

Come to think of it, there's probably a CD player somewhere in Trina's room, just out of sight. She's put on a favorite piece of music, and you can hear the distant sound of silvery horns.

Now take another look.

The Least You Need to Know

➤ Remembering groups of objects actually in front of you takes a different technique. It is necessary to organize them in your mind in a way that makes them easy to retrieve from memory.

➤ We have devised what we call the MOMA system, which stands for **M**ajor, **O**rder, **M**inor, **A**ttach.

➤ First decide what the major objects in view are. In a room, they usually would be the larger pieces of furniture.

➤ Next decide in what order you are going to group them: linear, circular, zigzag, or whatever. As long as it makes sense to you and is easy to remember, feel free to use it.

➤ Group minor objects around the major object they are most closely associated with.

➤ Mentally attach the minor objects to their associated major object and the major objects to each other.

➤ Listening to Mozart's music has been shown to aid memory and intelligence. Other composers? The jury is still out.

Chapter 26

I've Got a Little List

> ### In This Chapter
>
> ➤ Seven is a lucky number
>
> ➤ Snow White and her little friends
>
> ➤ Only one of the seven survives!
>
> ➤ A good constitution—and 10 great amendments
>
> ➤ A visit to an imaginary town

In this chapter, you'll get a chance to use many of the techniques we taught you in the earlier parts of this book. We've gathered together some lists of things that you always meant to memorize but never got around to, and we've put them here for you to practice on.

Remember all the times at parties or sitting around after dinner with your best friends when it suddenly became incredibly important, for reasons you never could figure out afterward, to be able to name all seven of Snow White's dwarfs, or all seven of the wonders of the ancient world? Well, we'll give them all to you in this chapter.

We'll wrap up the chapter with a section on the Bill of Rights. It will be fun, informative, and a great example of the world's oldest known mnemonic technique, the Loci System that you learned about a few chapters ago.

Lucky Seven

Seven was considered one of the luckiest numbers, being the sum of the two lucky numbers four and three. The seventh son was the most favored, and many magicians used to claim they were "the seventh son of a seventh son," presumably for twice the luck. There were seven days in the week, seven planets known to the ancient peoples, and seven days in creation. Among the ancient Hebrews, every seventh year was a sabbatical (and some universities still give their top professors a "sabbatical year" once every seven years, to spend on research or writing without having to meet any classes), and seven times seven years brought the jubilee.

All of these sevens—and a great many other ideas about lucky and unlucky numbers—go far back in history. In Western society, numerology dates at least to the development of the Kabala by Hebrew scholars in the seventh (!) century. Actually, numerology, like alchemy and astrology, is an ancient magical art and pseudo-science. Each was the forerunner of a *real* science—mathematics, chemistry, and astronomy. Eastern cultures, including those of ancient China and India, had their own versions of these magical arts.

> ### Instant Recall
>
> If a seventh son was lucky, maybe the seventh son of a seventh son wasn't just twice as lucky—he might have been *49* times as lucky! After all, why does luck have to work by simple addition? Aren't we supposed to "be fruitful *and multiply*"?

Short People

The seven dwarfs are among the most famous short people in all of children's literature. In the version of the Snow White story written by the Brothers Grimm, the seven dwarfs are not mentioned by name. Disney, however, has remedied that. So now, and probably for all time, Snow White's dwarfs will be known as:

Dopey

Grumpy

Sneezy

Happy

Sleepy

Bashful

Doc

How can you remember these names? Well, you probably already know the names; your problem is just how to recall them when necessary. How about an acronymic sentence? Here's one:

Do Green Snails Have Slippery Backs, Doc?

As we're sure you've noticed, the first two letters of each word correspond to the first two letters of a dwarf's name. Clever, eh? And Doc is, well, Doc.

The Seven Wonders

Everybody knows there were seven wonders of the ancient world, but how many people can name them? Well, we can. And shortly you will be able to as well. There are several different versions of just what these seven wonders were. Here's the most commonly accepted one:

1. The Pyramids of Egypt
2. The Walls and Hanging Gardens of Babylon
3. The Statue of Zeus at Olympia
4. The Temple of Diana at Ephesus
5. The Mausoleum at Halicarnassus
6. The Colossus at Rhodes
7. The Pharos (lighthouse) at Alexandria

Some Memorable Facts

The Pyramids of Egypt are the oldest of the seven wonders of the ancient world. Estimates of their age go as high as 5,000 years or even more! The other wonders all were built several thousand years after the Pyramids, although all were built in the era that historians now call "B.C.E." (before the Common Era), previously known as "B.C." All the wonders have been destroyed, whether by fire, earthquake, war, or simple neglect—except the Pyramids, which endure wondrous, serene, and eternal.

There are several ways to remember these wonders including the chain-link method, an acronymic sentence, and the Loci System. But let's refresh our memories, polish our skills, and use the number alphabet. You might remember that system as follows:

1 = t = hat

2 = n = hen

3 = m = ham

4 = r = hair

5 = l = hole

6 = sh = hash

7 = k = hook

The system goes on, of course, but we only need numbers 1 through 7 just now, so let's stop there. How do we remember the seven wonders? We can visualize each of them in a vivid and unforgettable combination with the word for its number. Here's an example:

1. The Pyramids are gigantic and hats are small, so let's create a silly image of a *hat*, perhaps a red fez, sitting upside down with the Great Pyramid of Giza dumped upside-down into it.

Some Memorable Facts

The Sphinx, the huge statue that lies near the Great Pyramid, appears on several "seven wonders" lists although not on ours. It is even older than the pyramids—and even more mysterious. Nobody knows exactly how old the Sphinx is, although estimates go back as far as 12,000 years. Nobody knows whose face was originally on the Sphinx, and it's impossible to tell, today, because (apparently) at least one of the pharaohs had the face re-cut into his own image. Speculation as to who built this magnificent statue of a lion with a human head has suggested the possibility of a mysterious civilization even more ancient and splendid than that of the Egyptians. But this is only speculation.

2. The hanging gardens hung from the walls of Babylon, so let's picture a *hen* squawking as it almost falls from atop the Walls and Hanging Gardens of Babylon.

3. Imagine a worshiper racing in from winning the Olympics, bowing low, and offering a *ham* to the god Zeus at his temple at Olympia.

4. "Effie says" just picture a luxuriant growth of *hair* sprouting from the Statue Diana in her Temple at Ephesus.

5. Mausoleums were named for King Mausolus's wonderfully ornate tomb at Halicarnassus. Most tombs are merely *holes* in the ground, but not King Mausolus's wonderful Mausoleum at Halicarnassus.

6. Picture a giant dish of *hash*, taking up the whole harbor at Rhodes, and from it is emerging this giant statue—the Colossus of Rhodes.

7. The gods are enraged! A giant *hook* is emerging from an angry, rolling storm cloud and carrying the Pharos (lighthouse) of Alexandria away, which is why we cannot find it in this modern era.

Remember This!

Once you have selected your pegs for the numbers (hat, hen, ham, and so forth), you must be consistent and apply the same system over and over. If you change your visual pegs, you will become confused. You must devote mental effort to visualizing the items on your list along with the pegs. This takes some work, but it is vital to your success!

The Bill of Rights

By now you know how to use the Loci System, one of the most powerful, flexible, and practical methods of memorizing lists. You'll recall that anyone can create her own set of Loci, as the Italian Father Ricci did with his "palaces of memory." In Chapter 23, "Foci on the Loci," we created two sets of Loci for demonstration purposes—a tour of the solar system and a baseball diamond with the players in position.

Many people use their own homes as Loci (or their hometowns, as Shereshevsky did). People using their homes already know the rooms and the layout. They need only imagine starting at the front door and then walking through the house, placing (or "imaging") objects in each room.

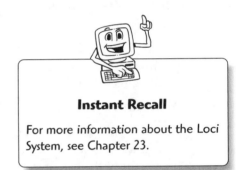

Instant Recall

For more information about the Loci System, see Chapter 23.

But now we're going to create a special-purpose set of Loci, an imaginary village we'll use to remember one of the most important documents we have—the Bill of Rights. How important is this document? Think back to your classes in American history and remember how our government was created. After 13 colonies won their independence from Great Britain and became the 13 original United States, they adopted a loose compact called the Articles of Confederation. This compact went into effect in 1781. Things didn't work out very well under the Articles, so a convention was called and a new Constitution was drafted. It went into effect in September 1788.

But many leading citizens were worried about a government with too much power. After all, this was what the Revolution had been all about—getting the Americans out from under the thumb of what they perceived to be a tyrannical government.

So one of the first orders of business of the new Congress was the adoption of 10 amendments to the Constitution that carefully stated the rights and powers of both the people and the government. These amendments were ratified in quick time and

Instant Recall

Remember that experiments conducted using college students as volunteer subjects show that nonsense syllables are harder to remember than words and that random words are harder to remember than a sentence created from these words. The more meaningful the material, the easier it is to learn it.

went into effect on December 15, 1791. It was a glorious day for freedom! These 10 amendments, collectively known as the Bill of Rights, are the foundation of the freedoms we enjoy to this day.

Everybody is at least vaguely aware of the Bill of Rights and some of its provisions. If you care enough to really get to know the Bill of Rights, however, here's a good way to learn. We're going to create a special set of Loci called Bill O'Rights Town (named after the town's legendary first mayor "Big Bill" O'Rights). We're going to set up this imaginary town so you can walk through it—in your mind—any time you want to. We urge you to spend time there. It's a wonderful place, and the rights that are placed there are very, very precious to us all.

First, let's take a look at the 10 amendments. You can find their text in most almanacs, civics texts, or other reference books. But just to make this convenient, we'll give them here.

When memorizing anything, it's helpful to understand what you're memorizing. As we go through the amendments, we'll follow the text of each with a brief explanation of what rights it guarantees.

Amendment One:

> Congress shall make no law respecting an establishment of religion, or prohibiting the free exercise thereof; or abridging the freedom of speech, or of the press; or the right of the people peaceably to assemble, and to petition the Government for a redress of grievances.

What It Means:

This amendment establishes several of our most important freedoms. It means that the government cannot force you to practice any religion against your will or prevent you from practicing the religion of your choice. You can worship a little green kitchen deity if you wish—it's your right. This amendment also states that you can speak up and write what you choose. The government cannot tell you, "You can't say that" or "You can't write that." If you and your neighbors want to get together and discuss dumping the mayor because you think he's a crook, he can't send the cops to break up your meeting (or break your skull). And if you don't like the government's policy on any issue, you have the right to demand that they change it.

Amendment Two:

> A well-regulated Militia, being necessary to the security of a free State, the right of the people to keep and bear Arms, shall not be infringed.

What It Means:

This amendment permits the establishment of a *militia*, an old term for what today we would think of as military reserves or National Guard units. Of course, they're allowed "to keep and bear arms." The amendment does *not* mean that your wacko neighbor is allowed to mount a howitzer on his roof or build a hydrogen bomb in his basement or that the gangsters down the block can carry Uzi's around and engage in gang wars. A lot of people don't seem to understand this distinction.

Amendment Three:

> No Soldier shall, in time of peace be quartered in any house, without the consent of the Owner, nor in time of war, but in a manner to be prescribed by law.

What It Means:

The British Army in America had a bad habit of requiring the King's colonial subjects to house and feed his soldiers without even asking permission. This saved the British Army money but created much ill will. This amendment hasn't been needed much since the Revolution, but it's there for our protection anyway. It means the army can't take over your living room and house a couple of infantry squads there. In peacetime, not at all. Even in wartime, it would take an act of Congress to make it okay.

Amendment Four:

> The right of the people to be secure in their persons, houses, papers, and effects, against unreasonable searches and seizures, shall not be violated, and no Warrants shall issue, but upon probable cause, supported by Oath or affirmation, and particularly describing the place to be searched, and the persons or things to be seized.

What It Means:

You're sitting in your living room one night, quietly reading Homer's *Odyssey* (in the original, classical Greek, of course) when a police officer knocks at the door and says he's there to search the place—and maybe to check you out into the bargain. "How come?" you ask. "'Cause I feel like it," the cop says. "Might be something shady going on in this house." No way! He has to have some evidence that criminal activity is going on in the house right then to enter (say someone screaming for help in the next room). Otherwise, he has to get a warrant from a judge first. To get the warrant, he must establish "probable cause" that something of interest to the police is going on or that something is concealed in the house that shouldn't be there, such as illegal drugs or weapons, or a stash of stolen goods. And the warrant has to say what the police officer is looking for and where he thinks he's going to find it.

Amendment Five:

> No person shall be held to answer for a capital, or otherwise infamous crime, unless on a presentment or indictment of a Grand Jury, except in cases arising in the land or naval forces, or in the Militia, when in actual service in time of War or public danger; nor shall any person be subject for the same offense to be twice put in jeopardy of life or limb; nor shall be compelled in any criminal case to be a witness against himself, nor be deprived of life, liberty, or property, without due process of law; nor shall private property be taken for public use, without just compensation.

What It Means:

The fifth amendment protects a lot of your rights, including some of the most important. First, it means that you can't just be dragged into court. The prosecutor has to get an indictment first (unless you're in the military, in which case a whole other set of laws apply). It means that, if you're tried and acquitted, they can't come after you and try you again for the same alleged offense. It means that nobody can make you testify against yourself. It's the prosecutor's job to prove you're guilty if he can, and you don't have to help him do his job. It also says the government can't decide to punish you just because someone thinks you're a bad guy and you deserve it. You have the right to a trial with all your *other* rights respected—that's what "due process" is all about! Finally, this amendment means that, if the government needs to take your property (maybe they want to build a freeway in your backyard), they can't just take it—they have to pay you fair market value for it.

Some Memorable Facts

The section of the Fifth Amendment that reads, "nor shall any person be subject for the same offense to be twice put in jeopardy of life or limb," is sometimes referred to as the "double jeopardy" clause. Like many legal principles, it can cut both ways. If an innocent person is accused of a crime, tried, and acquitted, the government cannot harass him by hauling him back into court and putting him on trial again for the same alleged offense. On the other hand, if a defendant is acquitted because the government failed to make its case, and new evidence turns up that proves conclusively that the accused person was guilty of that crime all along—he can thumb his nose at the law.

In recent years there have been attempts to get around this provision by changing the charge and the court. For instance, a person might be accused of murder, tried in a state court, and acquitted. The federal government might then accuse the same person of "violating the civil rights" of the victim and bring him to trial in a federal court. After all, being alive is a civil right, isn't it?

Another variation is for the family of the murdered person to bring a *civil suit* against the acquitted defendant. This, if he loses the suit, can stain his reputation and cause his financial ruin, but it is not double jeopardy because no criminal liability attaches—it cannot cause him to be imprisoned.

Many lawyers and civil libertarians are very nervous about some of these practices; they may spring from admirable intentions but they seem to go against the spirit, if not the letter, of the Fifth Amendment. You can expect to see this controversy pop up in the news from time to time.

Amendment Six:

> In all criminal prosecutions, the accused shall enjoy the right to a speedy and public trial, by an impartial jury of the State and district wherein the crime shall have been committed, which district shall have been previously ascertained by law, and to be informed of the nature and cause of the accusation; to be confronted with the witnesses against him; to have compulsory process for obtaining witnesses in his favor, and to have the Assistance of Counsel for his defense.

What It Means:

This is another biggie. It means that the government can't arrest you and keep you locked up for years on end "awaiting trial." They have to give you your day in court within a reasonable time. The trial has to take place in the "State and district" where the alleged crime was committed. They have to tell you what you're accused of and bring in the witnesses against you so you can see and hear them testify and cross-examine them; this means no secret trials on secret charges with secret evidence. It says that *you* have the right to subpoena witnesses, and you're entitled to have a lawyer and to have a jury decide your guilt or innocence.

Amendment Seven:

> In Suits at common law, where the value in controversy shall exceed twenty dollars, the right of trial by jury shall be preserved, and no fact tried by a jury, shall be otherwise re-examined in any Court of the United States, than according to the rules of common law.

What It Means:

Twenty dollars was worth a lot more in 1791 than it's worth today, but the principle still holds true. If someone sues you, you can demand a jury trial. After the jury makes its finding regarding the facts of the case, that's the end of it. The case can be appealed if the procedures were carried out wrongly or if misconduct was involved, such as collusion between the lawyers (if your lawyers were working for your opponent, for example). After the facts are settled, however, that's it. This only applies in federal courts. State courts set their own dollar limits and other rules.

Amendment Eight:

> Excessive bail shall not be required, nor excessive fines imposed, nor cruel and unusual punishments inflicted.

What It Means:

This means they can't demand $1 million bail for someone accused of stealing a honeydew melon (remember, no one's been *convicted* of anything, yet). It also means that the fine for stealing a honeydew melon must be appropriate to the offense—certainly not $1 million. And that "cruel and unusual punishment" clause is really, *really* important. It means that the law has to establish a reasonable penalty for any given offense. The judge can't sentence you to be eaten alive by alligators just because he doesn't like you—even if you *are* convicted of stealing a honeydew melon.

Some Memorable Facts

In recent years there have been many attempts to get chronic or "career" criminals off the streets in order to prevent their continuing to commit crimes. Among these are various "three strikes" (or even "one strike") laws. Again, the intention may be admirable and the laws may work in many cases. But in others, criminals have received sentences of many years for committing petty offenses, based on their number of "strikes."

Amendment Nine:

> The enumeration in the Constitution, of certain rights, shall not be construed to deny or disparage others retained by the people.

What It Means:

This is an amendment we don't hear about very often, but it's another gem. It means that, just because the Bill of Rights doesn't list a particular right, that doesn't mean you weren't meant to have it. Are you allowed to stand on your head and sing arias from your favorite opera? Gosh, the Constitution doesn't say you can. Maybe you can't! Right? No, wrong! If there's no law *against* it, you can do it. This is a free country!

Amendment Ten:

> The powers not delegated to the United States by the Constitution, nor prohibited by it to the States, are reserved to the States respectively, or to the people.

What It Means:

Every time a fight breaks out between your state's governor, legislature, or courts and the Feds, you can be certain that somebody's going to invoke this amendment. It says that the Constitution gives the federal government its powers and that any power it *doesn't* give to the federal government, the federal government doesn't have. Period. A lot of politicians don't believe this—that's why there are so many fights!

Bill O'Rights Town

Let's start by remembering, in the order we will mentally see them, the buildings in Bill O'Rights Town. Because we're creating this town for the specific purpose of memorizing the Bill of Rights, we can put the buildings best suited to our needs exactly where we want them. You'll see why we picked each one when we tie the amendments into their places.

We'll begin at the left end of town with the *church*, proceed down Constitution Avenue (you don't have to remember that) to the *armory*, and then visit a lovely two-story *private home* with a picket fence. From there, we'll go to the equally lovely *house next door*. At the end of the street we'll come to the *courthouse*, and next to it the town *jail*. Now we can head back across the street, where we'll come to the wide, well-tended, grassy *town commons*. The picturesque tranquillity of the town is somewhat offset by the *whipping post* at the edge of the commons. Next we'll encounter the large, colonial-style *town hall*, and past that we'll see the wide double-doors of the *People's Power Building*.

Now let's pick out the key features (or Loci) that we encountered in that quick tour of Bill O'Rights Town. Here they are, in the order in which we encountered them:

1. Church
2. Armory
3. Private home
4. House next door
5. Courthouse
6. Jail
7. Town commons
8. Whipping post
9. Town hall
10. People's Power Building

Freedom in Action

Now we'll wander through the town and observe freedom in action, as envisioned by the authors of the Bill of Rights. When you read each scene, refer back to the article in question. After two or three readings, you'll have the whole scene firmly fixed in your mind, at least as far as the meaning and intent of each article. To memorize the exact wording, you'll probably have to go over it a few more times.

1. We'll start at the church, which we can see has a printing press busily printing out a petition. In front of the church, a crowd of people have assembled and are discussing the government.

2. In the armory, the militia members are drilling in Revolutionary War uniforms with their long flintlock rifles over their shoulders.

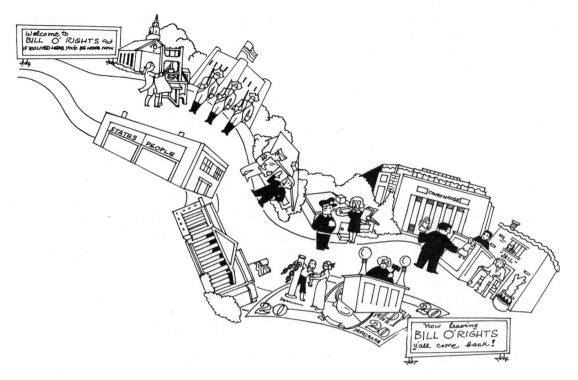

A map of Bill O'Rights Town prepared by the Tourist Board of the Bill O'Rights Town Chamber of Commerce.

3. Now we are at the private house, where a soldier with a pillow in his hand is being turned away from the door by the resident, who is screaming at him, "There's no war on! And even if there were, Congress has to pass a law!"

4. At the house next door, a woman is standing with a pile of papers and effects in her left arm. Her right arm is extended, palm out, to bar the policeman, who is trying to enter without a warrant.

5. In the courthouse, there are two rooms. In one courtroom, a grand jury—perhaps a jury with great funny hats, that's pretty grand—is handing an indictment to a judge, who is turning it away and saying, "I can't take it—that's twice!" In the second courtroom, a defendant is refusing to take the stand while the judge is handing back his life, liberty, and property. On the courthouse steps, a property owner is accepting some oversized coins in return for his property from a second man wearing a signboard reading "public use."

6. When we reach the jail, everyone is rushing around to conduct a speedy trial on the steps. The accused is standing on a box with his lawyer by his side while several witnesses are being held up for him to examine.

Some Memorable Facts

The concept of a public trial means that the defendant's family and friends, the press, and members of the general public must be admitted to the courtroom during the trial. In this manner, the rights of the defendant are protected against the more obvious sorts of abuse of state power, or at least the abuse is exposed to public view. Tyrants don't like this, and secret trials are common under dictatorships—when they bother with a trial at all. Even in our own country, the ideal of the "open courtroom" is not always observed. Using the rationale of "national security," spy cases have sometimes been tried in secret.

7. We next arrive at the commons, where another trial is being held on a giant $20 bill.

8. At the whipping post, a man is being untied from the post by a woman in a white gown with a bandage around her eyes. (You can name her "Justice" if you like.) "That's cruel and unusual," she says, handing a few small coins for bail to the chief torturer.

9. The town hall is full of people who have come to make sure their rights are not denied. Someone tries to make fun of this, and everyone disagrees with him. But he's allowed to state his opinion. The people exercising their rights don't deny the protester his.

10. The People's Power Building has a sign on one front door saying "Reserved to the States" and on the other door saying "Reserved to the People."

The Least You Need to Know

➤ The seven dwarfs are Dopey, Grumpy, Sneezy, Happy, Sleepy, Bashful, and Doc. Just remember: Do Green Snails Have Slippery Backs, Doc?

➤ The seven wonders of the ancient world are a little more difficult to remember, but with some concentrated effort the number alphabet should work just fine.

➤ The Loci System enables us to remember the Bill of Rights.

➤ A walking tour of the imaginary Bill O'Rights Town will take us through the Bill of Rights and imprint it on our memory.

The Waters of Lethe

In This Chapter

➤ A river runs through it

➤ "Don't you touch my brain!"

➤ "You put your left foot in..."

➤ "I'd know you anywhere—who are you?"

➤ Some things you *want* to forget

Thousands of years ago, the Greeks created an elaborate mythology that purported to explain the universe. Among other subjects, it included a kind of underworld where the souls of the dead went. Through this shadowy world, called Hades, there flowed the river Lethe (pronounced *Leeth-ee*). One sip of the water from this river and all one's memories were wiped away.

Well, just between you and us, you don't have to die to forget. In fact, you forget 99 percent of your daily experiences. Make that 99 and a fraction. And it's a good thing you do!

"I Took a Step and Then I Took Another Step"

Remember the schematic we looked at, laying out the levels of memory. First there's sensory input, which goes into your immediate memory. There's almost no retention here. There's a constant stream of input: every step you take, every sight you see, every fleeting thought or emotion. Each impression replaces the one that came before and is in turn replaced by the one that follows.

From this initial memory "holding area," an image or thought moves into short-term or working memory. It stays here as long as you concentrate on it, typically 5 to 10 seconds if that. (Different researchers come up with different measurements for this phenomenon.)

Finally, it moves on to long-term memory. It can stay in long-term memory for a very long time, even for a lifetime, available for recall into working memory and your active consciousness.

You have several layers of memory so unimportant information can be filtered or edited out. This is very important. Let's see why. When you wake up in the morning, you probably go through a process something like this:

1. Sit up.
2. Yawn.
3. Stretch.
4. Turn sideways on the edge of your bed.
5. Put your feet in your slippers.
6. Stand up.
7. Take a step.
8. Take another step.
9. Take still another step.
10. Reach for the bathroom doorknob.
11. Turn the doorknob.
12. Open the bathroom door.
13. Take another step...

...and so on in endless, tiresome detail. You perform one routine task after another after another.

Do you really want to remember all that?

Do you really want to remember every breath you take, every sip of orange juice, every bite of toast, every word you read in your morning newspaper?

Hey, neither do we.

Fortunately, your brain has developed a very clever system for evaluating your sensory inputs and deciding which ones to pass on to the deeper and more enduring levels of memory. The great majority of sensations don't even make it from immediate memory to short-term memory, and still fewer make it from short-term to long-term memory.

At least, that's the way it seems. Some psychologists maintain that *everything* gets remembered and is stored away somewhere in your brain. Experiments performed on patients undergoing brain surgery offer limited support to this theory. These experiments suggest that your brain stores a lot more information than you can normally gain access to. This notion carries us back to our "library" model of memory. What if there are books in the attic with wonderful information in them—but you normally can't get up there to read them?

Surgeons have applied electrical stimulation to precise points on the brains of patients. This is a painless procedure. The brain itself is apparently incapable of experiencing any sensation. The patients, after the procedure, do not make any reports to the effect of, "I felt you touch my brain, Dr. Pretorius."

Refresh Your Memory

"The past is not something fixed and unalterable. Every age has their own Greece and Rome, their own Middle Ages."

—Aldous Huxley

Remember This!

Any medical experimentation on human beings—*especially* experimentation on their brains!—presents serious ethical and legal problems. In all the cases described here, brain surgery was required for other, medical, reasons. Even in these cases, it was necessary for the surgeon to obtain the informed consent of the patient before any experiment was performed.

Instead, they say things like, "I experienced a moment from my sixth birthday party. It wasn't like a normal memory; I was *there*. I had a ribbon in my hair, and I was wearing my new green dress and my patent leather shoes. I ate cake, we played games, and there were presents. My Mommy and Daddy were there, and they looked so young. And all my friends were there. I know what kind of day it was. We sang songs. My doggie came running in and stole a piece of birthday cake, and everybody was laughing. It wasn't just remembering. I was there, it was happening, and it was all *absolutely real*."

Certainly the experience was "absolutely real" to the patient, but did the surgeon's touch to her brain summon a memory of an actual event in the patient's childhood? Or was this a "created memory"? Alas, at this early stage of research, this question has yet to be answered. Keep monitoring the scientific journals for news.

This is puzzling in another regard. How much capacity does the human brain have? Considering the number of neurons and the number of possible connections among them, the capacity is utterly staggering. Remember Ray Kurzweil's estimate of 100 *billion* neurons in your brain and 100 *trillion* connections between them.

Let's assume each of these connections represents one memory unit. We don't know yet exactly what a memory unit contains. Is it the equivalent of a single bit (binary digit) of computer memory? Or a byte (a number or letter) or a complete image or incident?

We just don't know—yet.

If those neural connections do represent 100 trillion memory units, just how much information is that? To get even a slight idea of the amount, try looking at the quantity 100 trillion written out in ordinary numerals:

100,000,000,000,000

It looks as if memory *capacity* isn't the problem. Why, then, did you develop that system of filtering memories? When you were a newborn infant, you probably didn't have it. *Everything* made an impression on you. And yet, if your infancy made it to your long-term memory, you don't know how to retrieve it. Nobody does.

As you grew older and your capabilities developed, you learned to concentrate your attention. If you've ever watched a young child learning to walk, you have observed how intent that child has to be on the act of walking. It is quite a remarkable feat. Walking on two feet is very different from walking on four feet. Most of our four-footed friends can stand up and take at least a few tottering steps the day they're born.

After you master the art of walking on two feet, you can assign that function to a part of your brain other than your conscious mind. Despite the old saying about not being able to walk and chew gum at the same time, most people *can* do two things at once, very well, whether it's walking and eating an ice-cream cone or walking and carrying on a conversation with a friend.

Some Memorable Facts

As a matter of fact, you can do a lot more than two things at once. While you're walking down the street, chatting with a friend, and eating an ice-cream cone, you're also observing other pedestrians, watching out for traffic lights, and pausing at corners, glancing occasionally into shop windows, worrying about your daughter's scoundrelly new boyfriend, and thinking about what you're going to have for dinner tonight. You also are breathing in and out, your heart is beating, your digestive system is carrying out its usual duties, and a myriad of other bodily functions are taking place—all under automatic (or "autonomic") control. Your brain is taking care of these jobs, and you don't even have to think about them!

You don't remember learning to walk (or at least you don't unless you're a very unusual individual), but you probably remember learning to ride a bicycle. Remember how, as a beginner, you had to concentrate on balancing and pedaling and steering? If someone so much as asked you a question, you were likely to crash into a wall!

Once you mastered the art of riding a bike, however, that skill, like the art of walking, became automatic. What's going on here?

All Those Little Cubby Holes

You have some wonderful software in your head, and in the cases we just described—learning to walk, learning to ride a bike, learning to drive a car—that software has taken over and has routed the "skill memory" you've been developing in your conscious, working memory to long-term storage. You don't need to think about it any more. Your body will take care of it for you the next time you have to walk across the room or ride your bicycle in the park or drive your car to the supermarket.

You don't *need* the conscious memories of learning how to walk or ride or drive, and you don't *need* to devote conscious thought to the mechanics of walking or riding or driving, so your mind gets rid of them and sends the mechanics to long-term memory. There, you retain the skills you do need. And when you utilize those skills, you usually do so with little or no conscious thought.

Of course, if you're walking on a very icy sidewalk, riding your bike through an obstacle course, or driving in especially difficult traffic, the routine act becomes anything but routine, and your conscious mind comes back into the picture.

Remember This!

We can think of memory as **immediate**, **short-term**, and **long-term**. Or we can think of it as **fact**, **skill**, and **event** memory. Is one metaphor right and the other wrong? No! In fact, the most useful approach is to think of memory as *containing* fact, skill, and event memories. But these are all memory **functions**. They're not separate little devices inside your head, the way a RAM chip, hard disk, and tape backup are separate units inside your computer.

Refresh Your Memory

"Blessed are the forgetful: for they get the better even of their blunders."

—Friedrich Wilhelm Nietzsche (1844–1900) from *Thus Spake Zarathustra*

But what about *fact memory*? Whoa, let's pause for a moment and review. Remember that there are different ways of thinking about memory. These are different concepts, or *metaphors*, for what goes on inside your brain. When we look at memory in different ways, it doesn't mean one way is right and other way is wrong. These *metaphors* are just *images* or *models* we use to help us understand real-world phenomena.

So after you've learned something you want to hang onto and use again, such as how to walk, your brain stores that information or skill but "throws away" your specific recollection of events in obtaining the skill.

You don't need to clutter your mind with vast amounts of uninteresting trivia for which you have no use!

"I Know I Know It!"

Sometimes you try to recall something you did know at one time, and you just can't "find" it mentally. For example, you meet someone you haven't seen in a long time. "I don't know the name but the face is familiar." We devoted an entire chapter to dealing with the problem of matching names with faces, but it still might plague you from time to time.

This is especially true if you meet someone in an unfamiliar context. You see a bus driver in her uniform every morning, cap and all, driving her bus. You've exchanged friendly greetings hundreds of times.

She knows you, and you know her. Sure you do.

Then one evening you're dining with your significant other in your favorite restaurant, and you happen to catch the eye of a lovely woman seated at another table. She's wearing an elegant gown, her hair is elaborately coifed, and she's holding hands romantically with her companion.

To your surprise, the glamorous woman leaves her seat, walks over to you, and says, "What a pleasant surprise, Mr. Shaw! And I assume this is Mrs. Shaw?"

You rise and bow and manage to blurt a few embarrassed words. The glamorous woman smiles and returns to her own table. Your significant other says, "What a beautiful woman! Who was she?"

You stammer in reply, "I haven't the foggiest idea! I know that I know her. I'm sure of it. But I just can't place her!"

Monday morning you board your regular bus and nod to the driver. She smiles back. "Mr. Shaw, nice to see you again." At this moment, you realize to your shock that she was the woman in the restaurant!

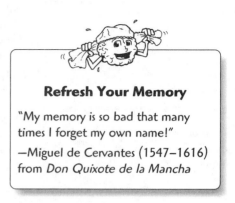

Refresh Your Memory

"My memory is so bad that many times I forget my own name!"

—Miguel de Cervantes (1547–1616) from *Don Quixote de la Mancha*

But what happened? Did you forget her? No. You knew her only as a bus driver. You hadn't made the right neural connections to recognize her in a restaurant, wearing an elegant dress.

You do forget things, however. Facts you learned in school fade away. Skills you haven't used in a long time also fade. To understand why, we have to revert to our model of memory as an electrochemical process that takes place in the brain. Remember, every time you exercise a neuron, you strengthen it. You reinforce that memory.

If you don't use it for a long time, it may well fade away.

Learning and Relearning

Relearning is a phenomenon that supports the idea that we do not *totally* forget anything once we've learned it. We mentioned the experience of our actor friend who could relearn a role in a play he had not performed for many years far more quickly and easily than he could learn a new role. His experience suggests that the "circuits" were still in place. They merely needed to be reactivated and reinforced.

Instant Recall

Another common experience is relearning in later years a language you knew as a child but had then forgotten. Relearning a language is much easier than learning it.

This also applies to people who have learned to play musical instruments and then stopped playing for years or even decades. They forget everything they ever knew, or so they think. When they start music lessons over from scratch, however, they find that they can learn (actually, relearn) far more quickly and easily than they did the first time around.

Instant Recall

Some psychotherapists, including Dr. Sigmund Freud, have developed elaborate theories about emotional problems, tracing them to forgotten and suppressed memories of harmful childhood experiences. Freud called these suppressed memories **traumas** or **traumata**. He blamed them for many **neuroses**. Some later therapists developed Freud's ideas further, taking them in varied directions and sometimes substituting other terms for those which Freud used, but the basic notions remain in use today.

What's going on? Apparently, the connections in the brain that stored the knowledge of that musical instrument or that language grew weak through disuse. But they're still there and, once reactivated, can be readily restored.

"But I *Want* to Forget This!"

One of the toughest problems of memory is *wanting* to forget. You've probably had the experience, after some unpleasant event, of saying, "I just want to forget about that."

Can you do this? Is it a good idea to do it, even if you can? Ah, that's a very tricky matter.

For a number of years, it was almost impossible to go to the movies or turn on a television set without seeing some poor, confused individual lying on a psychiatrist's couch, painstakingly dredging up childhood recollections. After a couple hours of dark and depressing images, the patient (or "analysand") would discover that, "Yes, Doctor, I remember it now! I was just three years old, and my mommy was trying to make me eat my broccoli, and my grandma was dying, and..."

Ah, the *trauma* was discovered. The poor sufferer was at last able to confront the cause of all her troubles, and she was able to eat broccoli again!

Such dramas, thank heaven, are far less common nowadays. But the question remains, are our ongoing problems the result of past experiences? If so, can we ever really get rid of them? Are we better off just putting them our of our minds? Or will we benefit more by confronting them and conquering them?

Some Memorable Facts

Forgetfulness

The name of the author is the first to go
followed obediently by the title, the plot,
the heartbreaking conclusion, the entire novel
which suddenly becomes one you have never read, never even heard of,
as if, one by one, the memories you used to harbor
decided to retire to the southern hemisphere of the brain,
to a little fishing village where there are no phones.
Long ago you kissed the nine Muses goodbye
and watched the quadratic equation pack its bag,
and even now as you memorize the order of the planets,
something else is slipping away, a state flower perhaps,
the address of an uncle, the capital of Paraguay.
Whatever it is you are struggling to remember
it is not poised on the tip of your tongue,
not even lurking in some obscure corner of your spleen.
It has floated away down a dark mythological river
whose name begins with an L as far as you can recall,
well on your own way to oblivion where you will join those
who have even forgotten how to swim and how to ride a bicycle.
No wonder you rise in the middle of the night
to look up the date of a famous battle in a book on war.
No wonder the moon in the window seems to have drifted
out of a love poem that you used to know by heart.

—Billy Collins from *Questions About Angels*

"Yes, Yes, That's Called a..."

Hardly anyone has gone through life without experiencing that "It's right on the tip of my tongue" feeling. Isn't it frustrating? And it's so common that there's even a name for it. It's called *aphasia*. This is a peculiar form of a more general problem called *amnesia*.

Amnesia has always been a favorite device for soap opera writers. Oscar or Laura is forever getting hit on the head and wandering off in a fog, getting into all sorts of trouble, and providing fodder for many, many scripts.

Words to Remember

Aphasia: Partial or total loss of the ability to articulate ideas in any form, resulting from brain damage or other causes.

Amnesia: Partial or total loss of memory, especially through shock, psychological disturbance, brain injury, or illness.

Some Memorable Facts

A recent case of "traumatic amnesia" was reported in a California newspaper. (The location and victim's name have been changed in the interest of his privacy.) The story described a high school student who was victimized by a gang of toughs. When he recovered and returned to school, the toughs caught him and delivered a second beating. The trauma of the second attack apparently wiped out Clark's memory of the period immediately preceding it. "When I woke up in the hospital, the first thing I thought was that I'd had a diabetic emergency or was in a car accident," Clark said as he recovered at his Smallville home. "Yesterday as a whole was pretty cloudy for me." Police found his locked car in the school parking lot, making it likely he was beaten at school.

If you're suffering from a general deterioration of your memory, we don't want to alarm you, but you'd better see a doctor and not waste any time in doing so. It may be a minor or temporary problem, but it also could be a very serious matter that needs to be taken care of.

Actually, total amnesia is a pretty rare condition. Aphasia, on the other hand, is very common. In fact, it's almost universal. It's that "It's right on the tip of my tongue" phenomenon. For such a common experience, it's odd that we don't know what causes it. One friend of ours suggested that it happens whenever a cosmic ray happens

348

to hit your brain and accidentally disconnect a synapse. We asked him whether he was serious about that, and he replied, "Of course I am. Why, it's obvious. It's as plain as the nose on your ... uh, uh ... as the nose on your ... uh ... "

"Face?" we offered.

"That's exactly the word I was looking for," said our friend.

Sometimes single-word aphasia strikes on a seemingly random basis. If it happens to you, you might work around it by using a synonym. Another friend of ours suddenly blanked one day on the word "house." It really was an amazing moment, and he was understandably

Words to Remember

Neurosis: Any of various mental or emotional disorders, such as hypochondria or neurasthenia, arising from no apparent organic lesion or change and involving symptoms such as insecurity, anxiety, depression, and irrational fears.

upset. But he had presence of mind to simply substitute "dwelling," and we went on with the conversation. We didn't even notice anything odd until he told us about it afterward.

On the other hand, sometimes you might consistently have trouble remembering a particular word. This is an even more puzzling event, and again, there's a way to overcome it. Another friend of ours reported that he couldn't remember the word "synchronicity." This term was used by the psychologist Carl Jung, who believed that coincidences weren't really accidents. They all have meaning (according to Jung), and to indicate as much, he applied the other term.

But our friend just kept blanking on "synchronicity." Time after time, he would have to describe Jung's theory to acquaintances until he found someone who could tell him the word. As he describes the situation, "It was driving me crazy!" Finally, he devised the following little story:

Childhood sweethearts are separated when their families move to different parts of the country. After 20 years, they happen to be in the same city on business. They both happen to stop in the same book store. It's early in February, and they're both looking at a display of Valentine's Day cards.

They look up, recognize each other, and without either of them saying a word, hand each other identical "I Love You" cards.

They then agree to meet for dinner that night. They arrange the time and the place where they will meet. To make sure they are both on time, just before parting, they *synchronize* their watches.

Ever since our friend invented that story, any time he needs to remember "the s-word," he calls up the story. He says he can see it as a little movie in his mind. When the happy lovers *synchronize* their watches, he remembers his problem word—*synchronicity*.

Maybe a needlessly elaborate and roundabout way to remember one word—but it works for our friend, and now he's as happy as a ... as a ... darn it, you know, that thing, it's something like an oyster!

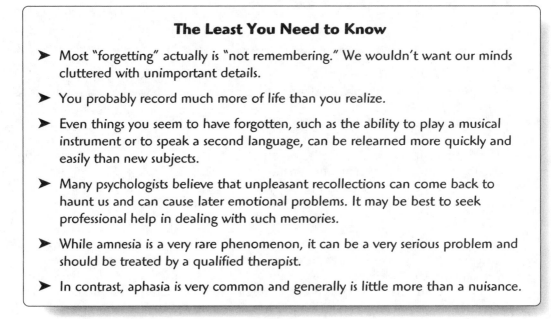

The Least You Need to Know

➤ Most "forgetting" actually is "not remembering." We wouldn't want our minds cluttered with unimportant details.

➤ You probably record much more of life than you realize.

➤ Even things you seem to have forgotten, such as the ability to play a musical instrument or to speak a second language, can be relearned more quickly and easily than new subjects.

➤ Many psychologists believe that unpleasant recollections can come back to haunt us and can cause later emotional problems. It may be best to seek professional help in dealing with such memories.

➤ While amnesia is a very rare phenomenon, it can be a very serious problem and should be treated by a qualified therapist.

➤ In contrast, aphasia is very common and generally is little more than a nuisance.

Chapter 28

The Last Roundup

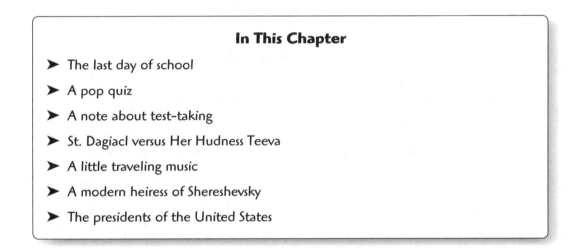

In This Chapter

➤ The last day of school

➤ A pop quiz

➤ A note about test-taking

➤ St. Dagiacl versus Her Hudness Teeva

➤ A little traveling music

➤ A modern heiress of Shereshevsky

➤ The presidents of the United States

You've been a wonderful student, and we want to thank you. If you've paid close attention and applied yourself to the methods and exercises we've laid out for you, you should now have a good general idea of how your memory works. What's more, you should have a solid working command of several practical mnemonic systems. Which ones you find most useful and most to your liking, will, of course, be up to you. But everyone can benefit from these techniques.

We'd like to think of this final chapter of *The Complete Idiot's Guide to Improving Your Memory* as, well, the last day of school.

Remember how exciting that was? The year's work was completed, and you were ready for promotion to the next grade (or graduation into the real world!) and the summer of fun before you.

A Little Review, a Little That's New

But don't turn in your schoolbooks, close your desktop, and head for the door quite yet. We're going to take a little more time to review some of the high points of the past school year—or the past 27 chapters. We'll also toss in a few helpful hints to use in conjunction with the material you've learned, and we'll show you a couple "tricks of the trade" that professional mentalists and mnemonists have used over the past couple thousand years.

You can use these tricks to amaze and amuse your family and friends. You can also adapt them to practical, everyday situations. You will discover that, like the mnemonic methods we've already shown you, they're not "just tricks" at all but solid, handy techniques.

Some Memorable Facts

Some things can't be learned or remembered by conscious effort. With practice, however, your brain and body can learn and retain them automatically. One such example is the use of bifocal eyeglasses. A friend of ours recently switched to bifocals. At first she thought the lenses had been installed upside-down in the frames—she was having a terrible time. Then one day everything came back into focus. Her brain had figured the thing out.

In a university study of this phenomenon, volunteers wore special glasses that literally turned the world upside-down (or its image, anyway). At first the volunteers were totally disoriented, but their brains quickly adjusted to the "new view," and the volunteers got along just fine.

Pop Quiz Time

Let's begin with a little quiz to see how much you've learned, how much you remember (ah ha!), and what you might want to go back and look over. The nice thing about this pop quiz is that it's designed for fun and not for grades.

Even if you can't pull all the answers out of that elusive memory of yours, that's okay. You can go back through this book as many times as necessary, and you can learn whichever of the mnemonic systems seems most useful to you at that moment. Practice with the examples given and then adapt them to any applications of your own for which you need them. Like any other skill—from playing the violin to flying an airplane—the more you do it, the more confident and relaxed you will become, and the better your performance will be.

The Test

The number of the chapter we pulled the material from is in parentheses after each question. Write your answers on a separate sheet of paper. If there are any questions you can't answer, go back to the corresponding chapters and review the material.

1. Where in the brain is language located? (Chapter 5)

2. Name three things to which memory has been compared. (Chapter 8)

3. a. What are the effects of a lobotomy? (Chapter 6)

   b. Why have neurosurgeons stopped performing this operation? (Chapter 6)

4. Name two products said to help improve memory. (Chapter 9)

5. How dependable is eyewitness testimony? (Chapter 10)

6. In what year was the Captain Marvel radio show broadcast? (Chapter 11)

7. What do we mean by the numeric alphabet? (Chapters 15, 17, and 18)

8. The letter equivalents in the number alphabet are: (Chapter 18)

   1 = _____   6 = _____

   2 = _____   7 = _____

   3 = _____   8 = _____

   4 = _____   9 = _____

   5 = _____   0 = _____

9. The peg words for the numbers from 1 to 20 are: (Chapter 18)

   1 = _____   11 = _____

   2 = _____   12 = _____

   3 = _____   13 = _____

   4 = _____   14 = _____

   5 = _____   15 = _____

   6 = _____   16 = _____

   7 = _____   17 = _____

   8 = _____   18 = _____

   9 = _____   19 = _____

   10 = _____   20 = _____

10. What are the colors of the rainbow? (Chapter 19)

11. What do we mean by "Every Good Boy Deserves Favor"? (Chapter 19)

12. Name Snow White's seven dwarfs. Hint: Do Green Snails Have Slimy Backs, Doc? (Chapter 26)

13. What is the Loci System? (Chapter 23)

14. Create a 12-position Loci System using a town or city with which you are familiar. (Chapter 23)

15. Summarize the 10 amendments to the Constitution of the United States that make up the Bill of Rights. (Chapter 26)

16. Memorize the following items using any of the techniques you like. See how many you remember in an hour, in a day, and in a week. (Chapters 12, 18, 26, and others)

    1. A dozen roses

    2. A 10-inch nonstick frying pan

3. The state of Nebraska

4. An empty urine-specimen jar

5. King Kong

6. The Andromeda galaxy

7. A pound of butter

8. A Colonial rocking chair

9. The last unicorn

10. Captain Marvel

11. A digital alarm clock

12. Elvis Presley

13. A pink Cadillac convertible

14. Tinky Winky, the purple Teletubby

15. The space shuttle Atlantis

16. The Great Wall of China

17. A cup of cocoa

18. Wonder Woman

19. A strawberry ice-cream cone

20. Your belly button

Well, that's it. How did you do? Remember, this test was for you to evaluate how much of the techniques in this book you've taken away already. If you've only skimmed the book and haven't practiced any of the techniques, you probably didn't do all that well. If you have practiced a few of them, then you've been pleasantly surprised at how well you've done.

Congratulations!

Memorable Facts

"Good heaven!" said Scrooge, clasping his hands together as he looked about him. "I was bred in this place. I was a boy here!" ... The Spirit gazed upon him mildly. Its gentle touch, though it had been light and instantaneous, appeared still present to the old man's sense of feeling. He was conscious of a thousand odours floating in the air, each one connected with a thousand thoughts, and hopes, and joys, and cares long, long forgotten! "Your lip is trembling," said the Ghost. "And what is that upon your cheek?" Scrooge muttered, with an unusual catch in his voice, that it was a pimple; and begged the Ghost to lead him where he would ...

"You recollect the way?" inquired the Spirit.

"Remember it!" cried Scrooge with fervour, "I could walk it blindfold."

"Strange to have forgotten it for so many years!" observed the Ghost. "Let us go on."

—Charles Dickens, *A Christmas Carol*, 1843

Some Thoughts About Test-Taking

Did your heart beat a little faster when you suddenly found out you had to take a test? Did you feel flustered and unprepared? Did the thought "That's cheating! They didn't tell us there was going to be a test!" run through your mind?

Even though you knew you could avoid the test if you wanted to and that nobody but you would ever know how well you did, you still may have found yourself getting just a little upset when we sprang this on you.

The anxiety you feel when faced with taking a test, going on a job interview, or public speaking has another ill effect in addition to making your hands sweat, your knees shake, and your heart pound. It's absolute murder on your memory.

To improve the situation, you can do the any or all of the following:

Instant Recall

Fear of test-taking is right up there with fear of public speaking as one of the biggies. A common recurring dream of college students is that they are entering a classroom to take the final exam when they suddenly realize they haven't attended any of the classes and they don't even know what the course is about.

➤ Practice some deep-breathing exercises.

➤ Take a few moments of silent meditation.

➤ Imagine a peaceful and tranquil scene.

➤ Focus intently on what's happening and on mentally putting aside your apprehensions. (Imagine putting them in a briefcase, closing it, and placing it aside to be opened later.)

And in Closing

Here are a few items you might find useful or at least interesting. You can use them to exercise your new memory talents.

Our Favorite Saint Meets a Warrior Queen

When you took a high school civics class, it's likely you were asked to memorize the order of presidential succession or maybe the Cabinet departments in the United States government. We know that, if the president dies before his (or her!) term expires, the vice president becomes president. After that, the order of succession is the Speaker of the House of Representatives, the president pro tempore of the Senate, and then the various Cabinet secretaries in order of seniority.

That's a tricky one—what matters is the seniority of their departments. This means which one was created first, which second, and so on. Some of these take some funny twists, too. The Department of Defense wasn't created until 1947, for example, but it replaced the Department of War created in 1789. The postmaster general used to be a Cabinet officer, but that position ceased to exist when the U.S. Postal Service became an independent agency.

At any rate, you can remember the Cabinet officers in order of seniority if you visualize a truly weird television show. It's about a holy woman named Saint Dagiacl and her archrival, an evil monarch who insists on being addressed as Her Hudness Teeva. It's the *St. Dagiacl/Her Hudness Teeva* show.

As you've probably figured out by now, we're using   to jog our memory on this one. Here's how to decode the secret message:

S = Secretary of State

T = Secretary of the Treasury

D = Secretary of Defense

AG = Attorney General

I = Secretary of the Interior

A = Secretary of Agriculture

C = Secretary of Commerce

L = Secretary of Labor

H = Secretary of Health and Human Services

HUD = Secretary of Housing and Urban Development

T = Secretary of Transportation

E = Secretary of Energy

E = Secretary of Education

VA = Secretary of Veterans Affairs

You have to remember that Energy comes before Education, but that's easy enough because you need a hearty breakfast before you go to school! You also need to remember that the Department of Justice is the only Cabinet department without a secretary—it has a general instead.

Any time you need this information, just sit back, close your eyes, and watch St. Dagiacl go up against Her Hudness Teeva!

Some Memorable Facts

Pulitzer Prize winning novelist Norman Mailer was a freshman at Harvard University in 1938. In 1998, Mailer was interviewed by a journalist who thought he'd spring a surprise question on the famous author. The journalist had learned that Mailer was embarrassed on his first day at Harvard because he wore a pair of garish trousers while all the other students dressed in navy blue blazers and gray flannel slacks.

"Is it true that you wore bright green pants that day?" asked the journalist.

"No!" Mailer growled fiercely. "They were green and orange striped!"

Mailer had remembered that embarrassing detail after 60 years.

I Hear a Rhapsody

You may have read the odd story about the stroke patients who were unable to speak but could still sing familiar songs. Music is a very powerful memory tool. You may even be able to make use of the power of music to aid your own memory. Many music appreciation students have memorized lines that were tacked onto classical pieces of music. Did you ever hear, "This is the symphony that Schubert wrote but never finished?" What about, "Barcarole / from Tales of Hoffman / written by Offenbach?"

Song lyrics are memorable because they are reinforced three times: by the melody of the song, by its rhythm, and by the rhyming structure of the words themselves. This applies to any song with these three elements: melody, rhythm, and rhyme.

Not all music, of course, has all three elements. It would be hard to memorize the words of a Gregorian chant (if there are any words to memorize!) because the chant doesn't work the way popular songs do. The chant creates a wall of sound, perhaps even a sea of sound. It's wonderful for meditation. Many people achieve a profound sense of serenity and clarity of mind through chanting or through hearing chants. This is a far cry, however, from "How Much Is that Doggie in the Window?"

Instant Recall

Mystery writer Colin Dexter, creator of the popular *Inspector Morse* series, is one of the world's great solvers—and devisers—of crossword puzzles. He calls himself a "cruciverbalist." If you take the word apart, you'll discover it means crossworder.

Dexter believes that spending 30 to 60 minutes each morning with a good crossword puzzle tunes up his mental circuits and prepares him for a successful day.

You might want to try it!

As You Leave These Hallowed Halls

Are you still with us? Good! Here we are at the end of *The Complete Idiot's Guide to Improving Your Memory* (well, except for a few appendices, but what's an appendix or two between friends?). We hope it's been as much fun for you as it has been for us.

Instant Recall

If you want to remember the lyrics of a favorite song, use the tune of that song to help you remember.

We've found that, in the course of researching and writing this book, we've refreshed our own memories and have learned (or relearned) some mnemonic techniques that we wish we'd mastered a long time ago. And there's still a lot more for all of us to learn. Research into the nature of memory and how it works is still in its infancy, and fascinating and important discoveries are being made almost daily.

If we've managed to interest you in the subject in general, in addition to improving your own memory, we suggest you keep an eye on the science columns of your favorite newspapers and magazines. Stay alert for news on the subject of memory. You'll be surprised and delighted at how much new information is coming along.

Most important, we urge you to apply the mnemonic systems you've learned in *The Complete Idiot's Guide to Improving Your Memory*. Any time you're uncertain of a point, go back and reread the chapter that explains the system you're using.

Feel free to invent a new system of your own, to modify any of the systems we've explained, or to find new ways to apply and utilize these systems.

You'll be amazed and pleased at how well your memory works, now that you know how to use it!

A Modern Shereshevsky

Being the sharp-eyed and perspicacious individual you are, you have doubtless noticed that we make frequent mention of Mr. Shereshevsky, the Russian mnemonist about whom Dr. Luria wrote his famous book. This isn't by accident, and it isn't just because we find Shereshevsky fascinating. The fact is that Shereshevsky is one of the most important subjects in the history of memory research—just as Luria is one of the most important researchers.

Shereshevsky is not a unique case, however. Every once in a while, a person comes along who possesses astonishing powers of memory. When such an individual comes to the attention of researchers, the person almost always responds with an astonished statement to the effect of, "But I thought everybody could do what I do!" Remember Shereshevsky's reply when his editor complained that he wasn't taking notes at the staff meeting? (See Chapter 13, "Very Special Memories.")

The most recent natural mnemonist to come to our attention is Tatiana Cooley. In 1999 Ms. Cooley won the title of USA National Memory Champion for the second time, besting a field of 16 challengers. An Associated Press dispatch dated February 21, 1999, described the 27-year-old Ms. Cooley's triumph in a national competition. Ms. Cooley won her first championship in 1997.

Ms. Cooley can remember "strings of 4,000 numbers or 500 words." How does she do it? She calls her two techniques *visualization* and *association*. Associated Press writer Arlene Levinson quotes Ms. Cooley as explaining

Refresh Your Memory

"The ideal condition would be, I admit, that men should be right by instinct. But since we are all likely to go astray, the reasonable thing is to learn from those who can teach."

—Sophocles, *Antigone*

that visualization "entails looking at material and mentally photographing it." This, of course, is exactly the method Shereshevsky used. Remember the table of 50 numbers Luria showed him and Shereshevsky's remarkable ability not merely to remember the numbers but to mentally "read" them up, down, or diagonally? This method is called *eidetics*.

Tatiana Cooley's second method, which she calls association, apparently is a combination of the chain-link and Loci methods, both of which you learned in this book.

When Tatiana Cooley attended college, she never had to study. She attended lectures and she did take notes. As you now know, this was a means of reinforcing her audio input with visual and body memories of the items she wrote down. "It sort of didn't occur to me that it was anything extraordinary," she now says. "It was nice. It was just a means to get me more free time."

Can you hear Shereshevsky's comments echoing down the years? He, too, thought his powers were nothing out of the ordinary.

The champion mnemonist, Tatiana Cooley, first won her crown when she and her boyfriend were out looking for fun and stumbled across the competition. She had no time to prepare—and no time to get nervous! She says that an important factor in her success is breathing deeply and reminding herself to take it easy. Her advice to people who fear that the stresses of modern life are causing their memory to slip is very simple: "Relax."

Our hats are off to her!

Ladies and Gentlemen, the Presidents of the United States!

We have one last little memory exercise for you. Here is a list of the presidents of the United States in the order in which they served:

George Washington	James Knox Polk
John Adams	Zachary Taylor
Thomas Jefferson	Millard Fillmore
James Madison	Franklin Pierce
James Monroe	James Buchanan
John Quincy Adams	Abraham Lincoln
Andrew Jackson	Andrew Johnson
Martin Van Buren	Ulysses S. Grant
William Henry Harrison	Rutherford B. Hayes
John Tyler	

Instant Recall

Grover Cleveland served again after Benjamin Harrison and is sometimes listed as both the twenty-second and twenty-forth president of the United States. You may remember that if you like.

James A. Garfield	Franklin Delano Roosevelt
Chester A. Arthur	Harry S Truman
Grover Cleveland	Dwight D. Eisenhower
Benjamin Harrison	John F. Kennedy
William McKinley	Lyndon Baines Johnson
Theodore Roosevelt	Richard Milhous Nixon
William Howard Taft	Gerald R. Ford
Woodrow Wilson	Jimmy (James Earl) Carter
Warren G. Harding	Ronald Reagan
Calvin Coolidge	George Bush
Herbert Hoover	William Jefferson Clinton

If you feel like memorizing the list in order, this mnemonic sentence might help:

"What a joy! Mom made a junior varsity hockey team pennant—the football player's big loose jersey gets high grades as clothing—he may remember the whole history class having returned the entire knit jersey—not for credit refunds but cash!"

With that, and our good wishes, we leave you. We wish you great success in using the methods you've learned here. Relax and have a good life.

The Least You Need to Know

➤ Our little quiz should give you some idea how well you've done and what needs to be reviewed.

➤ If you've practiced the mnemonic techniques we've provided, you should have little trouble with memorizing any list.

➤ The key to test-taking, in addition to being prepared and knowing the material, is to relax.

➤ Lyrics are easier to remember than other text because both music and rhyming patterns are great memory aids.

➤ Tatiana Cooley, a modern memory champion, uses methods similar to those of Shereshevsky: visualization and association.

Glossary

Acronym   A word formed from the first letters of other words, such as NATO (formed from North Atlantic Treaty Organization).

Alzheimer's disease   Named for German neuropathologist Alois Alzheimer (1864–1915). In 1906, Alzheimer was the first person to give the illness, which then was called presenile dementia, a full clinical and pathological description.

Amnesia   Partial or total loss of memory, especially through shock, psychological disturbance, brain injury, or illness.

Anthropoid   Resembling a human being, especially in shape or outward appearance.

Anthropomorphize   To attribute human motivation, characteristics, or behavior to inanimate objects, animals, or natural phenomena.

Antioxidant   A substance that scrounges up and neutralizes free-radical molecules in the body before they can cause harm.

Antiretrograde   Moving or tending forward. In cases of antiretrograde amnesia, refers to the ability to remember only events and experiences that occurred after the onset of the amnesia. *See also* Retrograde, Amnesia.

Aphasia   Partial or total loss of the ability to articulate ideas in any form, resulting from brain damage or other causes.

Bilateral   Having two sides; two-sided.

Binary   Of or relating to a system of numeration that has the number 2 as its base.

Blood-brain barrier   The name given to the capillary system that isolates the brain from foreign objects that might be circulating in the blood and from unpredictable fluctuations in the normal makeup of the blood plasma.

Conditioned   In psychology, exhibiting or being trained to exhibit a predetermined response.

Conditioned reflex   A reflex is an action that takes place automatically and without conscious thought in response to a given stimulus; a conditioned reflex is a an unconscious reaction caused by training.

Conflated   Combined, as when two memories are merged into one, with parts of one being "overwritten" by the other.

Consciousness   A sense of one's personal or collective identity, especially the complex attitudes, beliefs, and sensitivities held by or considered characteristic of an individual or a group.

Chromosome   The part of a cell that transmits hereditary information.

DNA (deoxyribonucleic acid)   A complex chemical that holds a cell's genetic information and is capable of self-replication.

Encephalitis   An inflammation of the brain, usually caused by a virus, that can be serious or even fatal if not promptly treated. Unfortunately, its early symptoms (headache, stiff neck, and fever) can be misdiagnosed as the flu.

Entomologist   A scientist who studies insects.

Feral   Existing in a wild or untamed state; having returned to an untamed state from domestication; of or suggestive of a wild animal; savage.

Gene   A site on a chromosome that encodes specific hereditary information.

Glial cells   Cells that support, protect, and nourish the neurons.

Haptic   Pertaining to the sense of touch. Haptic memory is your memory of how something feels when you touch it.

Hominids   Primates of the family *Hominidae*, of which *homo sapien* is the only extant species.

Howitzer   A cannon with a relatively short barrel that delivers shells at a medium muzzle velocity, usually by a high trajectory.

Intelligence   The ability to acquire, organize, and evaluate data and to make meaningful decisions based on this data.

Loci   (pronounced *LO-sigh*) The plural form of the Latin word "locus," which means location.

Medulla oblongata   Latin for "elongated marrow," although the actual object isn't all that elongated. It takes up the first inch of the three-inch brain stem.

Meg   Short for "megabyte," one million units or characters of storage capacity in computer memory.

Memory   In computer lingo, describes a machine's capacity for storing information as well as the device in which the information is stored.

Midbrain   The part of the brain that sits atop the brain stem, surrounded by the rest of the brain.

Mnemosyne   The ancient Greek goddess of memory, who was the daughter of heaven and earth (Uranus and Ge) and the mother of the Muses. (This shows you how important the Greeks thought memory was.) The word "mnemonic"—things that help memory—is named after the goddess.

Motor In the nervous system, of, relating to, or designating nerves that carry impulses from the nerve centers to the muscles; involving or relating to movements of the muscles.

Neurobiologist A person who studies the functions of the brain from the deep level of the neurons and other brain cells to the higher levels of how thoughts and memories are formed. The root "neuro" (nerve) also is used in the words "neurologist," a doctor who treats diseases of the brain; "neurosurgeon," a doctor who operates on the brain; "neuropsychologist," a specialist in testing for brain impairment; "neurophysiologist," a scientist who studies how the brain works; and the general term "neuroscientist," for anyone who studies the brain in any way without a more specific title.

Neurons The cells that transmit information and sensory impulses (vision, hearing, pain, heat, touch, and so on) around the body.

Neurosis Any of various mental or emotional disorders, such as hypochondria or neurasthenia, arising from no apparent organic lesion or change and involving symptoms such as insecurity, anxiety, depression, and irrational fears.

Neurotransmitter A chemical that carries nerve impulses from one neuron to the next.

Pons Latin for "bridge." In the body, it serves as a bridge for information and instructions between the spinal cord and the brain.

Primate A mammal of the order *Primates* (which includes the anthropoids) characterized by refined development of the hands and feet, a shortened snout, and a large brain.

RAM (random access memory) A term devised in the early days of computers, it is in direct contrast to sequential memory. In the latter, the machine had to move through long series of locations to reach the item desired. With RAM, it can move directly to the desired address. In the modern era, RAM often is synonymous with "main memory." It is possible to write or read (that is, to record data or retrieve it) in RAM.

Reflex In physiology, something produced as an automatic response or reaction.

Retrograde Moving or tending backward. In cases of amnesia, this refers to all events and experiences occurring prior to the onset of the amnesia.

ROM (read only memory) Computer memory that is burned in, so to speak, and cannot be changed. It is used for permanent functions that are part of the computer's basic system and need never be altered by the user. There also are special cases such as CD-ROMs, which contain programs or data.

Semantics The study of meaning in language forms; the study of relationships between signs and symbols and what they represent.

365

Symmetry   Exact correspondence of form on opposite sides of a dividing line.

Trauma   An emotional wound or shock that creates substantial, lasting damage to the psychological development of a person, often leading to neurosis.

Tropism   The turning or bending of an organism or part of an organism toward or away from an external stimulus such as light, heat, or gravity.

A Mnemonic Word List to 100

With thanks to Max Maven.

Here is a numeric alphabet list up to 100 with five choices for each number.

1. hat, tea, hood, yacht, Yoda
2. hen, knee, hun, gnu, yawn
3. ham, home, hum, Moe, yam
4. hair, wire, year, whore, oar
5. hole, ale, hail, yellow, eel
6. hash, ash, wish, jaw, shoe
7. hook, hack, hag, cow, hookah
8. hive, wave, ivy, Eve, oaf
9. hoop, ape, whip, pie, boy
10. dice, Otis, toss, DOS, Hades
11. tide, doo-doo, teat, date, idiot
12. tin, den, tuna, ton, Odin
13. team, dome, dime, dame, atom
14. tear, door, deer, udder, tray
15. tail, dial, tile, idol, yodel
16. dish, dish, Yiddish, douche, attache
17. duck, dike, dog, Tiki, tag
18. dove, taffy, daffy, dive, tough
19. top, tape, dope, daub, tub
20. nose, noose, Heinz, ENSA, nice
21. note, net, wand, hand, newt
22. nun, noon, neon, Onan, nanny
23. enema, enemy, nim, gnome, numb
24. honor, Nair, near, Henry, owner
25. nail, Nell, only, in-law, Nile

26. niche, nosh, inch, hunch, honcho
27. nuke, ink, hank, knock, Yankee
28. knife, knave, nova, envy, navy
29. knob, nape, nap, nib, honeypie
30. mouse, moose, moss, mace, maze
31. mitt, maid, mat, meat, moat
32. moon, man, woman, human, amen
33. mime, mom, imam, yum-yum, maim
34. mare, moor, hammer, homer, amour
35. mail, mall, mule, homily, homely
36. mush, mash, mooch, mage, image
37. mike, mug, hammock, amigo, Mickey
38. muff, move, movie, humvee, mo'fo'
39. mop, mob, hemp, amp, mope
40. rose, horse, race, rice, hearse
41. rat, rod, heart, yard, art
42. rain, horn, earn, yarn, run
43. ram, rum, ream, harm, arm
44. roar, rear, rare, error, horror
45. rail, roll, roil, hurl, Harley

46. rash, arch, roach, Hershey, urge
47. rock, rake, rug, rook, rag
48. roof, revue, Harvey, wharf, reef
49. rope, robe, harp, rib, Arab
50. lace, lass, also, Alice, louse
51. light, lute, welt, halt, hold
52. line, lean, Ellen, loan, loon
53. lime, loom, elm, lame, llama
54. lyre, Lear, holler, Larry, lure
55. lolly(pop), lull, Lola, loll, El Al
56. leech, leash, lash, Welsh, Alicia
57. lake, lick, Alec, log, leg
58. leaf, love, halvah, Alf, wolf
59. lip, lap, lab, help, elbow
60. juice, jazz, cheese, choice, chase
61. jet, sheet, shot, shed, chat
62. gin, chin, genie, chain, ocean
63. gem, gym, jam, shmoo, chum
64. jar, chair, shore, usher, shrew
65. shell, jail, jelly, chill, chili
66. cha-cha, josh, hashish, Jewish, shush
67. jack, joke, jog, chick, shock
68. shave, chief, chef, Jove, jive
69. ship, shop, sheep, cheap, chap
70. goose, case, cuss, axe, haggis
71. cat, coat, kite, kid, act
72. cane, cone, con, Agnew, gone
73. gum, game, cam, acme, comb
74. car, gear, ogre, crow, core
75. coal, goal, clay, claw, kill
76. cash, cage, gush, waggish, coach
77. coke, gag, cook, geek, kick
78. coffee, café, cave, cove, gaff
79. cap, cab, gap, cub, copy
80. face, phase, vase, visa, vice
81. foot, fat, vat, vote, fade
82. fan, van, fin, hyphen, phone
83. foam, fame, fume, femme, ovum
84. fire, fur, fair, hover, weaver
85. file, fool, veil, evil, vial
86. fish, fudge, veggie, Vichy, fuchsia
87. fig, fake, vogue, fog, folk
88. fife, fief, Fi-Fi, viva, Fauve
89. fib, vibe, fop, faux pas, VIP
90. buzz, bass, pass, pussy, busy
91. pot, bed, bat, habit, boat
92. pen, pan, bone, pine, weapon
93. poem, bomb, boom, puma, palm
94. pear, boar, eyebrow, bar, bare
95. pail, pool, ball, bill, apple
96. bush, push, bash, pasha, posh
97. book, bike, peak, OPEC, bug
98. puff, poof, beef, bevy, buff
99. pipe, pip, bib, pub, pop
100. disease, decease, disuse, hot sauce, odysseus

Selected Bibliography

Baddeley, Alan. *Your Memory: A User's Guide.* New York: Macmillan, 1982.

Bryan, C.D.B. *Alien Abduction, UFOs, and the Conference at M.I.T.* New York: Knopf, 1995.

Cytowic, Richard E. *The Man Who Tasted Shapes.* New York: Warner Books, 1995.

Estabrooks, G.H., *Hypnotism.* New York: Dutton, 1957.

Flesch, Rudolf. *The Art of Clear Thinking.* New York: Harper & Row, 1951.

Furst, Bruno. *The Practical Way to a Better Memory.* New York: Fawcett, 1957.

Furst, Bruno. *Stop Forgetting.* New York: Doubleday, 1948.

Higbee, Kenneth L., Ph.D., *Your Memory: How It Works and How to Improve It,* New York, Prentice Hall, 1988.

Hilts, Philip J. *Memory's Ghost: The Nature of Memory and the Strange Tale of Mr. M.* New York: Simon & Schuster, 1996.

Kurzweil, Ray. *The Age of Spiritual Machines.* New York: Viking, 1999.

Loftus, Elizabeth and Katherine Ketchum. *The Myth of Repressed Memory.* New York: St. Martin's Press, 1996.

Loftus, Elizabeth and Katherine Ketchum. *Witness for the Defense.* New York: St. Martin's Press, 1991.

Loisette, Prof. A. *Assimilative Memory.* New York and London: Funk & Wagnalls, 1896.

Lorayne, Harry. *How to Develop a Super-power Memory.* New York: Stein and Day, 1957.

Lorayne, Harry. *Remembering People,* New York: Stein and Day, 1975.

Lupoff, Richard A. *Mnemonics.* Indianapolis: United States Army Publication, 1957.

Luria, A. R. *The Man with a Shattered World.* Cambridge: Harvard University Press, 1987.

Luria, A. R. *The Mind of a Mnemonist.* Cambridge: Harvard University Press, 1987.

Restak, Richard M., M.D. *The Brain.* New York: Bantam, 1984.

Restak, Richard M., M.D. *The Modular Brain.* New York: Scribners, 1997.

Rosenfield, Israel. *The Invention of Memory.* New York: Basic Books, 1988.

Roth, David M. *Roth Memory Course.* New York: Sun Dial Press, 1918.

Rupp, Rebecca. *Committed to Memory,* New York: Crown, 1998.

Shepard, Paul. *Thinking Animals: Animals and the Development of Human Intelligence.* Athens, GA: University of Georgia Press, 1998.

Wade, Nicholas, ed. *The Science Times Book of the Brain*. New York: Lyons Press, 1998.

Waters, T. A. *Psychologistics: An Operating Manual for the Mind*. New York: Random House, 1971.

Weeks, David and Jamie James. *Eccentrics: A Study of Sanity and Strangeness*. New York: Kodansha, 1996.

Winchester, Simon. *The Professor and the Madman: A Tale of Murder, Insanity, and the Making of the Oxford English Dictionary*. New York: HarperCollins, 1998.

Wood, Ernest E. *Mind and Memory Training*. New York: Occult Research Press, 1936.

Index